PARIYATTI

STUDIES IN PĀLI LANGUAGE AND LITERATURE

EDITORS

BIMALENDRA KUMAR
UJJWAL KUMAR

ADITYA PRAKASHAN
NEW DELHI

PARIYATTI

STUDIES IN PĀLI LANGUAGE AND LITERATURE

EDITORS

BIMALENDRA KUMAR

UJJWAL KUMAR

Publisher

Aditya Prakashan

Ansari Road

New Delhi- 110002

Phone: +91-11-232-780342

E-mail: contact@adityaprakashan.com

ISBN 978-81-7742-163-7

First Edition- 2017

New Delhi

Bimalendra Kumar started his academic career as a Lecturer in the Department of Indo-Tibetan Studies, Visva Bharati University, Santiniketan (W.B.). At present, he is Professor of Pali, Department of Pali and Buddhist Studies, Banaras Hindu University, Varanasi (U.P.). His publications include over eighty articles in various scholarly journals published from India and abroad. He has edited and authored nine books namely, *Theory of Relations in Buddhist Philosophy* (1998), *Gandhavaṃsa: A History of Pali Literature* (1992), *Perspectives of Tibetan and Buddhist Studies (2005), Paṭṭhānuddesadīpanī* (2005), *Dāhtuvaṃso* (2006), *Dhammadesanā: A Buddhist Perspective (Prof. Mahesh Tiwari Commemoration Volume)* (2007) (jointly edited), *Buddhism and Social Ideals* (2009) (jointly edited), *Meghadūta: Critical Edition with Sanskrit and Tibetan Index* (2011) (jointly edited) and *Bhesajjamañjusā* (Devanagarī Edition): 1-18 Paddhati (2015), *Bodhi: Recent Studies in Pāli Buddhism* (2016) (jointly ed. with U. Kumar). He is the editor of *Dharmadoot* Journal (Sarnath), published by Maha-Bodhi Society of India.

E-mail: bimal_bhu_60@yahoo.co.in

Ujjwal Kumar started his academic career as an Assistant Professor in the Department of Pali, University of Pune, Pune, Maharashtra in 2006. At present, he is Assosiate Professor in the Department of Buddhist Studies, University of Calcutta, Kolkata, West Bengal. In his credit, three books and number of articles are published. His area of research is Pāli Nīti Literature. His major publication includes *Lokanīti: Devanāgarī Edition with Hindi Translation* (2015), *Bodhi: Recent Studies in Pāli Buddhism* (2016) (jointly edited with Prof. B. Kumar).

E-mail: ujjwal1980@gmail.com

PREFACE

The present volume entitled "*Pariyatti: Studies in Pāli Language and Literature*" contains some valuable essays of the Pāli scholars of the world representing all the Theravada Buddhist countries and highlighting different divisions of Pāli literature like *Sutta, Abhidhamma, Vyākaraṇa* etc. It is said that '*Pariyatti*' (thought) and '*Paṭipatti*' (practice) are the two aspects of Pāli Buddhism, which move together side by side, just like the two wheels of a chariot for righteous and smooth way faring in the life. The *Pariyatti* (thought) does not refer to mere imaginative flight but as real fact moving pace to pace with the process of life. It unfolds the nature of reality (*dhamma-svabhāva*), eradicates the ignorance (*moha*) and presents admonition for visualization of truth face to face.

The thought revealed through Pāli literature has occupied an enormous value in the discipline of Buddhist Studies. The main tenets of Buddhism like Four Noble Truths, Eight-fold Path, Law of Dependent Origination, Karma and Rebirth, Nirvāṇa etc. have been explicated in Pāli literature, which plays an important role in critical exposition of all teachings of the Buddha. Hence, an effort has been made to show the wider role of Pāli literature in interpreting the thoughts available in the teachings of the Buddha through the research papers in this volume. The present volume consists of sixteen papers altogether. Four papers in the beginning of this volume are directly related to the profound and excellent teachings of the Buddha namely *Abhidhamma*. Next four papers are dealing with the literary and critical analysis of the *sutta-s* available in the *Sutta Piṭaka* as well as in the post-canonical texts. Other papers in the third section attempt to reveal various aspects of Kātantra and Kaccāyana Grammars along with some methodological reflections in translating *sutta-s* from Pāli to English. The research papers of the last section are devoted to many aspects of Buddhism with special reference to philosophical and historical expansion of Buddhism.

In this way, this volume covers all aspects of thoughts available in Pāli literature and will be helpful to the researchers in Pāli Studies. We take this opportunity to put on record our sincere thanks to all the contributors for their papers. Finally, we express our thanks to Shri Aditya Goel, Proprietor, Aditya Publishers, New Delhi for his full cooperation in bringing out the present volume in time.

Varanasi
Kolkata — Editors

Contents

Vyākaraṇa

Pakiṇṇaka

Abhidhamma: Its meaning in the Theravāda and Sarvāstivāda

Uma Shankar VYAS*

Abhidhamma or *Abhidharma* is an exclusive Buddhist term, not available in non-Buddhist Indian literature of all phases. In fact, this term occupies most important position in the vocabulary of Buddhist philosophical tradition and is nucleus of the psycho-ethical analysis of all schools of Buddhist thought. The study of the *Abhidhamma* remains indispensable even today for the clear understanding of the history of Buddhist philosophical thought and spiritual practice. A careful reading of the Pāli canonical texts and Buddhist Sanskrit texts, reveal the fact that, prior to expressing the meaning of "supplementary (*atireka*) and superior (*visiṭṭha*) doctrine (*Dhamma*), the term *Abhidhamma* conveyed various meanings in the early phase of Pāli literature.

In common usage *Abhidhamma* represents either specific method in which the *Dhamma* is propounded in the third collection of Buddhist canonical texts or the latter. This is confirmed by the fact that sometimes in the *Nikāya*-s (see A IV.274-79), *Āgama*-s and *Vinaya*-s of different schools, the term seems to refer to an *Abhidhamma-piṭaka* and sometimes only to those types of expositions (see D III.267, M I.472), out of which the *Abhidhamma-piṭaka* was elaborated later on. In the earliest occurrence of the term *Abhidhamma* in the

---

* Professor (Retired) and Former Director, Nava Nalanda Mahavihar, Nalanda, Bihar, India. E-mail: drumashankarvyas@hotmail.com

Nikāya-s and *Vinaya* texts of the Theravāda tradition there are two types of statements wherein the term *Abhidhamma* appears together with *Abhivinaya* in locative case. These are:

a) A monk loves the Buddha's doctrine, the utterance of it is clear to him, he finds exceeding joy in *Abhidhamma* and *Abhivinaya*- "*abhidhamme abhivinaye uḷārapāmojjo*" (D III. 267).
b) Concentration on *Abhidhamma* and *Abhivinaya* should be made by a monk who is living in the forest- "*āraññikenāvuso, bhikkhuneva abhidhamme abhivinaye yogokaraṇīyo*" (M I.472).

While keeping in view such usages of the word *Abhidhamma* in the canonical Pāli literature, it is also essential to keep in mind that etymologically the word is a prepositional compound consisting of preposition *abhi* and the noun *dhamma*. In the traditional interpretations, the prefix *abhi* has been interpreted in different ways resulting in the various types of interpretation of the compound word, *Abhidhamma*. Some of the attempts by the modern scholars for the interpretation of the word *Abhidhamma* are also mainly based on the variety of the traditional interpretations of the prefix *abhi* itself. These modern attempts may be classified under three heads:

1. Attempts to interpret *abhi-dhamma* as a prepositional compound,
2. Attempts to interpret the prefix *abhi* as an adjective qualifying the noun *dhamma*,
3. Attempts to accept both these interpretations correct according to their contexts.

As Fumimaro WATANABE (1983: 19) quoted W. and M. Geiger's *Pali Dhamma*, the word *Abhidhamma* has no philosophical meaning. The terms *Abhidhamma* and *Abhivinaya* are used here in the locative case and simply express the meaning "about the *Dhamma*" and "concerning the *Vinaya*." Further WATANABE (1983: 19) quoted A. K. WARDER's *Introduction to Pali*, where WARDER also expresses almost similar opinion and adds that in these passages the word *Abhidhamma* does not convey specific meaning of a systematic analysis of the *Dhamma*, which was done only in the later stage. As far as the usage of the terms, *Abhidhamma* and *Abhivinaya* in the Pāli *nikāya*-s is concerned, it is undoubtedly in the locative case (WATANABE 1983: 19). However, in the parallel Chinese *Āgama*-s the term *Abhidhamma* appears in the accusative case also. WATANABE (1983: 20) cites the following passage as an example of the said usage:

> "The Buddha realized that the monk Rāhula had not been released to perfection and had not been capable of receiving *Abhidhamma* from the, Buddha".

The interpretations of T. W. and C. A. F. Rhys DAVIDS are based on the traditional belief that the prefix '*abhi*' is an adjective and means 'special' or 'extra'. Accordingly, in PED (65) of PTS, they translate the term *Abhidhamma* as special *Dhamma*. Thus, both propound the view that the terms *Abhidhamma* and *Abhivinaya* in the Pāli *Nikāya*-s mean the advanced teaching of both, the *Dhamma* and the *Vinaya* (RHYS DAVIDS 2007: III.246). F. L. WOODWARD translates these terms as extra doctrine and extra discipline (WOODWARD 2006: I.267) or further *Dhamma* and further discipline (WOODWARD 2006: V. 19, 139, 217 etc). E. M. HARE (2006: III.85) translates *Abhidhamma* as 'more-*dhamma*'.

Scholars like I. B. HORNER puts more emphasis on the fact that while trying to ascertain the exact meaning of the word *Abhidhamma* a reference to that particular context is essential in which the term *Abhidhamma* is used. She minutely examines the usages of the terms *Abhidhamma* and *Abhivinaya* in the *Sutta-piṭaka* and *Vinaya-piṭaka* (see HORNER 1941: 219-310). As a result of her deep study she translates both these terms as "further *Dhamma*" and "further discipline" in some cases (HORNER 2004: II.145). She also translates the same words as "what pertains to *Dhamma*" and "what pertains to discipline" in some other cases (HORNER 1971: IV.83-84). Thus according to I. B. HORNER (1969: III.X), the particular meaning ascribed to the term *Abhidhamma* in any one particular context must depend largely on the sense, linguistical style and terminology of that whole context, which should therefore be considered on its own merits.

It is also worth mentioning here that all these interpretations of the word *Abhidhamma* are based on the traditional expositions appearing in the Pāli canonical and Post canonical texts and in Chinese translations of the Buddhist texts. Therefore, it is essential to trace-out clearly these traditional expositions.

The word *Abhidhamma* also occurs in the *Mahāvagga* (see Vin I.64). However, it is used there in connection with the instructions in the rules of the monastic life (*Abhivinaye vinetuṁ*). Thus, it still has no special meaning, which was given to it in later Pāli works. If one goes through different sections of the *Vinaya-piṭaka*, it becomes clear that in these texts the word *Abhidhamma* does not refer to anything deeper.

Thus it is almost certain that in these references of early Pāli texts the term *Abhidhamma* neither refers to *Abhidhamma* books, constituting the third Canonical collection nor the specific meaning proposed by the Pāli writings of later stages. However, there are some passages in the same Pāli *nikāya*-s representing the second stage of the historical evolution of *Abhidhamma*. The following types of Pāli *sutta*-s are especially significant because they contain such features, which, most probably, contributed for the development of the meaning of *Abhidhamma* in the specialized sense. These are as follows:

A. The *sutta*-s featuring the term *Abhidhamma-kathā* contains a dialogue between two monks regarding the spiritual-path. The *Mahāgosiṅga-sutta* (M I.212 ff) is the best example of these kinds of *sutta*-s. In this *sutta* elder Moggallāna in reply to a question raised by elder Sāriputta, replies that only that kind of monk can illuminate this *Gosiṅga-Sālavana* garden, who, being engaged in an *Abhidhamma-kathā*, answers without floundering and in accordance with the *Dhamma*. It is to be noted here that *Buddhaghosa* has linked the word *Dhammakathika* with the word *Abhidhamma* (As 25). I. B. HORNER (1941: 299) also remarks, "The word *Abhidhamma* occurring in the *Sutta* and the *Vinaya* although not indicating a complete and closed system of philosophy, had been intended to stand for something more than *Dhamma* and *Vinaya*, perhaps in the sense of some more than usually complete grasp and mastery of them due to further study and reflection".

B. There are some Pāli *sutta*-s wherein the *Abhidhamma* is used with the word *Vedalla* or the *Sutta*-s in the form of questions and answers on serious doctrinal matters. The scope of these questions and answers is clearly broader than that in the *Abhidhamma-kathā*. *Vedalla* is one of the nine divisions of the Buddhist teaching (*Navaṅga-satthu-sāsana*). In this nine-fold classification of the teachings of the Buddha, *Vedalla* occurs as the last member, which may suggest that it came to be incorporated into the scheme at the time of the evolution of *Abhidhamma* into the genre of which it was considered to correspond. In the Sarvāstivāda and Yogācāra systems of Buddhist thought, *Vedalla* has been equated with *Vaipulya* or *Vaitulya* and Saṅghabhadra, a Sarvāstivāda *Abhidhārmika* explains the term, *Vaipulya* as a word referring to the extensive analytical clarification of *dharma*-s by logical reasoning, as all the *dharma*-s have different natures and characteristics which cannot be clarified without extensive discussion (see DHAMMAJOTI 2009: 7-8). He also calls it *Vaitulya* or matchlessness as this extensive discussion (of the *Vedalla*) has subtle principles, which cannot be matched.

C. The *Sutta*-s featuring the *Vibhaṅga*-exposition of a brief and summarized teaching either by the Buddha or by one of his prominent disciples also indicated further development in the exposition of the term *Abhidhamma*. The twelve *Sutta*-s grouped under *Vibhaṅga-Vagga* indicate that the method of the expositions of brief teachings came to predominance at least by the time of the formation of *Nikāya* collections. Thus like *Vedalla*, *Vibhaṅga* (a method) also came to signify the explanation of the profound meanings intended in the Buddha's brief teachings. Such a development was obviously connected with the emergence of the *Abhidhamma* in its specific sense.

Finally, later Pāli writers interpreted the term in the specific sense. According to Buddhaghosa, the famous Pāli commentator and the author of the *Aṭṭhasālinī*, the prefix '*abhi*', when prefixed to word '*dhamma*', conveys the meaning of 'supplementary *dhamma*' and 'special *dhamma*': "*atireka-visesattha-dīpako hi ettha abhi-saddo*" (As I.2). Elsewhere in his *Samantapāsādikā* he says that the prefix '*abhi*' conveys as many as five meanings. Thus according to Buddhaghosa *Abhidhamma* is so called because it excels in and is distinguished by several qualities.

According to Asaṅga, a famous teacher of Mahāyāna Buddhism, these excellent qualities are four. These are as follows:

1. It is face to face (*abhimukha*) with the highest goal and the nature of reality,
2. *Abhīkṣṇato*- It presents the teaching of the way for the attainment of the goal from various view-points,
3. *Abhibhava-gatito*- It stands to petty controversies regarding the nature of reality and has capacity to come to a definite answer.

4. *Abhigatito*- It penetrates into the deeper meaning of the Buddha's teachings.

Buddhaghosa declares that the *Abhidhamma* does not only mean the teaching of the *dhamma* but it also means the instruction in the ultimate nature of things: "*Abhidhammo nāma paramattha-desanā*" (As III.488). In his opinion the ultimate way of explanation or the non-discursive style (*nippariyāya-desanā*) is an outstanding quality of the *Abhidhamma* (As III. 304, 484, 486). This, according to him, is in clear contrast to the discursive style (*sappariyāya-desanā*) of *Sutta-piṭaka* wherein the *Dhamma* is taught with the frequent use of similes, metaphors and the anecdotes. The *Abhidhamma* uses a very select, precise and thoroughly impersonal style, which is certainly technical in meaning and function. Buddhaghosa also declared that the tradition recognized distinct character of each *Piṭaka*. It is as follows: the *Vinaya* is the discourse on injunctions (*āṇā-desanā*), the *Sutta* is the popular teachings (*Vohāra-desanā*) and the *Abhidhamma* is the discourse on the ultimate reality (*paramattha-desanā*) (As I.21).

Thus, in the Pāli literature the word *Abhidhamma* was used as a masculine gender word in the Vinaya, in the Nikāya-s and more frequently in the post-canonical works (sees Mil 344, As I.2, Dip V.37). In its earlier usages, it refers generally the meaning of concerning the *Dhamma*. Sometimes it also refers to the distinct technique for the exposition of the special *Dhamma* (M I. 472; A I.14).

However, in some of the later interpolations in the *Sutta-piṭaka* (Ap 4), in the Pāli chronicles (Dip V.37) and in the commentaries, the word *Abhidhamma* was used in its literary sense and referred to the texts of a special collection. Finally, in the Pāli-Commentaries of Buddhaghosa, it conveyed these specific senses:

1. Supplementary *Dhamma*.
2. Special/ Superior *Dhamma*

3. Supreme *Dhamma* (Mp III.271)

In the Sarvāstivāda tradition the meanings of the two components (*abhi* and *dhamma*) are elaborated even in more details than in the Pāli literature.

The Chinese translation of the *Mahāvibhāsā-śāstra* mentions various theories regarding the meaning of the word *Abhidharma*. Some of them are as follows:

(A) It is so called because it is able to investigate and discriminate the characteristic of phenomena thoroughly well, it is able to reflect on the various natures of phenomena and penetrate into them, it is able to perceive and realize phenomena, its dharma is very profound and reaches the very foundation, it is able to reveal the subtle nature of things and it can conquer all doctrines.

(B) According to Vasumitra, the *Abhidharma* is so called because it is always able to investigate the nature and characteristics of phenomena expounded in the *sūtra* etc. It explains the twelve member casual law and the inherent nature of phenomena, it helps us to understand the four noble truths thoroughly, it studies and practices the law of the noble eightfold path, it enables one to realize *Nirvāṇa* and it arranges phenomena in various ways by profound doctrines.

(C) According to Bhadanta Dharmatrāta it is called *Abhidharma* because it collects, arranges and discriminates such problems as defilements, purity, bondage, emancipation, degeneration, elevation by means of phrases, words and sentences.

(D) According to Pārśva it is called *Abhidharma* because it is ultimate, excellent and infallible wisdom (*prajñā*).

(E) According to Ghoṣaka's theory, it is called *Abhidharma* because through it one, who seeks emancipation, following the right practice, gets clear insight as to suffering, cause and cessation of suffering etc.

(F) According to the Dharmaguptaka's theory, it is called *Abhidharma* because of the predominance of the *dharma*.

(G) The Mahīśāsaka holds that it is called *Abhidharma* because its wisdom ably illuminates the phenomena.

(H) The theory of the Dārṣṭāntika-s is that *Nirvāṇa* is supreme among all the *dharma*-s and the *Abhidharma* is next to it. Therefore, it is too called *Abhidharma*.

(I) According to the opinion of Śabdavāda here '*a*' stands for removal and '*bhi*' for discrimination. As it removes *dharma*-s like fetters, trivial studies, the outburst of organs and perception and discriminates *dharma*-s like *skandha*-s, *āyatana*-s and *dhātu*-s. Therefore, it is called *Abhidharma*.

(J) In the opinion of Venerable Buddhapālita it is called *Abhidharma*, because the prefix "*Abhi*" means "face to face" and this *dharma* can induce all the skillful *dharma* (the *Bodhipakṣīya-dharma*-s etc.) to appear face to face.

(K) According to Venerable Buddhadeva '*abhi*' means predominant and this *dharma* is predominant.

(L) According to Vāmalabodha '*abhi*' means veneration and this *dharma* is venerable. (For detail discussion see WATANABE 1983: 23-24; DHAMMAJOTI 2009: 7-8).

Thus, twenty-three meanings of the term *Abhidharma* are given in the *Mahāvibhāṣā*. Some of them are, more or less overlapping while some correspond to the meanings propounded in the Theravāda tradition. Two broad meanings expressed by them may be identified thus:

A. The meaning of *dharma-pravicaya* or the decisive discernment of the nature of the *dharma*-s. There is more emphasis in this on the intellectual function of *Prajñā* and it inspired the later *Abhidharmika*-s such as *Vasubandhu* and *Saṅghabhadra* for their interpretation of the term *Abhidharma*. Here the term *Dharma* is explicitly interpreted as fundamental constituents or elements of existence. Their exposition of the term *Abhidharma* is clearly based on this meaning.

B. In the *Abhidharma-kośa-bhāṣya* (AKB), Vasubandhu defines the term *Abhidhamma* and says: "A *Dharma* is so called because it sustains its own characteristic. This *dharma* faces (*abhi*) towards the *dharma* in the highest sense, i.e. *Nirvāṇa*, or towards the characteristics of *dharma*-s, thus it is *Abhidharma*", "*svalakṣaṇa-dhāraṇād dharmah. tad ayaṁ paramārtha-dharmaṁ vā nirvāñaṁ dharma-lakṣaṇaṁ vā praty ābhimukho dharma itya abhidharmaḥ*" (tr. and quotation taken from DHAMMAJOTI 2009: 9, note 35). The same author, further explaining the term, says that in the highest or real sense *Abhidharma* is none other than the pure wisdom (*Amalā-prajñā*) which is defined as the discernment of (*Dharma-pravicaya*)- "*Prajñā'malā sā'nucarā'bhidharmaḥ*" (AKB I.2).

C. In keeping with the numerous definitions of the term *Abhidharma* given in the *Mahā-vibhāṣā-śāstra*, Saṅghabhadra, *a* Vaibhāṣika teacher, clearly spells out the meaning of prefix '*abhi*' as *abhisamaya* or direct realization.

D. Now, why the pure (*anāsravā*) wisdom (*prajñā*) alone is called *Abhidharma*? Because, when the characteristics of *dharma* are directly realized through it, one will no longer be deduced (therein) (DHAMMAJOTI 2009: 9).

E. Both, Vasubandhu and Sanghabhadra, declare that conventionally *Abhidharma* also refers to that tainted wisdom (*sāsravāprajñā*) which is acquired through listening (*śrutamayī*) reflection (*cintanamayī*) and cultivation (*bhāvanāmayī*) or which is acquired innately (*upapattipratilambhikā*) and which helps to attain the pure wisdom, (*amalāprajñā*). Similarly the *Abhidharma-śāstra*-s (texts) are also to be considered as *Abhidhar-*

ma, as they serve as a means of as prerequisites' (*sambhāra*) to its acquisition.

F. The meaning of being face to face or being direct to the *dharma*, which is *Nirvāṇa*, the supreme *dharma*, unfolds the spiritual function of the *Abhidharma*. In fact, the soteriological aspect of the *Abhidharma* is amply testified in the writings of both the Theravāda and the Sarvāstivāda. Buddhaghosa, the most celebrated commentator of the Theravāda tradition says that the Buddha revealed *Abhidhrama* while residing in the heaven of the *Tāvatiṁsa* gods (As I.76). The expressions such as "the divine world" or the "world of gods" should be taken as symbolic expression of the fact that in the *Abhidharma* attention has been drawn away from the surface of sensuous world and has been directed towards the within, the source of everything and no amount of discursive reasoning will be able to convey that which is to be experienced within and is to be known independently of any logical method. In fact, prince Siddhārtha became the Buddha only by internally knowing the true nature of elements of existence. Therefore, Buddhaghosa says: "*Sammā saṁbuddho hi paṭhamataraṁ abhidhammiko. So hi naṁ mahābodhi- pallaṅke nisīditvā paṭivijjhi*" (As I.44)

G. Furthermore, it is also said that the *Abhidhamma* is the sphere of the omniscient Buddha-s, but not the sphere of others: "*abhidhammo nāma esa sabbaññu buddhānaṁ yeva visayo, na aññe saṁvisayo*" (As I.73). Similarly, the film conviction in the soteriological function of the *Abhidharma* is clearly confirmed by the *Abhidharmika*-s of *Sarvāstivāda* tradition. Thus in the *Abhidharmakośa- bhāṣya*,Vasubandhu declares that *Abhidharma* has been taught by the Buddha because there is no efficient means for the appeasement of the mental defilement apart from the discernment of the *dharma*-s, and it is on account of the mental defilements that beings wander in the ocean of existence. "*dharmāṇāṁ pravicayamantareṇa nāsti kleśānāṁ yata śāntaye 'bhyupayaḥ, kleśaiśca bhramati bhavārṇave'tra lokastaddhetorata uditaḥ kilaiṣa śāstrā*" (AKB I.2).

Thus, this discussion on the meaning of the *Abhidhamma/ Abhidharma* indicates that *Abhidhamma* should not be mistaken for mere scholarly debate or mental exercise. It should be made amply clear that *Abhidhamma* originated with a spiritual motivation for attaining inner experience. Taken together the main tenets, the *Abhidhamma* constitutes the true spiritual praxis taught by the Buddha for the attainment of *Nibbāna/Nirvāṇa.*

Abbreviation (Pāli texts quoted here are from the PTS, London.)

A *Aṅguttara-nikāya*
AKB *Abhidharma-kośa-bhāṣya*, Ed. by P. PRADHAN. K. P. Jaiswal Research Institute, Patna, 1975.
As *Aṭṭhasālinī*
Ap *Apadāna*
Dīp *Dīpavaṃsa*
Mil *Milindapañho*
M *MajjhimaNikāya.*
Vin *Vinaya Piṭakaṁ.*
Mp *Manorathapūraṇī*
PED Pāli English Dictionary, PTS, London.

Selected Bibliography

DHAMMAJOTI, Bhikkhu K. L.
(2009). *Sarvāstivāda Abhidhamma.* The University of Hong Kong, Hong Kong: Centre of Buddhist Studies. 1st Ed. 2002 Colombo.

HARE, E. M.
(2006). *The Book of the Gradual Sayings.* Tr. Vol. III-IV. 1st Indian ed. Delhi: Motilal Banasidas Publishers Private Limited. 1st Pub. PTS, U.K. 1934-35.
HORNER, I.B.
(1941). *Abhidhamma and Abhivinaya in the first Piṭakas of the Pāli Canon.* Vol. XVII, No. 3, 219-310. Indian Historical Quarterly.
(1969). *The Book of the Discipline.* Tr.Vol. III. (*Suttavibhaṅga*). London: PTS. 1st Pub. 1942.
(1971). *The Book of the Discipline.* Tr. Vol. IV. (*Mahāvagga*). London: Luzac & Company LTD. 1st Pub. 1951.
(2004). *The Middle Length Sayings.*Tr. Vols. 1-II. 1st Indian Ed. Delhi: MotilalBanasidas Publishers Private Limited. 1st Pub. PTS, U.K. 1954.
RHYS DAVIDS, T.W. & C.A.F.
(2007). *Dialogues of the Buddha.* Tr. Vol. I-III. Re. Delhi: MotilalBanasidas Publishers Private Limited. 1st Pub. U.K. 1921.
WATANABE, Fumimaro.
(1983). *Philosophy and its Development in the Nikāyas and Abhidhamma.* Delhi: Motilal Banarsidass Private Limited.
WOODWARD, F. L.
(2006). *The Book of the Gradual Sayings.*Tr. Vol. I-II, V. 1st Indian ed. Delhi: Motilal Banasidass Publishers Private Limited. 1st Pub. PTS, U.K. 1933.

Buddha's *Paññā* that Purifies and Liberates

Angraj CHAUDHARY*

Of the three kinds of *paññā- sutamayā* (knowledge gained by listening to what others say), *cintāmayā* (knowledge gained by thought and reflection) and *bhāvanāmayā* (knowledge gained by a virtuous person's own experience) the Buddha regards the last one as the most important. The purer the mind the deeper the experience and the clearer and sharper is the *paññā* (wisdom). The experience of a person can be pure only when his mind is free from defilements like anger, jealousy, greed, and other unwholesome *dhamma*-s. According to the Buddha, defilements can be removed by observing *sīla*-s (precepts). That is why it has been said that *paññā* is purified by morality. The following quotation from the *Soṇadaṇḍa Sutta* brings out the characteristic of *paññā*:

> "*sīlaparidhotā paññā, paññāparidhotaṃ sīlaṃ. yattha sīlaṃ tattha paññā, yattha paññā tattha sīlaṃ. sīlavato paññā, paññavato sīlaṃ. sīlapaññāṇañca pana lokasmiṃ aggamakkhāyatī"ti*" (D I.108)
>
> 'For wisdom is purified by morality, and morality is purified by wisdom: where one is, the other is, the moral man has wisdom and the wise man has morality, and the combination of morality and wisdom is called the highest thing in the world' (tr. WALSH 1995: 131).

It is clear from this that wisdom and morality mutually

* Professor (Retired), Nava Nalanda Mahavihar, Nalanda, Bihar, India. E-mail: angraj.c@gmail.com

purify and strengthen each other. One more aspect of this *paññā* is that it is not only a means to an end but it is an end in itself. When one attains the highest knowledge he becomes the Buddha who is the embodiment of the highest knowledge.

The *paññā* which Siddhārtha was interested in to attain was not the *jñāna* which would enable him to master physical, chemical, biological, or geometrical formulas or laws. How was he going to benefit from knowing that the three angles of a triangle are together equal to two right angles, or the two sides of a triangle are together greater than the third side or $2H^2+O^2= 2H^2O$ or say the Laws of Newton. The knowledge of these laws was not going to help him get rid of suffering which is an existential problem of mankind. And the *ariyan* quest for which he had left home for a homeless life was to find out the way of ending suffering.

In the *Mūlapariyāya Sutta* the Buddha has shown that only a virtuous man can have understanding, wisdom or insight. Of the three kinds of people viz. *puthujjana* (a worldling), *sekkha* (a learner) and an Arhant, a Buddha or a Tathāgata, the last has developed complete understanding because he is virtuous. This is the only *sutta* in the whole of Buddhist literature which was not understood by the *bhikkhu*-s who were present when it was preached because the Buddha talks here of the happy union of epistemology and ontology being a *sine qua non* for attaining *paññā*. It is here that the Buddha divides people into three categories, namely, *assutavā* (*puthujjana, adasssāvī, akovido, avinīto* are all his synonyms), *sekkha* (*appattamānaso* or *anuttarayogakkhemaṁ patthayamāno*) and *khīṇāsava*.

A *khīṇāsava* has six categories, four categories of *arahat*-s and two categories of the Tathāgata-s. All have achieved destruction of taints because all of them do not take delight in worldly objects. Because taking delight means developing desire or *taṇhā*, so all categories have destroyed the root cause of *taṇhā* and have thus destroyed taints.

This categorization has been done on the basis of their degree of knowledge attained by them. There are different degrees of knowledge expressed by the verb *jānāti* (knows) when it is prefixed by *upasarga*-s like *sañ—sañjānāti* (recognizes and experiences), *vi—vijānāti* (knows it out of many), *pa—pajānāti* (knows it clearly), *pari—parijānāti* (knows it surely for whatever is to be known about something) and *abhi—abhijānati* (knows it rightly at the experiential level). A *puthujjana* has the lowest degree of knowledge and the Tathāgata has the highest. An *Arhat* also has been put into four categories. The first category has fully understood the reality of an object and does not delight in it as a *puthujjana* does. The second category of *Arhat* does not take delight in an object because he is free from lust as he has destroyed it. The third category does not have hatred because he has destroyed it, he is free from aversion and the fourth category of *Arahat* has rent the veil of ignorance completely and is free from it.

Of the two types of the Tathāgata-s the first has fully understood the reality to the end. The Pāli word used for his degree of knowing is *parijānāti.* The second type has not only understood reality to the end, i.e., as far as it has to be known but he has also understood that delight is the root of suffering. He has also understood the *Law of Dependent Origination* which explains why *taṇhā* causes suffering. Because he completely destroys, gives up and relinquishes cravings he becomes the Tathāgata- *the fully Enlightened One*. The degree of his knowledge is expressed by the Pāli word *abhijānāti.*

The *Mūlapariyāya Sutta* was not understood by the *bhikkhu*-s. Why? Because here the Buddha explains different degrees of knowledge attained by different persons. Attainment of knowledge by a person is directly proportional to his observance of precepts of morality. The greater the purity the deeper and sharper is the knowledge. In the *Aṭṭhakathā* of this *sutta* it has been shown that complete understanding or comprehension *(pariññā)* consists of three stages; viz. *ñātapariññā, tīraṇapariññā* and *pahānapariññā* (Ps I.29). *Ñātapariññā* is a stage at which one becomes thoroughly familiar with an object, say, the earth (*pathavī*) in terms of its characteristics (*lakkhaṇa*), its function (*rasa*), its manifestation (*paccupaṭṭhāna*) and its immediate cause (*padaṭṭhāna*), i.e. one does not know only its characteristics, function and how it manifests but also knows its immediate cause. *Tīraṇapariññā* is a higher stage of comprehension at which one realizes that nothing is permanent. All that look permanent reveal their three characteristics of impermanence, suffering and no-self. This is a stage at which a meditator penetrates into *dhamma*-s and knows their true nature. *Pahānapariññā* is the highest stage at which one begins to practice what he knows, i.e. one begins to live up to his understanding or wisdom. In other words, he gives up his attachment to worldly objects knowing their impermanent nature and becomes completely free from *rāga* (craving) for them.

Paññā, as said above is to know thoroughly and comprehensively. What to know? To know penetratingly the nature and ingredient of something, *pajānāti paññā, yathāsabhāvaṃ pakārehi paṭivijjhatī'ti attho* (Sv-pṭ I.4). *Paññā* pierces into the real nature of things, *nibbijjhatī'ti nibbedhikā paññā* (Sv-pṭ III.150). It also grasps the real nature of things completely. And every object has three characteristics namely impermanence, suffering and no-self. (*sammasanaṃ paññā, sā maggasampayutta aniccādisammasana kiccaṃ sādheti niccasaññādi pajahanato* (Sv-pṭ III.231). When a meditator practicing *Vipassanā* knows at the level of his experience that what looks stable and permanent is not so, but it is characterized by the three characteristics of impermanence, suffering and no-self then it is *paññā* or insight attained through *Vipassanā*.

In the *Mahāvedalla Sutta* of *Majjhimanikāya* (I.291-298), Sāriputta explains the purpose of *paññā* (wisdom). He says that "*paññā kho, āvuso, abhiññatthā pariññatthā pahānatthā*"*ti* (M I.293), "the purpose of wisdom is, friend, direct knowledge, its purpose is full understanding, its purpose is abandoning" (tr. ÑĀṆAMOLI and BODHI 1995: 389). From these quotations it is clear that *paññā* is not intellect, which according to Oxford English Dictionary is defined as 'the faculty of reasoning and understanding.'

What is meant by knowing something at the experiential knowledge? It is not knowing by hearing from somebody or by reflection that it is sweet because it contains sugar but knowing by personal experience. The difference between them is knowing from somebody that *rasamalāi* (an Indian sweet) is sweet and knowing that it is sweet by tasting it. When you taste it you know all about it, not only that it is sweet but also the degree of its sweetness and how it differs from other sweetnesses say the sweetness of mango and the sweetness of that. The latter is real understanding or wisdom or insight.

Aldous HUXLEY (quoted in DHARMASENA 2008: 20) has brought out the difference between knowledge and understanding in these words:

> "Understanding can only be talked about, and that very inadequately, it cannot be passed on, it can never be shared. There can, of course, be knowledge of such an understanding, and this knowledge may be passed on. But we must always remember that knowledge of understanding is not the same thing as understanding, which is the raw material of that knowledge. It is different from understanding as the doctor's prescription for penicillin is different from penicillin. Understanding is as rare as emeralds, and so is highly prized. The knowers would dearly love to

> be understanders; but either their stock of knowledge does not include the knowledge of what to do in order to be understanders, or else they know theoretically what they ought to do but go on doing the opposite all the same. In either case they cherish the comforting delusion that knowledge, and above all pseudo-knowledge are understanding."

HUXLEY's 'understanding' comes very close to 'direct experience', which is *prajñā*. *Prajñā* is made up of prefix *'pra'* which means *'pratyakṣa'* 'direct' and *'jñā'* means 'to experience'. So *prajñā* means direct knowledge, i.e. knowledge at the experiential level. It is wisdom born out of one's direct experience which can move one to the depth of his heart when he sees that all things that he is attached to are impermanent and changing at an inconceivably fast rate.

This wisdom is different from knowledge. Of the different types of knowledge such as Revealed Knowledge, Speculative knowledge, Scientific Empirical Knowledge and Practical knowledge it may be called Scientific Empirical Knowledge. But here also there is a difference. Scientific Empirical knowledge is gained by observation and experiment in a laboratory outside but *paññā/prajñā* is gained by observing what happens within when mind and matter work together. This experiment is carried out in one's fathom long body. In the former you observe things happening outside but in the latter you observe what happens within you. This one does again and again within himself. This is technically called *bhāvanā* which means increasing, cultivating, and developing, "*bhāvanāti vaḍḍhanā, brūhanā*" (Sv-pṭ III.237). But where to do this? Unlike a scientist who experiments in an outside laboratory one does it within oneself. He knows that what arises in his mind passes away and he experiences that again and again. Thus he verifies the truth, "*attano santāne uppannaṃ jānāti, paṭisaṃveditaṃ karoti, anubhavati*" (Mp II.274). A stage comes to him when he begins to see its impermanence because it soon passes away. At a higher stage he sees it as *dukkha* because it does not last. At a still higher stage he experiences that there is nothing like soul here—"*yadaniccaṃ taṃ dukkhaṃ yaṃ dukkhaṃ tadanattā* (S III.22)...*attano santāne aniccaṃ dukkhaṃ anattāti tividhānupassanā karaṇaṃ*" (Mp IV.86).

There is another difference. As far as physical, chemical and biological laws are concerned they are observed with five senses but psychological and psycho-ethical laws that operate within him are observed by his own mind. It is common knowledge that you can increase the power of seeing with eye, ear etc. by using microscope and telescope and other suitable apparatuses and machines but how to increase the power of mind? The power of mind can be increased by practicing *Vipassanā*, which is a technique of meditation discovered by the Buddha.

There is yet another difference. As far as the physical, chemical and other laws are concerned, they have been discovered by persons who were not necessarily absorbed in meditation. They kept on observing what happened in nature and why and propounded these laws. Of course, some amount of concentration on their part must have been there but leading an ethical life to achieve concentration of pure mind was not a necessary condition, was not an absolute condition for them.

Besides, the laws discovered by them can be experimented by others in any suitable lab. Neither the discoverers of the laws nor those who make experiments to prove their veracity are required to lead a life of virtue, concentration and wisdom.

On the other hand, as the Buddha discovered the laws like the Law of Dependent Origination, or *vedanāpaccayā taṇhā* (Vin I.1) (sensation gives rise to desire) or *pubbe hanati attānaṃ, pacchā hanati so pare* (Th 19), (he first hurts his own self before he hurts others), so a man walking on the path shown by him can verify these laws. These laws will remain a sealed book to those who do not walk on the path shown by him—the path consisting of *sīla, samādhi* and *paññā.* Only those who achieve purity of mind are capable of verifying and understanding these laws.

One may call them spiritual laws or psycho-ethical laws and know them at the intellectual level but one cannot understand them in depth. One who wants to know how sweet a *rasamalāi* is he has to taste it himself as shown above. Somebody else tasting it and telling him that it is sweet will not enable him to know the kind and degree of sweetness.

The Buddha himself could discover these laws by living a pure and ethical life, by making his mind 'concentrated, purified, bright, unblemished, rid of imperfection, malleable, wieldy, steady and imperturbable'. Because these laws are related to how mind and matter work together, they cannot be understood outside of one nor can they be experimented in any lab outside of one's fathom-long body, where the veracity of these laws can be proved if the mind of the man making experiment is purified. For precisely understanding these laws one has to concentrate one's mind. And how can one's mind with various defilements be concentrated unless he observes ethical precepts to free his mind from them.

Buddha's scientific discoveries based on observation by a mind purified and sharpened by leading an ethical life:

Buddha's scientific discoveries are, therefore, based on observation by a mind purified and sharpened by leading an ethical life. All the laws that he discovered relate to how one's mind works, how cravings are caused, where precisely they arise and why they cause suffering. If one knows all these, one can know the causes of suffering and get rid of it by annihilating them.

One of the constituents of the discovery of these laws is observation. But this is not an ordinary observation. It is an observation made by a virtuous man who leads a pure ethical life as said above and who has made his mind so sharp, pointed and pure that he can observe all the minutes things that happen within him. He can also understand how he hurts himself first when he is angry with somebody before he hurts him if he enables himself to see what happens inside him when he is angry.

No great scientist, not even a Nobel Laureate, can understand the laws propounded by the Buddha unless he walks on the path shown by him and unless he achieves concentration of his mind by purifying it.

Buddha's Philosophy of suffering is not speculative but born out of his own experience:

The philosophy of suffering propounded by the Buddha is not speculative but it is born out of his own experience. It was the direct experience not of a common man but of a very sensitive and pure man, who was free from defilements such as greed, aversion, jealousy, anger etc. which he had annihilated by practicing *vipassanā*. His philosophy, therefore, is not based on abstractions. It does not speculate on 'empty first principles' in the words of Robert N. BECK- a pragmatic thinker. Buddha's attitude to speculative philosophy becomes clear from what he says to Poṭṭhapāda (D I.177-202) and Mālunkyaputta (M I). When Poṭṭhapāda put ten questions relating to the world and the soul like, "Is the world eternal or not eternal? Is the world finite or not finite? Does the Tathāgata live after death or not?" and so on, the Buddha did not answer these questions. Why? Because he called them indeterminate. Answering such questions, according to him, is not 'conducive to the purpose, not conducive to *Dhamma*, not the way to embark on the holy life, it does not lead to disenchantment, to dispassion, to cessation, to calm, to higher knowledge, to enlightenment, to *Nibbāṇa*'. Instead he explained the Four Noble Truths because their enunciation 'is conducive to the purpose, conducive to *Dhamma*, the way to embark on the holy life; it leads to disenchantment, to dispassion, to cessation, to calm, to higher knowledge, to enlightenment, to *Nibbāṇa*'. From this it is clear that the philosophy propounded by the Buddha is not speculative but it is born out of his direct experience. So it is pragmatic because knowing the cause of suffering he tries to destroy it to end suffering.

This is also clear from what he says to Mālunkyaputta who also like Poṭṭhapāda wanted to know from him the answer to such speculative questions. The Buddha said to Mālunkyaputta that to insist on knowing the answer to such questions before one agrees to lead the holy life is as foolish and fruitless as a man pierced with a poisoned arrow not agreeing to have the arrow taken out by a surgeon until he knows all about the arrow and the person who shot it. What would be the result? The result would be that he would suffer great pain and die but the questions would remain unanswered (see M I.428).

The Buddha was a different kind of philosopher. The philosophies propounded by other philosophers are based on logic and reasoning and abstract thinking. They, therefore, may be controversial even if they are logical. But certainly they are not useful at all for solving the existential problems of man. Mind, as the Buddha says is very fickle and unsteady. It keeps on moving from one object to another. If this mind is controlled, then it can attain concentration. When it develops concentration and becomes sharp then it can observe things more clearly, not in a blurred manner, just as a mirror free from dust can reflect better and clearer. As a scientist makes experiment several times to prove whether any physical, chemical, and biological law is true or not, in the same way one makes experiment again and again to see whether the laws propounded by the Buddha are true or not. 'Mind is fickle' can be easily understood but *vedanā paccayā taṇhā* (sensation produces desire) cannot be so easily understood.

The Buddha wanted to grapple with the problem of suffering which is ubiquitous and universal. Suffering is an existential problem not only of mankind but also of all living beings. All are subject to different kinds of suffering, physical and mental. One who is born is subject to old age, disease and death. This is physical suffering. He is also separated from one he likes. He also has to live with somebody he does not like. He does not get what he wants. This is mental suffering. All these are sufferings from which no body is free. The Buddha saw it very sensitively and wanted to find a way out of it.

This is from where he started. He started with the real problem that faced mankind, not with the abstract and speculative problem. He saw the problem facing him starkly. He saw the disease. His effort was to know the cause of the disease and find out its remedy.

In his spiritual journey he learned from his own experience. While practicing meditation he went deep into it and realized that one's suffering is caused by one's desires for the things one likes. One's desires are never fulfilled because the things one desires are not permanent. They are in a constant state of flux. This realization came to him after practicing *Vipassanā* meditation. This was a sort of 'eureka' for him.

For practicing *Vipassanā* meditation concentration of mind even for a short while is a *sine qua non.* This is not possible without observing moral precepts. This was another big discovery. Gradually he learned that observation of *sīla* helps one to achieve concentration of mind and with the help of this concentration one realizes the true nature of the objects of the world by directly experiencing it.

When one comes to know the true nature of things, ignorance goes away. In other words, true knowledge dawns upon him. He sees the objects of one's attachment as impermanent, becomes disillusioned and concludes that if the objects he longs for are so transient and impermanent how can they make him happy? This again was a great realization born out of his direct experience.

Thus the Buddha concluded that one's suffering is caused by one's desires and one has desires for things the real nature of which one does not know. There is a built-in dynamo inside everybody. So long as one is ignorant of the real nature of the objects of the world the dynamo within one fuelled by desires keeps on generating desires. And multiplication of desires causes endless suffering. But once he comes to know the real nature of the objects he hankers after, he begins to develop non-attachment for them. Practice of *Vipassanā* meditation helps him a lot. Whenever one practices *Vipassanā* one experiences that what arises passes away. Nothing is permanent. So he experiences impermanence (*aniccatā)*. And whatever is impermanent is *dukkha*. Thus he either reduces his desires and reduces his suffering proportionately or he completely annihilates his desires and completely eradicates his suffering.

Practice of *Vipassanā* helps one understand this law as it had helped the Buddha. The Buddha thus realized the cause of suffering. It was then just the second step for him to know that suffering can be eliminated by removing the cause.

Thus he propounded the philosophy of suffering from his own experience. He had realized the great importance of observing moral precepts and the great role of a concentrated mind in seeing things sharply and clearly as they are and by practicing *vipassanā* he could see how cravings cause suffering and how it can be eliminated. By practicing *Vipassanā* it became clear to him that, "*yaṃ loke piyarūpaṃ sātarūpaṃ, etthesā taṇhā uppajjamānā uppajjati, ettha nivisamānā nivisati*" (D II.

308) "wherever in the world there is anything agreeable and pleasurable, there this craving arises and establishes itself" (tr. WALSHE 1995: 346).

It did not take the Buddha long to conclude that cravings can be eliminated by eliminating the cause of cravings. And what is the cause of cravings? The agreeable and pleasurable in the world are the causes of cravings. By practicing *Vipassanā* he knew that even the most beautiful objects of the world are impermanent. They do not last forever. The natural question was then why crave for them? Thus he trained his mind to see the transitory nature of objects and give up his craving for them. In this way he ended his suffering. It means that anybody can end his suffering by practicing *Vipassanā*. Because he had realized how suffering is caused and also because he had realized the role of morality *(sīla)* in eliminating it so while propounding the philosophy of suffering he ethicized it. He was also a great psychologist. He saw the role of our mind in causing craving; he also saw how to tame this monkey mind, which now craves for this object and now for that.

The Buddha thus propounded his philosophy of suffering with his *bhāvanāmayā paññā*, (experiential wisdom) which is *yathābhūtañāṇadassana* (wisdom arising from seeing the truth as it is). *Bhāvanāmayā paññā* means insight wisdom developed at the experiential level. There is no question of its being false or speculative or abstract. It is experiential knowledge *(paññā)* with which he saw the cause of suffering. The philosophy of suffering propounded by the Buddha, therefore, is based on his direct experience. Anybody who practices *Vipassaṇā* can see for himself why craving is caused, where suffering arises and how craving and suffering can be ended.

Thus he propounded the Four Noble Truths of suffering, viz. suffering, its cause, its cessation and the way leading to its cessation and preached them to the first five disciples. He explained three aspects of each truth. One should know the

First Noble Truth. This is the first aspect of the First Noble Truth. The First noble truth of suffering should be comprehended *(pariññeyaṃ)*. This is called *kicca ñāna,* i.e. knowledge gained while doing. This is its second aspect. When it is thoroughly comprehended *(pariññātaṃ)* it is called *kata ñāna,* i.e. knowledge gained when done. This is its third aspect. Similarly the rest of the truths should also be known comprehensively. The Second Noble Truth of suffering should be abandoned *(pahātabbaṃ).* This is *kicca ñāna* and when it is completely abandoned *(pahīnaṃ)* it is called *kata ñāna*. The Third Noble Truth should be realized *(sacchikātabbaṃ)*. This aspect of this truth is *kicca ñāna* and when it is realized *(sacchikataṃ)* it is called *kata ñāna.* The Fourth Noble Truth should be developed *(bhāvetabbaṃ)*. This is called *kicca ñāna* and when it is developed *(bhāvitaṃ)* it is called *kata ñāna.* As the Buddha propounded the philosophy of suffering by developing his *bhāvanāmayā paññā* so his philosophy of suffering can be understood by developing *bhāvanāmayā paññā* for which practice of *vipassanā* meditation is inevitable.

Requisites necessary for practicing Vipassanā

For practicing *Vipassanā* the nature of mind has got to be understood. Mind is very fickle and unsteady, "*phandanaṃ capalaṃ cittaṃ*" (Dhp 33). This is Psychology. And for concentrating mind observation of *sīla* is inevitable. *Sīla* comes under Ethics. When one understands the true nature of the objects of the world for which one craves, this is Metaphysics, Buddhist Metaphysics if one may call it so. Apart from these, *Vipassanā* also means training one's mind to give up the old habit pattern of reacting to sensations that arise on one's body. Thus *vipassanā* is a very comprehensive practice to know the nature of mind and nature of reality. Besides, it is also an effective tool to train one's mind to learn to behave in a particular way.

Practicing *Vipassanā* the Buddha propounded the Law of

Dependent Origination, which explains how one creates *saṅkhāra*-s in ignorance, how *saṅkhāra*-s give rise to consciousness, consciousness to *nāma-rūpa*.... and how *bhava* gives rise to *jāti* and *jāti* gives rise to old age, disease, death and all sorts of sorrows and suffering. The Buddha also concluded that as effect has a cause and as it can be eliminated by eliminating its cause, so suffering can be extirpated by eliminating cravings. All the links of *Paṭiccasamuppāda*, each of which is a law, can be understood by practicing *Vipassanā*.

One's fathom long body is the only laboratory where the Laws propounded by the Buddha can be experimented:

But there is a basic difference between the physical laws and the laws connected with the Four Noble Truths. In no other laboratory outside this fathom-long body can it be proved that sensations cause desire. This will be possible only when one, who wants to prove it, lives a pure life, practices *Vipassanā* and observes one's sensations pleasant or unpleasant or neutral. He will see that he wants to have more of pleasant sensations and none of the unpleasant ones. The former is craving and the latter is aversion. Both are the causes of suffering. He will also see that sensations are not permanent. They keep on changing.

Physical laws can be experimented and proved in outside laboratories by anybody. He may be of greedy temperament. He may have several defilements. It does not matter. But the laws relating to the Four Noble Truths propounded by the Buddha can be experienced and proved by those, who live a virtuous life, i.e. who observe *sīla*, practice *samādhi* and are on the way to develop *paññā*. Buddhaghosa in his *Visuddhimagga* gives a beautiful simile to show how to develop *paññā*. He is quoted here in extenso:

> "*ettha pana yasmā imāya paññāya khandhāyatana dhātu indriya sacca paṭiccasamuppādādi bhedā dhammā bhūmi. sīla visuddhi ceva citta visuddhi cāti imā dve visuddhiyo*

> *mūlaṃ. diṭṭhi visuddhi, kaṅkhā vitaraṇavisuddhi, maggāmaggañāṇa dassana visuddhi, paṭipadāñāṇa dassanavisuddhi, ñāṇa dassana visuddhīti imā pañca visuddhiyo sarīraṃ. tasmā tesu bhūmibhūtesu dhammesu uggaha paripucchāvasena ñāṇa paricayaṃ katvā mūla bhūtā dve visuddhiyo sampādetvā sarīrabhūtā pañca visuddhiyo sampādentena bhāvetabbā*" (Vism 443).
>
> "Now the things classed as aggregates, bases, elements, faculties, truths, dependent origination, etc., are the *soil* of this understanding, and the [first] two purifications, namely, Purification of Virtue (*sīlavisuddhi)*, and Purification of Consciousness *(cittavisuddhi)*, are its *roots* , while the five purifications, namely, Purification of View *(diṭṭhivisuddhi)*, Purification by Overcoming doubt (*kaṅkhāvitaraṇavisuddhi*), Purification by Knowledge and Vision of What is the Path and What is not the Path, Purification by Knowledge and Vision of the Way *(maggāmaggañṇadassanavisuddhi)*, and Purification by Knowledge and Vision (*ñāṇadassanavisuddhi*) are the *trunk*. Consequently one who is perfecting these should first fortify his knowledge by learning and questioning about those things that are the 'soil' after he has perfected the two purifications that are the 'roots', then he can develop the five purifications that are the 'trunk' (tr. ÑĀṆAMOLI 2010: 439)

Developed *paññā,* according to Buddhaghosa is like a big tree of which the roots are the two Purifications of Virtue and Consciousness. These roots are struck in the soil of aggregates, bases, elements, faculties, and truths etc., which draw sustenance from them and then grow into a big tree with five purifications as its trunk.

When Buddhaghosa says that Purification of Virtue *(sīlavisuddhi)* and Purification of Consciousness *(cittavisuddhi)* are the roots of understanding, he underlines the importance of both *sīla* and *samādhi.* Only a virtuous man can attain concentration of mind, which can enable him to see the real nature of reality. When he sees the reality as it is at the experiential level he is on the way to develop non-attachment to so-called attractive things because the darkness of ignorance is now over.

These two Purifications, which are roots, derive their nourishment from the soil of aggregates, bases, elements, faculties, truths, dependent origination and so on as said above. When they are studied in detail and their characteristics (*lakkhaṇa*), function *(rasa)*, how they are manifested *(paccupaṭṭhāna)* and their immediate cause (*padaṭṭhāna)* are known it becomes clear that all things of the world are dependently originated. All this is experienced at the experiential level.

When things are seen in such a way then Purification of View *(diṭṭhi visuddhi)* is developed. This is followed by the development of Purification by Overcoming Doubt *(kaṅkhāvitaraṇa visuddhi)*. Further progress is made and what is the Path and what is not the Path is known. Thus purification by knowledge and vision of what is the path and what is not the path *(maggāmaggañāṇadassan visuddhi)* is made. This is followed by the development of Purification by Knowledge and Vision of the Way *(paṭipadāñāṇadassanavisuddhi)* and finally Purification by Knowledge and Vision *(ñāṇadassanavisuddhi)* is developed. This is the *paññā* that simultaneously purifies and liberates and is highly prized by the Buddha.

Abbreviation (Pāli texts quoted here are from PTS, London.)

D	*Dīghanikāya*
Dhp	*Dhammapada*
M	*Majjhimanikāya*
Mp	*Manorathapūraṇī (Aṅguttara-nikāya-aṭṭhakathā)*
Ps	*Papañcasūdanī (Majjhima-nikāya-aṭṭhakathā)*

S Saṃyutta-nikāya (*formerly* SN)
Sv-pṭ *Dīghanikāyaṭṭhakathāṭīkā (sīlakhandhavaggaṭikā)*
Th *Theragāthā*
Vin *Vinayapiṭaka*
Vism *Visuddhi-Magga*

References

DHARMASENA, C. B.
(2008). *Purification of View.* The Wheel Publication No. 40. Kandy: Buddhist Publication Society (Online Edition). 1st Pub. 1962.

ÑĀṆAMOLI, Bhikkhu.
(2010). *Visuddhimagga: The Path of Purification.* 4th ed. Kandy: Buddhist Publication Society.

ÑĀṆAMOLI, Bhikkhu, and BODHI, Bhikkhu
(1995). *The Middle Length Discourses of the Buddha: A New Translation of Majjhima Nikāya.* Kandy: Buddhist Publication Society.

WALSH, Maurice
(1995). *The Long Discourses of the Buddha: A Translation of the Dīgha Nikāya.* Boston: Wisdom Publications.

Anattā and *Suññatā* in Indian Sociology

Suniti Kumar PATHAK*

Anattā vs Sakkāyadiṭṭhi

A general allegation is labelled against Gotama, the Buddha for his negation of the self-existent soul-like entity *attā/ātmā* as permanent, with its individual manifestation *jivātmā.* In respect to the individual sentient being, the Jaina propounder Mahāvīra declared that as many living beings are, so many souls existed in probable of the *Anekāntavāda.* In the context of the Indian Sociology, the impact of *Anattā* negation of the self-existent permanent entity did stir the socio-spiritual vision of the animate life since the middle of the first millennium before the Christ.

On the other hand, seers of the ancient Indian Vaidika cults had established opposite view in the *Nāsadīyasūkta* of the *Ṛg-veda.* [1] That claimed that the existent *sat* reality generated out of the indeterminable. The *Ṛg-veda* further enumerated three primary factors in origination of the universe, namely *ṛtam*, the mobility of the universal potential in kinetic function, *satyam*, the would-be existent matter *a-priori* to function and *tapas*, the heat. In order to generate objective contents out of the mobility in action three above were

---

* Professor (Retired), Visva-Bharti University, Shantiniketan, West Bengal, India. E-mail: geetaniti@gmail.com

1 nāsadyasīnno sadāsittadāniṃ nāsīdradho no vyomoparoyan।
kimāvarīvah kuhū kasya śarmannbhah kimāsidgahanam gabhīram॥
na mrityurāsidamṛnam na tarhi na rātrayā ahu āsīt prakenah।
ānīdavānaṃ svadhayā tadekaṃ tasmāda dhānānnah parā kiṃ cānase॥ (*Parmātmadevatā, Prajāpatiṛsi, Ṛg-veda* 10/129/1-2)

essential.[2] These preconditioned states of the Universe were the unchangeable being *ka*, otherwise named the golden essence *hiraṇyagarbha.*[3] Resultantly, the Vaidika ontology had accepted the self-existent *svayambhū* with multiple appositions like *sad, parama, brahman, viśvam* to signify the 'that latent'.

The Buddhist literatures, as they have come down up till date, disown what as the *Vedist Upaniṣada* claim. Some Indians, who hold the legacy of the *Vaidika* heritage, fail to fallow what the Gotama Buddha had meant. Because, the Buddha remained silent when ontological questions had been put regarding the existent permanent real like the *Brahman* to govern the functioning of the universe, visible or invisible. He denied *sakkāyadiṭṭhi*, the notion of self-existent reality to manifest in origination of pluralistic universe. Later on, the Buddhist logicians entered intellectual wrestles of dialectic dilemma in the questions of 'is' and 'is not'.

In the *Vinayapiṭaka Anattapariyāya* Gotama makes his position explicit by three-fold rationale in sequence.

1. That, which is conditioned to change, is changeable not permanent *anicca.*

---

2 cakhuṣah pinā manasā hi dhīrodhṛtamene aghanannabhnamāne ।
yadedantā adadahanta pūrva ādiddhyāvāpṛthivī aprayenām ॥
(*Viśvakarmādevatā, Viśvakarmaṛsi, Ṛg-veda* 10/88/1)
ataṁ ca satyaṁ cābhīdadhāttapasoadhyadhāyana ।
tato ratryadhāyana tatah samudro arṇavah ॥
samudrādarṇatādadhi saṁvatsaro aghāyana ।
ahorātrāṇi nidaghadviśvasya bhiṣato vabhī ॥
sūryācandramasau ghātā yathāpūrvamakalpayan ।
divaṁ ca pṛthivīṁ cāntarikshamatho svah ॥
(*Sṛṣṭidevatā, Aghamarṣaṇaṛsi, Ṛg-veda* 1/190 l1-3)

3 hiraṇyagarbhah samavartatāgre bhūvasya ghātah patireka āsīd ।
sadyapāra pṛthivīṁ dyābhūtemāṁ kasmai devāya hviṣā vidhema ॥
(*Prajāpatidevatā, Hiraṇyagarbhaṛsi, Ṛg-veda* 1/121/1)

2. That which is changeable or impermanent, is the not pleasant *dukkha*, but is to suffer.
3. That which is to suffer for being impermanent[4], is not self-existent like soul i.e. *anatta* otherwise essence-less. Because, the time plays an important role in changing a matter or a psychic trait incessantly. A Vedic seer also admitted that changeableness of what a wavering ocean appeared, as designed *aprioi*. So, manifestations of the universe, as viewed upon as real by a seer, are liable to be wrong, *micchādiṭṭhi*. That is the logical basis of the Buddhists for refutation of *sakkāya-diṭṭhi*, the viewpoint of holding the assemblage of permanent existent as real. Before entering into the relative understanding of *suññatā*, substantive otherwise the nature of the universe in the Buddhist literature, a few words about Indian Sociology may be relevant here.

Indian Sociology

In the race-course of the humans, since bio-physical change over from the biped homo-sapiens (circa 10 crore BCE), the human inhabitants of the Indian peninsula followed a circular lane of eco-balance with all necessities. In that respect, they may be of distinct from the other peoples of the eastern hemisphere. The olden settlers of the peninsula might be multiethnic during the hoary past. Presumably, they were hydraulic as the oldest evidences of Harappa Mohenjodaro speak so far our knowledge goes. The remains of the

---

4 *atha kho bhagavā pañcavaggiye bhikkhū āmantesi- rūpaṁ bhikkhave anattā, rūpaṃ ca hidaṃ bhikkhave, attā abhavissa, nayidaṁ ābādhāya saṁvatteyya, labbhetha ca rūpe- evaṁ me rūpaṃ hotu, evaṁ me rūpaṁ mā ahosī ti.... taṁ kiṁ maññatha, bhikkhave, rūpaṁ niccaṁ vā aniccaṁ vā ti? aniccaṁ bhante. vepanāniccaṁ dukkhaṁ vā taṁ sukhaṁ vā ti. dukkhaṁ bhante. yaṁ panāniccaṁ dukkhaṁ vipariṇāmadhammaṁ, kallaṁ nu taṁ samupassituṁ- etaṁ mama, eso hamasmi, eso me attā ti. no hetaṁ bhante.* (*Anattapariyāya, Mahāvagga* 1.8.20-21, *Vinayapiṭaka*- Nalanda)

lost peoples who had that civilization proved the nucleus of the Indians in the following lines.[5]

i) Toilsomeness is the basic criterion of Indian Sociology. That means the Indian peoples, in general, tend to toil along with pace of time since they had become aware of their existence on this geo-physical land. In the Indian diction, the toilsomeness is termed as *karma* with extensive connotations in multiple contexts.

ii) Any human being becomes a part of the wholesomeness of the universe, as far as the Indian seers could visualize. Thereby humans have been sailing on the same boat along with the other animate sentient beings like animals, worms etc. in the Nature as a whole. An Indian therefore is not concerned only with the same class of biped humans. All species of animate and even inanimate beings come in purview. Tendencies of animating the inanimate prevail among the Indians since time immemorial. That means eco-balance *pūrṇāta/akhaṇḍatā* is presumed the primary condition of Indian Sociology.

iii) Alike innumerable animate beings humans toil untiringly to combat and confront against the Nature around with the best of their ability. Therefore, the Indian Sociology stands on the moderate process of distributing social emphasis in qualitative degrees like intellectual toils, manual toils inclusive inner appeasement. Because, an animate body is constituted physiologically by innumerable cells. They function in animate organs in multifarious ways in coordinating process for origin, development and decay. In that respect, Indian Sociology is primarily organic in cellular structure, *kauṣikī* in the Indian diction.

---

5 See, *Pre Aryans and pre Dravidians in India*. Ed. and Tr. by P C Bagchi, Calcutta University, 1938.

iv) In course of incessant toils of the human organs like intellect, physique, multiple progressive effects and enterprises are conditioned to undergo changes towards intellectual attainments and material prosperity as well. As regards individual persons their psychic growth along with those of other physical strength, one claims individual superiority *svātantrya* to others. Human beings socially claim to be superior to animate beings in their brainpower and they endeavour to safeguard from the nails and fangs of animals and serpents. Competitive rivalries, physical assaults, psychic challenges ego-strifes, superiority claims and direct or indirect exploitations have society made the Indian Societies no less uneven than that of others.

Thereby repeated warnings by the seers have been laid on the Indian peoples. Some Indian spiritual leaders, seer, sages, saints and the socio-ethical leaders through the ages appeared in manifested forms *avatāra*. By the growth of material gains and psychic traits simultaneously, many Indian hydraulic societies have been bifurcating in either agro-based rural societies or trade based urban societies since the first millennium BCE if not earlier. A tendency of social integration among the pluralistic structure of the peoples of the peninsula India has become unique. Those integrated structures hold four columns of material relevance with a lien tospirituality complacence.

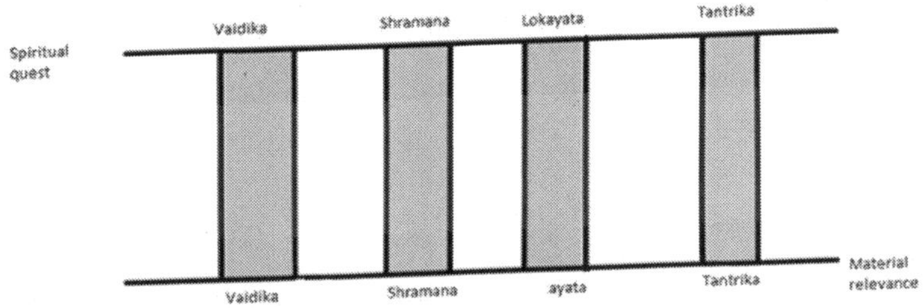

Is *anattā* negative?

Indian Sociology, as stated above, holds the Nature-modelled postulates of generation, sustenance and mergence at the socio-economic levels. In that case, *anatta* a negation of the self-existent permanent reality may appear negative. The viewers of *sakkāyadiṭṭhi*, referred above may claim their rationale as positive and affirmative to accept the permanent existent reality. The followers of Gautama the Buddha are therefore alleged to be the destructive and non-formative in ontological quest of the universe.

The Buddhist however hold a dialectic by two opposite ideas for an analytical critique, i.e. *attā* as postulate 'B' and *anattā* as postulate 'A'. The position of 'B' may be drawn in a monolith tri-angular diagram. Z= psyche, Y= material phenomena and X= preconditioned self-existent reality. *Attā*, as a whole, the *paramātmā* vis-à-vis the Brahman universal extensive reality is self-existent.

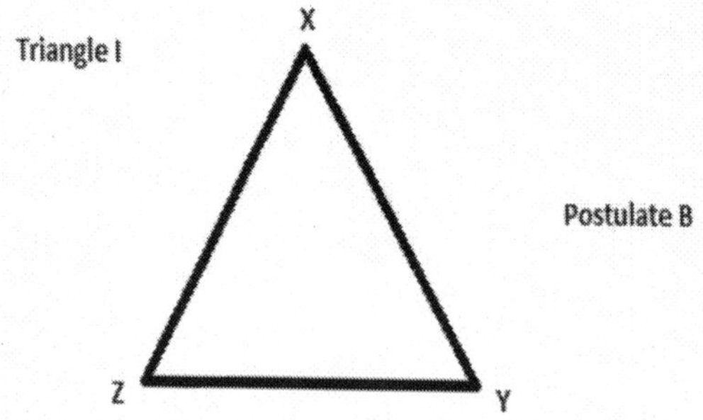

Whereas the postulate 'A' may be placed in other way in an opposite direction of a tri-angular diagram since, the Buddhists disown the authority of the Veda-s, as they are Anthology of Revelations (*apauraṣeya*).

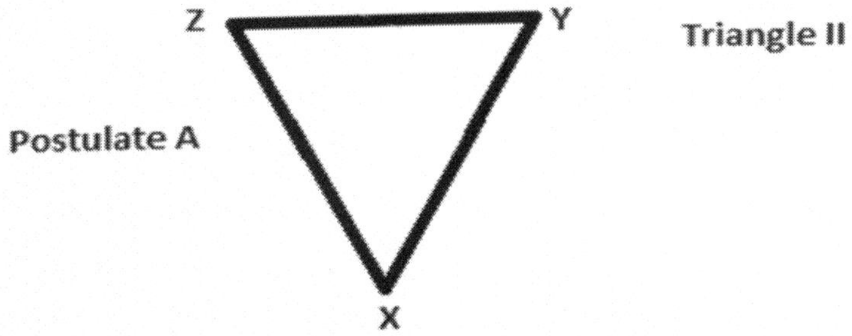

Z= psyche, Y= material phenomena, X= conditionally existent reality building no scope of pre-determination, nor that is accidental.

Gautama the Buddha's view of no-self-existent reality *anattā* is not the abstaining for what is real. But that disowns pre-conditioned factor in establishing the self-existent as real on account of relative origination and decay.

A *Ṛg-veda* seer had forecast *a-priori* conditionally for 'being' *sad* out of 'not-being' *asad* as that was predetermined *yathāpūrvam-akalpayat*. Conditionality is however dependent to the time and the locality. Otherwise, a condition leads to no-condition if it be predetermined. Causation and effectuation function with conditionality in the time and the space context. Here *anattā* is not-unconditioned in the case of admitting self-existent reality *atta* as the latter is pre determined to function *apriori* in cause(s) and effect(s).

Linguistically, the negative particle *an* in Sanskritic expression is contradictory to the existence of *attā*, a permanent substance. According to epistemological understanding the particle *an* is used for negating an alternative *prasajyapratiṣodha* instead of *paryudāsa*. In other words, that which is conditioned becomes constituted or effectuated by cause(s). Logically the proposition may be substantiated by reading thus- *ye dhammā hetuppabhavā hetuṁ tesaṁ tathāgato āha.*

tesaṁ ca yo nirodho evaṁ vādī mahāsamaṇo (*Mahāvagga* 1.17.601).

Universal proposition: Conditionality always changes to effect(s) out of cause(s) processing through sequence of origination, growth and decay.

<X: The triangle under II above justifies that, conditionality point that correlates two other angles.

< Z: Connects <X by XZ referring to the psyche of the sentient beings with changeable frequency unless properly exerted to functional appeasement.

<Y: Connects < X by XY referring to the matter of the visible and unvisible universe with intrinsic changeable characteristic under the conditions of the time and the space.

Therefore, *anattā* affirms the conditional changeability of the mind and the matter.

Social relevance of *anattā*

What is the pragmatic value of holding *anattā* no self existent reality in the material world? A question may be raised. What the Buddha endeavoured to establish was the measures how to eradicate ego-ness of the individual. *Dhammapada* justifies his stand. The notion of 'self' *atta* i.e. narrowness of egoistic hindrance of I-ness or mine-ness does not extend up to wholesome all-extensive *Brahman paramātmā*. As long as the mental cravings for nurturing I-ness prevail, every sentient being remains self-centered. My possessions, my prestige, my voice, my power, my my etc. promote the cravings for bigger and biggest I-ness. Thereby, any person withdraws from the others, ego-strifes, identity struggles etc. generate out of the egoistic causes like superiority or inferiority complexes in the individual psyche or those in multitude.

Anattā in that respect may become a guiding principle of dedicating for the cause of others. The Buddhist literature therefore lays emphasis on self (*sva*) and others (*para*) repeatedly[6]. In due course, the Buddhists innovated the ideal of selflessness by enunciating the models of *pāramitā* practices par excellence for becoming a Bodhisattva. Vast literature of *Jātaka, Apadāna, Avadāna* and *Vyūha* texts speak about selflessness inspite of numerous procurement for one's own self. Because, the so-called I-ness or mine-ness is conventional, then individual is not an embodiment of a mono-item like self or one's own. A *pudgala*, under the process of metabolic changes in every fraction of a second, is constituted by five *skandha-s* with no particular self-existent item to reckon.

Suñña, Suññatā, Shūnyatā

The Buddhists Pāli literature occasionally refers to *suñña, suññatā* in the sense of that which is not in existence. Lexiconists usually translate them void, open space, or vacuum. The significance of emptiness is not always phenomenal but that of psyche to experience by a person with elevated purified sense organs including that of the individual mind[7]. In the phenomenal context, *suññaṃ* may refer to the space with no item to hold by the sense organs like the eyes, ears etc., which in the course of experiencing the psycho-spiritual attains emptiness status *suññaṃ.* Those words usually connote a status in withdrawal of phenomena either psychic or those cognitions of matter. *Suñña* as an adjective suggests vacant. For instance, *suññāgāra* a vacant

---

6 khantī paramaṁ tapo titikkhā nibbānaṁ paraṁ vadanti buddhā ।
na hi pabbajito parūpaghātī samaṇo hoti paraṁ viheṭhayanto ॥
(Dhp 184).
attadatthaṁ paratthena bahunā pi na hāpaye ।
attadatthaṁ abhiññāya sadatthapasuto siyā ॥ (Dhp 166)

7 yesaṁ sannicayo natthi ye pariññāta-bhojanā ।
suññato animitto ca, vimokho yesaṁ gocaro ।
ākāse va sakuntānaṁ gati tesaṁ durannayā ॥ (Dhp 92)
yassāsavā parikkhīṇā āhāre ca anissito ।
suññato animitto...... (Dhp 93)

state of room is congenial for look within in course of *vipassanā* meditation, *suññatā* goes upto the experience of *samatha*, as the *Majjhima Nikāya* (III: 111) reads, equivalent to *nibbāna*. Because of being entered into seclusion, the entrant experiences the joy that transcends.

> suññāgaram paviṭṭhassa santa-cittassa bhikkhuno।
> amanusi rati hoti sammā dhammaṃ vipassato॥ (Dhp 373)

In due course, the Buddhist Sanskrit text *Prajñāpāramitā Sūtra*, while leads to the status of experiencing *the wisdom-par excellence*, Ārya Nāgārjuna (circa 2nd CE) propounded the *śūnyatā* in the four dimensional dialectics of a, not-a, a-not-a and not a-not-a. His dialectics are neither affirmation, nor negation. The same idea may be traced as the *Kaṅkhāvitaran-avisuddhi-neddeso* (of *Visuddhi Magga*-2) as it reads.

> kammaṃ natthi vipākamhi pāko kamme na vijjati।
> aññamaññaṃ ubho suññā na ca kammaṃ vinā phalaṃ॥

Karma holds no *karma-vipāka*, nor *karmavipāka* remains in *karma*, those two are as vacant (as the sky), despite that, no effects occurs without (thing caused by) *kamma.*

Nāgarjuna's analysis in an eight-pronged diagram may be:

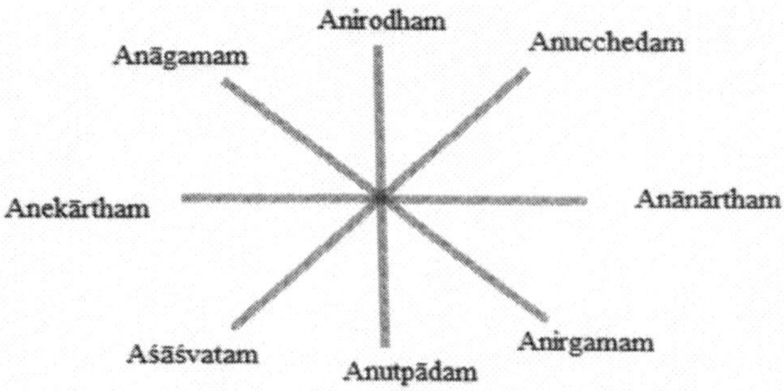

> anirodhamanutpādamanucchedamaśāśvatam।
> anekārthamanānārthamanāgamamanirgamam॥

yaḥ pratītyasamutpādaṁ prapañcopaśamaṁ śivam।
deśayāmāsa saṃbuddhastaṃ vande vadatāṃ varam॥

(*Madhyamakaśāstram* 1:1-2)

Evidently, the moot point of Indian Sociology remains open to accept the apparent views of *ātman* an individual existent real with no hindrance to hold conventional grasping of existent material object or that of subjective phenomenon in day to day livelihood to promote the cause of existence.

Bibliography

A. Root texts (Mūlagrantha)

Atharvaveda Saṃhitā Bombay edn. 1938. Eng. tn. W.D. WHITNEY, Harvard Oriental Series vol VII, VIII, Cambridge, 1905

Apastampa Dharmasūtra (Gautama BodhayanaVashistha) S.B.E. 2, 14, ed. G. BUHLER

Aṣṭasāhasrikā Prajñāpāramitā. 1925. Asiatic Society Calcutta

Ṛg-Veda Samhitā. 1925. Bombay edn. With Eng. tn. Of H. Wilson, Nag Publishers, Delhi 1977.

Aitareya Brāhmaṇa. ed. B. G. APTE. Poona edn. Eng. Tr. Martin Hang. 2 vols. Bombay Govt-Central Book Depot. 1963.

Aitareya Aranyaka ed. A. B. KEITH. 1909. Oxford. Eng. Tr. F. Max Muller, Sacred Books of the East Series (SBE) Oxford 1879.

Dhammapada. ed. Sumangala Thera. 1914. London: PTS. English tr. Ed. N. H. SAMTANI, Central Institute of Higher Tibetan Studies, Sarnath, Varanasi, 1989.

Bhagavadgita Gita Press edn. Gorakhpur 1926 Eng. Tr. S. RADHAKRISHNAN, 1933, W. D. P. Hill ed. London.1928

Madhyamakaśāstram. ed. P. L. VAIDYA. 1945. Darbhanga : Mithila Research Institute.

B. Secondary Sources

BAHADUR, Mol.

1967. *The Religion of the Buddha and its Relation to the Upanisadic Thoughts*. New York: Genge Broziler.
BANERJEE, Nitya Ranjan.
1966. *Peace Through Hinduism*. Calcutta.
BAPAT, P.V.
1956. *2500 Years of Buddhism*. New Delhi: Publication Division, Govt. of India.
BASAM A.
1954. *The Wonder that was India.* New York: Grave Press Inc.
BASU Jagiraj
1975. *India of the Age of Brahmanas*. Calcutta: Samskrita Pustaka Bhandar.
CHATTERJEE S. C.
1956. *An Introduction to Indian Philosophy*. 3rd ed. Calcutta: Calcutta University.
DANDEKAR R. N.
1977. *Insight into Hinduism*. Poona: Bhandarkar Oriental Research Institute.
KAUSAMBI D. D.
1950. *The Culture and Civilization of Ancient India*. Bombay: Popular Prakashan.
1965. *An Introduction to the Study of Indian History*. Bombay: PopularPrakashan.
MALL, Linnart.
2003. *Studies in the Aṣṭasāhasrikā Prajñāpāramitā and other Essays*. Taru: Centre for Oriental Studies, Uni-Tark.
MARSHALL, John.
1951. *Mahenjodaro and Indian* Civilization. Probstein.
MUKHERJEE, B. N.
1976. *The Genesis of Buddhism Its Social Content*. Vol I . Calcutta.
NARAIN A. K.
1980. *Studies in History of Buddhism*. Delhi: B R Publishers.
PATHAK S. K.
1983. Ekayāna Buddhayāna. Proceeding of *International Buddhist Conference*. Bodhagaya: Indosan Nipponji.
WALPOLA, Rahula.

1978. *What the Buddha Taught*. Ondon: Gordon Fraser Gallery ltd.

YAKUB, Mashi.
1985. *The Hindu Religions Thought.* Delhi: Motilal Banarsidas.

BAGCHI, P C.
1938. *Pre Aryans and pre Dravidians in India*. Ed. and Tr. Calcutta: Calcutta Universit.

Nature of Buddhist Theory of Well Being

Wadinagala PANNALOKA*

Abstract

Among the few scholars who have discussed the Buddhist theory of well-being, Charles GOODMAN's (2009) characterization of the Theravāda Well-Being is illustrative and comprehensive. GOODMAN characterizes Theravāda Buddhist theory of well-being as an Objective List theory (OLT), a theory proposed by the consequentialist ethics in the west. OLT produces lists of elements of well-being and attaining these good makes one living well. In this paper, it is intended to examine the plausibility of the claim that Theravāda Buddhism has an Objective List as its well-being theory. The reasons given to prove the theory by GOODMAN is examined and then will point out the Buddhist theory of well-being has to be understood in relation to the key doctrine, '*Paṭiccasamuppāda*,' the Causal Interdependence.

Key Terms: Well-being, Objective List Theory (OLT), *Paṭicca-samuppāda*, Value

Introduction

Within the western philosophical tradition, we can find different views about what constitutes well-being. Generally, well-being is understood as leading a happy life. In western

* Senior Lecturer, Department of Buddhist Philosophy, Postgraduate Institute of Pali and Buddhist Studies, University of Kelaniya.
E-mail: wadinagala@gmail.com

philosophy, Aristotle's eudaimonia, John Stuart Mill's utility and Immanuel Kant's happiness all at least bear resemblance to the concept of well-being. Further the concepts such as welfare, prudential value, self-interest and flourishing are concerned with well-being.

Charles GOODMAN (2009: 59) has made an attempt to produce a Buddhist theory of well-being in line with his interpretation of Theravāda Buddhist ethics as Rule-consequentialism. According to the Rule-consequentialist reading of Theravāda Buddhism, there are rules to be followed by the Buddhists, which will bring about morality of the society. In a society where moral codes are the major method teaching morality, there should be a kind of conception how to lead a good life, which would bring about happiness or pleasure and more other goods that are basically considered as goods. As Charles GOODMAN understands, Theravāda Buddhism maintains a well-being theory that is similar to the OLT. After a brief reference to the *Lakkhaṇa Sutta*, GOODMAN reaches the following conclusion about the well-being theory in Theravāda Buddhist moral system:

> According to the *Lakkhaṇa Sutta*, to wish for people's well-being is to wish for them to have both worldly success and virtue. But it seems that wealth and other forms of worldly success are valuable only as means to the happiness of oneself and others. If we combine these teachings in the most natural way, we will get an objective list theory of well-being, which regards well-being as consisting of two main components: worldly happiness and virtue (GOODMAN 2009: 61).

In the present paper, I will examine the plausibility of GOODMAN's interpretation of Buddhist theory of well-being as OLT. The OLT considers elements of well-being are objective and mutually exclusive. There areseveral independent fundamental goods but there is no interconnection. I will examine whether as GOODMAN says, Buddhist well-being theory considers happiness and virtue as two values intrinsically good. Then, I will propose the Buddhist theory of well-being needs to be based on the key Buddhist doctrine of Causal Conditioning (*Paṭiccasamuppāda*) and try to see what kind of well-being is derivable from it. Finally, I will show that inner transformation of the personality gained through wisdom (*Paññā*), what Buddhists accepts as the penetrative knowledge into the nature of reality as an incessantly being conditioned process, will help to lead the ultimate level of well-being.

Objective List Theory (OLT)

We can recognize three major theories about well-being among the western philosophers, Hedonistic Theory of Well-being, Desire-Satisfaction Theory and OLT. According to Hedonism and the Desire-satisfaction Theory, happiness is a matter of subjective mental states. Hedonism counts subjective mental states of pleasure and pain are the contents of well-being; desire-fulfillment theory considers the satisfaction of personal desires is well-being. According to OLT, apart from the subjective mental states, there are objective goods such as knowledge, friendship etc which also components of well-being (GRIFFIN 1988: 33-34). The theories related to well-being share one common feature, that is, they all agree general goods play an important role in bringing out well-being (GOWANS).

Further, OLT differs from hedonism as to the question of whether there is only one element of well-being or more than one. The OLT claims that other things can also constitute benefits— for example, knowledge of important matters, friendship, significant achievement, and autonomy. First time in western philosophy, Derek PARFIT (1984: 493–502) used the name 'OLT.' In shortened form, it is referred to as the 'List Theory'. From the OLT's point of view, life contains more welfare to the extent that it contains pleasure, knowledge of important matters, friendship, significant achievement, and autonomy (GRIFFIN 1988: 29–35, 58–72).

The OLT consider that some goods exist outside the mind states. So, they are objective. There is a list normally given as ordinary goods that are also accepted to be *ordinary goods.* From OLT view point, these goods are recognized by any reflective person as goods. The list normally includes life, health, marriage, children, knowledge, achievement and friends. According to List Theory, these goods are not mutually connected, that is why they are called *list* (GOWANS: Buddhist Well-Being).

There are few questions to address regarding the Buddhist theory of well-being from the Buddhist point of view. What is the basic understanding that on which the theory of well-being is built? Since there are two categories of persons, one as enlightened and the other as unenlightened, are there two theories of well-being? Is Buddhist theory of well-being objective or subjective? It is useful to know the scope of OLT-s of well-being. Brad HOOKER (2002: 41) provides the following description about the OLT:

> Views holding that something benefits a person if and only if it increases the person's pleasure or desire fulfillment are in a sense 'subjectivist' theories of personal good. For these theories make something's status as a benefit depend always on the person's subjective mental states. In contrast, 'objective list' theories claim that the contributions to personal good made by such things as important knowledge, important achievement, friendship, and autonomy are not exhausted by the extent to which these things bring people pleasure or fulfill their desires. These things can constitute benefits beyond the pleasure they involve and even when they don't involve pleasure. Likewise, they can constitute benefits even when they are not the objects of desire. These 'list'

> theories will typically add that pleasure is, of course, an objective good. List theories also typically hold that delusion, failure, friendlessness, servitude, and pain constitute objective harms.

The doctrine of Causal Conditioning would help to find the doctrinal basis on which the Buddhist theory of well-being is set. So, the well-being has to be discussed in relation to two kind of nature of experience, one is conditional and the other is unconditional. The conditional realm is recognized with the mark of suffering, the key issue that the Buddha sought to find answer. And the unconditional is recognized with the liberation. Let us examine first the nature of these two kinds of experience as given in the Pāli textual tradition.

Happiness and Virtue

The claim of Charles GOODMAN that Theravāda Buddhism has an OLT as its theory of well-being is formed on the assumption that both happiness and virtue are considered intrinsically valuable in this tradition. As GOODMAN (2009: 47) puts:

> The conception of well-being in this tradition includes both happiness and virtue as intrinsic goods. Although attachment to wealth and craving for sensual pleasures are very bad, the pleasures themselves have some small but genuine value, and wealth can be an instrumentally valuable means to benefit one-self and others.

For the OLT, happiness and virtue are two separate phenomena. As GOWANS (see Buddhist Well-Being) illustrates, for the well-being theorists, happiness and virtue are not necessarily connected. However, as we see the *kamma* theory of Buddhism, happiness and virtue are closely connected. It is evident from the Buddhist theory of existence. For the Buddhists, the virtue and cosmic terrain are not distinct. The basic cosmological division goes as realm of sensuality, realm of fine material and realm of immateriality. The person who keeps precepts and practices charity etc. is possible to be reborn in the realm of sensuality (*kāmaloka/kāmabhava*), which is composed of six divine realms, human world and four places of retribution, animal, angry-gods, ghosts and hell-beings. Those who have practiced mental trances, *jhāna* of material realm (*rūpa-jhāna*) will be reborn in the abodes of fine matter and there is no sensual enjoyment. Further, if one's mental development reaches to the immaterial *jhāna*-s (*arūpa-jhāna*), he will be reborn in immaterial realm. This stratification of the cosmic realm is based on the level of virtue one maintains, more one increases spiritual capacity transcending material desires, higher is his reward in the cosmic realm. Generally, it is considered being reborn in *rūpa* and *arūpa* realms is far happier than the *kāma*-realm. What we can observe is in Buddhism, happiness and the degree of virtue are not separate but invincibly connected. This makes us to rethink and re-assess the validity of claim that Buddhist well-being theory is an OLT for Buddhism embraces both happiness and virtue.

The list like health, education, long life, important knowledge, achievement and children are considered as basic goods in well-being theories (HOOKER 2015:18). From the Buddhist point of view, the achievement of these fundamental goods is related to one's previous life as well as certain conditions in this life. More significantly, one's conduct of behavior throughout the existence and the experience at the moment show one continuation. Once a young Brahmin called Subha met the Buddha and questioned what is the cause and condition, why human beings are seen to be inferior and superior, short-lived and long-lived, sickly and healthy, ugly and beautiful, uninfluential and influential, poor and wealthy, low-born and high-born, stupid and wise. The Buddha's reply was:

> *kammassakā, māṇava, sattā kammadāyādā kammayonī kamma bandhū kammappaṭisaraṇā. kammaṃ satte vibhajati yadidaṃ – hīnappaṇītatāyāti* (MN: III.203).

> Student, beings are owners of their actions, heirs of their actions; they originate from their actions, are bound to their actions, have their actions as their refuge. It is action that distinguishes beings as inferior and superior (ÑĀṆAMOLI and BODHI 1995: 1053).

The reply here given to the question why there is variety in the achievement of basic goods like wealth and longevity etc. indicates that those goods are connected with the actions (volitional actions are meant) one committed. The Theravāda tradition maintains one's previous life's conduct may be influential in deciding one's pleasure and pain that is undergone in this life. What the Buddhist tradition maintains is that moral conduct and one's nature of life well-being are inseparable.

The brief reference to the *kamma* theory was made in order to show that in Theravāda tradition, though there is appreciation both worldly happiness and virtue in equal weight, these goods are not separable as it is met in list theory. In the following sections, let us turn to the Buddhist worldview as conditionality and how far it is significant in a discussion about the nature of Buddhist theory of well-being.

Well-being in Conditional Experience

The understanding about the nature of reality the human being exists is recognized as a state subject to conditionality. To put in other words, human life is subject to be conditioned by multitude of factors. In the Theravāda Buddhism, the basic process of existence of the individual is explained through the doctrine of Causal Conditionality (*Paṭiccasamuppāda*) and the Conditionality (*Idappaccayatā*). The second term is recognized with the concept of conditionality.[1] The typical

1 The fourth characteristic of causation, 'Conditionality' (*idappaccayatā*), is by far the most significant in that it steers clear of the two extremes- the unconditional necessity implied in strict determinism

formula of twelve links explains the existence of the human being. The first order which describes how the human predicament is formed due to the chain of causes is the one that manifests the conditional realm of experience; the reverse order of the formula explains how one gets rid of the conditional realm.

> *iti imasmiṃ sati idaṃ hoti. imassuppādā idaṃ uppajjati. imasmiṃ asati idaṃ na hoti. imassa nirodhā idaṃ nirujjhati. yadidaṃ: avijjā paccayā saṅkhārā, saṅkhāra paccayā viññāṇaṃ...jāti paccayā jarāmaraṇaṃ, sokaparideva- dukkhadomanassūpāyāsā sambhavanti. evametassa kevalassa dukkhakkhandhassa samudayo hoti. avijjāya tveva asesa virāga nirodhā saṅkhāra nirodho. saṅkhāra nirodhā viññāṇa nirodho...jāti nirodhā jarāmaraṇaṃ, sokaparideva dukkhadomanassūpāyāsā nirujjhanti. evametassa kevalassa dukkhakkhandhassa nirodho hotī'ti* (SN II.28).
>
> Thus when this exists that comes to be; with the arising of this, that arises. When this does not exist, that does not come to be; with the cessation of this, that ceases. That is with ignorance as condition, volitional formations come [come to be]; with volitional formations as condition, consciousness....such is the origin of this whole mass of suffering. But with the remainderless fading away and cessation of ignorance comes cessation of volitional formations; with the cessation of volitional formations, cessation of consciousness....such is the cessation of this whole mass of suffering (BODHI 2000: 522).

The conditionality is understood in this context as human life is subject to be conditioned by factors beyond his/her control. Particularly, the conditional realm is characterized with the three characteristics of the nature, impermanence, unsatisfactoriness and non-substantiality (*anicca*, *dukkha*,

---

and the unconditional arbitrariness assumed by accidentalism (KALUPAHANA1976: 28).

anatta). And the three characteristics are mutually connected, *yadaniccaṃ taṃ dukkhaṃ, yam dukkhaṃ tadanattā* (SN III.66). The first truth of the Four Noble Truths, the Truth of Suffering (*dukkha saccaṃ*) illustrates the experience of the conditioned existence. There are list of eight and thirteen in different texts what the conditional existence is undergoing. The brief description is given as follows:

> *idaṃ kho pana, bhikkhave, dukkhaṃ ariya saccaṃ– jātipi dukkhā, jarāpi dukkhā, byādhipi dukkho, maraṇampi dukkhaṃ, appiyehi sampayogo dukkho, piyehi vippayogo dukkho, yam picchaṃ na labhati tampi dukkhaṃ– saṃkhittena pañcupādānakkhandhā dukkhā.*
>
> Now this, monks, is the Noble Truth of Suffering: birth is suffering, aging is suffering, disease is suffering, death is suffering; association with the unbeloved is suffering, separation from the beloved is suffering, not getting what is wanted is suffering. In short, the five clinging-aggregates are suffering.

Irrespective of the variety of the manifestations of suffering, the underlying experience is recognized as 'unsatisfactorinness'. The reason for the unsatisfacotoriness is craving. These things are seen as inevitable experiences and they are experienced through the conditional things which form the complex of psycho-physical personality of human being, the five aggregates, physical body, feeling, perception, mental formations and consciousness. These five aggregates are conditioned by the factors and it is always ongoing the process of conditioning again and again until one escapes from the entire realm of conditionality.

As GOODMAN (2009: 69) points out, the Theravāda Buddhism accepts the worldly pleasures have intrinsic value as it accepts of the *Nibbānic* happiness; the former is lower to the latter in the ultimate sense. No matter, whether the Theravāda Buddhism accepts the material pleasures or values having intrinsic value, it is remarkable to note that they are all lacking selfness. So, they are momentary and unsatisfactory. In the discourse of the *Cakkavattisīhanāda Sutta* (DN III.58ff), the Buddha praises the seven treasures of the universal ruler and places the universal rule as the ideal of worldly life. In contrast to this compliment, the Buddha declares the value of the pleasures of the universal monarch does not worthy to a one sixteenth of the value of the stream-entrant of the path towards enlightenment (SN. V.342).

Moreover, the approval and instructions given by the Buddha to the householder Dīghajānu Koliya is expressive of the Buddhist attitude towards the well-being connected with the sensuous life of the lay community. Dīghajānu describes charms of the life leaded by him amidst sensual objects. The life of householders is absorbed in pleasure; their time is spent among children and wives; they delight in the muslins from Benares and in sandalwood; they deck themselves with flowers, garlands and cosmetics; they enjoy the use of both silver and gold. At his request, the Buddha offers some instruction for the well-being of the next life (AN IV.281). In this discourse, the householder refers to almost all ordinary goods; in which participation is recognized as well-being by the OLT (the OLT holds that all instances of a plurality of basic objective goods directly (or non-instrumentally) benefit people. These can include goods such as loving relationships, meaningful knowledge, autonomy, achievement, and pleasure (RICE 2013: 196-211). The reason for the Buddha's approval for sensual life is clear in another discourse where a householder states that the life of renunciation looks like a fathomless hole for the one who enjoys the pleasures of the family life (*papāto viya khāyati yadidaṃ nekkhammaṃ*). Then, the Buddha agrees with him for it is natural to see the life free of sensuality like a bottomless hole since the ordinary person is unaware of the happiness in the renunciation (AN

IV.438).

To understand the goods that produce the well-being that rule consequentialism aims for, was experienced by the young prince Siddhartha prior to his renunciation from those ordinary goods. The Text called *Māgandiya Sutta* (MN I.501) puts his luxurious life as follows:

> *ahaṃ kho pana, māgaṇḍiya, pubbe agāriyabhūto samāno pañcahi kāmaguṇehi samappito samaṅgībhūto paricāresiṃ cakkhuviññeyyehi rūpehi iṭṭhehi kantehi manāpehi piyarūpehi kāmūpasaṃhi tehirajanīyehi, sotaviññeyyehi saddehi...pe...ghānaviññeyyehi gandhehi... jivhāviññeyyehi rasehi... kāyaviññeyyehi phoṭṭhabbehiiṭṭhehi kantehi manāpehi piyarūpehi kāmūpasaṃ hitehi rajanīyehi. tassa mayhaṃ, māgaṇḍiya, tayo pāsādā ahesuṃ - ekovassiko, ekohemantiko, ekogimhiko. so kho ahaṃ, māgaṇḍiya, vassike pāsāde vassike cattāro māse nippurisehi turiyehi paricāriyamāno na heṭṭhāpāsādaṃ orohāmi.*

> Māgandiya, when I was a householder, I was well provided with the five strands of sensual pleasures. Such as pleasing agreeable forms cognizable by eye consciousness arousing fondness and sensual desires. Pleasing agreeable sounds, --pleasing agreeable smells-- pleasing agreeable tastes, and pleasing agreeable touches cognizable by body consciousness, arousing fondness and sensual desires. I was provided with three palaces, for the three seasons, one for the rainy season, one for the cold season and another for the hot season. Māgandiya, I spent four months in the palace for the rainy season, without males and provided with music. Not coming down to the lower storey, for any reason (Bodhi and Ñāṇamoli 1995: 609).

After making a comprehensive account about the nature of sensual life, the Buddha questions the Brahmin Magandiya whether it is possible for a recovered patient from an itch to desire the itch sensation once again.

This indicates the issue of the well-being faces at the conditional level. Buddhism does not consider the enjoying ordinary goods gained through morally as an evil; desire for gratification is not an evil but the course of looking for gratification would result in lot of pain both psychological and physical. The *Alagaddūpama Sutta* has come out of number of vivid similes about the goods of the ordinary life. One of the similes is the contention among vultures or dogs for the piece of meat (MN I.130ff). The ordinary goods obviously possess their own intrinsic value in one sense; similarly, in Benthamian words, they also have intrinsic disvalue (pain is perceived as intrinsic evil by Bentham) (see HURKA 2001: 100). The Buddha sees when we compare the amount of pleasure we gain through the ordinary goods with the pain they simultaneously bring, the pain outdoes pleasure (*appassādo bahū dukkhā*).

According to the *Ariyapariyesana Sutta* describes what leaded him for the enlightenment. His spiritual seeking was oriented at finding freedom from birth, disease, decay and death (ÑĀṆAMOLI and BODHI 1995: 260). This explains what sort of well-being was sought after by the Buddha. The reason why did he strive for such kind of well-being is related to the nature of the experience the person undergoes in the conditional realm. Concerning the nature of the things within the sway of conditionality, PAYUTTO (1994: 14) has summarized in his explanation about the suffering of conditioned things (*Saṅkhāra-dukkha*) well:

> The most important kind of suffering is the third kind, which describes the nature inherent to all conditions, both physical and mental. *Saṅkhāra-dukkhatā* as a natural attribute a psychological significance when it is recognized that conditions are incapable of producing any

> perfect contentment, and as such will cause suffering for anybody who tries to cling to them.

The explanation of this life under the conditional realm, depicted as shaky state of affairs, anytime possible to occur a change to the experience one is undergoing, has been understood as unsatisfactory. This understanding underlying the Buddhist view of the nature of the well-being found in the conditional realm, has led scholars to see it as lower level of well-being irrespective of the participating in goods in the common-sense. G. W. GOWANS (see Buddhist Well-Being) is helpful here:

> Buddhism supposes that there is a lower form of well-being that consists of participation in ordinary goods. This is the well-being that is available to unenlightened persons...

Buddhism encourages for the people to go beyond the power of causal conditioning, which is free from continuous debilitating met in the conditional realm. This is known as unconditional realm. So, the well-being in the Buddhist tradition has inseparable relation to its world view expressed in the doctrine of causal conditioning. Let us examine for clarification what is the nature of well-being in conditional realm and unconditional realm as the Pāli canonical text reveal. This is not a matter something is intrinsically valuable or instrumental, yet, the things are deeper than the face appearance, which we know through our ordinary sense perception.

Well-being in Unconditional Realm

Happiness in the unconditional realm is to understand and from the accounts given about the enlightened persons. The unconditional realm in Buddhism is the *Nibbāna*. The one who attains the *Nibbāna* crosses the world of conditionality. The *Nibbanic* experience is twofold: the *Nibbāna* with the residue- *sa upadhisesa nibbāna-* (*nibbāna* with five aggregates) and the *Nibbāna* without residues - *nirupadhisesa nibbāna-* (*Ni-*

bbāna without the five aggregates). The former is the experience that enlightened person undergoes till his death. The latter is the experience that the enlightened person receives after the death. Information about this stage is less. It is sufficient to read into some texts about the *Nibbāna* in this life to know about the well-being of the enlightened being who has gone beyond the conditional realm.

Does the enlightened one participate in the ordinary goods? The enlightened one is unbroken in his senses. So, he feels pain, pleasure and neutral feelings. In this regard, he is not different from the unenlightened person. Where does the demarcation lie between the enlightened and the unenlightened? The *Itivuttaka Nibbānadhātusutta* reports as follows:

> *tassa tiṭṭhanteva pañcindriyāni yesaṃ avighātattā manāpāmanāpaṃ paccanubhoti, sukhadukkhaṃ paṭisaṃvedeti. tassa yo rāgakkhayo, dosakkhayo, mohakkhayo- ayaṃ vuccati, bhikkhave, saupādisesā nibbānadhātu.* (Itivuttaka: 38)
>
> His five sense faculties remain unimpaired, by which he still experiences what is agreeable and disagreeable, still feels pleasure and pain. It is the destruction of lust, hatred and delusion in him that is called the nirvana element with residue remaining.

So, at the biological level, enlightened person and the unenlightened are the same. The latter part of this sentence asserts that enlightened one does not have the psychological tendencies in his experience. What is characterized the experience of the ordinary person is desire, anger and ignorance. If I gain, thousand dollars, I desire it to keep with me as a possession. If I am going to lose it, then I am not happy and going to take whatever step to stop loosing, even the violent acts.

The theory of well-being of the enlightened person is connected with the removal of craving and the ignorance. In this context, craving is the wishing for more and ego-centric conception. The enlightened person whatever feeling or perception arises in the mind body, is of the capacity to observe the experience without identification. What the issue of the confusion that the ordinary person makes is that his sensory experiences and the psychological process relate to him and perceive them as 'mine'. This identification would activate the psychological tendencies of craving, rejection and obscurity. Once, the person is enlightened, he eradicates the mental tendencies leading to 'identification'. So, he maintains an imperturbable attitude in face any kind of experience. This makes the person balanced avoiding the swinging towards liking, disliking and inclinations.

To know the nature of the well-being of the enlightened person, there is a contrast between the enlightened person and unenlightened person filled with every kind of ordinary goods. The life of peace that the Buddha spends, who has nothing as material possession, is an instance recorded as follows:

> *sabbadā ve sukhaṃ seti brāhmaṇo parinibbuto,*
> *yo na limpati kāmesu sītibhuto nirūpadhi.*
> *sabbā āsattiyo chetvā vineyya hadaye daraṃ,*
> *upasanto sukhaṃ seti santiṃ pappuyya cetasoti.* (SN I.212).
>
> The enlightened one, done with sensual pleasures, free from acquisitions and with a cool heart, always sleeps happily. When attachments are chopped off, the heart is carefree, and the mind is at peace, and the serene one sleeps well.

The reason that to lead a life of happiness for the Buddha is his mental composure and the purity from anxieties and worries which come with the ordinary goods. Though the king is over flowed with the ordinary goods he is not free from the dangers inherent in them.

The metaphor used to indicate the *Nibbāna* is 'serenity'; one who is calmed or serene is called one who has attained

Nibbāna, (*tyamhā khīṇāsavā dantā sītibhūtāmha nibbutāti*. Therigāthā: 130). This metaphor is very useful to comprehend its opposite side, which is, burning. The discourse called *Ādittapariyāya Sutta* describes that our six senses, eye, ear, nose, tongue, body and mind are burning; they are burning from craving, hatred and ignorance. The text runs as follows:

> Monks, the All is aflame. What All is aflame? The eye is aflame. Forms are aflame. Consciousness at the eye is aflame. Contact at the eye is aflame. And whatever there is that arises in dependence on contact at the eye-experienced as pleasure, pain or neither-pleasure-nor-pain- that too is aflame. Aflame with what? Aflame with the fire of passion, the fire of aversion, the fire of delusion (SN IV.19).

The opposite of the serenity is burning. The enlightened person or the one who has from this side to the other side of the shore (this is an allusion to *Nibbāna*; the realm of conditionality is called this shore and the realm beyond the conditionality is called the other shore: one who has gone to the other side is called '*pāramgata*' in Pāli). Such a person has no burning.

From the brief reading over the well-being in relation to realm of conditionality where the well-being is measured in proportion to the participation in ordinary goods and the realm beyond conditionality where there is serenity, we can see that Theravāda Buddhism maintains a stark difference and the higher well-being is located in the unconditional realm in utilitarian terms.

It can be said that the well-being theory of Theravāda Buddhism is a form of pluralism. It becomes pluralism by allowing for many causes to come into produce and effect. For a single act of giving a gift, there need three phenomena to come into contact: the donor, the recipient and the object. An effect is not a result of a single factor but several factors.

One problem of OLT is that they propose several goods; yet, they do not show us the unity among those goods. Or they are separate goods, so they are called 'list'. Further, OLT produce 'insouciant pluralism', that is, one is not concerned with the other. For Buddhists, each and everything is interdependent. Theravāda Buddhism accepts the value as plurality but it is in mutual relation with each and every factor that contributing to one's well-being.

Liberation from Conditional Realm

The doctrine of *paṭiccasamuppāda* explains the 'conditional-/relational existence'. One aspect of the doctrine explains the problem of existence and the other aspect explains how to get liberation from relational web (*apica lokasamudayanti anulomapaccayākāraṃ. lokanirodhanti paṭilomapaccayākāraṃ.* SNA II.33). Due to ignorance and craving, sentient beings experience the cyclic process of birth and death. This conditional experience is ethical for the reason that force of ignorance is a deciding factor about the 'happiness and pain', the person goes through. Ignorance leads to craving or grasping (*upādāna*) and in turn grasping conditions 'becoming'. Once we are in the becoming, we get a variety of forms of birth. When, one is born, somewhere, then, the unsatisfactoriness naturally follows.

The life within the conditional realm is entirely ethical and moral. The moral action both good and evil determines the happiness and pain at this level. The persons can lead ethical life following the rules (as rule-consequentialism advices) and cultivating character traits such as bravery (in Aristotelian terms). For the good things one does he gets the good results and the so for the bad actions get bad results. At this level, one can follow any kind of moral theory, utilitarian, deontological or consequentialist as they all guide the person to be ethical (SIDERITES 2008: 110).

The world we are living in is the world of conditions. The

concept of *saṅkhāra* (volitional formations) is called by that name because "they construct the conditioned" (BODHI 2000: 915). The *saṅkhāra* is understood as the *kamma* (the sphere of moral actions). Putting together statements from various *sutta*-s, we can see that the *saṅkhāra*-s are the *kammically* active volitions responsible for generating rebirth and thus for sustaining the onward movement of *saṁsāra*, the round of birth and death (BODHI 2011). The *kamma* leads to rebirth and eventually to the associated phenomenal suffering. The *saṅkhāra* are conditioned by the view of self (*avijjā*) and not-knowing the Four Noble Truths. The Four Noble Truths, if we understand in the ethical sense, then, the person do not know how to eliminate the 'ego-centric' worldview. So, he/she continues committing actions conducive to prolong the existence in the conditional realm.

The precedent factor that conditions volitional formations is ignorance, the 'deep-rooted subjective perspective.' So, every volitional act, committed through body, speech and mind are influenced by ignorance. Here the *Parivīmaṃsanasutta* is illustrative as:

> *avijjāgato yaṃ, bhikkhave, purisapuggalo puññaṃ ce saṅkhāraṃ abhisaṅkharoti, puññūpagaṃ hoti viññāṇaṃ. apuññaṃ ce saṅkhāraṃ abhisaṅkharoti, apuññūpagaṃ hoti viññāṇaṃ. āneñjaṃ ce saṅkhāraṃ abhisaṅkharoti āneñjūpagaṃ hoti viññāṇaṃ* (SN II.82).
>
> Monks, if a person immersed in ignorance generates a meritorious volitional formation, consciousness fares on to the meritorious; if he generates a demeritorious volitional formation, consciousness fares on to the demeritorious; if he generates animperturbable volitional formation, consciousness fares on to the imperturbable (BODHI 2000: 587).

Here, we can observe that the sphere of moral/ethical activity, which is composed of meritorious actions and demeritorious actions is the result of volitional actions conditioned by ignorance. According the commentary on this passage, three kinds of actions given here, good, evil and stable represent the round of existence (Bodhi 2000: 765).

The life called *saṃasāric* life definitely brings certain goods for the person, sensual pleasures and pleasures beyond sensuality (in the realms of material and immaterial realms in which there is no sensual pleasure but subtle form of mental enjoyment gain from the spiritual practices). The life in the conditional realms is full of material goods such as marriage, children and achievements (as the OLT enumerates the goods). One can lead both at individual and social level an ethical life. Then, there arises a question, if the life in the conditional realm is good, why Buddhism tries to guide people to an unconditional realm.

The rational for the encouragement lies in the understanding of the nature of the conditional existence. The conditional existence at whatsoever level is understood to be unsatisfactory. Conditioned by the 'egocentric perception', the person commits ethically evaluative actions (*saṅkhāra*) leading to produce the rebirth consciousness (*viññāṇa*) and it in turn gives rise to the 'psycho-physical personality' (*nāma-rūpa*). The psycho-physical personality generates the six senses through the person relates to the external world. The human being is recognized as the psycho-physical personality with six senses. The formulation of the five aggregates, form, feeling, perception, volitional formations and the consciousness is the way that the human personality is composed and functions through. The five aggregates are subject to the three characteristics that are inherent in the conditionality, that is, impermanence, suffering and insubstantiality (*anicca*, *dukkha* and *anatta*). So, the human experience is perceived as deprived of any permanent, satisfactory and substantial existence. In other words, there is no any substance behind the human personality that keeps him going through eternally changeless, satisfactory experience. This is understood as the problem human being faces and what the Buddha aims at, is to show the path to get out of the realm of conditionality to a state free of conditionality or unconditional.

The psychological process how the liberation is attained is explained through the reverse order (*paṭilomanaya*) of the *Paṭiccasamuppāda* doctrine. As the first step towards liberation, the individual must remove the ignorance (*avijjā*) and then the course of elimination follows through the other factors till one totally eliminates potential of rebirth and thereby all the phenomenal suffering. However, the *Paṭiccasamuppāda* doctrine has to be elaborated through the other doctrines, then it becomes clear the interconnection between it and the other key doctrines, especially the Four Noble Truths. The *Paṭiccasamuppāda* doctrine connects with the doctrine of Four Noble Truths as a way to practical ethical program, through which the psychological factors given in the *Paṭiccasamuppāda* formulation are gradually eliminated leading to *Nibbāna*.

The Buddha approached to the problem of getting out of causal nexus; the existential suffering is inseparable from the understanding about the sense perception. A proper understanding about the sense perception would give insight into the origin of suffering as well as into the way for one to get freedom from suffering. So, the text in the *Saṃyutta Nikāya*, asserts that the purpose of living religious life under the Buddha is aimed at understanding the sense organ, the sense object, the sense contact, sense perception, for the very reason of suffering is sensory process (SN IV.138).

> Dependent on the eye and forms, eye-consciousness arises. The meeting of the three is contact. With contact as condition there is feeling. What one feels, that one perceives. What one perceives, that one thinks about.

> What one thinks about, that one mentally proliferates. With what one has mentally proliferated as the source, perceptions and notions tinged by mental proliferation beset a man with respect to past, future, and present forms cognizable through the eye (ÑĀṆAMOLI and BODHI 1995: 203).

This text presents the key issue of the sense perception, namely, the origin of the egoistic conception. The text initiates with the mechanical sensory process leading to the 'proliferated thinking', (*papañcasaññāsaṅkhā*), this is recognized as the beginning of the perceptual error of understanding about the reality. The sensory generates the concept of 'I am', the egoistic conception. Here, we can see that the explanation of the sensory process is given in the formulae of *Paṭiccasamuppāda*. Through the proliferated thinking, the agent begins to perceive the conditioned world through all the senses, eye, ear, tongue, nose, body and mind.

In the Pāli canon, the existential problem is also recognized as a matter of distorted sense perception. How the sense perception gives rise to this distortion has been explained in the former text. There are other texts that the Buddha says that his dispensation is dedicated to understand the problem of senses. The text mentions that if the other sectarian ascetics would ask what the suffering are for the holy life is undertaken under the Buddha, the answer should be given as follows:

> The eye is suffering: it is for the full understanding of this that the holy life is lived under the Blessed One. Forms are suffering: it is for the full understanding of this that the holy life is lived under the Blessed One. Eye consciousness is suffering...Eye-contact is suffering...whatever feeling arises with eye-contact as condition-whether pleasant or painful or neither-pleasant nor painful-that too is suffering: it is for the full understanding of

this that the holy life is lived under the Blessed One (BODHI 2000: 1214).

The Buddhism also recognizes the process of the sense perception as the beginning of the world (*lokassasamudayo* – SN II.73).

Text I

sotañcapaṭicca sadde ca uppajjati sotaviññāṇaṃ...pe... ghānañca paṭicca gandhe ca...pe... jivhañca paṭicca rase ca...pe... kāyañca paṭicca phoṭṭhabbe ca...pe... manañca paṭicca dhamme ca uppajjati manoviññāṇaṃ. tiṇṇaṃ saṅgati phasso. phassapaccayā vedanā; vedanā paccayā taṇhā. tassāyeva taṇhāya asesavirāganirodhā upādānanirodho; upādānanirodhā bhavanirodho; bhavanirodhā jātinirodho; jātinirodhā jarāmaraṇaṃ sokaparidevadukkhadomanassupāyāsā nirujjhanti. evametassa kevalassa dukkhakkhandhassa nirodho hoti. (SN II.73).

In dependence on the ear and sounds...In dependence on the mind and mental phenomena, mind-consciousness arises. The meeting of the three is contact. With contact as condition, feeling [comes to be]; with feeling as condition, *craving.* But with the remainder less fading away and cessation of that same craving comes cessation of clinging...cessation of existence...cessation of birth; with the cessation of birth, aging-and-death, sorrow, lamentation, pain, displeasure, and despair cease. Such is the cessation of this whole mass of suffering. This is the passing away of suffering (BODHI 2000: 581).

Text II

katamo ca, bhikkhave, lokassasamudayo? cakkhuñca paṭicca rūpe ca uppajjati cakkhuviññāṇaṃ. tiṇṇaṃ saṅgati phasso. phassapaccayā vedanā; vedanāpaccayā taṇhā; taṇhāpaccayā upādānaṃ; upādānapaccayā bhavo; bhavapaccayā jāti;

> *jātipaccayā jarāmaraṇaṃ sokaparidevadukkhadomanassupāyāsā sambhavanti. ayaṃ kho, bhikkhave, lokassasamudayo* (SN II.73).
>
> And what, bhikkhus, is the origin of the world? In dependence on the eye and forms, eye-consciousness arises. The meeting of the three is contact. With contact as condition, feeling [comes to be]; with feeling as condition, craving; with craving as condition, clinging; with clinging as condition, existence; with existence as condition, birth; with birth as condition, aging-and death, sorrow, lamentation, pain, displeasure, and despair come to be. This, bhikkhu-s, is the origin of the world (BODHI 2000:581).

The text I describes the origin of suffering is traced to the sense perception process culminating in craving. Once the craving is eliminated, then the following factors such as clinging, becoming, rebirth and associated suffering cease. The text II refers to the origin of the world (*lokassasamudayo*); it is also traced to the sense perception activity. Sense perception produces the subjective evaluation of craving and then follows the other psychological factors resulting in suffering. In the text, we can find the factors given in the twelve-linked formulation are applied in different forms of explanations. The selected passages deal with the causal factors of feeling (*vedanā*), craving (*taṇhā*) and grasping (*upādāna*). However, there is no deeper analysis about the sense perception as factor to create distortion of the reality. In the *Aṅguttara Nikāya*, the Buddha has mentioned four types of perception distortions:

> *anicce niccasaññino, dukkhe ca sukhasaññino;*
> *anattani ca attāti, asubhe subhasaññino;*
> *micchādiṭṭhihatā sattā, khittacittā visaññino.* (AN II.52).
> Sensing no change in the changing,
> Sensing pleasure in suffering,

> Assuming "self"where there's no self,
> Sensing the un-lovely as lovely —
> Gone astray with wrong views, beings
> Mis-perceive with distorted minds (OLDENZKI 2013).

In sum, the sense perception process given in the texts highlight the role of craving (*taṇhā*) in forming subjective reaction to and subjective involvement in perceptual things, which leads to a construction of a distorted world, to false values and to suffering (JOHANSSON 1985: 97). Once we eliminate desire, the rest of the process is arrested. Then, the person becomes realistic. As the text runs, one who has control over desire becomes disinterested in forms. When he sees a form, he is mindful. With detached mind he senses it, but he remains without clinging. When he sees the object and follows the sensation, he is reduced, not increased "*yathāssa sāyato rasaṃ, sevato cāpi vedanaṃ; khīyati nopacīyati, evaṃ so caratī sato; evaṃ apacinato dukkhaṃ, santike nibbāna-muccati*" (SN. IV.74). According to this description, the Buddhist practitioner receives information offered by the senses and makes use of it (*sevatovedanaṃ*) but not be subject to seduction by them. Consequently, there is chance for grasping (*upādāna*) to arise.

To stop the construction of perceptual misunderstanding about the reality, one must practice mindfulness. When a practitioner meets an opposite sex, practitioner's proper reaction is 'not seeing' (*adassana* DN.II.141); if he/she speaks to the practitioner, the latter must develop mindfulness (*sati*). The release from the erroneous perception of the reality is gained by exercise of understanding. And the deconstruction of the subjective perceptual process is called by the Buddha as 'ending of the world' (*lokassanirodho*).

> "*yattha ca kho, samiddhi, natthi cakkhu, natthi rūpā, natthi cakkhuviññāṇaṃ, natthi cakkhuviññāṇaviññātabbādhammā, natthi tattha loko vā lokapaññatti vā...pe...natthi jivhā-*

> *...pe...natthi mano, natthi dhammā, natthi manoviññāṇaṃ, natthi manoviññāṇaviññātabbā dhammā, natthi tattha loko vā lokapaññatti vā*"ti (SN IV.40).
>
> Where there is no eye, Samiddhi, no objects, no visual consciousness, no things cognizable through visual consciousness, there is no world no manifestation of the world. Where there is no ear...no mind, no mental phenomena, no mind-consciousness, no things to be cognized by mind-consciousness, there the world does not exist nor any description of the world.

When this process is stopped, there is no temptation (*māra*), no suffering (*dukkha*) and no being (*satta*). The elimination of the causal factors given within different contexts, finally resort to the idea that we need to break the causal nexus and freedom. Sometimes, the texts have selected one causal factor and examine how it is removed through the mind cultivation and understanding.

As G. C. PANDE illustrates, in Buddhism, the ethical program related to *kammic* process is not sufficient in bringing about well-being in perfect sense, since 'Karma is inadequate to the attainment of final peace, which can come only through perfect awakening (*sambodhi*). The goal is attained not merely by the transformation of body and mind, themselves necessarily involved in transformations, but by the Intuition which dispels Ignorance and reveals the eternal (*amatapadaṃ*)' (PANDE1995: 410). The view that the doctrine of *kamma* is not sufficient to gain the liberation is supported by the twelve-linked formulation and the emphasis of abolition of ignorance as the way to liberation. According to the twelve-linked formulation, the sphere of action (ethical realm) is governed/conditioned by the self-centered psychology of the individual, which is called 'ignorance' (*avijjā paccayā saṅkhārā*). Prior to the ethical behavior, the perceptional level exercises its influence over selecting the actions.

Moreover, the doctrine of *paṭiccasamuppāda* offers an account of the morality and its genesis through the view of conditional nature of all the phenomena including the actions or ethical behavior.

In order to facilitate the discussion on the Theravāda Buddhist theory of conditionality, I will refer to the following texts from the Pāli canon, the discourse titled *Proximate Cause* and the *City Discourse.*

i. *The Proximate Cause Discourse* (*Upanisāsutta*):

The *Paṭiccasamuppāda* doctrine has been explained in regard to the both movements, one about the cyclic existence and the other about the liberation. The discourse titled *Upanisā* (*Proximate Cause*) explains the two processes as follows:

Process I: (Existence)

> *avijjūpanisā saṅkhārā, saṅkhārūpanisaṃ viññāṇaṃ, viññāṇūpanisaṃ nāmarūpaṃ, nāmarūpūpanisaṃ saḷāyatanaṃ, saḷāyatanūpaniso phasso, phassūpanisā vedanā, vedanūpanisā taṇhā, taṇhūpanisaṃ upādānaṃ, upādānūpaniso bhavo, bhavūpanisā jāti, jātūpanisaṃ dukkhaṃ* (SN II.32).
>
> ...with ignorance as proximate cause, volitional formations [come to be]; with volitional formations as proximate cause, consciousness; with consciousness as proximate cause, name-and-form; with name-and-form as proximate cause, the six sense bases; with the six sense bases as proximate cause, contact; with contact as proximate cause, feeling; with feeling asproximate cause, craving; with craving as proximate cause, clinging; with clinging as proximate cause, existence; with existenceas proximate cause, birth; with birth as proximate cause, suffering (BODHI 2000: 555).

Process II: (Liberation)

> *dukkhūpanisā saddhā, saddhūpanisaṃ pāmojjaṃ, pāmojjūpa-*

> *nisā pīti, pītūpanisā passaddhi, passaddhūpanisaṃ sukhaṃ, sukhūpaniso samādhi, samādhūpanisaṃ yathābhūtañāṇadassanaṃ, yathābhūta-ñāṇadassanūpanisā nibbidā, nibbidūpaniso virāgo, virāgūpanisā vimutti, vimuttūpanisaṃ khayeñāṇaṃ* (SN.II.33).
>
> ...with suffering as proximate cause, faith; with faith as proximate cause, gladness; with gladness...rapture; with rapture ...tranquility; with tranquility ...happiness; with happiness ...concentration; with concentration... the knowledge and vision of things as they really are; with the knowledge and vision of things as they really are ...revulsion; with revulsion ...dispassion; with dispassion...liberation; with liberation as proximate cause, the knowledge of destruction (BODHI 2000: 555).

The process I explains how the suffering arises with each factor having its precedent condition as the cause. This discourse remarks the knowledge of destruction (attachment to the five aggregates which compose the human personality) as the last stage of the path to liberation (*khayeñāṇa*). As the text indicates, suffering becomes condition to arising of faith/confidence (*saddhā*). The rational faith (*ākāravatī saddhā*) is considered to be the initiative step in the path towards liberation. The significance of the text quoted above is that it connects the two relational processes and the possibility of the conditional process to be directed to liberation. Both, the human predicament as well as the liberation are explained with the causal relation. This presentation of the doctrine has sometimes been called "transcendental dependent origination (BODHI 2000: 524)."

ii. *The City Discourse* (*Nagarasutta*):

This text is significant for two reasons: the first is, it does not refer to ignorance as the fundamental cause of suffering but consciousness. The mutual conditional relation between consciousness and name-and-form (*nāma-rūpa*) gives rise to rebirth leading to a mass of suffering headed by aging and death; the origin of suffering is comprehended as the consciousness and related conditional process. And the cessation of suffering is conceived in terms of cessation of consciousness. Once the consciousness is abolished, then there is no rebirth and consequently suffering ceases. The Buddha before his Enlightenment, through the penetrative wisdom realizes the causal relations that give rise to suffering. The comprehension covers the suffering, its origin and the cessation. The second important factor is the Buddha's comprehension that the path to cessation is practice of the Eight Noble Path, the ethical program of the early Buddhism.

> *katamo ca so, bhikkhave, purāṇamaggo purāṇañjaso pubbakehi sammāsambuddhehi anuyāto? ayameva ariyo aṭṭhaṅgiko maggo, seyyathidaṃ - sammādiṭṭhi...pe... sammāsamādhi. ayaṃ kho so, bhikkhave, purāṇamaggo purāṇañjaso pubbakehi sammāsambuddhehi anuyāto, tamanugacchiṃ; tamanugacchanto jarāmaraṇaṃ abbhaññāsiṃ; jarāmaraṇasamudayaṃ abbhaññāsiṃ; jarāmaraṇa-nirodhaṃ abbhaññāsiṃ; jarāmaraṇanirodhagāminiṃ paṭipadaṃ abbhaññāsiṃ* (SN II.106).

> I saw the ancient path, the ancient road travelled by the Perfectly Enlightened Ones of the past. And what is that ancient path, that ancient road? It is just this Noble Eightfold Path; that is, right view....right concentration. I followed that path and by doing so I have directly Known aging-and-death, its origin, its cessation, and the way to cessation (BODHI 2000: 605).

The pertinent point in this discourse is the connection between the causal conditioning in its both aspects, origin of suffering and cessation and the way to cessation are given in one context. The Buddha asserts the ancient path to cessation of suffering is the Eight Noble Path (*ariya aṭṭhaṅgika magga*). Here, both ontology and ethics in Buddhism, have been put to one discussion and reveals their invincible interconnection.

Conclusion

The interpretation that Buddhist theory of well-being presented in the Pāli canonical literature shows similarity to OLT, a theory that does not show inter connection between one fundamental good with the other, faces problem with the very nature of Buddhist ethical system, which is inclined to see the things in a context of multiplicity of factors, mutually connected. The analysis carried out on the key Buddhist doctrine of 'causal conditioning' shows that well-being is a concept invincibly connected with the Buddhist worldview. In the first stage, the *Paṭiccasamuppāda* doctrine reveals how human beings lead a life that is rich of ordinary goods such as wealth, children and wealth etc. in the process of *kammic* activity. At the same time, the doctrine reveals the life in the conditional realm, despite the attainment of material happiness, is affected with unsatisfactoriness. In order to live a life that is not subject to conditioning, the source of change, suffering and lacking essence, one must transcend the conditionality.

In the well-being theories in the western philosophical tradition, there is no close connection with morality and happiness. In contrast, the aspect related to the doctrine of 'causal conditioning' reveals that Buddhist theory shows very close connection between morality and happiness. Further, the western well-being theories do not discuss in detail how to attain the life of well-being. The teachings inducing the individual to practice Buddhist ethical path, the Eight Noble path, shows how to reach well-being both in conditional realm and unconditional realm.

Finally, it is to be noted that doctrine of *Paṭiccsamuppāda* being the Buddhist theory of ontology, indicates a close connection with the theory of well-being. This is aspect is to be discussed in detail in a forthcoming research.

Abbreviations

AN *Aṅguttara Nikāya*
DN *Dīgha Nikāya*
OLT Objective List Theory
MN *Majjhima Nikāya*
SN *Saṁyutta Nikāya*
SNA *Saṁyutta Nikāya Aṭṭhakathā*
PTS Pali Text Society

Bibliography

Pali Texts and Translations

BODHI, Bhikkhu.
(2000). *The Connected Discourses of the Buddha: A New Translation of the Saṁyutta Nikāya.* Boston: Wisdom Publications.
CARPENTER, J. E.
(1992). *TheDīgha Nikāya.* Vol.III. (ed.). Oxford: PTS.
CHALMERS, Robert.
(1993-94). The *Majjhima-Nikāya.* Vol.II. (ed.). Oxford: PTS.
HARDY, E.
(1979). (ed.) The *Anguttara-Nikāya* Part IV&V. London:PTS.
IRELAND, John D.
(2007). *The Udāna and Itivuttaka: Two Classics from the Pali Canon.* Kandy: Buddhist Publication Society.
LEON Feer, M.
(1975). *Saṁyutta-Nikāya.* Part III. (ed.). London: PTS.
(1989-94). *Saṁyutta-Nikāya.* Part I, II, IV, V. (ed.). Oxford: PTS.
MORRIS, Richard.
(1976). *The Anguttara Nikāya.* Part I. (ed.). London: PTS.
(1989). The *Anguttara Nikāya.* Part II. (ed.). (Revised by A. K. Warder). Oxford: PTS.
ÑĀṆAMOLI, Bhikkhu; BODHI, Bhikkhu.

(1995). *The Middle Length Discourses of the Buddha: A New Translation of the MajjhimaNikāya.*Kandy: Buddhist Publication Society.

NORMAN, K. R.; ALSDORF, L.,

(1990). *The Thera- And Theri-Gāthā.* (eds.). Oxford: PTS.

NYANAPONIKA,Thera; BODHI, Bhikkhu.

(2001). *Numerical Discourses of the Buddha: An Anthology of Suttas from the AnguttaraNikāya.* New Delhi: Vistaar Publications.

RHYS DAVIDS, T.W., and CARPENTER, J.E.

(1975-82). *The Dīgha Nikāya.* Vols. I & II. (eds.). London: PTS.

TRENCKNER, V.

(1993). *The Majjhima-Nikāya.* Vol. I. (ed.). Oxford: PTS.

Secondary Sources

GOODMAN, Charles.

(2009). *Consequences of Compassion: An Interpretation and Defense of Buddhist Ethics.* Oxford: Oxford University Press.

GRIFFIN, James.

(1986). *Well-Being.* in B. Hooker, 'The Elements of Well-Being,' Pp. 29–35, 58–72 . *Journal of Practical Ethics,* Volume 3, Number 1. June 2015, p.18.

(1988). *Well-Being: Its Meaning, Measurement and Moral Importance.* Oxford: Clarendon Press.

HOOKER, Brad.

(2002). *Ideal Code, Real World.* Oxford: Clarendon Press.

(2015). The Elements of Well-Being. *Journal of Practical Ethics,* Vol. 3.1.

HURKA, Thomas.

(2001). *Perfectionism.* Oxford: Oxford University Press.

JOHANSSON, Rune E.A.

(1985). *The Dynamic Psychology of Early Buddhism.* Re. London and Malmo: Curzon Press.

KALUPAHANA, David J.

(1976). *Buddhist Philosophy: A Historical Analysis.* Honolulu:University of Hawaii Press.

PANDE, Govind Chandra.

(1995). *Studies in the Origins of Buddhism.* Re. Delhi: Motilal Banarsidass Publishers.

PAYUTTO, P. A.

(1994). *Dependent Origination: The Buddhist Law of Conditionality.* Bangkok: Buddhadhamma Foundation.

SIDERITS, Mark.

(2008). *Personal Identity and Buddhist Philosophy: Empty Persons.* Re. Hampshire: Ashgate Publishing.

Internet Sources

Chatthasamgayana Online Version

BODHI, Bhikkhu.

(2011). "Anicca Vata Saṅkhara," in *Access to Insight* (Legacy Edition).URL:http://www.accesstoinsight.org/lib/authors/bodhi/bps-essay_43.html.

GOWANS, C.W. "Buddhist Well-Being". URL: www.cbs.columbia.edu/files/gowans-essay.pdf

OLDENZKI, Andrew. (2013). "VipallasaSutta: Distortions of the Mind," in *Access to Insight* (Legacy Edition), URL: http:// www.accesstoinsight.org/tipitaka/an/an04/-an04.049.olen.html

RICE, Christopher M. (2013). "Defending the Objective List Theory of Well-Being," in *Ratio*, 26, no. 2, pp.196-211. URL: http://onlinelibrary.wiley.com/doi/10.1111/rati.2013.26.issue-2/issuetoc

The Sutta-s as Literary Genre: A Study of the Sīlakkhandha-vagga

G. A. SOMARATNE*

Introduction

This article aims to critically assess the 13 *sutta*-s (discourses) of the *Sīlakkhandha-vagga* of the *Dīghanikāya* as of a particular literary genre called the '*sutta*-s'. It views these *sutta*-s as oral texts composed by following a specific *sutta* model or template known as the 'Long *sutta*-s' of that *sutta* literary genre in order to transmit the Buddha's message from one person to another and from one generation to another.

Dīghanikāya Collection

The *Dīghanikāya* is the first book of the *Suttanta-piṭaka.* It contains comparatively long texts some of which depict dialogues taken place between the Buddha and his contemporaries. The *sutta*-s of this collection were originally oral compositions taken shape during the time of the Buddha himself in North India, orally transmitted to Sri Lanka within three to four centuries after the Buddha's *parinibbāna* (passing away), put into writing around the first century CE in Sri Lanka and from there transmitted as written texts to Southeast Asia, if not earlier, around the 12th century CE.

The whole *Dīghanikāya* collection consists of 34 *sutta*-s

---

* Assistant Professor, Centre of Buddhist Studies, The University of Hong Kong, Hong Kong, former Professor in Pali & Buddhist Studies, University of Peradeniya, Sri Lanka; former Associate Professor, Miyazaki International College, Japan. E-mail: gsomarat@yahoo.com

divided into three *vagga*-s (groups). The *Sīlakkhandha-vagga* has 13 *sutta*-s, and many of its *sutta*-s contain, often in abbreviated form, a repetitive long section on morality (*sīla*), perhaps inserted in order to make the *sutta* fit to be included in the *vagga*. The next *Mahā-vagga* contains 10 *sutta*-s (14-23) and most of its *sutta* titles have the word *mahā* (great or big). The final *Pāṭika-vagga* has 11 *sutta*-s (24-34), and Pāṭika is the name of its first *sutta* (#24). However, it is also possible to opine that not only the last but also the other two *vagga*-s have gotten their names from each *vagga*'s very first *sutta* to which *sutta* the other *sutta*-s now in the section were later linked.

The *Dīghanikāya* as a whole corresponds to the *Dīrgha-āgama* of some early Buddhist schools, though some of its *sutta*-s in some versions appear now not in the *Dīrgha-āgama* but in the *Madhyama-āgama*. It should be noticed that all the 13 *sutta*-s of the *Dīghanikāya* have their counterpart *Dīrgha-āgama* parallels in either Sanskrit or Chinese, or both (see DHAMMADINNĀ 2014). The Pāli commentaries too sometimes identify the *nikāya* texts as *āgama*. For example, we read: *majjhe visuddhi maggo, esa catunnampi āgamānaṃ* (*Sumaṅgalavilāsinī* I 2; *Papañcasūdanī* I 2; *Sāratthappakāsinī* I 2; *Manorathapūraṇī* I 2). This shows that these collections have a common origin. The *Dīghanikāya* together with the other four *nikāya*-s of the *Suttanta-piṭaka* constitutes the early authority for the *Dhamma* in contrast to the *Vinaya* that finds its authority in the *Vinaya-piṭaka*. In its early stages of transmission, the *Dīgha-bhāṇakas* ("reciters") took the responsibility of maintaining the quality of the text as a whole by checking it from all forms of unauthorized text contaminations.

Texts in Stocks

The *sutta*-s in the *Sīlakkhandha-vagga* showcase all these *sutta*-s as having been composed according to the standard large *sutta* model, by knitting together many stock phrases, passages, verses,[1] and lists containing basic doctrinal and ethical points, perhaps originally designed by the Buddha himself, in a narrative, often embellished in mythology, mixed with subtle humour, in a language pleasing to the ear when recited or chanted, with a certain intended religious purpose. It is likely that these pithy statements and stock passages were originally used in teaching the *Dhamma*, often with the teacher's explanations (commentaries), and over the time came to form expanded stock passages, which in turn came to produce large *sutta*-s as we now have them. These *sutta*-s then contain the Buddha's well-spoken words (*sutta*) in pithy statements (*sutta*) connected to each other through the thread (*sutta*) of narrative context and purpose. Such perception will help us understand the large quantity of repetitions, from small phrases to large sections, running through several pages, within a larger collection like a large *sutta*, the *Sīlakkhandha-vagga* or the *Dīghanikāya*. It is also evident from this *vagga* that a *sutta* is also called *suttanta* (chapter, discourse, dialogue, or text), *dhamma-pariyāya* (exposition of the *dhamma*)[2] or *veyyākaraṇa* (explanation).

Sutta Classification

The *sutta* models or templates seem vary. The more popular traditional classification constitutes long *sutta*-s, middle length *sutta*-s, topic-based *sutta*, and numerical *sutta*-s; the latter two types are mostly composed of short *sutta*-s. According to another traditional classification the *sutta*-s could be divided into those that convey the path to *nibbāna* and those that convey the path to worldly fortunes (*dve suttāni vāsanābhāgiyañca nibbedhabhāgiyañca*, Nett: 48). The modern scholars have come up with more innovative classifications. J.

---

1 The *Sīlakkhandha-vagga* contains, beside the *uddāna-gāthā*, only four (actually three, one repeated twice) verses that are to be found at DN I 99 & 223.

2 The Bhābrā edict of Asoka uses the word *dhamma-pāliyayāni* to refer to the Buddhist discourses (see, Bloch 1950: 154-5).

MANNE (1990: 29-87), for example, identifies three categories of *sutta*-s: sermons, debates and consultations. She identifies the interlocutor's becoming a covert of the Buddha's teaching at the end of the *sutta* as a characteristic of the 'debates' *sutta*-s. If so, contrary to the identification of von HINÜBER (2001: 29) that all 13 *sutta*-s of the *Sīlakkhandha-vagga* are debates, we find the *Brahmajāla-sutta* and both the *Mahāli-* and the *Jāliya-sutta-s*, and the *Kevaṭṭa-sutta* in this *vagga* not coming under this category for in these *sutta-s* no mention is given to conversion; so there are no formal conversion statements built into the *sutta*. The *Brahmajāla-sutta* was addressed to Buddhist monks (*bhikkhu*-s). Licchavi Oṭṭhaddha of the *Mahāli-sutta* and the householder Kevaṭṭa of the *Kevaṭṭa-sutta* could already have been Buddhists. The only failure to be converted to Buddhism could be the case of the *Jāliya-sutta*'s two *pabbajjā*, the wanderer Maṇḍissa and Jāliya the student of Dārupattika. In the remaining nine *sutta*-s in this *vagga*, we find the formal conversion statement. The total number of converted persons in these *sutta*-s is ten, all elites that include a king (Ajātasattu), five *brāhmaṇa*-s (Pokkharasāti, Soṇadaṇḍa, Kūṭadanta, Lohicca), an *acela* (Kassapa), a *paribbājaka* (Poṭṭhapāda), an elephant trainer (Citta Hatthisāriputta), and three *māṇavaka*-s (Subha, Vāseṭṭha, Bhāradvāja). As we are told, both Kassapa and Citta Hatthisāriputta receive ordination and later practicing the path become *arahat*-s. The rest become lay male devotees (*upāsaka*) for in these super elite *sutta*-s in the *vagga* no recognition is awarded to female devotees and nuns.

A Sutta Template

As I understand, all *sutta*-s of the *Sīlakkhandha-vagga* showcase a *sutta* template or a *sutta* model that belongs to the category long *sutta*-s. This template reveals that a text to be one belonging to this particular *sutta* model, it must have composed following a certain *sutta* style which includes having a formal beginning that locates the living Buddha, a story in which the Buddha dialogues with a possible convert, a specific long stock block of texts on the Buddhist path and practice, and a conclusion in which the listener, rather the interlocutor, appreciates the new teaching mostly by way of becoming a convert. In the following pages, I will demonstrate this *sutta* model while critically reviewing the content of each *sutta*.

DN#1. Brahmajāla-sutta:

The episode of the *sutta* takes place between Rājagaha and Nālandā, and the Buddha is located as traveling along the main road that links these two cities. Such beginning which shows the Buddha is travelling deviates from the standard template which shows the Buddha is dwelling in a particular monastery or park or river bank or foot of a tree. The word *Brahma-jāla* means "supreme or all-embracing net", and it is one of the five titles that the Buddha proposes to identify this *dhamma-pariyāya* (exposition of the *dhamma*), as he called it in the *sutta*. The other titles are *attha-jāla, dhamma-jāla, diṭṭhi-jāla,* and *anuttaro-saṅgāma-vijaya.* The *sutta* contains a highly systematized and fully comprehensive summary of the belief systems in India prevalent at the time of the Buddha.

The *sutta* could be divided into two parts. The part I provides an introduction in which the Buddha tells his monks not to be affected by either praise or blame of the worldly persons who praise him for superficial reasons (p. 3, PTS edition, *here and throughout*), not for that he realized the *dhamma.* Here the *sutta* presents morality in three sections: *cūḷa-sīla*, *majjhima-sīla*, and *mahā-sīla* (pp. 4-12), that express mainly the Buddha's outer behaviour. *Cūḷa-sīla* consists of 26 restraints; *majjhima-sīla* has 9 restraints that are mostly the expanded versions of several *cūḷa-sīla* restraints; *mahā-sīla* contains 7 categories of *micchā-ājīva*. In explaining *micchā-ājīva*, the *sutta* refers to varying occupations such as arts, crafts, and sports of early India. It is interesting to notice that no item of restraint is to be found on *surāmeraya*!

The part II (pp. 12-46) is a well-organized section which introduces the Buddhist net by which all 62 types of non-Buddhist philosophical and speculative views concerning the self and the world could be trapped. The holders of the 62 types of views, rather the holders of speculative views, are classified into two main groups: *pubbanta-kappika*-s (18 types) (pp. 12-30) and *aparanta-kappika*-s (44 types) (pp. 31-39). The *pubbanta-kappika*-s are further classified into five groups: *sassata-vādin*-s (4 types), *ekacca-sassatika-ekacca-asassatika*-s (4 types), *antānantika*-s (4 types), *amarā-vikkhepika*-s (4 types), and *adhicca-samupannika*-s (2 types). The *aparanta-kappika*-s are also subdivided into five groups: *saññī-vādin*-s (16 types), *asaññī-vādin*-s (8 types), *neva-saññī-nāsaññī-vādin*-s (8 types), *uccheda-vādin*-s (7 types) and *diṭṭhadhamma-nibbāna-vādin*-s (5 types). The proclaimers of these views are the "worldly persons" (*puthujjana*) who do not know and see things as they really are. They express these views based on their feelings (p. 40). Their views are mere reactions to six types of sensory contact (p. 42). *Tathāgata* understands as they really are the arising and the passing away of the six types of sensory contact and feeling, their attraction and peril, and the deliverance from them, and as such he has gone beyond these views. At the end of the discourse, the monks were satisfied and the tenfold world system shook. As it is evident, it is the framing story with its both a dramatic beginning and a wonder creating end that gives life to otherwise highly theoretical and dull content of the *sutta*.

DN#2. Sāmaññaphala-sutta:

Sāmañña-phala means "fruits of the contemplative life". King Ajātasattu of Magadha asks the Buddha about the benefits of being a *samaṇa*, obtainable in this life. This event takes place in Rājagaha and the Buddha is dwelling in a mango-grove belongs to Jīvaka Komārabhacca. The *sutta* first provides, as presented by the king, the replies to the question given by the six non-Buddhist teachers: Pūraṇa Kassapa, Makkhali Gosāla, Ajita Kesakambala, Pakudha Kaccāyana, Nigaṇṭha Nāṭaputta, and Sañjaya Belaṭṭhaputta (pp. 52-59). The Buddha's reply comes with a presentation of a gradual path culminating in becoming an *arahat*. Some twelve stages in the path beginning with the first *jhāna* are identified as benefits that could be enjoyed by a *samaṇa* here and now, and each of these inner experiential fruits is illustrated with vivid out door similes.

The Buddhist path and practice presented in this *sutta* (pp. 62-84), sometimes with slight adjustments, becomes standard for the rest of the *sutta*-s in the *Dīghanikāya*, and it consists of the following: listening to the Buddha's teaching and becoming a monk, practicing morality as discussed in the *sutta* #1, restraining the six sense doors, practicing mindfulness and clear awareness (*sati-sampajañña*), developing contentment, removing the five hindrances (*nīvaraṇa*) while being in a seated meditation and concurrently attaining the first *jhāna*, attaining the second, the third and the fourth *jhāna*-s, turning the mind to knowing and seeing (*ñāṇa-dassana*) and realizing the impermanent nature of the body and the attachment of the mind (*viññāṇa*) to that body, projecting from the physical body a mind-made body with all physical components and senses, attaining the skills in performing psychic powers, in hearing divine and human sounds afar, in reading others' minds, in recollecting one's past lives, in seeing other people's dying and being born, and attaining the knowledge in the destruction of *āsava* and attaining the freedom from *āsava* together with the confirmation that one has now ended rebirth (*puna-bbhava*). The last attainment consists of a fourfold realization—problem, cause, solution, path—with reference to both *dukkha* and *āsava*.

The *sutta* discloses that, though convinced, converted, and gone for refuge in Venerable Gotama (*bhavantaṃ gotamaṃ*), the *Dhamma* and the *Saṅgha*, King Ajātasattu failed to attain the pure and spotless *dhamma*-eye (stream-entry) due his patricide (pp. 85-86). At the end of the *sutta*, the king confesses to the Buddha his patricide and informs that he now sees it as a serious mistake in his part.

DN#3. Ambaṭṭha-sutta:

The *sutta* is on the subject of caste hierarchy, and the episode takes place in a *brāhmaṇa* village Icchānaṅgala in Kosala. The Buddha has taken temporary residence there in the forest bordering the village. Two main parts of the *sutta* could be identified.

In the first part, we find the young *brāhmaṇa* Ambaṭṭha is sent by his teacher the *brāhmaṇa* Pokkharasāti to find whether the Buddha possesses the 32 bodily marks of a great man (the *sutta* #30, *Lakkhaṇa-sutta* of the *Dīghanikāya* has detailed all of the 32 marks). On arrival the proud Ambaṭṭha behaves impolitely towards the Buddha on grounds of the latter's *khattiya* descent. The Buddha responds stating that the world, including the *brahmā* Sanaṅkumāra, treats *khattiya*-s as superior ranking than *brāhmaṇa*-s, and in that sense he is actually higher born than Ambaṭṭha. He also reveals here what he considers as superior beings are those who have fulfilled in conduct (*caraṇa*) and wisdom (*vijjā*). The *sutta* describes conduct and wisdom by dividing the Buddhist path and practice as of *sutta* #2 into two. All stages of practice from morality to the attainment of the fourth *jhāna* are treated here under conduct and all stages of attainment from *ñāṇa-dassana* to *āsava-kkhaya-ñāṇa* are treated under wisdom (pp. 99-100). In this section of the *sutta* at p.99 we meet the very first *gāthā* (verse) in the *Dīghanikāya*, as spoken by the *brahmā* Sanaṅkumāra, and approved by the Buddha.

In the second part of the *sutta* (pp. 106-7) we find, after listening to the report of Ambaṭṭha, the *brāhmaṇa* Pokkharasāti, being unhappy of Ambaṭṭha's conduct, himself visits the Buddha on the following day, witnesses the 32 marks including the two not normally visible: 'the sheathed genitals and the large tongue' (p. 109: *kosohite ca vattha-guyhe pahūta-jivhatāya ca*), and extends an invitation to the Buddha for a meal. At the residence of the *brāhmaṇa* Pokkharasāti the Buddha delivers a graduated discourse on morality, generosity et cetera and then preaches the Buddhas' exalting *Dhamma* (*buddhānaṃ sāmukkaṃsikā dhamma-desanā*): suffering, its origin, its cessation and the path. At the end of the discourse, Pokkharasāti attains the pure and spotless *Dhamma*-eya and, together with his family and officials, goes for refuge in Venerable Gotama, the *Dhamma* and the *Saṅgha* (p. 110).

DN#4. Soṇadaṇḍa-sutta:

This *sutta* too showcases a change taking place in the social hierarchy: who are superior? *brāhmaṇas* or *khattiyas*? The event takes place in Campā in the country of Aṅga, where the Buddha is dwelling on the bank of the Gaggarā pond. The *brāhmaṇa* Soṇadaṇḍa, being praised by the *brāhmaṇa*-s with reference 11 points, praises the Buddha with reference to 29 points supporting his decision to visit the Buddha, against the advice of the *brāhmaṇa*-s who think visiting the Buddha will contribute toward the decrease of Soṇādaṇḍa's fame. Soṇadaṇḍa accompanied by a group of *brāhmaṇa*-s visits the Buddha who asks the visitor on the essential qualities that make a man a *brāhmaṇa*. Soṇadaṇḍa presents five qualities (pure descent, versed in the *mantra*-s, and being handsome, virtuous, and wise), but at the Buddha's instance admits that these five could be reduced to two, morality/character (*sīla*) and wisdom (*paññā*). At this point, the *brāhmaṇa*-s seeing Soṇadaṇḍa agreeing with the Buddha on the triviality of the caste and birth make a noise. The Buddha explains what he meant by morality and wisdom. Here he presents the Buddhist path and practice as elaborated in the *sutta* #2, and as it could be seen from the abbreviated context (p. 124), the four *jhāna*-s are treated here under *paññā* (DN of the Buddha Jayanti Series, p. 244 treats them under *samādhi.*). At the end, Soṇadaṇḍa expresses that he goes for refuge to Venerable Gotama, the *Dhamma*, and the *Saṅgha* (p. 125) and invites the Buddha for a meal on the following day. The concluding section (p. 125) shows that Soṇadaṇḍa, perhaps considering the reactions of the *brāhmaṇa*-s in previous two occasions, fearing the possible blame from them, expresses that he will limit the outer expression of his devotion to the Buddha to a certain extent. This expression also conveys the triviality of the outer expression over the inner conviction.

DN#5. Kūṭadanta-sutta:

The *sutta* mirrors a transition that is taking place in the ritual context from cruel animal sacrifices to vegetarian offerings; from hoarding wealth to sharing excesses; from externally directed practices to internally directed ones. The event takes place in the *brāhmaṇa* village Khāṇumatta in Magadha, where the Buddha is dwelling in a mango grove. Strangely, the *brāhmaṇa* Kūṭadanta who is preparing to hold a great sacrifice with the slaughter of many hundreds of animals asks the Buddha about how to perform a sacrifice as someone who knows the three modes and the sixteen paraphernalia required for performing an effective sacrifice. This is noted by scholars as an example for the use of humour in the Buddhist texts (See RHYS DAVIDS 1899/2002: II. 160).

The Buddha tells a story from his past lives (a *jātaka* story not to be found in the *Jātaka*), where he is chaplain to King Mahāvijita. With the advice of the chaplain, the king prepares an economic plan, implements it and brings the country to economic prosperity (pp. 135-6). Here he keeps his subject informed on his intension of performing a sacrifice, and gets their consent and cooperation. The chaplain informs the king that maintaining an un-regretting mind at the three stages of the sacrifice, before, during, and after, are the three modes, and the 16 requisites consist of the king receiving the support of the four divisions of his people: the nobles, the officials, the *brāhmaṇa*-s and the householders; the king having eight personal qualities and the chaplain having four personal qualities (p. 138). At pp. 137-8 where this list appears, it seems, with reference to the king's qualities, we could count only 7 qualities; it seems one quality, the most plausibly *sīlavā vuddhasīlī vuddha-sīlenasamannāgato* is missing from the list. The Sinhalese BJ edition (pp. 264-7) breaks *ubhato sujāto* phrase into two and identifies *akkhitto anupakkuṭṭho jāti-vādena* as the second. But this is hard to accept when we consider the four qualities of the chaplain given next, where all four items are there, taking whole of the *ubhato sujāto* phrase as one. Both RHYS DAVIDS (1899/2002: II. 177) and WALSHE (p. 136) without providing any notes, it seems, break *bahussuto... attho ti* phrase into two and identifies *tassa tasseva kho pana bhāsitassa atthaṃ jānāti ...* as the other. The Burmese Chaṭṭhasaṅgāyanā's newest print also agrees with this. Though it makes sense, it is still doubtful on the ground that all other phrases begin with a noun: *sujāto, abhirūpo, aḍḍho, balavā, saddho, bahussuto*, and *paṇḍito*. At p. 140 (PTS) where this list appears again, the text adds the phrase *no ca kho* to *tassa tasseva kho pana...* identifying it as a separate quality. This settles the issue, but could this be a later adjustment!

Following the advice the king, with support from volunteers, performs a sacrifice consisting of making vegetarian offerings to both the good and the bad recipients, while concentrating his mind only on the good people who have abstained from 10 evils.[3] Kūṭadanta who listens to the story asks the Buddha whether there are any other sacrifices that are less complicated but highly effective (p. 143), and the Buddha,

---

3 This list given here is the same as the tenfold *akusala* and *kusala-kamma-s* divided into bodily, verbal and mental actions in later analyses.

placing the above sacrifice in the lowest level, recommends in succession making an offering to the virtuous monks (*sīlavantepabbajite*),[4] making a *vihāra* for the *Saṅgha* of the four directions (*cātuddisaṃ saṅghaṃ*), going to the Buddha,[5] the *Dhamma* and the *Saṅgha* for refuge, observing the five precepts[6] and reaching various stages in the Buddhist path and practice as discussed in the *sutta* #2 to be better and superior sacrifices, and concludes by recognizing the attainment of *āsava-kkhaya-ñāṇa* as the best of sacrifices (p. 147).

After listening to all these, Kūṭadanta converts himself to Buddhism by expressing that he goes to Venerable Gotama, the *Dhamma*, and the *Saṅgha* for refuge and liberates hundreds of animals destined for slaughter. The Buddha then continues his teaching and delivers the Buddha's *sāmukkaṃsikā-dhamma-desanā* with which Kūṭadanta's *Dhamma*-eye opens (p. 148).

DN#6. Mahāli-sutta:

The Buddha is in Vesāli and many *brāhmaṇa* emissaries from Kosala and Magadha came to see the Buddha who was living there in a hall in the Great-forest; Oṭṭhaddha (=Mahāli) also came there with a group of Licchavis. At this time, the Buddha's attendant (*upaṭṭhāka*) was the monk Nāgita, but the one who really arranged the meeting between the visitors and the Buddha was Sīha, a novice monk (*samaṇuddesa*). The *sutta* discusses the ways and means of attaining divine eye and divine ear. In replying to a question asked by Oṭṭhaddha, as to why a certain monk, in this case Sunakkhatta, a Liccha-

4 For such a *dāna* it is possible that *arahats* or those who have entered into the path to *arahatta* participate as recipients (*arahantovāarahatta-maggaṃ vāsamāpannā*) (p. 143).

5 Here is the only place in the Sīlakkhandha-vagga the phrase *buddhaṃ saraṇaṃ gacchati* is given (p. 145). All other places *bhavantaṃ gotamaṃ saraṇaṃ gacchāmi* is to be found.

6 The term *pañca-sīla* is not used but the five are given as *sikkhā-padāni* (p. 146).

vian, sees divine sights but fails to hear divine sounds (p. 152), the Buddha explains that it is because of the "one-sided" way the monk has practised his *samādhi* (p. 153). The PTS p. 153 & p. 154 identify and define it fully the *puratthimāya disāya ekaṃsa-bhāvito samādhi*, and then presents in abbreviated form *dakkhiṇāya disāya ekaṃsa-bhāvito samādhi, pacchimāya disāya ekaṃsa-bhāvito samādhi*, and *uttarāya disāya ekaṃsa-bhāvito samādhi*. Next comes in abbreviated form *uddhamadho tiriyaṃ ekaṃsa-bhāvito samādhi*. Here it is unclear whether we should understand the last as one *samādhi* or as three (= *uddhaṃ ekaṃsa-bhāvito samādhi, adho ekaṃsa-bhāvito samādhi* and *tiriyaṃ ekaṃsa-bhāvito samādhi*). If the latter is correct, the text should be presented as *uddhaṃ/m ...adho ... tiriyaṃ ekaṃsa-bhāvito samādhi*. This should also apply to pp. 154-5 where *ubhayaṃsa-bhāvito samādhi* is presented. After listing several ways of practicing the *samādhi-bhāvanā*, the *sutta* states that the monks lead a holy life under the Buddha not for realizing these *samādhi* but for attaining stream-entry, once-return, non-return and *arahatta* (p. 156). This section is noteworthy for it is where important stock phrases for explaining Buddhist soteriology are found: here the concepts of both *saṃyojana* and *āsava* without identifying them (except the naming of *rāga, dosa* and *moha*) are given; the word *anāgāmi* is not to be found and this noble person is identified as *opapātiko* which is again another obscure term. The phrase used to explain *arahat* also appears for the first time and is worth comparing with *āsava-kkhaya-ñāṇa* at p. 84. The Noble Eightfold Path, a mere listing, is presented next as the path to reach those higher attainments (p. 157).

It seems the actual *sutta* ends there, and the rest that discusses whether the body and the self are the same or different could be an extension (See the *sutta* #7), as immediately after identifying the Noble Eightfold Path, the Buddha continues with a story almost unrelated to what is being discussed. The redactor's intention could be to find a way to present the

Buddhist path and practice consisting morality as in the *sutta* #2 and the rest of the *sutta*-s. Asked by two *pabbajitā*, Maṇḍissa and Jāliya, whether the self and the body are the same or different, the Buddha presents the Buddhist path and practice, and says when it comes to define, rather when one has fulfilled and attained, the higher states of attainments from the first *jhāna* to *arahatta*, this talk on duality or identity of the body and the self is irrelevant. Mahāli becomes happy, and nothing is said about the reaction of the *brāhmaṇa* emissaries and the other Licchavis who were in the audience.

DN#7. Jāliya-sutta:

This *sutta* (pp. 159-160) is exactly the extended section of the *sutta* #6 (pp. 157-8), and the event takes place in Kosambi where the Buddha is dwelling at its Gosita grove. It discusses the relationship between the self and the body by bringing in the Buddhist path and practice. Is this *sutta* then a redundant piece? Yes, but also no, because this could be the original *sutta* which was in the original *Dīghanikāya* or the *Sīlakkhandha-vagga* collection, and in this sense the *Mahāli-sutta* without its *Jāliya-sutta* section could be a later addition to the collection, and it was during the *vagga* formation period, the latter part was added to qualify it for inclusion. There is another possibility, that is, during its early transmission period, this *sutta* could be the one in the *Sīlakkhandha-vagga*, and due to its abbreviated nature (less than two pages in print) came to be confused in deciding whether it was part of the *Mahāli-sutta* or an independent one. The decision of the redactors could be to count it as part of the *Mahāli-sutta* as well as to keep it as an independent one. This could also be supported by the fact that even though logically as the Buddha recalls the content of the *Jāliya-sutta* in the *Mahāli-sutta*, in this *vagga* the *Jāliya-sutta* should have presented first as the *sutta* number 6 of the collection. Further, unlike the former's location Vesāli, this *sutta* is connected to Kosambi. It should be noted that the conclusion of both the *Mahāli-sutta* and the *Jāliya-sutta* are the same; in the case of the latter, the two *pabbajitā* do not get converted to Buddhism but become happy with what the Buddha said.

DN#8. Mahāsīhanāda-sutta:

The *sutta*'s aim is to give new definitions to the old words *samaṇa* and *brāhmaṇa*, and is also titled in the manuscripts as *Kassapa-sīhanāda-sutta* or *Sīhanāda-sutta*. The word *sīha-nāda* means "lion's roar" and the name comes from p. 175 where the Buddha explains the comprehensiveness of his teaching mission with reference to ten points: he teaches the *Dhamma* to people in public; he teaches them with confidence; people ask him questions; he answers them; he wins them over with his answers; people think that they should listen to him; they are pleased after listening to him; they show they are pleased; they practice to attain the goal; those who have practiced are satisfied. The event of the *sutta* takes place at Kaṇṇakatthala in Ujuññā where the Buddha is dwelling in a deer park. The naked ascetic Kassapa asks if it is true that the Buddha condemns all forms of ascetic practice and ascetics (p. 161). The latter denies and says he distinguishes between those that lead one to hell and those that lead one to heaven. With reference to some points he says he agrees with other *samaṇa*-s and *brāhmaṇa*-s but with reference to some others he disagrees; other *samaṇa*-s and *brāhmaṇa*-s also do the same. However, the Buddha says, it is with reference to what both parties claim that they are in agreement that the wise should make a comparison regarding both the teachers and the disciples. Such a comparison will reveal that the Buddha and his disciples have completely eradicated *akusala* and fully cultivated *kusala*, while other teachers and their disciples have done so only partially (pp. 162-5).

The *sutta* adds that by practicing the Noble Eightfold Path one could by oneself see and know that only the Buddha is *kāla-vādī, bhūta-vādī, attha-vādī, dhamma-vādī,* and *vinaya-vādī* (p. 165). Kassapa presents a range of standard three sets of ascetic practices due to which practices one is identified as a *samaṇa* or *brāhmaṇa* (p. 166). The Buddha says that if one's morality, concentration and wisdom are not developed with these practices, one is still far from being a *samaṇa* or *brāhmaṇa*, and that it is one who practices loving-kindness (*mettā*) and is here and now an *arahat* who is a *samaṇa* or a *brāhmaṇa* (pp. 167-9). The *sutta* finds space here to present the Buddhist path and practice divided into three: the cultivation of morality, concentration and wisdom (pp. 171-4). The Buddha here concludes his discourse by stating that as regards to *adhisīla, adhijeguccha* (super austerity), *adhipaññā, and adhivimutti* there is none who surpasses him. It could be noted that no mention is given to *adhicitta* or *adhisamādhi.*

Kassapa becomes a convert, and seeks going-forth and ordination under the Buddha. It is noteworthy that here we find the statement *bhagavantaṃ saraṇaṃ gacchāmi dhammañca bhikkhu-saṅghañca* (p. 176) that in other contexts occurs with *bhavantaṁ gotamaṁ ....* Though the usual practice is to make those who come from other religious sects undergo a probationary period of four months, considering "personality types" (*puggala-vemattatā*), Kassapa is allowed to become a monk who by following the path turns into an *arahat* (pp. 176-7).

DN#9. Poṭṭhapāda-sutta:

The *sutta* context is in Sāvatthi where the Buddha is dwelling at Jeta's grove. The wanderer Poṭṭhapāda asks the Buddha how the "higher perception" (*abhisaññā-nirodha*) ceases. The Buddha answers that it is through training, and explains to him the Buddhist path and practice as in the *sutta* #2 up to identifying the four *jhāna*-s, and then presents for the first time in the *Dīghanikāya* the first three formless states: the sphere of infinite space, the sphere of infinite consciousness, and the sphere of nothingness (pp. 183-4). He explains how the new perceptions relevant to each state arise by ridding the perceptions of the previous state. In this way, the practitioner gradually reaches the apex of perceptions (*saññagga*) and by deciding not to think and to mentally construct, he touches the state of cessation (*nirodha*) (pp. 184-5). Here Poṭṭhapāda's acceptance that *anupubbābhisaññā-nirodha-sampajāna-samāpatti* is something unheard before seems to confirm the Buddhistic nature of this attainment and the path leading to its attainment.

The *sutta* confirms that perception arises first and then arises knowledge (*ñāṇa*) (p. 185). This could be a reference to how those who have attained the cessation state come out of it as *arahat*-s; first reappearing perception (*saññā*) and then immediately arising knowledge (*ñāṇa*) in the destruction of *āsavā* taking place. The *sutta* then refutes three kinds of possible self (pp. 186-7), and discusses the undeclared issues and the reason for their not being declared. To the question what then he has declared, the Buddha says he has declared "this is *dukkha*", "this is the arising of *dukkha*", "this is the cessation of *dukkha*", and "this is the way leading to the cessation of *dukkha*", for these four are conducive to *nibbāna*.

The Buddha leaves the place (p. 189) and the other wanderers abuse Poṭṭhapāda for approving everything what the Buddha said. With a clear interruption of two to three days, the wanderer Poṭṭhapāda and Citta, son of elephant trainer, come to the Buddha again. The discussion on the undeclared issues continues. The Buddha explains how he questions those who declare that after death the self is entirely happy and is in a permanent state. He presents two popular similes, one on a man's love for an unseen beauty queen (p. 193) and the other on one preparing a ladder to climb an unseen multi-floored building (p. 194), and shows how baseless their claim as they do not have any experience of what they say. At the end, both Poṭṭhapāda and Citta become converts of

Buddhism and declare the statement *bhagavantaṃ saraṇaṃ gacchāmi* ... and Citta receives ordination and, after following the path, becomes an *arahat* (p. 203).

DN#10. Subha-sutta:

The *sutta* context takes place in Sāvatthi, shortly after the passing away of the Buddha; deviating from the standard way, the *sutta* locates the living Venerable Ānanda[7] as that he is dwelling in the Jeta's grove there, who in this case explains the aggregates of morality, concentration and wisdom, to the young *brāhmaṇa* Subha Todeyyaputta who has taken temporary residence in Sāvatthi for some matter, and who somewhat strangely (not for a meal as in many cases) invites Ānanda to visit him. We are also informed that Ānanda is on medication. The Buddhist path and practice as given in the *sutta* #2 is treated here for the first time under the three headings of *sīla*, *samādhi*, and *paññā*, also with the same similes as in the *sutta* #2. The *sīla* is defined with the sections of *cūḷa-*, *majjhima-*, and *mahā-sīla*-s (p. 206). The *samādhi* section begins with the restraint in the sense doors and goes up to the fourth *jhāna* (pp. 207-8). The section on *paññā* begins with *ñāṇa-dassana* and goes up to the attainment of *arahatta* (pp. 208-9). The young *brāhmaṇa* becomes a lay devotee by taking refuge in Venerable Gotama, the *Dhamma*, and the *Saṅgha* (p. 210).

DN#11. Kevaṭṭa-sutta:

Some manuscripts title this *sutta* as Kevaddha or Kevaḍḍha. The event takes place in Nālandā where the Buddha is dwelling in a mango grove. The *sutta* discusses the topic of miracles and demonstrates that the Buddha who recommends and performs the miracle of teaching is the teacher far-excellence. Kevaṭṭa asks the Buddha why he does not gain

---

7 It is unusual to find that many manuscripts read in both places as in the words of Subha: *bhagavantaṃ ānandaṃ* (see the variants of given on p. 185 of De (pilot edition).

disciples by working a miracle of psychic power (p. 211);[8] the Buddha explains that people would simply dismiss such wonder-work as magic and that, for the Buddha, real miracle is education (p. 214), training his followers to become *arahat*-s. Here the *sutta* presents the Buddhist path and practice as in *sutta* #2. Such instruction cannot be given by the divine beings including Brahmā, who are not free from *saṃsāra.* Here he tells a story (pp. 215-22) of the monk who wants to know "where the four great elements cease without remainder", and who by way of a meditative state finds the way to the world of the gods and the way to the world of the *brahmā*-s in search of an answer. After not getting an answer from both the gods and *brahmā*-s, the monk finally meets Mahābrahmā who too admits his ignorance but is kind enough to direct the monk back to the Buddha. The Buddha first corrects the question to "where do the four great elements find no footing?", and gives his answer. Here both the question and the answer are given in verse, making the *sutta* a *sagāthaka* text. There is no conversion statement appearing in it.

DN#12. Lohicca-sutta:

The *sutta* is a discussion on blameworthy and blameless teachers, and the ethics of teaching. The event takes place in Sālavatikā in Kosala (p. 224) to which place the Buddha just arrived in. The *brāhmaṇa* Lohicca believes that whoever discovers a good doctrine should not try to teach it to others. He invites the Buddha for a meal. In this visit, the Buddha points out the danger of the misperception as it blocks people the opportunity to learn the *Dhamma* whose practice conduces them the fruits of stream-entry (*sotāpatti-phala*), once-return (*sakadāgāmi-phala*), non-return (*anāgāmi-phala*) and the *arahatta* (p. 229). Lohicca poses some questions: If the *Dhamma* is

8 Kevaṭṭa, a fisherman as the name suggests, may be thinking why the Buddha not use *iddhi* for a big catch!

something that one must realize for oneself, then what is the role of a teacher? Are there any teachers who don't deserve criticism? The Buddha replies by identifying three types of teachers who deserve some criticism (p. 230), and says that the teacher who has attained *arahatta* and guides others to reach it deserves no criticism. The teacher who deserves blame is the one who has not attained the goal but teaches others to attain it, and whose students do not listen to him and not arouse the thought of enlightenment; one who has not attained the goal but teaches others to attain it, and whose students listen to him and arouse the thought of enlightenment; one who has attained the goal and teaches others to attain it, and whose students do not listen to him and arouse the thought of enlightenment. In explaining the one who does not deserve blame, the *sutta* explains the Buddhist path and practice as in the *sutta* #2 (pp. 232-3). Lohicca goes for refuge to Venerable Gotama, the *Dhamma* and the *Saṅgha*.

DN#13. Tevijja-sutta:

The event takes place in the *brāhmaṇa* village Manasākaṭa in Kosala where the Buddha has taken temporary residence at a mango grove on the bank of the river Aciravatī. The *sutta* is a criticism of the *brāhmaṇa*-s of the *Three Veda*-s, who profess a path to union with Brahmā while they themselves leading a life incompatible with the qualities of Brahmā. Vāseṭṭha and Bhāradvāja, the two young *brāhmaṇa*-s who disagree with each other on the paths to the union with Brahmā as taught by two different *brāhmaṇa* teachers come to the Buddha to settle the dispute (pp. 235-6). The Buddha gets them to admit that none of those teachers and others in the religion have ever seen Brahmā face to face, that they teach the path to union with Brahmā whom they do not know and see. Such *brāhmaṇa*-s have been compared to a file of blind men who go on clinging to each other, seeing nothing (p. 239). Asked about the path to union with Brahmā (p. 248), the Buddha switches it to the world of *brahmā*-s and explains the Buddhist path and practice up to the first *jhāna* (pp. 250-51), and then explains the practice of the four *brahma-vihāra*-s: *mettā, karuṇā, muditā*, and *upekkhā*. Unlike in other *sutta*-s, the path discussed here does not culminate in the attainment of *arahatta*. Both Vāseṭṭha and Bhāradvāja become lay followers of the Buddha (*mayaṃ bhavantaṃ gotamaṃ saraṇaṃ gacchāma dhammañca bhikkhu-saṅghañca*, p. 252).

Compositional Imperfections

As it could be observed in the *Sīlakkhandha-vagga*, the *sutta*-s sometimes contain certain compositional imperfections often common to oral texts. These defects could also be the remnants of a deliberate attempt in making things fit to the *sutta* template concerned. However, it is also possible to find internal inconsistencies within a large *sutta* or between large *sutta*-s that could be hypothesized as due to the gradual and natural process in the formation, composition and redaction of these large *sutta*-s. Some examples for such internal inconsistencies could be pointed out from the most important *sutta* #2 of the *vagga* under review. The order of listing the names of the six non-Buddhist teachers at pp. 52-59, for example, differs from its previous listing at pp. 47-48 where Nigaṇṭha Nāṭaputta is placed after Sañjaya Belaṭṭhiputta. Again the first five paragraphs of the same *sutta*-s how that each of the first five teachers, while presenting their doctrines, addresses King Ajātasattu with 'Great King' (*mahārāja*): *karato kho mahārāja kārayato* (p. 52), *natthi mahārāja hetu* (p. 53), *natthi mahārāja dinnaṃ* (p. 55), *sattime mahārāja kāyā* (p. 56), *idha mahārāja nigaṇṭho* (p. 57) where as the last teacher misses to address the king, *atthi parolokoti itice ...* (p. 58) which could be a possible evidence for showing that these passages were brought in from a third source and attempted to contextualize them by addition the world *mahārāja*. Further, we could notice a difference in the way the king addresses each teacher, some with the first name: *bho ajita* (p. 55), *bho sañjaya* (p. 58); some with the last name: *bho kassapa* (p. 52), *bho gosāla* (p. 53), *bho kaccāyana* (p. 56), and one with a totally different name: *bho aggivessana* (p. 57).

As an example to show the inconsistencies between the *sutta*-s, we could examine the way the four *jhāna*-s are treated in different *sutta*-s. At pp. 73-6, in the *sutta* #2, they appear forming a part of a continued listing, without any divisions; at p. 124, in the *sutta* #4, they are listed and identified under *paññā* for the context requires its inclusion with either *sīla* or *paññā*; at p. 100, in the *sutta* #3, they are treated under *caraṇa* as the context requires the presenting of the whole Buddhist path and practice divided into two: *caraṇa* and *vijjā*; and at pp. 207-8, in the *sutta* #10, Venerable Ānanda arranges the four *jhāna*-s under *samādhi* (*idam pissa hoti samādhismiṃ*), the standard way of treating them.

Sometimes, it is noticeable that in the *vagga* as a whole or in the individual *sutta*-s of it, either things are half done or done are undone. A good example for such incompletions could be noticed with reference to the *bhāṇa-vāra* identification in the *vagga*: The first and the second *bhāṇa-vāra*-s are identified at p. 9 and p. 32 respectively, both within the *Brahmajāla-sutta*, but again at p. 99 (inside the *Ambaṭṭha-sutta*) the first *bhāṇa-vāra* is identified. However, no other *bhāṇa-vāra* identification is to be found in the remaining sections of the *Sīlakkhandha-vagga*, even though one could expect at least 25-30 *bhāṇa-vāra*-s marked there, out of the total 64 of the whole *Dīghanikāya* as mentioned in the *Samantapāsādikā-ṭīkā* (See von HINÜBER 2001: fn. 29). Perhaps this is due to the impracticability of marking such boundaries in a text with a large number of abbreviated texts as in the *Sīlakkhandha-vagga*. Further, when a new *sutta* is brought into a collection, new counting and marking are required in the *bhāṇa-vāra* system and it seems this was also the reality with regard to the *Sīlakkhandha-vagga*. Further, in such transportation of texts into a collection required adjustments in the *uddāna-gāthā*, often upsetting their metre. This could be the reason that the *uddāna-gāthā*-s in the Pāli Canonical texts are often metrically corrupt, and it is also the case of the *uddāna-gāthā* of the *Sīlakkhandha-vagga* (p. 253). Perhaps, this movement from collection to collection was made easy by the self-sufficient nature of the large *sutta*-s.

As the *sutta*-s are formed and brought into different collections in stages, the original intention of composing a *sutta* for use in self-understanding or teaching in a particular oral community such as of Sāvatthi, Rājagaha, Nālandā, Vesāli, Campā or Kosambi could differ from its actual functional role within a collection such as of the *Sīlakkhandha-vagga* or of the *Dīghanikāya*. Therefore, it is important to treat a *sutta* first as an independent entity and see the consistency or inconsistency within its multiple components before treating it as a dependent entity and seeing the reason behind that *sutta* forming a part of that larger collection of *sutta*-s.

Conclusion

Our conclusion is that all *sutta*-s in the *vagga* showcase they belong to one literary genre, the *sutta*-s, more specifically 'Long *sutta*-s'. The beginnings and ends of these *sutta*-s follow a similar format. Almost all *sutta*-s locates the living Buddha and the content within attempts to glorify him. Even in the exceptional *Subha-sutta*, it is still the Buddha that is the centre-focus. Overall, each *sutta* in this *vagga* is presented embedded into a beautiful story in which the interlocutor comes to the Buddha, listens to the *Dhamma* and in most of the cases becomes a convert. All *sutta*-s contain a large section on morality in the same verbatim, and all *sutta*-s present the Buddhist path and practice almost using a one large stock section divided into smaller portions appropriating to different contexts. At the end, the interlocutor accepts the Buddha's teaching and some ends up taking refuge in the Buddha, the *Dhamma* and *Saṅgha*. Though these *sutta*-s are beautifully composed they are also not without compositional defects as compositions of a particular ancient oral literary genre.

References

Buddhajayanti Tipiṭaka Series
(2005). *Dīghanikāya.* Vol. 1. Dehiwala, Sri Lanka: Buddhist Cultural Centre.
Dhammachai Tipiṭaka Project.
(2013). *Dīghanikāya Volume I: Sīlakkhandhavagga Pilot Version.* Thailand: Dhammakāya Foundation, Dhammachai Institute.
BLOCH, Jules.
(1950). *Les Inscriptions d'Asoka.* Paris: Les Belles Lettres.
Dhammadinnā.
(2014). *Research on the Dīrgha-āgama.* (ed.). Taipei: Dharma Drum Publishing Corporation.
HARDY, E.
(1902/1995). *The Netti-pakaraṇa with Extracts from Dhammapāla's Commentary.* (ed.). Oxford: PTS.
MANNE, J.
(1990). Categories of Sutta in the Pāli Nikāyas and Their Implications for Our Appreciation of the Buddhist Teaching and Literature. *JPTS.* no. 15, Pp. 29-87.
RHYS DAVIDS, T. W.
(1899/2002). *Sacred Books of the Buddhists Vol II: Dialogues of the Buddha Translated from the Pali.* Oxford: PTS.
RHYS DAVIDS, T.W., and J. Estlin Carpenter.
(1890/1995). *The Dīgha Nikāya* Vol. 1. Oxford: PTS.
von HINÜBER, Oskar.
(2001). *A Handbook of Pāli Literature.* Delhi: Munshiram Manoharlal Publishers Pvt. Ltd.
WALSHE, Maurice.
(1997). *Thus Have I Heard: The Long Discourses of the Buddha Digha Nikaya: Translation from the Pali.* London: Wisdom Publications.

An Attempt to Derive a Chronology of the Majjhima Nikāya Objectively, Using Grammatical Markers

Venerable Medhāvī Bāhiya*

This article describes a PhD research project currently being conducted by the author which attempts to use changes in Pāli grammar as the language developed over the course of history as markers to show which texts in the *Majjhima Nikāya* (hereafter M) of the Pāli Canon are early and which are late. The approach is broadly based on that of Paul KINGSBURY (2002) who compared the relative frequency of different types of aorist in the Pāli Canon, and showed that later texts were marked by a higher proportion of sigmatic aorists to thematic/root aorists. The current study sets out to take the approach one step further by comparing a wide variety of linguistic features in a much more rigorous manner, limited to prose text of the M. A relational database containing the text of the M is currently being constructed with detailed grammatical information attached on a word-by-word basis, enabling a much more detailed and multifaceted analysis than would otherwise be practicable. The project is currently at an early stage of preparation of the database.

Textual Traditions

Although the Pāli Canon is regarded according to Buddhist

* Sitagu International Buddhist Academy, Sagaing Hills, Myanmar. E-mail: medhavi1@gmail.com

tradition as the original teaching of the Buddha which has been preserved perfectly and unchanged since the time of the Buddha, there are a variety of reasons to believe that some changes in the texts have taken place during the course of the last 2500 years since the time of the Buddha, for example:

1. The Commentaries on the Pāli Canon typically analyse the texts methodically phrase by phrase, commenting on how to understand the meaning. There are numerous instances, however, where the commentary analyses each phrase consecutively and then suddenly skips a section of the text as it is currently preserved in the Pāli Canon, and continues methodically from a subsequent point as though the intervening text did not exist in the copy of the text examined by the commentator, Venerable Buddhaghosa. This might be interpreted as indicating that the intervening text has been added to the original text at some time after Buddhaghosa edited the Commentaries in the 5th CENTURY CE (ADIKARAM 1946: 34-35; ABEYNAYAKE 2000: 179-181; NANDAMĀLĀBHIVAṀSA 2012).

2. Similarly, there are other instances where the Commentary appears to add an extra section of text to the text as it is preserved today – as though contiguous with the text before and after the point at which it appears to be inserted – in that the Commentary comments on a section of text that does not exist in the Pāli Canon as we find it today. This might be interpreted as indicating that the relevant section of text was included in the Pāli Canon as it was preserved in the time of Venerable Buddhaghosa, but was subsequently lost.

3. The Pāli Canon is not a single uniformly preserved body of texts – there are differences between the national editions of different countries, such as Myanmar, Thailand, Sri Lanka etc. Differences also exist between

individual palm leaf manuscripts within each country. In most instances the differences are simply differences in spelling, or a single character difference which might result in a different meaning, different grammatical suffix or construction, the substitution or addition of one word, etc. However there are also instances where the text is completely different and the different versions are hard to reconcile. The question then arises which is the correct version, which is the original version, which version gives the correct meaning.

4. For several hundred years the texts of the Pāli Canon were preserved orally until they were first written down in the first CENTURY BCE. Various non-canonical texts and inscriptions known to have been written during different periods in history clearly show that the Pāli language was in a state of flux during that period; the Pāli language of the Commentaries, for example, is significantly different to that of most of the Pāli Canon. At the same time changes in society, traditions, folklore, technology (for example building technology, farming technology), geography, flora and fauna, etc, could be expected to have influenced the way the texts in the Pāli Canon were understood. For example some authorities today maintain that the Yakkhas and Nāgas were (human) ethnic tribes living in India at the time of the Buddha, but that these two ethnic groups were unknown in Sri Lanka at the time of Buddhaghosa and were subsequently assumed to have been non-human beings (MARASINGHE 1974: 74-75). ABEYNAYAKE (1984: 99, 104) cites a number of cities – including some beyond the borders of India such as *Yonakā*, *Tambapanni* and *Suvannabhūmi* – and tribes which do not occur in the Pāli Canon except in the *Niddesa* and *Apadāna*, and suggests they refer to regions and tribes that only experienced the Buddha's teaching during a later age. By the time of the Commentaries certain techn-

ological terms would also have fallen into disuse so that their exact meaning was no longer known. Modern studies of oral traditions have indicated that oral traditions from all cultures and traditions all over the world and throughout history appear to follow certain common features: one of these is that the oral tradition tends to gradually evolve with changing understanding and world-view, as a natural consequence of the way the human mind and human memory works. Human memory is – unlike computer memory – critically dependent on meaning, and when the perceived meaning changes as a result of words falling into disuse, changes in traditions and in the structure of society, etc., the memory is influenced by those changes – the mind has a tendency to unconsciously "reconstruct" the text where it appears to conflict with current understanding, so as to counteract that apparent conflict. Sometimes a change of just one consonant could give rise to a quite different meaning for a passage of text as a whole, and in such circumstances the mind may very easily but quite unconsciously institute such a change in order to try to bring the recollected text in line with current views and experiences.

5. From the first CENTURY BCE until the 19th CENTURY CE – a period of two millennia – the texts of the Pāli Canon were preserved primarily in the form of collections of palm leaves on which the texts were carefully inscribed. Under optimal storage conditions with minimal or no handling the palm leaves could be preserved relatively intact for up to 300 years, but in practical circumstances in humid tropical countries such as Myanmar, Thailand and Sri Lanka the usual usable lifetime of palm manuscripts if minimally handled would be vastly less than this – a figure of 70 to 100 years would be more realistic. If the manuscripts are heavily used it may well be that even within 5 or 10 years they will already no longer be prese-

rved intact and are in need of replacement. Furthermore a single copy does not suffice – the texts need to be used by many different individuals in different monasteries, different regions, and different countries and written in different national scripts. Thus the history of the Pāli Canon since it was first committed to text is marked by constant and countless copying and recopying. Errors inevitably occur during the course of such copying, including lexical errors, grammatical substitutions, and text omissions, repetitions, and substitutions. It is also the case that emissaries from one country have often transcribed texts from another country into their own script and taken it back to their own country; for example there are certain textual traditions among manuscripts in particular districts of Sri Lanka that display certain specific orthographic errors that appear to indicate that they are derived from a single manuscript in Burmese script, since the errors appear to be related to the similarity of certain characters in Burmese script where the equivalent characters in Sinhalese script are quite distinct. The Pāli Canon comprises about 4 million words, and when copying it even a single time the probabilities of making an error are very high. Various projects to digitise the Pāli Canon in the modern age demonstrate the scale of the problem: Japanese scholars have found that all the available digital editions of the Pāli Canon have error rates averaging at least one per page (THANISSARO 2000). THANISSARO cites an 8-step error-checking protocol used in the preparation of the PĀLITEXT CDROM version of Wat Dhammakāya (including, *inter alia*, entering each text twice followed by a digital comparison of the two versions, and use of a digital spell-check program – neither of which could have been used by the manual scribes copying texts over the millennia). CONE (2007) draws attention to the same problem, noting that the PTS editions of the Pāli Canon contain large numbers of errors compared to other editions.

6. According to the Pāli commentaries and the ancient Sri Lankan chronicles, many learned monks died during a twelve year long Brāhmaṇatissa famine prompting urgent efforts to protect the collective memorisation of the Pāli Canon, and leading to the subsequent decision to commit the Pāli Canon to writing in the first CENTURY BCE (ADIKARAM 1946: 73-79). At that time the memorisation of some sections of the Pāli Canon was confined to a very small number of individuals, and the memorisation of one section of the Vinaya was even supposed to have been confined to a single monk who was criticised as having poor moral conduct. Furthermore substantial changes had taken place in the way of life of the Bhikkhus from the time of the Buddha in India to the first CENTURY BCE in Sri Lanka where the texts were first written down, and these changes might have influenced the interpretation and correct recollection of the texts. It seems likely that the texts may have been influenced by such constraints. Furthermore in view of the practical considerations of committing the Pāli Canon to writing for the first time, KULASURIYA (2000: 156, 160) argues that it was necessarily subjected to substantial prior editorial handling.

7. Enumerations within the Pāli literature of the number of texts, the number of sections, the length of the sections, and their overall organisation are difficult to reconcile with the text of the Pāli Canon as we know it today, and there are indications that the texts might have been reorganised and in places perhaps even reformulated at certain times (ABEYNAYAKE 1984). In the *Papañcasūdanī* (Majjhima-nikāya-aṭṭhakathā), for example, Buddhaghosa states on the authority of the *Porāṇas* that the M consists of just 80,523 words (*pada*) (ADIKARAM 1946: 20) – just one third of the number of words in today's editions (240,051

words including verse in the Myanmar Chaṭṭhasaṅgīti edition).

Therefore we must be vigilant in our interpretation of the texts of the Pāli Canon, and use our best efforts and all means at our disposal to try to ensure that possible errors and changes can be recognised and taken into consideration. The teachings of the Buddha have the property of *akāliko* – timelessness – as they are general properties of human nature which are just as true today as they were 2500 years ago. Nevertheless, it is only the deeper meaning of the teachings which has this property of *akāliko* and not the expressions and linguistic formations habitually used to express those teachings. If it is the case that different texts were written during different periods and under different linguistic, cultural, social and technological conditions, then we must be aware of those differences in order to be able to understand those expressions and linguistic formations correctly, and in order to ensure that we understand the deeper meaning of the text correctly. Otherwise we may find that we have errors in our understanding of the proper practice which obstruct our progress.

The use of Grammatical Markers to Date Texts

Paul KINGSBURY (KINGSBURY 2002, 2003) studied the relative frequencies of different types of aorists in texts from the whole of the Pāli Canon, in an attempt to derive a chronology of the Pāli Canon based only on grammatical features in the text, and thereby independent of any subjective evaluations of what constitutes an "early" or a "late" text. He showed that compared to root or thematic aorists, sigmoid aorists are increasingly common in late texts relative to early texts, and that the relative frequencies of sigmoid to non-sigmoid aorists can be used as an indicator of text age.

Texts used by KINGSBURY (2002: 171-172, 219-221, 229) in his study were classified into the three groups (predominately) verse, mixed, and (predominately) prose. One aspect clear from KINGSBURY's results is the necessity of adequately discriminating between verse and prose. The type of language used in verse is frequently skewed by metrical constraints, with the result that verse from a late period tends to have much higher frequencies of archaic word forms than would otherwise be expected on the basis of its actual age. In addition for a variety of reasons it can be suspected that verses may sometimes have been composed during a different period to that of the underlying prose text. In some cases for example, already pre-existing verses might have been used in a new composition, while in other cases verses might have been added later[1]. Some verses could even date from a pre-buddhist era, i.e. they might plausibly have originated from earlier non-Buddhist sources (*ārogyaparamā lābhā, nibbānaṁ paramaṁ sukhaṁ*, for example, in *Māgaṇḍiya-sutta* M 75 §215 PTS 1: 508, could plausibly be included in this category). As there are many difficulties associated with dating verse from its linguistic forms, verse text is completely excluded from the corpus used for the current study.

The Pāli Canon Relational Database

A relational database is currently under construction containing the text of the M. A major advantage of the relational database format is that detailed grammatical information can be included on a word-by-word basis, including part of speech, root, tense, voice, person, number, case, gender, sentence position, and so on, all linked to tables of conjugations and declensions, unique word forms, and word roots.

1 For example, Ven. Yakkaduwe Sri Pragñārāma has established that there are four stanzas in Sinhala Prakrit in the *Sammādiṭṭhi-sutta* of the M, added to highlight topics discussed in the *sutta*; three of the four stanzas – if assumed to be Pāli – are cryptic, and have been removed from some editions (ABEYNAYAKE 2000: 172).

The M comprises 236,526 words of prose (plus 3525 words of verse) and around 20,000 different lexical forms. The majority of the grammatical data can be entered once for each of the 20,000 different word forms, but some word forms must be checked against each grammatical context in which they appear. Construction of this database is therefore a mammoth undertaking by any reckoning. However, by attaching detailed grammatical information to each word a tremendously powerful research tool is created, and the possibilities for comparing the frequency of different linguistic forms in different groups of texts are almost endless.

The database is prepared by running a special program which scans a digital form[2] of the Myanmar Chaṭṭhasaṅgīti edition of the M, analysing and interpreting structure, and recording all structures and text in an SQLite[3] relational database in a format well suited to subsequent analysis. In the first stage the text is recorded in the database paragraph by paragraph; during subsequent specialised scans individual words are extracted and separated from punctuation, quotation marks, and *pe* ellipsis markers (all of which are retained in separate tables). The position of every word is available with respect to text blocks of any desired size, such as *sutta*, section, subsection, paragraph or sentence, and sentence word order is also available for further processing. Page markers for the Myanmar, PTS, Thai and Vipassana Research Institute editions are also included. Words at the end of direct speech are converted to the form without *'ti* (i.e. the last vowel is shortened where required). The result of the subsequent scan is a word table comprising every prose word in the M, together with its exact location, and to which grammatical information is subsequently to be attached;

---

2 Derived from Ven. YUTTADHAMMO's excellent Digital Pali Reader software (pali.sirimangalo.org)

3 SQLite is an open source implementation of a Structured Query Language (SQL) relational database (www.sqlite.org).

distinct from the word table, an additional scan prepares a table of unique words, i.e. a list of all word forms that exist in the word table, with references to all the instances where they appear. These unique words will be indexed both on a left-to-right and a right-to-left lexical basis[4]. Most of the various automised scan processes described in this paragraph are now nearing completion.

The program performing these scanning operations is in principle capable of scanning the entire Pāli Canon, commentaries and subcommentaries. However it has so far been run only on the M. In order to get it working on other Pāli texts some relatively minor differences in structure of the digital texts – and various inconsistencies – have to be specified, and coded in the program. For some texts that would be expected to be a relatively trivial change, while for others it could potentially be somewhat tedious and time-consuming. The database structure is sufficiently general that it can incorporate all the data from the Pāli Canon and commentaries – and even supplementary texts – without intrinsic difficulties of compatibility.

The next stage of the database development is a very tedious and time-consuming one – the mammoth task of inputting grammatical properties for all the 236,526 prose words of the M. In principle, it should be adequate in many cases to input these properties for each of around 20,000 unique words. The complication here is that some of these unique words – each of which may occur in many different locations in the text – may represent different grammatical elements (cases, tenses, etc.) in different instances, and sometimes even different

---

4 That is, ordered according to characters of the word selected successively from left-to-right or from right-to-left respectively. The left-to-right sort order sorts words with similar word stems together, while the right-to-left sort order sorts similar inflections together. This is useful for selecting words from the database according to word stem or inflection.

parts of speech. Therefore where one unique word can represent several different grammatical elements, it has to be mapped to a list of all those possible elements[5]; each instance of that word in the word table then has to be mapped manually onto the correct one of those elements using a drop-down menu in a view of the sentence. A problem which will have to be addressed is that of ensuring that all possible alternative grammatical elements are included in the list, for each unique word; failing to include the possibilities exhaustively can be expected to lead to errors during the mapping of words in the word table onto individual grammatical elements in the unique word table.

Each word in the unique word table has to be manually marked according to part of speech as verb, noun, pronoun, adjective, adverb, or indeclinable, and its stem and inflection marked. In the case of a verb, its root and prefixes must also be selected from tables of roots and prefixes. From the stem and inflection, links can be made to various grammatical elements – in part this can be done on an automatised basis.

As mentioned above, the different grammatical elements lexically corresponding to the same unique word will be linked to it; conversely – and crucially for the purposes of this study – alternate lexical forms corresponding to the same grammatical element[6] will also be tabled, and linked

5 Here each element in the list represents a different grammatical element for the same lexical form. These may represent for example different cases with the same inflection on the same root, such as *lokehi* ⇨ the instrumental plural *or* the ablative plural of *loka*; they may also represent different parts of speech such as *santi* ⇨ the feminine noun *santi* in the nominative *or* vocative *or* the verb *as* in the present 3rd person plural *or* also as an auxiliary verb.

6 For example the verb *gam* has numerous forms of the aorist in the first person singular which include: the root aorists *agaṁ* or *agamā*; the thematic aorists *gacchiṁ* or *agamaṁ*; or the sigmatic aorist *agamāsiṁ* or *agamisaṁ* (Duroiselle 1906, Kingsbury 2002).

both to tables of inflections and to tables of word stems and roots.

It will be apparent from the above description that the database will incorporate substantial Pāli grammatical data in a relational[7] format. This is a particular benefit to be derived from the decision to use a relational database for the project. It has many very important implications in terms of the powerful potential of the database for easily performing statistical grammatical analyses on subsets of the text which can be selected in any way that might be desired, and also has the result that it could be extended comparatively easily to other books of the Pāli Canon. It also means that the database could be used to assist the translation of the M (and of Pāli texts in general) into other languages[8], and for other research purposes.

Ven. Yuttadhammo's Digital Pali Reader[9] includes both dictionary entries from the PED and extensive inflectional information (in the form of conjugations and declensions which are available by clicking on any word in the text, in that software). It is hoped to be able to find a way to import that information into the present relational database (with the correct relations to the unique word table and root tables), which will then facilitate the entry of grammatical information in the word table – significant parts of this process can then be automised.

7 Quasi a *procedural* grammar!

8 It is notable that the benefit applies equally, irrespective of the intended destination language, as it is specific to the Pāli side of the translation! The translation memory technology frequently used today by professional translators is related to this.

9 Ibid.

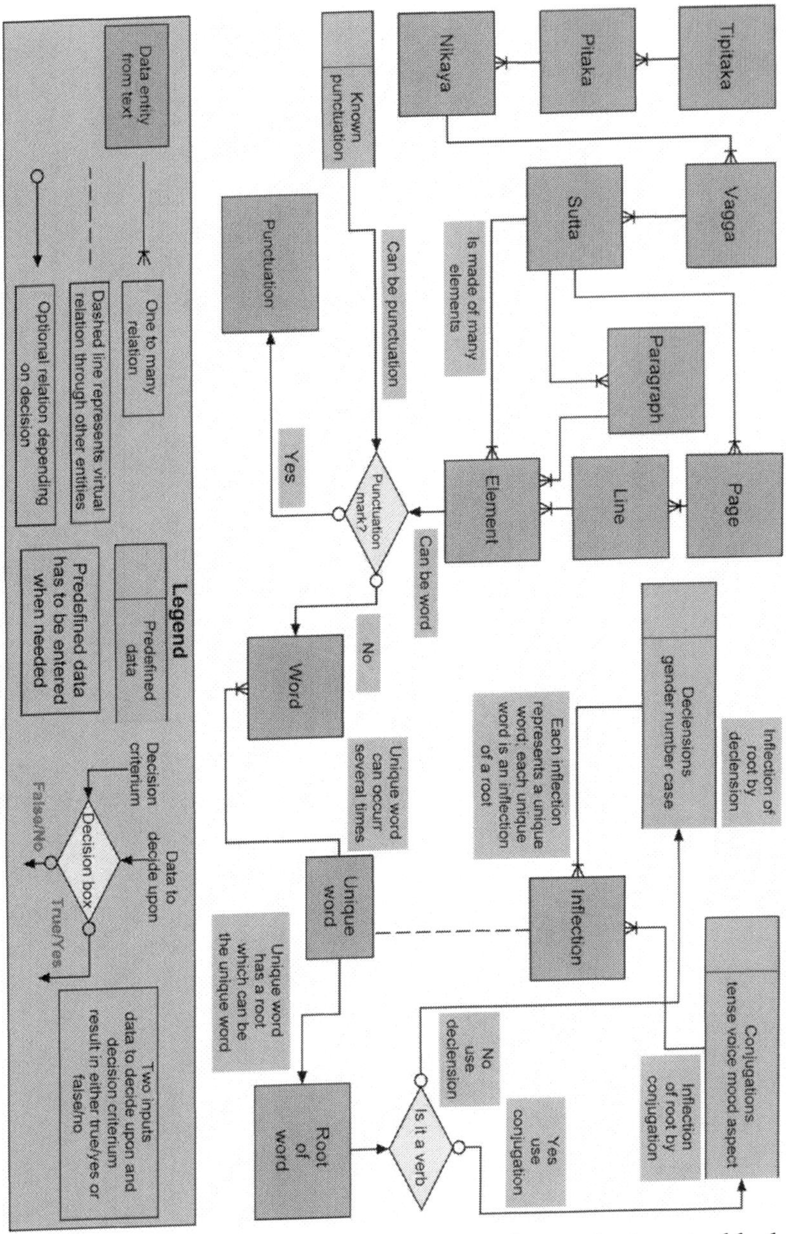

Figure 1: A portrayal of some of the database relations in block diagram format.

The leap from frequency comparisons to a chronology

In his dissertation KINGSBURY takes two steps which should be viewed as methodologically distinct. In the first step[10] (KINGSBURY (2002: 98-224) he takes pre-existing categories of "Old", "Middle", "Late", "Mixed", and "Uncertain" texts from the Pāli Canon which had already been asserted in the literature (his specific groups of texts are taken from PANDE 1974, although other sources are treated in his discussion). Using these groups of texts as a putative chronology, he compares the incidence of different types of aorists in each of PANDE's categories to see whether and how the aorists can be used to test the age of texts. In doing so he shows that the ratio of sigmoid aorists to non-sigmoid aorists was greater in those texts classified by PANDE as late[11] than those classified as early. In other words the sigmoid aorists tend to become relatively more common in later texts.

The second step taken by KINGSBURY (2002: 225-238) was an attempt to apply a mathematical model – the Constant Rate Effect (KROCH 1989 and others). The Constant Rate Effect model aims to explain the typically logarithmic plot of linguistic changes over time by arguing that the frequency of contexts in which a linguistic change is found itself changes over time at a constant rate. KINGSBURY used this model to derive a statistical distribution of different types of aorists in different texts of the Pāli Canon, and then assumed that that statistical distribution is, or approximates to, a chronology. That is quite a jump, and a problem with this approach is that it attempts to distribute the texts over a particular time-scale even though no single text has a definitive date. This is a cyclic argument which confounds two core variables–

[10] This step is not mentioned in KINGSBURY 2003, thus the 2002 dissertation is necessary to understand the data underlying his discussion in the later paper.

[11] The effect was more pronounced in prose texts; in verse texts the results were mixed.

namely the probability ratio of sigmoid to non-sigmoid aorists, and the timescale of the distribution – because the timescale is itself derived from the aorist probability ratio.

Aside from the confounding of the two core variables, the applicability of the Constant Rate Effect to the texts of the Pāli Canon is in any case far from clear. The Constant Rate Effect model was developed to describe linguistic changes between texts of known ages (such as Old English, Yiddish, and Ancient Greek language corpi, described by KROCH 1989, SANTORINI 1993, and TAYLOR 1994 respectively, cited in KINGSBURY 2002, 2003). The problem with the Pāli Canon, in contrast, is that we are trying to estimate the ages of the texts; the timescale of the linguistic change is completely unknown. In other words, we are trying to determine both the ages of the texts and the timescale of the linguistic change at the same time, although they are interdependent. KINGSBURY relied instead on a disturbingly large number of assumptions and arbitrary "stretching", "compressing" and "rescaling" of the data to derive his chronology, and we are left with an uneasy feeling that all is not quite as it seems (see in particular KINGSBURY 2002: 227-229). Furthermore, actual statistical comparisons of the frequencies of different types of aorists are nowhere evident[12]. Looking closely at this study, the only statistical test explicitly mentioned is a logistical regression on page 227. This test is very cursorily dealt with, and appears to be limited to showing that in a comparison between three logistical regression curves done on prose, verse, and mixed texts, the three curves were

---

12 What is also worrying is that in several cases KINGSBURY's description of his results conflicts with his tables of data, eg on p 220: in prose "ay-aorists are minimally attested in any stratum" – yet the corresponding table of data for prose cites the highest value 691 for ay-aorists in the late stratum, against 252 for e-aorists; a changeover from counting text blocks to counting individual aorists notwithstanding, there is no correspondence apparent between the tables of data on pp 220-221 and the corresponding charts and descriptions.

found to be different from each other (whether even this difference was statistically significant was not made explicit).

Despite serious problems with KINGSBURY's methodology, analysis and data presentation including important deficiencies in rigor, his study was nevertheless pioneering in its attempt to use historical linguistic changes to distinguish between early and late texts in the Pāli Canon and compare his results with prior groupings of early and late texts asserted on a non-linguistic basis. KINGSBURY used only one grammatical change out of many, and this was certainly a major cause of many of his difficulties. Limitations in the specificity of his text selections – especially with regard to the crucial distinction between prose and verse (but also the length of each of his text blocks) – was another.

The current study attempts to go a long way to redressing these deficiencies through crucial changes in methodology and approach, including: (1) many different grammatical changes will be evaluated; (2) the study will be confined to prose text in the M; (3) a custom-built relational database edition of the text will be used, thereby radically changing the technical possibilities for comparisons and enabling a rigorous approach; (4) prose and verse can be discriminated on a line-by-line basis[13] (although verse is explicitly excluded from the current study, a direct comparison with KINGSBURY's results will nevertheless readily be possible, because technically verse text can be switched at will in or out of inclusion in frequency comparisons of specific lists of words); (5) the

13 KINGSBURY, by contrast, grouped the whole of the M as prose, on the basis that it consisted predominantly of prose. The significant portions of verse present in some *sutta*-s in the M – the maximum percentage (74% verse) is found in the *Vāseṭṭha-sutta* M 98; the average for the whole of the M is 1.5% (3525 words) – might plausibly have contained substantial proportions of some specific types of aorists compared to the surrounding prose texts, thereby having the potential to considerably confuse his results.

length of text blocks to be analysed can be changed at will between *sutta*-s, sections, numbered subsections, paragraphs and sentences; (6) by pooling the results from many different linguistic changes – thereby substantially increasing the numbers and frequencies of indicators by which early and late text segments can be distinguished – the discriminatory resolution is thereby considerably increased, so that it becomes feasible to compare much smaller blocks of text than whole *sutta*-s, such as subsections, paragraphs, or perhaps occasionally even sentences; (7) direct statistical comparisons will be used instead of the Constant Rate Effect model; (8) the statistical significance of any evidence of linguistic change found within the M will be rigorously evaluated[14]; and (9) Kingsbury faced particular problems as a result of very large numbers of aorists in certain specific texts – especially the *Apadāna*-s – which distorted his results, but all those texts are outside the scope of the present study, and in any case all or most of those problems involved verse which is also completely excluded from the present study. Some of these points will be elaborated on in the next section.

14 This, at any rate, will be the intention! Statistical rigor will present considerable challenges, however, on at least two bases: (1) whilst it is expected in all probability to be possible to find evidence of linguistic changes which mark a statistically significant difference between two previously asserted groups of texts (namely those asserted by Pande 1974 to be early or late), the approach adopted by this study will be dependent on finding many such changes, and it might be that in the case of several of the changes found, the numbers of occurrences might be too small to get a statistically significant result; and (2) combining evidence from many different linguistic changes – many of which might be found very unevenly in different texts, some very frequently, others scarcely, some may be mutually exclusive, others may represent slight differences in frequencies – without invalidating statistical paradigms will present some particular challenges.

Basing an Analysis of Linguistic Change on a Sounder Foundation

The basic problem of using linguistic change within the Pāli Canon to derive a chronology is that we have no texts within the Pāli Canon for which an independently corroborated date can be provided[15]. The mathematical model on which KINGSBURY depended, the Constant Rate Effect, was based on corpi of linguistic change derived from texts of known ages (Old English, Yiddish, and Ancient Greek – KROCH 1989, SANTORINI 1993, and TAYLOR 1994 respectively, cited in KINGSBURY 2002, 2003). As we have indicated above, the argument is circular in the case of the Pāli Canon because in order to apply the Constant Rate Effect model to the Pāli Canon we need to know the dates of the texts in the Pāli Canon before we can plot the graph of linguistic change against time, which in turn is required to derive the dates of the texts.

Step 1

Nevertheless another approach is possible, using the grouping of early and late texts asserted by PANDE in the literature (PANDE 1974) as a starting point. We can consider this approach as comprising four distinct steps. In Step 1 for each linguistic difference (between alternate forms α and β, say) that exists within the Pāli language, we can analyse the relative frequencies of both forms in each of the texts which PANDE asserts to be early, and in each of the texts which PANDE asserts to be late. This gives us the relative frequencies

---

[15] The traditional assertion that the whole of the Pāli Canon dates from the lifetime of the Buddha (which is a small period of time in the context of linguistic change) is of course on multiple grounds provably false. Various non-canonical texts of approximately known dates could provide some chronological information, although not necessarily from a truly comparable period. Dateable non-canonical texts should nevertheless form part of the corroboration for a chronology.

of α and β in each text in PANDE's Early group (hereafter P^E), and the relative frequencies of α and β in each text in PANDE's Late group (hereafter P^L)[16]. We are interested in the difference between the relative frequencies of α and β in the Late group compared to the Early group. We can then make a statistical analysis to show whether this difference is statistically significant or not. From that statistical analysis we get a measure of how confident we are[17] that (for example) α is more common than β in early texts, while β is more common than α in late texts, for that particular linguistic change. Subject naturally to a variety of caveats, if the result is significant that suggests that the linguistic change between α and β can be used as an indicator of early and late texts.

In the same way we can conduct a similar analysis for many other linguistic differences. Some of these may give significant results while others do not. Those which do not give significant results we can discard – they may represent a linguistic difference that does not reflect a difference in age of the texts but rather some other difference (for example, a difference in style, a difference in the local dialect of the

16 In some texts neither α nor β forms can be found, or the total number of α and β forms in those texts is too small. Those texts have to be excluded from the comparison, for that specific linguistic change. However as long as we have many different linguistic changes available to test, the texts which we have to exclude from one comparison will be compensated for by other linguistic changes. For example, one text may not have any sentences in the past tense, in which case that text must be excluded from a test for changes in aorist forms. That same text however might display specific forms of the present tense which can be used in another test, and specific dative forms which can be used in another test. Essentially the more tests we have available the better.

17 For example, in very much simplified terms, a result significant at the 5% level means we can be 95% confident that the result is true. In reality, of course, statistics have their own set of caveats, and have to be used in their proper context.

person the Buddha is talking to or of the dialect through which a particular group of texts was transmitted[18], a difference in the class of speech used by the Buddha when addressing royalty vs. brahmins vs. tradesmen, etc). It may also be that some of those analyses which did not yield a significant result could bear some relation to text age, but the associated α and β forms are too rare, or the difference is too small – still we should discard that measure, because the statistical analysis shows that it does not indicate text age reliably in those text samples which were compared. All those linguistic differences which yield a significant result, however, we should retain as measures that appear to be useful for distinguishing early and late texts.

Step 2

In Step 2 – using only those measures which yielded a significant result in Step 1 – we derive many putative early/late pairs of groups from all the texts[19] of the M[20], measured according to each linguistic measure in turn. To clarify this we can denote the series of linguistic measures (each of which gave a significant result in Step 1) as M^1, M^2, M^3, ... etc; the corresponding linguistic forms that we measure in M^1 we can denote as α^1 and β^1; likewise for M^2, M^3, ... we can denote the linguistic forms measured as α^2 and β^2, α^3 and β^3, ... etc. Using the measure M^1, we make a group of

---

18 The *Apadāna*, for example, shows linguistic anomalies such as masculine plurals in *-āni* and aorists in *-e* which appear to indicate a connection to eastern India (NORMAN 1983: 90-91)

19 By all the 'texts' we mean the set of blocks of text – we could use the 152 *sutta*-s as blocks, or we could use smaller units such as sections, subsections, paragraphs, etc.

20 That is, for each linguistic measure we divide all the text of the M into one group of putative early texts and one group of putative late texts, this constitutes one pair. Of course corresponding to each pair of groups there will also be a list of texts which are undetermined for that pair, because they do not contain either forms α or β.

texts called M^{1E} for all the texts in the M which have a ratio of α^1 to β^1 that indicates early texts, and a group of texts called M^{1L} for all the texts in the M which have a ratio of α^1 to β^1 that indicates late texts. We must exclude all those texts for which the ratios of α^1 and β^1 are too close, or where the total frequencies of α^1 and β^1 are too low to give a reliable result. Parallel to this we make another division of all the texts of the Majjhima Nikāya into M^{2E} and M^{2L}, based on the ratios of α^2 to β^2; another division into M^{3E} and M^{3L}, based on the ratios of α^3 to β^3; ... etc.

At the end of this process we have many parallel divisions of the M into putative groups of early and late texts, one pair of sets according to each linguistic criterion. There should be some degree of overlap between each of the groups of putative early texts (M^{1E}, M^{2E}, M^{3E}, ...), and there should be some degree of overlap between each of the groups of putative late texts (M^{1L}, M^{2L}, M^{3L}, ...). It must also be true that there will be some degree of overlap between the putative early texts suggested by one measure, and the putative late texts suggested by other measures (i.e. between M^{1E} and M^{2L}, M^{3L}; between M^{1L} and M^{2E}, M^{3E}; etc). This is the case both because the original division of PANDE between putative early and late texts (P^E and P^L) on which we conducted Step 1 is not perfectly correct, and because each of our linguistic measures M^1, M^2, M^3, ... is also not perfectly correct. Each of these divisions into putative early and late texts M^{1E}/M^{1L}, M^{2E}/M^{2L}, M^{3E}/M^{3L}, ... etc represents a 'theory' or 'view' of which texts are early and which late.

The next stage (which is still part of Step 2) is to perform statistical tests which measure on the one hand the degree of correlation between each of these 'views' individually with P^E/P^L, and on the other hand the degree of correlation collectively between all the 'views' (M^{1E}/M^{1L}, M^{2E}/M^{2L}, M^{3E}/M^{3L}, ... etc). Some measures will correlate better with P^E/P^L than others; those that correlate well are implied to be good measures of text age, while those that correlate slightly less well are implied to be slightly less effective as measures of text age (all the measures should in any case correlate at least fairly well with P^E/P^L however, as this is required from the significant result in Step 1).

Very important, however, is the correlation between each measure with all the other measures. If they all correlate well with each other and tend to reinforce each other, that is a good sign – it means that all the measures are in good general agreement with each other, and that the combination of these measures is likely to be a fairly reliable predictor of text age[21]; further, it means that for any group of texts, a combination of these measures will give better results than any one measure taken on its own – this would be a very important result. If a number of measures correlate well with each other, but a few show no correlation at all, that could indicate that those uncorrelated measures represent some other variable that is not relevant to the date of the texts, such as differences in ethnicity, or some other aspect of the texts which has been overlooked; such measures should be omitted from the combination of measures used in Step 3. If, on the other hand, none of the measures correlate with each other – each pulling in different directions and acting in apparent contradiction to each other, that would tend to indicate that we cannot use these measures as a consistent and reliable indicator of text age.

Step 3

If we get a good result in Step 2 – namely, we find that the results of M^{1E}/M^{1L}, M^{2E}/M^{2L}, M^{3E}/M^{3L}, ... correlate well with each other – we can combine the measures to get a more accurate and reliable result, and to improve the resolution. This is Step 3 of our approach. Combining results means that

21 There is a wide range of caveats that we need to consider of course, which for reasons of space it is not appropriate to cover here.

we have a much larger number of observations, which are likely to be better distributed throughout the texts. For any statistical analysis it is important to maximise the number of observations to get more reliable results. In addition, by having a much larger number of observations which are better distributed throughout the text, we should be able to use smaller text blocks (for instance, paragraphs instead of whole *sutta*-s) – this would enable us to detect late portions of text that have been added to early *sutta*-s; this is what we mean by improving resolution. Where some of the *sutta*-s are a mixture of early and late texts, this will tend to cause the various measures to give slightly contradictory results when compared at the *sutta* level; this is because the measures will be differently distributed across different portions of the texts. For example, if some paragraphs are late and contain many sigmoid aorists, while other parts are early and contain no aorists at all but many examples of some other measure that predicts early texts, then the aorist measure will tend to suggest it is a late *sutta* while the other measure will tend to suggest it is an early *sutta* – i.e. the measures tend to conflict when viewed at the *sutta* level, because the *sutta* is a mixture of early and late. In this case, we can expect that by testing individual paragraphs separately we may be able to show exactly which text portions were original and which were added at a later date. In so doing our statistical measure – the correlations between different measures – will actually become higher, i.e. it will become a more reliable predictor of text age as a result of using smaller text blocks, because it can discriminate correctly between late text blocks added to earlier text blocks, instead of confounding them.

Combining results from different measures is also very important for another reason. Over the course of history since the texts were first written down in the first CENTURY BCE the palm leaf manuscripts on which the texts were preserved were constantly being copied and re-copied, as the durability of the palm leaves is very limited. As we have seen already, every time the manuscripts are copied mistakes inevitably tend to be introduced. Any scribe with experience of copying many manuscripts will be aware of this risk, as he will have on occasion found some of his own errors and corrected them. If he is living in a later period his understanding of Pāli grammar will be based on that prevalent at that time, and as a result of an intervening linguistic change he might regard a particular early form which he comes across in the text he is copying as "incorrect". He might then "correct" it[22] to reflect what he believes it should have been. In this way a single error (or indeed a pattern of errors) is introduced. A linguistic measure based on this particular change will thus mark it as a "late" text, even though prior to the introduced error the same linguistic measure would have marked the earlier manuscript as early. In this case we would expect that any other linguistic markers in the *same* paragraph would most probably indicate an earlier period, corresponding to the linguistic form before the error was introduced. Thus we might be able to detect some such changes introduced to the manuscript while copying. We should fully expect in such cases to be able to find alternate readings coming from other manuscripts, in which the aforementioned change had not been introduced.[23] Again, the greater

---

22 Technically this constitutes what is known as a false positive. Commenting on the errors made by editors in the PTS editions of the Pāli Canon, CONE (2007: 96) observes a form of this phenomenon in modern texts: "I suspect ... that those who did know Sanskrit emended silently, especially in matters of sandhi. The *Dīgha Nikāya* and its commentary seem to me to have been tidied in this way."

23 The likelihood of a false positive being introduced is also substantially increased if the particular character(s) being changed are obscured in the older manuscript as a result of damage to the manuscript, such as holes due to physical damage to the brittle leaves or edges broken off, holes due to insect damage, mould damage etc, all of which are common occurrences in the tropical

the number of linguistic measures that we combine, the greater our chances of detecting such changes and the better the consistency and reliability of our results.

Step 4

Once we have completed Step 3, we have a series of linguistic markers which we will have shown to be effective indicators of relative text age; we will have divided the *sutta*-s into smaller units such as sections or paragraphs; and we will have used the linguistic markers in a combined form to produce one combined list of early text blocks and one combined list of late text blocks. Probably we will find that we have some whole *sutta*-s that are predicted to be early, some which are predicted to be late, and some which appear to be mixed – whereby those texts assessed to be mixed will consist of specific portions marked as early or late. In the final step we need to assess what sort of texts we have in each category, and try to consider the plausibility of our results. What sorts of teachings are covered by the texts in the early group? What is in the late group, but absent from the early group? How do the doctrinal differences between the texts in the early and late groups compare with the doctrinal grounds used by PANDE to assert his groupings (PANDE 1974: 17-50, 116-179)?

Do the texts we have classified as early conform to the original teachings of the Buddha on two crucial criteria, namely: (1) is the text "beneficial, relevant to the fundamentals of the holy life, and leads to revulsion (*nibbidā*), to dispassion (*virāga*), to cessation (*nirodha*), to peace (*upasama*), to direct knowledge (*abhiñña*), to enlightenment (*sambodha*), to *nibbāna*"? – the *siṁsapā* leaves analogy (*Sīsapāvana-sutta/Siṁsapā-sutta* S Vol 5 §1101 PTS Vol 5: 437) (2) and when reviewed in the light of the core of the Buddha's teaching in

---

environment in which most of these manuscripts have been maintained over the millennia.

the Suttas and the Vinaya, do they conform to those teachings? – the *catumahāpadesa* (*Mahāparinibbāna-sutta* D 16 §188 PTS Vol 2: 124). These two conditions are necessary conditions rather than sufficient conditions. We would surely not expect to find many blocks of text in the M which violate these two principles. Nevertheless if we find text blocks in our putative early group which do violate these two principles then we should indeed be concerned[24].

Some Thoughts Related to Pāli Linguistic Development

Concomitant with an improvement in our understanding of which texts are late and which are early – a chronology of the Pāli Canon – it follows naturally that our understanding of the chronology of developments in the Pāli language will also improve. As our understanding of the chronology of Pāli linguistic developments improves this in turn will assist in finding many more linguistic changes, which can then be fed back into the analysis of the chronology of the Pāli Canon as additional measures in Step 3 to further refine the accuracy and resolution of our tests, and thereby the quality of the resultant chronology. The next step after that would perhaps be to divide the Pāli vocabulary into those words which appear in early texts, and those which appear exclusively in later texts. Once we have a list of early text blocks and a list of late blocks derived from a large number of linguistic measures which correlate well with each other, it would be technically

24 An example of a text block which appears to violate the first principle is the whole of the *Bākula-sutta/Bakkula-sutta* (M 124 §209 PTS Vol 3: 124) for it is surely hard to see how this sutta is truly useful on the criteria given by the Buddha; we should definitely not expect to see this *sutta* in a list of early *sutta*-s. An example of a text that might violate the second principle is to be found in the *Cūḷataṇhāsaṅkhaya-sutta* (M 37 §393 PTS Vol 1: 253) where Mahāmoggallāna performs a feat of supernatural power, violating both the Buddha's teaching that everything is subject to the law of cause and effect, and his admonition in the Vinaya that the *bhikkhu*-s should not perform miracles.

trivial to plot a complete distribution of all unique words that can be found across the two groups of text blocks. We would want to exclude from this exercise all text blocks which have too few linguistic markers to reliably indicate their age, and we would also exclude all unique words which appear in both groups at comparable frequencies – likewise technically trivial to specify. Many exciting discoveries would surely immediately be uncovered! The list of unique words used in this exercise can also effortlessly be limited in dozens of other ways – by part of speech, case, tense, root, stem, inflection, etc.

What is the nature of the relationship between the development of the Pāli language over time, and differences between local vernaculars (Prakrits) and Sanskrit? How did the Pāli grammars of the 6th/7th to the 12th centuries incorporate these changes in the Pāli language, and to what extent did they themselves fuel those changes? To what extent did developments in the Sanskrit language and Sanskrit grammars during the period from Pāṇini to the 12th century give rise to changes in the perception of Pāli grammar by contemporary Theravāda Buddhist monks, causing a gradual sanskritisation[25] of Pāli? During certain periods of Sri Lankan history scholarship in Sanskrit was very fashionable, which naturally could have played a role in such developments[26]. It

25 Our use here of the term sanskritisation is intended to mean that there might have been a tendency for grammatical connections between Pāli and Sanskrit to have increased over time, as a result of perceived causality of connections, and perhaps a perception that Sanskrit rules of derivation *ought to* apply to Pāli, rather than because they necessarily do.

26 Also relevant here is the history of a strong Brahmin influence on the royal courts of Asian countries including Sri Lanka and Myanmar, and concomitant Brahmin influences on the Buddhist Saṅgha. When Sri Lankan royalty invited Siam in the mid 18th century to re-establish ordination of the Buddhist Saṅgha in Sri Lanka following a long period of decline, it was under the specific

could be expected that the current study might be able to bring some novel evidence to bear on such questions.

It is generally accepted that the Pāli language as we know it evolved out of earlier forms which were more closely related to one or more vernacular languages known and used by the Buddha (eg LAW 2007: 11-28; HINÜBER 1992: 185, 188; *vide* also WIJESEKERA 1993: vii-viii). Once Pāli had become a language in its own right distinct from the vernacular forms from which it had evolved, the situation would inevitably arise that the pool of word forms available in the Pāli Canon – as a finite body of texts – would be insufficient to cover the forms required for new texts being composed. For example, an author might want to use the feminine singular form of the demonstrative pronoun *amu* in the instrumental case[27] – this form does not exist in the Pāli Canon[28]. It could be conceived that

---

condition that the Siamese monks were only permitted to ordain monks from the higher castes of Sri Lankan society (MALALGODA 1976). It is conceivable that such a condition might have been implicit also even from early times, as the Sri Lankan Saṅgha was long connected with the political establishment. It can certainly be expected that any such condition would bring with it a measure of Brahmin influence on the Saṅgha, and thereby also an influence of Sanskrit on Pāli.

27 Whilst the feminine singular form of *amu* in the instrumental does not exist in the Pāli Canon, of course in practice some other form of expression could have been found instead. Nevertheless as this pronoun exists, it makes sense that some author might have wanted to use it. By the way, briefly reviewing the incidence of this pronoun in the first four nikāyas indicates that it is manifested exclusively as a late pronoun!

28 Of course, scholars of that day did not have the possibility to conduct a digital search for rare forms such as we can today so easily do. Furthermore formal grammars of Pāli as such do not seem to have existed prior to Kaccāyana's grammar of the 6th-7th centuries (DEOKAR 2016). Therefore irrespective of whether a particular form was truly non-existent in the then extant Pāli Canon, if the scholar was unaware of examples of a particular rare form, then the constraints of this paragraph would still apply.

the scholars composing such texts would be influenced in this regard by at least four forces: (1) studies of language acquisition by children have established that during natural language conversation the human mind has a tendency subconsciously to fill in any gaps in linguistic knowledge on the basis of pattern matching to known language forms. In other words, where a particular inflection does not exist in the known repertoire, a speaker will automatically and subconsciously tend to generate a form which fits with known patterns from the inflection of other similar words, or other tenses. This might explain to some extent the many different inflectional variations of some words that can be found in Pāli. (2) The scholar might in addition be influenced by the grammatical rules of his own mother tongue (especially in the case of languages closely related to Pāli such as early Sinhala or Māgadhī). (3) He may try to derive a word form using the Sanskrit rules of Pāṇini (as Buddhaghosa sometimes did in the commentaries when explaining the meaning or use of a word, DEOKAR 2017: 252-3). (4) Similarly he might try to derive a word form from Pāli grammars – nevertheless since the earliest known Pāli grammar is that of Kaccāyana in about the 6th/7th century the availability of this option in practice would have been somewhat limited until that time (by the same token, it is reasonable to expect that the need to use new Pāli word forms in contemporary compositions would have added an impetus to encourage the composition of a Pāli grammar).

There are two quite different perspectives on the relationship between Pāli and Sanskrit. According to modern philologists, Pāli is derived from Sanskrit. This is however denied by the Pāli grammars of the 6th/7th to 12th centuries (DEOKAR 2017), who insisted Pāli was independent of Sanskrit. DEOKAR points out apparent anomalies in this denial, such as the reduplication of the initial consonants of some verbal roots when they are preceded by a vowel (e.g. *niggaho*, *paggaho*), which is said to result from the 'underlying' Sanskrit forms *nigraha* and *pragraha*. The problem with this argument is that the reduplication of the consonants is a lexicographic phenomenon which cannot have taken place until the 1st CENTURY BCE when the Pāli Canon was first written down. Before that Pāli was an entirely oral language, therefore the question of duplication of consonants could not have arisen. At the time of first writing down the Pāli language in the 1st CENTURY BCE the Sri Lankan monks would have had to construct a means of representing the phonology of Pāli from scratch, and they would certainly have relied on the well-established Sanskrit models to do this – thus the influence from Sanskrit was inevitable, but in this case necessarily post-dates the early Pāli. WIJESEKERA (1993: 184) also points out certain anomalies with respect to the use of the genitive case which Sanskrit grammars are at a loss to explain, and notes conspicuous divergencies of Pāli with respect to both Vedic and Classical Sanskrit (*Ibid.*: vii).

GOMBRICH furthermore points out with respect to both Pāli texts and Buddhist Hybrid Sanskrit texts, that when they were first written down there was a tendency to move words towards their Sanskrit spellings (GOMBRICH 2005: xxviii). From that time on throughout history there has been a constant influence of Sanskrit on the Pāli literature (GOMBRICH 2005: xxix), therefore any observed influence of Sanskrit on Pāli can be expected on that basis, independent of the origins of Pāli.

Whilst no philologist, this author has difficulty accepting that Pāli is derived from Sanskrit on another ground, namely it is certain that Pāli is derived from one or more natural languages which were used by the Buddha in his discourses, while Sanskrit – both in name and by its nature – is a constructed language not a natural language. It is also a prescriptive language. Sanskrit was used at the time of the Buddha by Brahmins for liturgical purposes rather than as a normal spoken language, and as such was furthermore a language restricted on the basis of caste. The Buddha himself instructed the monks to disseminate his teachings in their native language (*sakāya niruttiyā*), and specifically proscribed the translation of his teachings into Sankrit (*chandaso*, the term *sanskritabhāṣā* being of much later origin; *Cullavagga* Vol 4 §285 PTS Vol 2: 139; LAW 2007: 13-15). Even the Rigveda was a highly specialised form of language, and it seems entirely unreasonable to argue that a normal spoken language (including even that spoken – or one derived from it – by the authors of the Rigveda themselves) could have been derived from such stylised hymns. By way of analogy, nobody would argue that modern English is derived from Shakespear's Sonnets, or from the King James edition of the Bible. To claim that Pāli is derived from the Rigveda is profoundly different to saying that Pāli may have been derived from a language diffusely related to that used by the authors of the Rigveda.

Of course, the Brahmins would like to assert the precedence of Sanskrit in all matters from their own particular perspective, which is intricately bound up with the Vedas, and with knowledge of the Vedas including *Vyākaraṇa śāstra* (Science of Grammar); that Western scholars have acquiesced to such a fundamentally Brahmin perspective of philology without objective criticism is surprising, however.

As its name implies Sanskrit was supposed by the Brahmins to be a perfected language, especially so in its classical form as prescribed by the grammar of Pāṇini. Surely it must be the Pāṇini Sanskrit grammar which has had by far the most prevalent and enduring influence on Pāli – both directly and indirectly – from the time it was first written down (and conceivably also during the period of its divergence from its original vernacular form) until the 12th century. The Pāli texts must necessarily have predated this influence of Pāṇini, notwithstanding the changes they would have undergone during the stages of preparation for being written down.

Pāṇini's grammar was certainly presupposed by Buddhaghosa's exegesis of certain syntactic constructions and word derivations, and he wrote his commentaries in a Pāli which was influenced by classical Sanskrit in syntax and style (GOMBRICH 2005: xxix)[29]. Gombrich also points out that following the scholarship of the Burmese grammarians of the 12th century onwards, Pāli came to be written in a style heavily modelled on Sanskrit and "any Sanskrit lexical item could be turned into Pāli by mechanically applying phonetic rules, and Sanskrit sentences could similarly be transposed into Pāli". Thus Pāli has been substantially influenced by classical Sanskrit throughout virtually all its period of existence, and it would be impossible to distinguish such influences from influences of a supposed derivational nature on the precursors of Pāli, without understanding the nature of the earliest forms of the Pāli language in some detail. The timescale of such influences of Sanskrit on Pāli as it developed – however that may have been – certainly should have had a tangible impact on the history of changes to the text of the Pāli Canon, and on the linguistic markers that could be used to trace those changes.

Conclusions

It should be entirely possible to make chronological comparisons of the prose texts of the M based on a variety of linguistic markers. We do this essentially in four steps. In Step 1 we take a large number of different measures based on the relative frequencies of various alternate linguistic forms (namely, forms which we consider may plausibly reflect different historical periods), and for each of these we measure the relative frequencies of the alternate forms in all the texts listed by PANDE as early or late (PANDE 1974). For each lingui-

---

[29] Note should also be made in this context of the fact that Buddhaghosa was born a Brahmin, and was very well versed in the Sanskrit texts of the Brahmins prior to his ordination as a Buddhist monk.

stic measure, we then run a statistical comparison to show whether or not the relative frequencies of the alternate forms are statistically different in the two text groups. Those linguistic measures which do not give a significant result we reject, while those with a significant result we retain for Step 2. This stage represents a direct comparison between chronological information previously asserted on non-linguistic grounds in the literature, and the linguistic information bound to the same text groups.

In Step 2 we take all those measures which were successful in Step 1 (i.e. those which appear to indicate text age successfully), and we use each of them – independently – to produce competing lists of putative "early" and "late" texts. We measure the degree of agreement or correlation of each of these lists with PANDE's lists of early and late texts, and the correlation between the various lists. Those measures which correlate particularly well with PANDE's lists we expect to be good predictors of text age. The correlation *between* the various measures however is very important. In general a high correlation between a group of measures implies that those measures are a reliable indicator of text age, and that a variety of measures taken together will give better results than any one measure taken on its own. A very low correlation between some measures by contrast indicates that they may be measuring some other variable rather than text age, and are not useful for predicting text age.

This brings us to Step 3 where those measures that correlate well with each other are combined. Using this combined set of measures smaller blocks such as sections or paragraphs of the texts are compared, to see which text blocks are early and which are late. In this way we increase the resolution of our test, and we should thereby be able to detect which *sutta*-s consist of a mixture of early and late sections, and we can specify exactly which sections are early and which are late. At the end of Step 3 we have a single list of *sutta*-s which we assess as early, a list which we assess as late, and *sutta*-s which comprise a mixture of early segments and late segments.

We expect to find a certain class of cases where a single word exists in a late form in a certain paragraph, while all other indicators point to that paragraph as being early. This might indicate a word which has been copied incorrectly sometime in the past; in this case we would expect that we might be able to find another version of the manuscript which gives an alternate – and earlier – reading for this word.

Finally in Step 4 we need to look at the doctrinal and stylistic contents of those texts assessed as early and late, and assess the plausibility of our results and the implications for our understanding of the original teachings of the Buddha.

References

(References given in the text to the Pāli Canon cite the *sutta* number or volume and the subsection number in the Myanmar Chaṭṭhasaṅgīti edition, followed by the volume and page number in the PTS edition.)

ABEYNAYAKE, Oliver.

(1984). *A Textual and Historical Analysis of the Khuddaka Nikāya.* Colombo.

(2000). Sri Lanka's Contribution to the Development of the Pāli Canon. In PERERA (ed.) *Buddhism for the New Millennium.* Sri Saddhatissa International Buddhist Centre (UK), 163-183.

ADIKARAM, E. W.

(1946). *Early history of Buddhism in Ceylon as revealed by the Pāli commentaries of the 5th century A.D.* Dehiwala: The Buddhist Cultural Centre (Sri Lanka).

CONE, Margaret.

(2007). *caveat lector.* The Journal of the Pali Text Society, Vol. XXIX, 95-108.

DEOKAR, Maresh A.
(2017). *A Comparative Study of the Pāṇinian Grammar and the Three Grammars of Pāli*. (In this volume).
DUROISELLE, Charles.
(1906). *A Practical Grammar of the Pāli Language*. First edition. Rangoon: Rangoon College.
GOMBRICH, R. F.
(2005). Introduction: What is Pāli? In GEIGER, Wilhelm *A Pāli Grammar*. Oxford: Pali Text Society.
HINÜBER, Oskar von.
(1992). Linguistic Considerations on the Date of the Buddha. In BECHERT (ed.) *The Date of the Historical Buddha,* Part II. Göttingen: Vandenhoeck und Ruprecht, 183-193.
KINGSBURY, Paul.
(2002). *The Chronology of the Pāli Canon: The case of the aorists.* PhD dissertation, Department of Linguistics, University of Pennsylvania.
(2003). *Inducing a Chronology of the Pāli Canon.* Unpublished article (submitted to *Language Variation and Change*, October 2003).
KULASURIYA, Ananda S.
(2000). Writing, Palm-leaf Manuscripts and the Sinhala Script. In PERERA (ed.) *Buddhism for the New Millennium.* Sri Saddhatissa International Buddhist Centre (UK), 163-183.
LAW, B. C.
(2007). *A History of Pāli Literature.* 2nd ed. Varanasi: Indica Books. First Pub. 1933.
MALALGODA, Kitsiri.
(1976). *Buddhism in Sinhalese Society 1750-1900 - A Study of Religious Revival and Change.* University of California Press.
MARASINGHE, M. M. J.
(1974). *Gods in Buddhism: A study in their social and mythological milieu as depicted in the Nikāyas of the Pāli Canon.* Kelaniya: University of Sri Lanka.

NANDAMĀLĀBHIVAṀSA, Sayadaw Dr. U.
(2012). *Personal communication.*
NORMAN, K. R.
(1983). *Pāli Literature: Including the Canonical Literature in Prakrit and Sanskrit of all the Hīnayāna Schools of Buddhism.* Wiesbaden: Otto Harrassowitz.
PANDE, Govind Chandra.
(1974). *Studies in the Origins of Buddhism.* 2nd ed. Delhi: Motilal Banarsidass.
THANISSARO, Ven. Bhikkhu.
(2000). Computerization of the Buddhist Scriptures for the Twenty-First Century. In *Buddhism for the New Millennium*, Sri Saddhatissa International Buddhist Centre (UK), 217-228.
WIJESEKERA, O. H. de A.
(1993). *Syntax of the Cases in the Pali Nikayas.* Kelaniya: University of Kelaniya.

A Critical Reading into the *Mahādukkhakkhandhasutta*《苦蘊 經》in the Pāli Canon

Wadinagala PANNALOKA*

Abstract

The teaching of suffering (Pāli: *dukkha*) forms the key teaching of Early Buddhism and its literature is found in Pāli Language and in Classical Chinese. In order to explain the teaching of suffering (*dukkha*), the texts have adopted various approaches. This paper is an attempt to understand the role of above mentioned discourse in presenting the teaching of suffering in Early Buddhism.

Introduction

For this paper, I have selected a discourse titled *Mahādukkhakkhandhasutta- The Great Mass of Suffering*《苦蘊 經》which is found in the collection named *Majjhima Nikāya* belonging to the Pāli Theravāda tradition of Buddhism. This discourse has been translated into the Classical Chinese and there are three different translations for it in the collection called《阿含經》of the Chinese Tripiṭaka《漢譯經典》. Through an account of sensuality (欲望/婬), material form (色), and feeling (痛/覺) the text provides us with a new outlook into the day to day life trapped in intra or inter personal struggle. However, in this paper, I am not going to discuss the social

* Senior Lecturer, Department of Buddhist Philosophy, Postgraduate Institute of Pali and Buddhist Studies, University of Kelaniya. E-mail: wadinagala@gmail.com

application of the text but its textual characteristics and doctrinal basis on which it has evolved. As to the textual form, I will point out that *sutta*-s in the Pāli canon talking about the teaching of suffering; can be divided into two categories, introductory/definitive and descriptive. With regard to the doctrinal basis, I will refer to the discussion still going on among the modern Buddhist researchers concerned with the main cause of suffering, whether craving (*taṇhā*-渴愛,愛欲) or ignorance (*avijjā*-無明). Finally, I will try to determine the textual characteristics of the *Mahādukkhakkhandhasutta*, whether it is introductory or descriptive and what is the doctrinal foundation, *taṇhā* or *avijjā*, the account of suffering in this *sutta* revolves on.

Two Categories of *Sutta*-s Dealing with *Dukkha*

As the Buddha himself states, his whole career of teaching is centered on the task of explaining what is suffering (*dukkha*-苦) and its cessation (*nirodha*-苦滅).[1] From this statement we can learn that the concept of suffering is so fundamental to the early Buddhism. The Buddha in his first discourse, *Dhammacakkappavattanasutta* 《轉法輪經》, briefly introduced his articulation of the teaching of suffering through the formula of the Four Noble Truths (四聖諦).[2] They are namely, the Noble Truth of Suffering (*dukkhaṁ ariya saccaṁ*-苦聖諦), the Noble Truth of Origin of Suffering (*dukkha samudaya ariya saccaṁ*-苦集聖諦), the Noble Truth of Cessation of Suffering (*dukkha nirodha ariya saccaṁ*-苦滅聖諦) and the Noble Truth of Path to the Cessation of Suffering (*dukkha nirodhagamini paṭipadā ariya saccaṁ*-苦滅道跡聖諦). These are truths achieved through wisdom (*paññā* -智慧) in that they are so deep to realize by the ordinary beings. Once the Buddha states that the shades of the meaning of *dukkha* are

---

1 MN I.140; SN III.119

2 SN V.421f , Vin.I.10f; T2, 103c~104a

numerous and this is a so deep concept.[3] A reading into the Pāli *Suttapiṭaka* (巴利經典) reveals us that the texts have manifested themselves in many ways to explain the concept of suffering. Some *sutta*-s only serve the purpose of defining or introducing the teaching of suffering whereas some other *sutta*-s deal with in detail. Thus, according to the nature of their function in presenting the teaching, the *sutta*-s dealing with the teaching of suffering can be divided into two groups:

1. Introductory *sutta*-s on the teaching of suffering
2. The *sutta*-s providing detailed accounts of the teaching of suffering.

The First Category: Introductory *Sutta*-s on *Dukkha*

As it was mentioned above, the discussion given by Buddha in the *Dhammacakkappavattanasutta* is limited to a brief account on suffering. As it presents:

> Now this, *bhikkhu*-s, is the Noble Truth of Suffering: birth is suffering, aging is suffering, illness is suffering, death is suffering; union with what is displeasing is suffering; separation from what is pleasing is suffering; not to get what one wants is suffering; in brief, five aggregates subject to clinging is suffering.
>
> Now this, *bhikkhu*-s, is the Noble Truth of the Origin of Suffering: it is this craving which leads to renewed existence, accompanied by delight and lust, seeking delight here and there; that is craving for sensual pleasures, craving for existence, craving for extermination.
>
> Now this, *bhikkhu*-s, is the Noble Truth of the Cessation of Suffering: it is remainder less fading away and cessation of that same craving, the giving up and

[3] Ibid.

> relinquishing of it, freedom from it, non reliance of it.
>
> Now this, *bhikkhu*-s, is the Noble Truth of the Leading to the Cessation of Suffering: it is this Noble Eightfold Path; that is Right View...Right Concentration.
>
> This is the Noble Truth of Suffering...the Noble Truth of the Leading to the Cessation of Suffering: thus *bhikkhu*-s, in regard to things unheard before, there arose in me vision, knowledge, wisdom, true knowledge, and light.[4]

It is clear that this text gives the reader an idea what is suffering. Yet, when it is compared with some other texts in the same line, we can see that this account is not detailed enough.[5] On the other hand, this discourse was offered to a group of spiritual seekers, the five ascetics (*pañcavaggiya bhikkhu*-s-五比丘), who had a lot of experiences about the problem of human life.[6] So, a brief explanation might be enough for them to get the insight into the truth of reality. It is evident from the fact that at the end of the sermon, Aññā Koṇḍañña (阿若憍陣如) attained the first stage of spiritual path, stream-entering (*sotāpanna*-須陀洹).[7]

However, the brief explanation on the four truths seems not clear enough for the followers who joined the Order later. When we examine the treatment given in the *Saccavibhaṅgasutta* 《分別聖諦經》[8] for the truth of suffering and the truth of leading to cessation of suffering, it is evident that the early Buddhists had engaged in the task of expanding the doctrine of four truths, *dukkha*. In the *Dhammacakkappavattanasutta*, the first truth of suffering is explained in terms of

---

4 CDB: 1844

5 W. Rahula, *What The Buddha Taught*,p.30

6 P. Harvey, *An Introduction to Buddhism*,p.47

7 Vin I.12; T22, 788b: 五比丘阿若憍陳如諸塵垢盡得法眼生。

8 MN III.248-252;T1,467a~469c

eight facts which are common experiences to every human being. And, we can say that this is a collection of events which are both physically and mentally unpleasant. Moreover, this short account of suffering can be considered as a definition given for suffering. In the *Saccavibhaṅgasutta*, going forward in the explanation as to what is suffering, Sāriputta adds five more items to the first truth and clarifies each item with more details.[9] For example, the *Dhammacakka-ppavattana- sutta* refers to birth (*jāti*-生) as one form of suffering without any clarification.[10] In the case of *Saccavibhaṅga-sutta*, after defining what is suffering in terms of ten modes, Sāriputta begins to gloss all of them one by one. First he takes up the topic of birth (*jāti*-生) and glosses it as follows:

> And what, friends, is birth? The birth of beings into the various orders of beings, their coming into birth, precipitation [in a womb], generation, the manifestation of aggregates, obtaining the bases for contact- this is called birth.[11]

---

9 MN III.249f: namely i. *soka* (sorrow), ii. *parideva* (lamentation), iii. *dukkha* (pain), iv. *domanassa* (grief), v. *upāyāsa* (despair). In the Chinese parallel of the *Saccavibhaṅgasutta* mentions only eightfold aspects given in the *Dhammacakkappavattanasutta*: T1, 467b: 云何苦聖諦？ 謂生苦、老苦、病苦、死苦、怨憎會苦、愛別離苦、所求不得苦、略五盛陰苦。

10 Vin I.10f

11 MLDB: 1098; MN III.249: *Katamā cāvuso, jāti? Yā tesaṁ tesaṁ sattānaṁ tamhi tamhi sattanikāye jāti sañjāti okkanti abhinibbatti khandhānaṁ pātubhāvo āyatanānaṁ paṭilābho, ayaṁ vuccatāvuso – 'jāti'*; T1, p 467c: 諸賢！說生苦者，此說何因？諸賢！生者，謂彼眾生、彼彼眾生種類、生則生、出則出、成則成、興起五陰、已得命根，是名為生。諸賢！生苦者，謂眾生生時，身受苦受、遍受、覺、遍覺；心受苦受，遍受、覺，遍覺；身心受苦受，遍受，、覺，遍覺；身熱受，遍受、覺，遍覺；心熱受，遍受、覺，遍覺；身心熱受，遍受、覺，遍覺；身壯熱煩惱憂慼受，遍受、覺，遍覺；心壯

When one closely examines this description, though it has put a step further than the *Dhammcakkappavattanasutta*, we can see that still only serves the purpose of defining what is suffering but does not describe how *jāti* becomes suffering. If we look into the *Visuddhimagga*, a work belongs to the fifth century CE, we can learn that the Theravāda tradition had felt the need of further clarifying for the modes of suffering given in the early discourses. Hence, we can say that in presenting certain ideas, the early texts have tended to be concise. Buddhaghosa has undertaken the duty of describing how birth becomes a suffering. The *Visuddhimagga* mentions:

> Here the suffering classed as 'rooted in the descent into the womb', and so on, is this: when this being is born in the mother's womb...like a worm in rotting fish, rotting dough, cess-pools, etc., he is born in the belly in a position that is below the receptacle for undigested food (stomach), above the receptacle for digested food (rectum).....And on being reborn there for ten months he undergoes excessive suffering, being cooked like a pudding in a bag by the heat produced in the mother's womb, and steamed like a dumpling of dough, with no bending, stretching and so on. So this, firstly, is the suffering rooted in the decent into the womb.[12]

What we can learn from these textual references is that since the first time of presenting the doctrine of suffering, up to later ages when the commentaries and summaries of the teaching (like the *Visuddhimagga*) were composed, the authors have tried to illustrate the concept of suffering.

熱煩惱憂慼受，遍受、覺，遍覺；身心壯熱煩惱憂慼受，遍受、覺，遍覺。諸賢！說生苦者，因此故說。
From the Chinese version, we can see that it is more detailed than the Pāli version.

12 *The Path of Purification*: 569

The Second Category: detailed *Sutta*-s on *Dukkha*

The four truths through which the Buddha's view and solution to human suffering was revealed, give rise to the production of a vast literature related to each aspect of them. As it is noted above, the *Dhammacakkappavattanasutta* is limited to the task of defining what is suffering, what is origin of suffering, what is the cessation of suffering and what is the method to eradicate suffering. Some other *sutta*-s just select one or two out of these four and try to explain in different angles. Here we can say that such an attempt is in line with the Buddha's guidance how to deal with each truth. In the *Saṃyutta-Nikāya*《相應部》, he says that first truth of suffering (*dukkha*) has to be well understood (*pariññāta*- 苦聖諦智當復知) and the second truth of arising of suffering (*samudaya*) has to be eradicated (*pahātabba*- 苦集聖諦已知當斷); the third truth of cessation of suffering (*nirodha*) has to be realized (苦滅聖諦已知當知作證) and the last one of the way of putting end to suffering (*paṭipadā*) has to be cultivated (*bhāvetabba*- 苦滅道跡聖諦已知當修).[13] In the texts, it is mentioned that it is not easy to realize suffering by ordinary persons. The aspect of '*pariññāta*' implies the need of perfect understanding concerning the nature of suffering or diverse forms of suffering as one aspect of the scheme to eradicate suffering. If we want to educate people on something, we need to adopt various teaching methods and provide them even with minute information. It was the same practice that was adopted by the redactors of Pāli texts. In order to make people aware of what they are experiencing every moment, the texts tried to look into the concept of suffering from various ways.

In order to realize how the second truth has been treated in the *Suttapiṭaka* in different ways, let us take a few *sutta*-s. The

---

13 SN V.421f; T2,103c

Dhammacakkappavattanasutta presents a brief account about craving (*taṇhā*) as the cause of suffering and marginally says it makes people hang in here and there and leads to continuous rebirth. It comes into appearance in three modes, craving for sensual pleasure (*kāmataṇhā*- 欲愛), craving for self-assertion (*bhavataṇhā*- 有愛) and craving for annihilation (*vibhavataṇhā*- 無有愛).[14] The *Saccavibhaṅgasutta*, though has treated the first truth and the fourth truth in detail, for the second and the third truths, only gives the same description found in the *Dhammacakkappavattanasutta.*[15] In some other *sutta*-s, we can find each of these modes has been provided with details. The *Dhammacakkappavattanasutta* only defines what sensual pleasure is and considers it as conducive to recurrent existence. Furthering the Buddhist understanding of sensual pleasure, many Pāli *sutta*-s have discussed in depth how it functions to create suffering in this life and next one. For example, by using similes from day to day life, the *Māgandiyasutta* 《鬚閑提經》 provides a very convincing message how sensuality causes sentient beings suffers. To take one simile:

> Māgandiya, it is like a leper, a man with his limbs all ravaged and festering, and who being eaten by vermin, tearing his open sores with his nails, scorches his body over a charcoal pit. But the more, Māgandiya, this leper, a man with his limbs... scorches his body over a charcoal pit, the more those open sores of his become septic and evil-smelling and putrefying and there is only a sorry relief and satisfaction to be had from scratching the open sores. Even so, Māga-

14 Vin I.10f: *Idaṁ kho pana, bhikkhave, dukkhasamudayaṁ ariyasaccaṁ - yāyaṁ taṇhā ponobbhavikā nandīrāgasahagatā tatratatrābhinandinī, seyyathidaṁ - kāmataṇhā, bhavataṇhā, vibhavataṇhā*; T22, 788a: 何等為苦集聖諦？緣愛本所生，與欲相應愛樂，是謂苦集聖諦。

15 MN.III.248-252

ndiya, do beings who are not yet devoid of attachment to pleasures of the senses, while being consumed by the craving fro sense-pleasures, pursue sense pleasures; and the more these beings who are not yet devoid of attachment to pleasures of the senses ... pursue them, the more their craving for sense-pleasures increases, the more they burn with the fever for sense-pleasures, and moreover there is only a sorry relief and satisfaction to be had from the five strands of sense-pleasures.[16]

---

16 MLS II.187; MN I.507: *Seyyathāpi, Māgandiya, kuṭṭhī puriso arugatto pakkagatto kimīhi khajjamāno nakhehi vaṇamukhāni vippatacchamāno aṅgārakāsuyā kāyaṁ paritāpeti. Yathā yathā kho, Māgandiya, asu kuṭṭhī puriso arugatto pakkagatto kimīhi khajjamāno nakhehi vaṇamukhāni vippatacchamāno aṅgārakāsuyā kāyaṁ paritāpeti tathā tathā'ssa tāni vaṇamukhāni asucitarāni c'eva honti duggandhatarāni ca pūtikatarāni ca, hoti c'eva kāci sātamattā assādamattā - yadidaṁ vaṇamukhānaṁ kaṇḍū-vaṇahetu; evam-eva kho, Māgandiya, sattā kāmesu avītarāgā kāmataṇhāhi khajjamānā kāmapariḷāhena ca pariḍayhamānā kāme paṭisevanti. Yathā yathā kho, Māgandiya, sattā kāmesu avītarāgā kāmataṇhāhi khajjamānā kāmapariḷāhena ca pariḍayhamānā kāme paṭisevanti tathā tathā tesaṃ tesaṃ sattānaṃ kāmataṇhā c'eva pavaḍḍhati, kāmapariḷāhena ca pariḍay-hanti, hoti c'eva sātamattā assādamattā - yadidaṃ pañcakāmaguṇe paṭi-cca;* T1, 671b~671c: 世尊告曰：鬚閑提！猶人病癩，身體爛熟、為蟲所食、爪擿瘡開，臨火坑炙。鬚閑提！於意云何？若病癩人，身體爛熟、為蟲所食、爪擿瘡開、臨火坑炙。如是，寧得除病有力、不壞諸根、為脫癩病、身體完健、平復如故，還本所耶？答世尊曰：不也，瞿曇！所以者何？若病癩人，身體爛熟、為蟲所食、爪擿瘡開，臨火坑炙。如是，更生瘡轉增多、本瘡轉大，然，彼反以癩瘡為樂。鬚閑提！如病癩人，身體爛熟、為蟲所食、爪擿瘡開，臨火坑炙。如是，更生瘡轉增多、本瘡轉大、然，彼反以癩瘡為樂。鬚閑提！如是，眾生未離欲、為欲愛所食、為欲熱所熱，而行於欲。鬚閑提！如是，眾生未離欲、為欲愛所食、為欲熱所熱，而行於欲。如是，欲轉增多、欲愛轉廣、然、彼反以欲愛為樂。彼若不斷欲，不離欲愛、內息心、已行、當行、今行者、終無是處。

Another example for descriptive discourses on suffering, particularly variety of modes in appearance of suffering from sensual pleasures is the *Piyajātikasutta* 《愛生經》. It refers to many sort of sensual objects and how their change brings about suffering. As the text follows:

> So, it is, Brahmin, so it is! Sorrow, lamentation, pain, grief, and despair are born from those who are dear; arise from those who are dear. It can be understood from this, Brahmin, how sorrow, lamentation, pain, grief, and despair are born from those who are dear, arise from those who are dear. Once in this same Sāvatthi there was a certain man whose mother died. Owing to his mother's death, he went mad, lost his mind, and wandered from street to street and from crossroad to crossroad, saying: 'Have you seen my mother? Have you seen my mother? And it also can be understood from this how sorrow, lamentation, pain, grief, despair are born from those who are dear, arise from those who are dear. Once in this same Sāvatthi there was a certain man whose father died...brother died...whose sister died...whose son died... whose daughter died...whose wife died. Owing to his wife's death, he went mad, lost his mind, and wandered from street to street and from crossroad to crossroad, saying: 'Have you seen my wife? Have you seen my wife? And it also can be understood from this how sorrow, lamentation, pain, grief, despair are born from those who are dear, arise from those who are dear.[17]

---

[17] MLDB 720; MN II.108: *Evametaṁ, brāhmaṇa, evametaṁ, brāhmaṇa! Piyajātikā hi, brāhmaṇa, sokaparidevadukkhadomanassupāyāsā piyappabhavikāti. Tadamināpetaṁ, brāhmaṇa, pariyāyena veditabbaṁ yathā piyajātikā sokaparidevadukkhadomanassupāyāsā piyappabhavikā. "Bhūtapubbaṁ, brāhmaṇa, imissāyeva sāvatthiyā aññatarassa purisassa mātā kālamakāsi. So tassā kālakiriyāya ummattako khittacitto rathikāya rathi-*

From these couple of evidence, it becomes clear that the formulaic statement concerning the doctrine of suffering in the *Dhammacakkappavattanasutta* has been elaborated in other texts.

The Cause of Suffering: *Taṇhā* or *Avijjā*

In the explanation of the cause of suffering, the Buddha states that it will never be a single cause and there are many causes and conditions which function together in generating psycho-physical pain.[18] In general, *taṇhā* (craving[19], thirst[20],

---

kaṁ siṅghāṭakena siṅghāṭakaṁ upasaṅkamitvā evamāha- 'api me mātaraṁ addassatha, api me mātaraṁ addassathā'ti ? Imināpi kho etaṁ, brāhmaṇa, pariyāyena veditabbaṁ yathā piyajātikā sokaparidevadukkhadomanassupāyāsā piyappabhavikāti.Bhūtapubbaṁ, brāhmaṇa, imissāyeva sāvatthiyā aññatarassa purisassa pitā kālamakāsi... bhātā kālamakāsi... bhaginī kālamakāsi... putto kālamakāsi... dhītā kālamakāsi... pajāpati kālamakāsi. So tassā kālakiriyāya ummattako khittacitto rathikāya rathikaṁ siṅghāṭakena siṅghāṭakaṁ upasaṅkamitvā evamāha – 'api me pajāpatiṁṃ addassatha, api me pajāpatiṁ addassathā'ti? Imināpi kho etaṁ, brāhmaṇa, pariyāyena veditabbaṁ yathā piyajātikā sokaparidevadukkhadomanassupāyāsā piyappabhavikāti; T01, 801b: 那利鴦伽梵志，受王教已、即詣佛所、共相問訊、卻坐一面，白曰：瞿曇！拘薩羅王波斯匿，問訊、聖體康強、安快、無病、起居輕便、氣力，如常耶？沙門瞿曇，實如是說：『若愛生時，便生愁慼、啼哭、憂苦、煩惋、懊惱耶？』世尊告曰：那利鴦伽！我今問汝，隨所解答。那利鴦伽！於意云何？若使有人，母命終者，彼人發狂、心大錯亂、脫衣、裸形、隨路遍走，作如是說：『諸賢！見我母耶？諸賢！見我母耶？』。那利鴦伽！以此事故可知，若愛生時，便生愁慼、啼哭、憂苦、煩惋、懊惱。如是，父、兄、姊、妹也；兒、婦命終，彼人發狂、心大錯亂、脫衣、裸形、隨路遍走，作如是說：『諸賢！見我兒、婦耶？諸賢！見我兒、婦耶？』。那利鴦伽！以此事故可知，若愛生時，便生愁慼、啼哭、憂苦、煩惋、懊惱。
Even though there is a difference how the discussion began between the Buddha and the counterpart, the the contents are same both in the Pali and Chinese.

18 W. RAHULA, *What The Buddha Taught*, p.45

19 MLDB translates '*taṇhā*' as 'craving': p.29, n.6, 138, 195; MLS I.133

20 W. RAHULA, *op.cit.*

desire[21]) and *avijjā* (ignorance) come to be emphasized normally as the causes of suffering. However, it should be mentioned that the discourses concerned with the second noble truth only refer to craving (*taṇhā*) as the sole cause of suffering. Moreover, we can find in the Pāli canon, discourses that trace to craving as the cause of suffering.

On the other hand, according to the twelvefold theory of causal condition, ignorance is placed as the first cause of suffering. As the texts describe, the nature of the individual's reactions to the environment, and the conditioning which promotes continued becoming, usually stem from ignorance, which is said to have no known beginning.[22] Further, it is mentioned that ignorance is correlated with volitional activities[23] and that when there is no ignorance there are no volitional activities and that with the cessation of ignorance there is a cessation of volitional activities.[24] And also, it is mentioned that when it is asked what is the causal condition (*upanisā*- 緣) of volitional activities, the reply should be 'ignorance'.[25]

The fact that making no reference to *avijjā* in the *Dhammacakkappavattanasutta* (in the second noble truth) and the indications to ignorance in some other *sutta*-s[26] as the head of causes conducive to *saṁsāric* existence, have led modern Buddhist scholars to form two theories for origin of suffering:

1. *Taṇhā* as the sole cause of suffering
2. *Avijjā* as the cause of suffering.

---

21 Ibid.

22 SN.II.178; AN.V.113

23 SN.II.7: *avijjāya kho sati sankhārā honti avijjā paccayā sankhārā*

24 SN.II.9: *avijjāya kho asati sankhārā na honti avijjānirodhā sankhāranirodho*

25 SN.II.31

26 SN.II.6, 9, 12; It 34:*yā kāc' imā duggatiyo asmiṁ loke paramhi ca avijjāmūlakā sabbā icchā -- lobha -- sammussayā*; Sn 199, 277, 729:*jāti -- maraṇa -- samsāraṁ ye vajanti punappunaṁ . . . avijjāy'eva sā gati*

Erich Frauwallner has tried to show a development in the Pāli *Suttapiṭaka* as to the cause of suffering. According to him, the *Dhammacakkappavattanasutta* establishes *taṇhā* as the sole cause of suffering and later through the theory of causal condition (*Paṭiccasamuppāda*- 緣起 法), ignorance (*avijjā*) was introduced as the cause functioning together with other conditions to generate suffering.[27] As the *Suttapiṭaka* reflects, there is no space to form a theory of a single cause as the origin of suffering. It is stated that there is no known 'first beginning' (*purimākoṭi*- 前際) of ignorance[28] and it is said that the causal formula beginning with ignorance is an effort of describing phenomena in terms of causally correlated factors 'in the middle' instead of seeking for initial or final causes.[29] The *Sammādiṭṭhisutta* states:

> With the arising of the taints there is the arising of ignorance. With the cessation of the taints there is the cessation of the taints.
>
> ....With the arising of ignorance there is the arising of the taints. With the cessation of ignorance there is the cessation of the taints.[30]

This is a well-illustrious mark to show that the Pāli *Suttapiṭaka* has not considered 'ignorance' as the fundamental cause of suffering but only as one of many factors which are causally conditioned.[31]

---

27 E. FRAUWALLNER, *History of Indian Philosophy*, Vol. I. pp.150-156sq; H.G.A. van Ziet, '*Avijja*' in *Encyclopaedia of Buddhism*, p.548 : he mentions of few scholars who tried to interpret 'ignorance' as the dominant cause of suffering in Buddhism.

28 AN.V.113

29 MN.I.265;SN.II.20,21

30 MLDB 143f ; T2, 797b: 彼云何名為無明？所謂不知苦、不知習、不知盡、不知道、此名為無 明。The Chinese version differs from the Pāli.

31 P. WILLIAMS and A. TRIBE, *Buddhist Thought*, p. 46

With regard to the hypothesis presented by FRAUWALLNER, Buddhist researchers have given consideration and have shown that it is groundless. However, they have tried to see a relationship between *taṇhā* and *avijja* as follows:

> Some fifty years ago Erich FRAUWALLNER highlighted the fact that at one time (in the formula of the Four Noble Truths) Buddhist thought sees 'thirst' (*tṛṣṇā/taṇhā*) as the root cause of suffering, at another time (in the formula of *Pratityasamutpāda*) ignorance (*avidyā/avijjā*); indeed, he saw this as something of an inconsistency. Yet what Buddhist thought seems to be suggesting here is that what is logically distinct- the cognitive and affective, fact and value-is empirically inextricably bound up together: a mind that does not see in accordance with the truth is a mind that tends to grasp.[32]

When we examine the way how some *sutta*-s have discussed the problem of suffering, it seems that what FRAUWALLNER has pointed out is partially acceptable. In the overall understanding, Buddhism does not accept a single cause as the root of suffering but a correlative mixture of causes and conditions. However, the Buddha has not followed a fixed theory in presenting his teaching and certain discourses were given by him according to the listener's capacity and interest. So, we can see that some discourses in showing why suffering arises, have referred to craving (*taṇhā*) as the cause of lot of issues confronted by unenlightened persons. For instance, in the *Mūlapariyāyasutta* 《想經》,[33] a deep philosophical scripture, after analyzing elements related to existence, express that delight in them is the cause of suffering (*nandi dukkhassa*

---

[32] R. GETHIN, 'Wrong View (*micchā-diṭṭhi*) and Right View (*sammā-diṭṭhi*) in the Theravada Abhidhamma' in *Recent Researches in Buddhist Studies Essays in Honour of Professor Y. Karunadasa*, p. 221

[33] MN I.1-6; T1, 596b~596c

mūlaṁ).[34] A close reading into the *Suttapiṭaka*, showing that though there is an obvious shortage referring to *avijjā* as the sole cause, there are number of discourses which talk only of *taṇhā* as the root of suffering. Thus, we can recognize a line of thought emphasized craving as the cause of suffering. Even we cannot agree with FRAUWALLNER's opinion complet-ely, his view causes us to look closer into the texts.

The Characteristics of the *Mahādukkhakkhandhasutta*《苦蘊經》

The main theme of this discourse is the truth of suffering and the origin of suffering. In the *Suttapiṭaka*, there are number of *sutta*-s dealing with the Four Noble Truths in different ways. A characteristic seen in the *Suttapiṭaka* is that each discourse has its own characteristic and an independent discussion related to the mainstream thought.[35] As we have noted above, we can recognize some characteristics common to these discourses. The discourses concerned with the conc-ept of suffering have functioned in two ways, definitive and descriptive. And, certain discourses in explaining the cause of suffering have inclined to trace to *taṇhā* as the cause of origin. In this section, I am going to point out that the *Mahā-dukkhandhasutta* belongs to the category of *sutta*-s that offer descriptive approach to explain the concept of suffering and it is based on the idea that suffering is resulted in from 'desire' (*taṇhā*).

---

34 MN I.6; This reference is not found in the Chinese version of this *sutta*.

35 R. GETHIN, *The Foundations of Buddhism*, p. 47: The Discourses of the Buddha as preserved in the Nikayas do not of themselves constitute a systematic exposition of Buddhist thought with a beginning, middle, and end. Each discourse is rather presented as a more or less self-contained piece on a particular theme. And yet, the discourses as a whole do contain quite explicit indications of how these various themes relate to each other and fit together to form and overall structure and pattern.

Mahādukkhakkhandhasutta: A Detailed Account

As we previously noted, the redactors of the *Suttapiṭaka* and later scholars (like Buddhaghosa) have attempted to present a more detailed description on the teaching of suffering. The Buddha himself accepted that the teaching of suffering is a so deep concept that people find it difficult to understand.[36] So, it was necessary to apply different teaching methods to convince the general public of his message. In an attempt to realize what is suffering and how it puts us in its sway, we have to have a deep knowledge regarding every aspect related to it. In this case, it was necessary to use descriptive method to present the idea needed to teach. The effort of producing detailed account on suffering-*dukkha* is clearly seen in the *Mahādukkhandhasutta* 《苦蘊 經》.

The discussion in this discourse concerned with suffering is mainly centered upon the *dukkha* and *dukkhasamudaya,* two truths. In order to educate the public about suffering, the text has selected three factors, which are very sensitive to deal and play a great role in human life. They are:

i. sensuality (*kāma*-欲望/婬)
ii. material form (*rūpa*-色)
iii. feeling (*vedanā*-痛/覺)[37]

To illustrate these three factors in relation to suffering and its arising, the text uses three angles to look at as gratification (*assāda*- 氣味/味), danger (*ādīnava*- 敗壞/患/過), and escape from them (*nissaraṇa*- 棄/出要/捨離).[38] Let us take one by one the three items and examine how far they have been described in comparison to the definitive *sutta*-s.

---

36 SN.V.430:*Idaṁ ariya saccanti bhikkhave mayā paññattaṁ. tattha aparimānā vaṇṇā aparimānā vyañjanā aprimānā samkāsanā itipidam dukkhaṁ ariya saccanti*

37 MN I.84

38 Ibid 85

Sensuality (*kāmā*- 欲望/婬)

In this *sutta*, sensuality has been analyzed in terms of gratification, danger and escape. The discourses defining what is craving, the cause of suffering, briefly mention craving for sensual pleasures (*kāmataṇhā*- 欲愛), craving for continuous existence (*bhavataṇhā*- 有愛), and craving for annihilation (*vibhavataṇhā*- 無有愛) as three modes of craving.[39] The *Mahādukkhakkhandhasutta* 《苦蘊經》 puts sensuality (*kāmā*) as the first topic to examine and first defines what is the gratification of sensuality. Neither in the *Dhammacakkappavattanasutta* nor in the *Saccavibhaṅgasutta*, there is reference to the definition of sensual gratification.[40] The *Mahādukkhakkhandhasutta* 《苦蘊 經》 defines (and also some other *sutta*-s) the gratification of sensual pleasures in terms of five codes of sense pleasures (*pañcakāmaguṇa*- 妙欲/五欲) as follows:

> What...is the gratification in the case of sensual pleasure?...there are these five codes of sensual pleasure. What are the five? Forms cognizable by the eye that is wished for, desired, agreeable and likeable, connected with sensual desire, and provocative of lust. Sounds cognizable by the ear...Odours cognizable by the nose...Flavours cognizable by the tongue...Tangibles cognizable by the body that are wished for, desired, agreeable and likeable connected with sensual desire, and provocative of lust. These are the five codes of sensual pleasure...the pleasure and joy that arise dependent on these five codes of sensual

39 Vin I.10f; MN III.250f; SN V.431

40 Ibid.

> pleasure are the gratification in the case of sensual pleasures.[41]

When we compare this description with the definitive discourses dealing with the second noble truth, which merely mentions sensual desire (*kāmataṇhā*- 欲愛) as one aspect of craving, the descriptive definition as to gratification given here can be understood as furtherance made to the brief reference to sensual desire in definitive discourses.

Moreover, we can point out even the definition of sensual gratification has been edited in the *sutta*-s by adding the mind and mind objects (*mano* and *dhamma*) as the sixth code of sensual pleasure to the list of five codes of sensual pleasures.[42] The *Satipaṭṭhāna-sutta* 《念處經》[43] in the *Dīghanikāya* 《長部》 has added the mind and mind-objects as the sixth code.[44]

In other words, the definition of sensual gratification in the *Mahādukkhakkhandhasutta* 《苦蘊 經 》does not differ from other *sutta*-s which offer the same description on this matter. Then, we can say that the definition given in this *sutta* is not a new thing but in line with the common definition found in many other *sutta*-s.

---

41 MN. I.85, 92, 144, 155, 173, 454, 504; II.42; III.114, 295; DN. I.245: *Koca bhikkhave kāmanāṁ assādo: Pañc'ime bhikkhave kāmaguṇā, katame pañca:cakkhuviññeyyā rūpā iṭṭhā kantā manāpā, piyarūpā kāmūpasamhitā rajaniyā,sotaviññeyyā saddā-pe-ghāṇaviññeyyā gandhā-jivhāviññeyyā rasā-kāyaviññeyyā poṭṭhabbā....Ime kho bhikkhave pañcakāmaguṇā. Yam kho bhikkhave ime pañcakāmaguṇe paṭicca uppajjati sukhaṁ somanassaṁ, ayaṁ kāmānaṁ assādo*; T2, 605a (EA): 欲有何味? 所謂五欲者是。云何為五? 眼見色，為起眼識; 甚愛敬念，世人所喜。若耳聞聲、鼻嗅香、舌知味、身知細滑，甚愛敬念，世人所喜。若復於此五欲之中起苦、樂心，是謂欲味。

42 E. FRAUWALLNER, *op.cit.*, p.150ff

43 T1, 582b~584b

44 DN II.308

The introductory *sutta*-s on the Second Noble Truth make no reference to the dangers of sensual attachment. However, in many places in the *Suttapiṭaka*, we can find that this aspect of sensuality has been provided with touching accounts, anecdotes and similes.[45] Because Buddhism is emphatic on the renunciation of sensuality (*nekkhamma*- 離欲) in favor of higher pleasures than sensual pleasures and perceives sensual pleasures as sources of suffering and fatigue, the texts has discussed how attachment to sensuality create conflicts in the human life.[46] The description contained in the *Mahādukkhakkhandhasutta* 《苦蘊 經》 is a new outlook shed to the course of life which is full of agonies, disappointments and conflicts but not perceived as painful experiences by the ordinary person. Let us refer to the first sort of unpleasant experience (*ādīnava*- 敗壞/患/過) undergone by the householder due to attachment to sensuality:

> And what, *bhikkhu*-s, is the danger in the case of sensual pleasures? Here, *bhikkhu*-s, on account of the craft, by which a clansman makes a living-whether checking...or whatever craft it may be– he has to face cold, he has to face heat, he is injured by contact with gadflies, mosquitoes, wind, sun, and creeping things; he risks death by hunger and thirst. Now this is a danger in the case of sensual pleasures, a mass of suffering visible here and now, having sensual pleasures as its cause, sensual pleasures as its source, sensual pleasures as its basis, the cause being simply sensual pleasures.[47]

In the ancient societies, it was very severe in executing punishments for those who were caught for committing

---

45 E. W. Burlingame, *Buddhist Parables*, pp. 274-279: He has collected seven parables that describe the problem of sensuality.

46 AN IV.438f

47 MLDB 180f

various criminal acts. According to this *sutta,* social crimes originate from the man's attachment to the sensual gratification and as a result of seeking illegal means to satisfy senses, the individuals become subject to dreadful punishments executed by the kings. As those punishments were familiar with the general public, the *Mahādukkhakkhandhasutta* 《苦蘊經》 brings forth the list of them in relation to suffering as follows:

> Again, with sensual pleasures as the cause...men break into houses, plunder wealth, commit burglary, ambush highways, seduce others' wives, and when they are caught, kings have many kinds of torture inflicted on them. The kings have them flogged with whips, beaten with canes, beaten with clubs; ...and they have them splashed with boiling oil, and they have them thrown to be devoured by dogs, and they have them impaled alive on stakes, and they have their heads cut off with swords- whereby they incur death or deadly suffering. Now this too is a danger in the case of sensual pleasures...[48]

If we evaluate the importance of this sort of descriptions in the context of suffering, it seems that these are so effective in teaching how people are affected by universally found experiences. Each aspect given to illustrate the ill effects of sensual desire carries a deep and touching image of suffering. These can be said as highly dynamic pictures to the experience of suffering.

---

[48] Ibid. p. 182; T1, 585b (MA): 復次，眾生、因欲、緣欲，以欲為本，著鎧被袍，持矟弓箭或執刀楯入村、入邑、入國、入城。穿牆發藏，劫奪財物，斷截王路或至他巷，壞村、害邑、滅國、破城。於中或為王人所捉；種種考治：截手、截足或截手足；截耳、截鼻或截耳鼻...彼在其中或死或怖，受極重苦。是謂現法苦陰；因欲、緣欲，以欲為本。

The third aspect to deal with sensuality, escape from issue of sensuality, has been marginally mentioned and advised to give up desire and lust for sensual pleasures. In this case, the discourse makes no special contribution as it did in the former aspect.

Material form (*rūpa*- 色)

The *Dhammacakkappavattanasutta* as a concluding remark to tell what is suffering, makes the statement that clinging to the five aggregates is suffering (*sankhittena pañcupādānakkhandhā dukkhā*).[49] There is no any clarification to this statement which is of philosophical character.[50] A further attempt made to explain why the five aggregates are subject to suffering, is seen in the *Anattalakkhaṇasutta* 《無我相經》, which is considered as the second talk (*veyyākaraṇa*- 解答) given by the Buddha.[51] Using the three characteristics, impermanence, unsatisfactoriness and non-substantiality of the phenomena (*tilakkhaṇa*: *anicca*, *dukkha*, *anatta*- 無常，苦，無我) as the measurement to decide whether five aggregates can be taken as substantial (*atta*- 我), the Buddha points out the body (*rūpam*- 色) is not self, if it were self, then this body would not tend to sickness.[52] Further he points out that if something is impermanent it is painful; something painful cannot be taken as the self; so is the body, feeling, perception etc. This was taught to the five ascetics who had attained the first

---

49 Vin I.10

50 MN III.250: The *Saccavibhaṅgasutta* takes up the role of defining and mentions cling to material form (*rūpa*-色), feeling (*vedanā*-受), perception (*saññā*- 想), mental formations (*sankhāra*- 行) and consciousness (*viññāṇa*-識) is suffering.

51 T22, 788~789b

52 *The Book of Discipline*, Part 4, p.20; T22, 789a: 比丘！色無我，若色是我者，色不增益，而我受苦。若色是我者，應得自在，欲得如，色不用如是色。以色無我故，而色增長，故受諸苦。亦不能得隨意，欲得如是色便得，不用如是色便不得。

stage of stream-entering (*sotāpanna*- 須陀洹). Thus, we can see that it is a philosophical discourse which is not easy for the ordinary listener to understand.

As to the *Mahādukkhakkhandhasutta* 《苦蘊 經》, it adopts the threefold analysis (gratification, danger and escape) to explain the reality of material form and describes how the persons experience body. The gratification of the body is the pleasure derived from the beauty of a girl at her prime youth and possessing all the characteristics which were considered as the measurement of feminine beauty.[53] This is a different way of understanding the pleasure of body and it has been done in terms of sensuality, which is the most dominant aspect in human psyche.[54]

In order to show the adverse aspects of body (*ādīnava* - 敗壞/患/過), the *sutta* describes how the same beautiful woman gradually becomes old, sick and finally dead. The *sutta* presents a picture of an old person's infirmity at his last days in life as follows:

> Again, one might see that same woman afflicted, suffering, and gravely ill, lying fouled in her own excrement and urine, lifted up by some and down by others. What do you think *bhikkhu*-s? Has her former beauty and loveliness vanished and the danger becomes evident?[55]

The nine stages of a dead body is a meditative object to

---

53 MN.I.88

54 Sue. HAMILTON, *Identity and Experience*, p. xxv: points out '*āsava*' as the most binding and deeply entrenched of all misplaced psychological tendencies. This insight to '*āsava*' is well applicable to sensual desire.

55 MLDB p.183; T2, 605b (EA): 復次，此，若見彼女人身抱重患，臥於床褥，失大、小便，不能起、止；云何比丘 本見妙色，今致此患，豈非大患乎？」 諸比丘對曰：「如是世尊！」世尊告曰：「諸比丘！是謂色為大患。」

contemplate the body. In the *Satipaṭṭhānasuttas*, it is given in abstract or a universal form whereas the *Mahādukkhakkhandhasutta* 《苦蘊 經》 relates those nine stages to the female body.[56] This is an attempt to describe the danger of body through common experience, which is easy to realize by the ordinary person. As for the escape from the perils of body, the *sutta* has not added any new idea.

Feeling (*vedanā*- 痛/覺)

Feeling, the second aggregate, is also treated through the three aspects of gratification, danger and escape. However, as it was seen in the sensuality section, there is no an attempt to describe in detail.

From the above analysis made regarding the textual form of this discourse, we can see that it has been a descriptive text when it explains sensuality in terms of three aspects: gratification, danger and escape; particularly, the treatment on the danger of sensual desire dramatically depicts how desire for sensual pleasures would cause suffering. This is a special discussion which is not found elsewhere in the *Suttapiṭaka*. The section on the material form also has been considerable descriptive, specially, on the problematic aspect of material form, which is related to the infirmities and the decomposing process happen to the body after death. As to the section on feeling, the text goes without much detail. As a whole, this *sutta* has been descriptive in examining the horror of suffering experienced due to attachment to sensual pleasures and changes occurred to the material form (human body).

The Doctrinal Basis of the Discourse- *Taṇhā* (渴愛)

As we have noted above, Pāli *sutta*-s have not got a fixed

---

56 MLDB p. 183f

single factor to show as the only cause of suffering. However, due to the diversity of listeners' capacity to realize the *dhamma* or due to their psychological inclinations or due to social factors or due to cotemporary religio-philosophical factors, there are number of *sutta*-s describe desire (*taṇhā*- 渴愛) as the origin of every sort of miseries. In this section, I am going to point out that the *Mahādukkhakkhandhasutta* 《苦蘊 經》 is based on the assumption that craving is the cause of intrapersonal and interpersonal psycho-physical conflicts and to avoid those melancholies one should root out craving appearing in various modes.

Sensuality (*kāmā*- 欲望/婬)

According to the *Mahādukkhakkhandhasutta*, the Buddha implements this discussion on sensuality, material form and feeling to show how his doctrine on them differ from the non-Buddhist religious practitioners' view on them. At the outset, the ascetics question what is the difference between the Buddha and ascetics (*paribbājakas*- 梵志) on the teaching of these three factors, they should be questioned what is the gratification, danger and escape in relation to these three factors. If they are asked so, they are not able to answer because it is beyond their capacity for knowing (*avisaya*- 非境界). As this statement indicates, we can assume that this discourse establishes the uniqueness of the Buddha's teaching on these three factors.[57]

The Buddha takes up three factors one by one and analyzed in terms of *assāda* (gratification), danger (*ādīnava*) and escape

---

[57] SN IV.7f : In this place, the Buddha says that before his enlightenment, while he was still a *bodhisatta*, the question occurred to him as to what are the gratification, the danger, and the escape in the case of six internal sense bases and six external sense bases.

(*nissaraṇa*).[58] We will try to follow the same way given in the *sutta* and discuss the three topics separately and finally to seek to form a generalization.

The psychological characteristics come under the names of *āsava* (漏)[59] (latent tendencies) and *anusaya* (隨眠)[60] form the deepest layer of the human psyche. *Kāmāsava* (欲漏), *bhavāsava* (有漏) and *avijjāsava* (無明漏)[61] (sometimes *diṭṭhāsava*-見漏) can only be removed by attaining the knowledge called *āsavakkhayañāṇa* (漏斷智) whose attainment establishes the enlightenment.[62] The desire to please senses with

58 This method has been used in many contexts by the Buddhists to reach a conclusion of a certain matter. MN I. 65 (*Cūlasīhanādasutta*)

59 S. Dasgupta, *A History of Indian Philosophy* Vol. I, pp.99-100 on *āsavas*: "Childers translates "*āsava*" as "depravities" and Mrs. Rhys Davids as "intoxicants". The word *āsava* in Sanskrit means "old wine". It is derived from "*su*" to produce by Buddhaghosa and the meaning that he gives to it is "*ciraparivāsikatthena*" (on account of its being stored up for a long time like wine). They work through the eye and the mind and continue to produce all beings up to Indra. As those wine which are kept long are called "*āsavas*" so these are also called *asavas* for remaining for long time. The other alternative that Buddhaghosa gives is that they are called *āsava* on account of their producing *saṁsāradukkha* (sorrows of the world), *Atthasālinī*, p. 48. (Contrast it with Jaina *āsrava* flowing in of karma matter). Finding it difficult to translate it in one word after Buddhaghosa, I have translated it as "depravities" after Childers".

60 *Anusaya* has been translated in to English as bent, bias, proclivities, the persistence of dormant or latent disposition, predisposition, and tendency (PED, 44). These are enumerated as seven in several places in the canon. They are: proclivity of sense desire (*kāmarāgānusaya*-欲貪隨眠), proclivity of anger (*paṭhighānusaya*-瞋恚隨眠), proclivity of view (*diṭṭhānusaya*-見隨眠), proclivity of doubt (*vicikicchānusaya*- 疑隨眠), proclivity of conceit (*mānānusaya*- 慢隨眠), proclivity for rebirth (*bhavarāgānusaya*- 有貪隨眠), and proclivity of ignorance (*avijjānusaya*- 無明隨眠): DN III.254

61 MN.I.55:*Tayo'me āvuso āsavā: kāmāsavo bhavāsavo avijjāsavo.*

62 MN.I.23; T2, 666c:我復以三昧，心清淨、無瑕穢，亦無結使、心意得定、得無所畏、得盡漏心，亦知此苦如實不虛。當我爾時得此

pleasant objects is called *kāmāsava* and the desire to continue in the existence is called *bhavāsava*. *Avijjā āsava* functions to form the wrong view of a 'self' (*atta*- 我), which provokes the person to seek gratification in an eternal existence.[63] The *Sammādiṭṭhisutta* has pointed out that *āsava*s function as the condition for ignorance and when they are removed (*khīnā-sava*- 漏斷) ignorance breaks up.[64] In the *Mahāmāluṅkyasutta* 《五下分結經》,[65] the Buddha says that latent disposition of sensual desire (*kāmārāgānusaya*- 欲使/欲貪隨眠) is active even in the baby lying with the back. As it is recorded:

> A young tender infant lying prone does not even the notion 'sensual pleasures', so how could sensual desire arise in him? Yet underlying tendency to sensual lust lies within him.[66]

It can be seen that craving for sense-pleasures has been understood by Buddhists as so deep phenomenon and it causes the being to continue in the cyclic course of birth and death.

According to the *Paṭiccasamuppāda* theory, craving (*taṇhā*) is conditioned by sensation (*vedanā*- 痛/覺/受)[67] and craving conditions attachment (*upādāna*- 取)[68] and attachment

---

心時，欲漏、有漏、無明漏，心得解脫。以得解脫，便得解脫智，生、死已盡，梵行已立，所作已辦，更不復受胎。如實知之，是謂梵志，我後夜時得第三明。

63 D.J. Kalupahana, *Buddhist Philosophy A Historical Analysis*,p.38

64 MNI.54: *Āsavasamudayā avijjā samudayo, āsavanirodhā avijjānirodho*

65 MN.I.432-437;T1,778c~780b

66 MN I.433; *MLDB. p.* 538; T1, 778c: 鬘童子！非為眾多異學來，以嬰孩童子責數喻詰責汝耶？鬘童子！嬰孩幼小，柔軟、仰眠，意無欲想。況復欲心纏住耶？然彼性使故，說欲使。

67 DN II.56; T1, 60b: 受是愛緣。

68 Ibid: *Taṇhā-paccayā upādānaṁ*; T1,60b: 愛是取緣。

conditions becoming (*bhava*- 有).[69] In this line of causes and conditions, *taṇhā* functions to get the person attached to sensual pleasures (*kāmūpādāna*- 欲取), views (*diṭṭhūpādāna*-見取), religious practices (*sīlabbatūpādāna*-戒取) and self-notions (*attavādūpādāna*- 我取).[70] The sensual objects are not understood in nature problematic but attachment to them causes suffering.[71] Attachment or inclination to a certain aspect of experience causes the person to wish to continuously get the same experience and in turn it leads to the continuous becoming. From the limb *taṇhā* to *bhava* (*kāma*, *rūpa*, and *arūpa*- 欲有,色有,無色有) all have included sensuality as one aspect of them. So, we can understand that sensual desire is a crucial factor to make the person turn in the cycle of existence. Based on this understanding, Buddhists have tried to explain it in various ways and to show how it brings about suffering.

The *Mahādukkhakkhandhasutta* 《苦蘊 經》 merely refers to the five codes of sense pleasures as the gratification of sensuality (*kāma*) but it does not try to explain the nature of this pleasure as it has been done in other places in the *Suttapiṭaka*. The *Khaggavisāṇasutta* in the *Sutta Nipāta* 《經集》 describes the alluring nature of sensual pleasures as follows:

> For sensual pleasures, variegated, sweet (and) delightful, disturb the mind with their manifold form.[72]

In the *Aṅguttara-Nikāya* 《增支部》, sensual pleasure is defined in the context of sexual pleasure by referring to the man

---

[69] Ibid: *Upādāna-paccayā bhavo*; T1,60b: 取是有緣。

[70] Ibid. 58; T1,60c

[71] D. KALUPAHANA, *The Principles of Buddhist Psychology*, p. 97

[72] Sn 50: *Kāmā hi citrā madhurā manoramā-virūparūpena mathenti cittaṁ*; Sn 766: *Kāmaṁ kāmayamānassa tassa ce taṁ samijjhati, addhā pīti mano hoti laddhā macco yadicchati*

and female as proving the highest sensual pleasure for each other.[73]

As this *sutta* was taught to the monks who have already left the sensual world, it might not need to deal in detail the aspect of gratification.

Following the short reference to sensual gratification, the *sutta* begins to describe the adverse effects (*ādīnava*) of sensual desire. There have been mentioned a few examples related to day to day struggles faced by people. The examples can be divided into two as personal suffering and interpersonal conflicts:

	Personal conflicts	Interpersonal conflicts
1	The householder undergoes suffering in earning the living[74]	
2	His all effort to earn wealth become fruitless[75]	
3	After gain property, he labours to guard and protect them[76]	

[73] AN I.1

[74] T1, 585a (MA): 族姓子者，隨其伎術以自存活，或作田業、或行治生、或以學書、或明算術、或知工數、或巧刻印、或作文章、或造手筆、或曉經書、或作勇將、或奉事王。彼，寒時則寒，熱時則熱；飢渴，疲勞；蚊、虻所蜇。

[75] Ibid. 作如是業，求圖錢財。彼族姓子，如是方便、作如是行、作如是求。若不得錢財者，便生憂苦、愁慼、懊惱、心則生癡；作如是說：『唐作、唐苦，所求無果。』

4		i. The kings, Brahmins, nobles, householders quarrels with one another[77] ii. Mother-son, father-son, brother-sister, and friend-friend quarrel mutually. [78]
5		People divide into two array and fight with one another using destructive weapons.[79]
6		Using various war techniques, people attack one another and get into serous injuries and finally go to death.[80]

---

76 Ibid.作如是求，若得錢財者，彼便愛惜，守護密藏...彼作如是，守護密藏。若有王奪、賊劫、火燒、腐壞、亡失，便生憂苦、愁慼、懊惱、心則生癡。

77 Ibid. 眾生，因欲、緣欲、以欲為本故，王，王共諍；梵志，梵志共諍；居士，居士共諍；民，民共諍；國，國共諍。See: Chapter III.III. 18 & 19 with the sub-sections regarding the differences in presenting this matter in the Pali and Chinese versions.

78 Ibid. 復次，眾生，因欲、緣欲、以欲為本故，母共子諍，子共母諍；父子、兄弟、姉妹、親族展轉共諍。彼既如是共鬪諍已；母說子惡，子說母惡；父子、兄弟、姉妹、親族更相說惡，況復他人？是謂現法苦陰；因欲、緣欲、以欲為本。This fact has been more elaborative by referring to the denial by each other whereas the Pali version only mentions of quarrel between two parties. See:Chapter III.III. 18 & 19 with the sub-sections.

79 T1, 846f (ACT): 此眾生，因婬故、至增上婬故，使著鎧、便執弓箭、或著皮鎧、持極利刀，相 圍聚鬪。

80 T1, 585a (MA): 復次，眾生，因欲、緣欲、以欲為本故，著鎧被袍、持矟弓箭、或執刀往奪他國、攻城破塢、共相格戰、打鼓吹角、高聲喚呼、或以槌打、或以鉾戟、或以利輪、或以箭射、或亂

7		Commit anti-social activities such as breaking into houses, plundering wealth and seducing others' wives etc. On being caught in offence, are subjected to fierce punishments and sometimes subject to death.[81]
8	Having conduct various misconducts, the person repents for them at his verge of death.[82]	
9	Engage in misconduct of body, speech and mind. Consequently,	

下石、或以大弩、或以融銅珠子灑之。彼當鬪時，或死、或怖，受極重苦。是謂現法苦陰；因欲、緣欲、以欲為本。

81 Ibid. 復次，眾生、因欲、緣欲，以欲為本故，著鎧被袍，持矟弓箭或執刀楯入村、入邑、入國、入城。穿牆發藏，劫奪財物，斷截王路或至他巷，壞村、害邑、滅國、破城。於中或為王人所捉；種種考治：截手、截足或截手足...彼在其中或死或怖，受極重苦。是謂現法苦陰；因欲、緣欲，以欲為本。

82 T1, 585b (MA): 復次，眾生、因欲、緣欲，以欲為本故，行身惡行，行口、意惡行，彼於後時，疾病著床，或坐臥地。以苦逼身，受極重苦，不可愛樂。彼若有身惡行，口、意惡行，彼臨終時，在前覆障，猶日將沒大山崗側，影障覆地。如是，彼若有身惡行，口、意惡行，在前覆障，彼作是念：『我本惡行，在前覆我。我本不作福業，多作惡業。若使有人作惡、凶暴，唯為罪；不作福，不行善，無所畏，無所依，無所歸。隨生處者，我必生彼。』從是有悔，悔者不善死，無福命終，是謂現法苦陰；因欲、緣欲、以欲為本。
This idea is found only in the MA and ACT versions whereas both the Pāli and EA versions miss it.

	after death, reappear in states of deprivation, in an unhappy destination, in perdition, even in hell.[83]	

The issues selected to show how people get into various perils due to sensual desire belong to the first category of suffering, *dukkha dukkha* (苦苦)[84] or ordinary suffering. W. RAHULA briefly explains the nature of ordinary suffering as follows:

> All kinds of suffering like birth, old age, sickness, death, association with unpleasant persons and conditions, not getting what one desires, grief, lamentation, distress-all such forms of physical and mental suffering, which are universally accepted as suffering or pain, are included in *dukkha* as ordinary suffering (*dukkha dukkha*).[85]

When we compare the above mentioned eight conditions with the RAHULA's explanation, it can be understood that the *sutta* has presented an account of ordinary suffering. And also, we can conceive it as an attempt to remind the people of the terror of ordinary suffering to which they are unknowingly subject.

83 Ibid. 復次，眾生，因欲、緣欲，以欲為本故，行身惡行，行口、意惡行；彼因身、口、意惡行故，因此，緣此，身壞命終，必至惡處，生地獄中。是謂後世苦陰；因欲、緣欲、以欲為本，是謂欲患。

84 Vism p. 499: divides suffering into tree types: 1. ordinary suffering (*dukkha dukkha*-苦苦) 2. suffering due to change (*vipariṇāma dukkkha*-壞苦) 3. suffering as conditioned states (*saṁkhāra dukkha*- 行苦).

85 W. RAHULA, *What the Buddha Taught*, p.19

The painful experiences given here reflect individual unrest, social instability and moral degeneration as phenomena arisen from attachment to sensual pleasures. In order to gain sensual objects, both at personal level and interpersonal, the human society struggles. This is a universal experience can be seen everywhere in the world.

On one hand, as the Buddha's teaching was an answer to the social unrest in contemporary India,[86] we can understand the description given to illustrate danger of sensuality as a criticism of contemporary social ideology. In the Brahmin society, the householder was the foundation of society and he was given to seeking sense pleasures both as personal pleasure and as a support to family life, to beget children. Without encouraging gratifying desires, it is difficult to maintain the secular society. The Brahmin society was a secular society and consequently its social foundation ideologically was based on 'desire'.[87] The desire based society encouraged people to gain more and more objects pleasing to minds and this trend led society to a competition. Finally, from the family level to the international level, every group in the society was forced to use quarreling, waging war, and committing immoral acts to possess what was wished. This unrest might have created a chaotic situation in the society, which is reflected in the *Mahādukkhakkhandhasutta* 《苦蘊 經》. The Buddha being an enlightened person understood that all conflicts in life were the results of the attachment to sensuality.

The religious groups, who denied the indulgence to sensuality, took an extreme attitude against it and selected the way of self torturing to eradicate desires. The Buddha's position was different from them; he pointed out that one should not fall to self-torture but should root out desire and lust to

86 R. GOMBRICH, *How Buddhism Began*, p.3

87 R. GOMBRICH, *Theravada Buddhism*, p.47

sensual objects, that is the way to avoid (*nissaraṇa*) all those anguishes come from desire.

Material Form (*rūpa*- 色)

The material form in this *sutta* means the female body. It is examined through the three aspects of gratification, danger and escape. The gratification of the material form (body) is the pleasure derived through the beauty and loveliness in the young girl who possesses all the feminine features which were the ideal qualities expected from a woman.[88]

In the *Suttapiṭaka*, *rūpa* (色) has been dominantly used in the two senses of visible object (*rūpāyatana*- 色處) and the physical body (*rūpakkhandha*- 色蘊).[89] As the context implies, the colourfulness (*vaṇṇanibha*- 美色/妙色) and the beauty in the body pleases the senses and thereby people get attached to it. Particularly, in the context of sensuality, female body (*rūpa*) functions as the highest pleasing object to the male.[90]

After brief reference to the gratification of the body, the text begins to discuss the danger (*ādīnava*) of the material form. The beauty and loveliness of the woman, which brought pleasure is subject to change. With the course of time, the lady gets old and loses the beauty of her bodily parts, teeth

---

88 MN.I.88: *Ko ca bhikkhave rūpānaṁ assādo: Seyyathāpi bhikkhave khattiyakaññā vā brāhmaṇakaññā vā gahapatikaññā vā paṇṇarasavassuddesikā vā soḷasavassuddesikā vā nâtidīghā nâtirassā nâtikisā nâtithūlā nâtikāḷī na accodātā, paramā sā bhikkhave tasmiṁ samaye subhā vaṇṇanibhā ti.– Evaṁ bhante.– Yaṁ kho bhikkhave subhaṁ vaṇṇanibhaṁ paṭicca uppajjati sukhaṁ somanassaṁ ayaṁ rūpānaṁ assādo*;T1,585c: 云何色味？若剎利女、梵志、居士、工師女，年十四、五。彼於爾時，美色最妙。若因彼美色，緣彼美色故，生樂，生喜。

89 SN III. *Khandha Vagga* and IV.*Saḷāyatana Vagga* have dealt in detail on these two shades of the '*rūpa*'.

90 AN.I.1; T2, 563a: 世尊告諸比丘：我於此眾中，不見一法最勝、最妙，眩惑世人，不至永寂，縛著牢獄，無有解已；所謂男子見女色已，便起想著，意甚愛敬，令人不至永寂。

broken, hair gets grey etc. No longer, we can find the beauty in her. This is an unpleasant experience for the person who once has admired and enjoyed the beauty of the female body.[91]

Getting older (*jarā-* 老) is one aspect of ordinary suffering and when one experiences it, he or she loses the bodily control and needs others' support to maintain any posture. Finally, one has to lie within one's own excrements.[92] In a person who undergoes such an infirmity, no beauty is available.

The *sutta* produces the list of nine stages (*navasīvathika-* 九墓節) which the dead body undergoes until it reaches to the state of dust.[93] It is obvious that this is the process to undergo by any person born into this world. By referring to this common life experience or universal truth of decay and death, the Buddha tries to show that what is madly loved and appreciated is not under our control and it is inevitable to destroy. In many places of the *Suttapiṭaka*, the decadent nature of the physical body has been explained.[94] The Buddhist understanding of the physical form is thus:

---

91 MN.I.88

92 Ibid.

93 Ibid.

94 MN II.65: *Añjanī'va navā cittā putikāyo alankato-alaṁ bālassa mohāya no ca pāragavesino*; SN.III.120: *kiṁ te Vakkali iminā pūtikāyena*; DN.II.293: *Puna ca paraṁ bhikkhave bhikkhu imaṁ eva kāyaṁ uddhaṁ pādatalā adho kesa-matthakā taca-pariyantaṁ pūraṁ nānappakarassa asucino paccavekkhati: 'Atthi imasmiṁ kāye kesā lomā nakhā dantā taco mamsaṁ nahāru aṭṭhi aṭṭhi-miñjā vakkaṁ hadayaṁ yakanaṁ kilomakaṁ pihakaṁ papphāsaṁ antaṁ anta-guṇaṁ udariyaṁ karīsaṁ pittaṁ semhaṁ pubbo lohitaṁ sedo medo assu vasā khelo singhānikā lasikā muttan ti'* ; T1,583b: 復次，比丘！比丘者，觀身如身：此身隨住、隨其好惡、從頭至足；觀見種種不淨充滿：我此身中有髮、髦、爪、齒、麤細薄膚、皮、肉、筋、骨、心、腎、肝、肺、大腸、小腸、脾、胃、摶糞、腦及腦根、淚、汗、涕、唾、膿、血、肪、髓、涎、膽、小便; T2,568a: 於是，比丘觀此身隨其性行，從頭至足，從足至頭；

> Four elements condition it. Which is conditioned it is subject to change. If some thing changes, it brings about suffering.[95]

This description frequently occurs in the context of bodily contemplation (*kāyānupassanā*- 觀身) in the *Satipaṭṭhanāsutta*-s.[96] In addition to the use of body as a meditation object, in many places, there are attempt to deconstruct the beauty of the female body, especially in the context where the male practitioners stand as the listeners of the discussion.[97]

In order to avoid the painful experiences arisen from the body (no matter it is male or female), one should give up the lust and desire for the body. Once the person realizes that the body and its beauty are not eternal and no one can control its changing, then it is easy for him to cultivate non-attachment to them (*nibbidā*- 厭離). Moreover, it is not a

---

觀此身中皆悉不淨，無有可貪；復觀此身有毛、髮、爪、齒、皮、肉、筋、骨、髓、腦、脂膏、腸、胃、心、肝、脾、腎之屬。皆悉觀知：屎、尿、生熟二藏、目淚、唾、涕、血脈、肪、膽。

95 CDB p.595:S.II.94

96 MN I.58; DN.II.294

97 *Theragāthā* I.279-280: Venerable Nandaka, according to the *Theragāthā commentary*, was going for alms and met his former wife who tried to seduce him. And then he said: A curse upon bodies, evil-smelling, on Mara's side, oozing; there are nine streams in your body which flow all the time; *Th*.I.p.1150-1160: Once Maggallāna has uttered this word to a female: You little hut made of a chain of bones, sewn together with flesh and sinew. Fie upon the evil-smelling body. You cherish those who have another's limbs. You bag of dung, tied up with skin, you demoness with lumps on your breast. There are nine streams in your body which flow all the time. Your body with its nine streams makes an evil smell and is obstructed by dung. A *bhikkhu* desiring purity avoids it as one avoids excrement.

solution to hate the body[98] and give pains to it as certain Indian religious seekers did.[99]

Feeling (*vedanā*- 痛/覺)

Feeling is understood in Buddhist psychology as present in every sort of experience. It is mentioned in the *Paṭicca-samuppāda* formula that feeling is conditioned by contact (*phassa paccayā vedanā*).[100] Here '*phassa*' (觸) means the contact between the internal sense organs with their corr-esponding external objects; according to the nature of the object, the feeling becomes three fold: pleasant, unpleasant and neutral. It is described in the texts as follows:

> *Bhikkhu*-s, in dependence on a contact to be experienced as pleasant, a pleasant feeling arises....In dependence on a contact to be experienced as painful, a painful feeling arises...In dependence on a contact to be experienced as neither- painful –nor pleasant , a as neither- painful –nor pleasant feeling arises.[101]

In order to understand the meaning of the term *vedanā*, it is useful to refer to the Mrs. RHYS DAVIDS' remark:

> *Vedanā* is term of great import, meaning sentience or reaction, bodily or mental, on contact or impression. Sensation is scarcely so loyal a rendering as feeling,

---

98 S. Hamilton, op.cit. pp.169-189: has well explained the early Buddhist attitude to body.

99 MN.I.92: '*kinnu tumhe, āvuso, nigaṇṭhā ubbhaṭṭhakā āsanapaṭikkhittā, opakkamikā dukkhā tibbā kharā kaṭukā vedanā vedayathā*'ti...? T1,587b:我往問曰：諸尼揵！汝等何故行此不坐行，常立、不坐，受如是苦？彼如是說：瞿曇！我有尊師尼揵，名曰親子，彼則教我作如是說； MN.II.218; T1,442c: 世尊告諸比丘：諸尼乾等如是見、如是說：謂人所受皆因本作，若其故業，因苦行滅，不造新者，則諸業盡；諸業盡已，則得苦盡，得苦盡已，則得苦邊。

100 DN II.58; T1, 60b: 觸是受緣。

101 CDB p.596

> for though *vedanā* is often qualified as ' born of contact', in sense activity, it is always defined generally as consisting of the three species- pleasure (happiness), pain (ill) and neutral feeling- a hedonistic aspect to which the term 'feeling' is alone adequate.[102]

According to the *Dhammasaṅganī*, the dominant character of *vedanā* is that it enjoys the taste of object.[103] The problem of the feeling is that they lead to the person to wish for, to thirst for the experience (*taṇhā*).[104] Pleasant feelings induce an attachment (*upādāna-* 取) to a pleasant object. There is potency in pleasant feelings to arouse sensuous greed (*rāgānusaya-* 貪隨眠), in painful feelings to arouse anger and hatred (*paṭighānusaya-* 瞋恚隨眠).[105] It is also mentioned in the Pāli canon that greed emerges due to unwise reflection (*ayonisomansikāra-* 非如理作意) on an attractive object and hate through unwise reflection on a repulsive object.

Greed (*lobha* or *rāga*) comprises all degrees of 'attractiveness' towards an object from the faintest trace of personal desire up to gross egoism, whilst hatred (*dosa-* 瞋) comprises all degrees of 'repulsion' from the faintest trace of ill-humour to the highest pitch of hate and wrath.[106]

It is a special characteristic in the *Mahādukkhakkhandhasutta* that it has discussed feeling in the context of *jhānic* experience. Here the Buddha sees the pleasure of four *jhānic* attainments as higher level experience of pleasurable feeling in relative to the pleasant feeling arisen from sensual gratification.

When a monk attains the first *jhāna*, which is gained

---

[102] C.A.F. Rhys Davids, *Buddhist Psychological Ethics*, p. 6

[103] *The Expositor*, p.145

[104] DN.II.58; T1,60b: 受是愛緣

[105] MN.I.303

[106] Nyanatiloka Thera 1980: 94

> through seclusion from sensual pleasure and unwholesome states, and is accompanied by applied and sustained thought, with rapture and pleasure born of seclusion, he does not choose for his own affliction, or for another's affliction, or for the affliction of both. On that occasion he feels only feeling that is free from affliction. The freedom from affliction is the highest gratification in the case of feelings. On attainment of the second, third and fourth *jhāna*-s with their characteristics, the monk only feels the feeling that is free from affliction for him, affliction for others, or for the both sides. He feels only the feeling that is free from affliction.[107]

In this case, the key word to get clarified is, freedom from affliction '*avyābajja*', which is recognized as the highest pleasurable feeling amidst feelings. The PTS Pāli-English Dictionary includes two entries for '*Avyāpajjha*' (*abyābajjha*). The first entry, which functions as a neutral noun, has the meanings of 'kindness of heart' (不念害者成就是樂) and 'freedom from suffering, that is *nibbāna* (Vin I.183: *avyāpajjhadhimutta*; *Itivuttatka* p.31: *abyābajjhārāma*). This word also functions as an adjective and then stands for the meanings, free from oppression or injury; not hurting and kind.[108] This word occurs in the *sutta*-s in combination with the word '*avera*' (avera+avyāpajjha).[109] In accordance with the context of the *Mahādukkhakkhandhasutta* 《苦蘊 經》, it can be said that the meaning of the "*avyābajja*" is confined to 'kindness', go beyond selfishness or it can mean 'loving-kindness' (*mettā*-慈悲)

---

107 MLDB p.184f; T1, 586a (MA): 云何覺味？比丘者，離欲， 離惡不善之法，至得第四禪成就遊。彼於爾時，不念自害，亦不念害他。若不念害者，是謂覺樂味。所以者何 ？ 不念害者，成就是樂，是謂覺味。

108 PED p. 86

109 DN II.242, 276

which is indicated as one of the fourfold immeasurable.[110]

What is significant is that instead of the pleasantness of the experience, it is subject to change and impermanent. In the *Anattalakkhaṇasutta* 《無我相經》, it is mentioned that feeling is not *atta* (我) because it is subject to impermanence and in turn brings about suffering.[111] Therefore, treating it as self is illogical. In many places in the Pāli canon, the evanescent nature of feeling has been discussed.[112]

The *jhānic* attainments are not considered as stable or final solution to the *saṁsāric* problem,[113] so is the certain experiences or feelings felt within a *jhānic* (*jhāna/dhyāna*-stance) experience. During the course of *jhānic* experience, if the practitioner attaches to the feeling of non-affliction, it would cause him to generate sensuous desire for (*rāgānusaya*-貪隨眠) the feeling,[114] whereby he generates sort of attachment to it. On the other hand, as the *jhāna*s are temporary states, they are very easy change, so the feeling of non-affliction. When the practitioner loses this pleasing experience, it is possible that he would feel anguish or disappointment. Such a condition will lead him to hang on the existence. This is the danger of feeling as discussed in the *Mahādukkhakkhandhasutta* 《苦蘊經》.

According to the *Mahādukkhakkhandhasutta* 《苦蘊 經》, based on the understanding that the feeling of non-affliction is the highest feeling to be experienced by an unenlightened

110 *Visuddhimagga* 296ff

111 Vin.I.13;T22,879a

112 SN. IV.214: *Tisso imā bhikkhave vedanā aniccā sankhatā paṭiccasamuppannā khayadhammā vayadhammā virāgadhammā nirodhadhammā.*

113 MN.I.163-166

114 P. DE. SILVA, *Buddhist and Freudian Psychology*, p.58: Pleasant feelings induce an attachment (*upādāna*) to pleasant objects and there is potency in pleasant feelings to arouse latent sensuous greed (*rāgānusaya*).

person and that it is still subject to change and is impermanent, one should give up the desire and lust for it, which is the way to freedom from suffering.

Conclusion

Three doctrinal topics discussed above, such as sensuality, material form (body) and feeling, all can be interpreted as the subtle manifestation of craving, *taṇhā*, which is recognized as the cause of suffering in the context of Four Noble Truths. In this discussion, the first and second topics show a great relation to the sensualistic people. In the Pāli canon, lay people are recognized as given to sensuality (*gihī kāmabhogino odātavasanā*), wherein the five strands of sense pleasures (*pañcakāmaguṇa*-妙欲/五欲) and feminine beauty function at head.[115] (However, the monks are also frequently advised not to fall back again to this realm). These two aspects in life are dominant in a society which is based on desire (*taṇhā*). Both the desire for five sense pleasures and desire for feminine beauty can be traced to latent tendency of sensual pleasure (*kāmāsava*- 欲漏), which is one mode of craving.

The third topic *vedanā* has been examined in the context of spiritual seekers, who possess contemplative states called *jhāna* (禪/靜慮). The Buddha finds that the feeling of non-affliction experienced during the first four *jhānic* states is the highest among the feelings felt by the unenlightened person, yet it is still subject to change. So, it can bring about suffering (*yadiniccaṁ taṁ dukkhaṁ*). Therefore, one has to give up the desire and lust for this feeling.

At the end of discussing the gratification and problematic aspect of these phenomena, the Buddha advises to give up

---

115 *Elders' Verses*, p. 47; *Theragāthā* I.455-456: *rūpā saddā rasā gandhā phoṭṭhabbā ca manoramā; pañca kāmaguṇā ete itthirupasmiṁ dissare.*

the desire (*chandarāgappahāna-* 除貪欲) for them. From this emphasis to eradicate lust and desire, we can assume that the cause of suffering, (*dukkhakkhandha-* 苦蘊) is desire or in the early doctrinal terminology, *taṇhā* (craving), which is understood in the *Dhammacakkappavattanasutta* 《轉法輪 經》 as the cause of suffering. So, we can conclude that the discussion of suffering in the *Mahādukkhakkhandhasutta* 《苦蘊 經》 has been revolved on the idea that craving is the reason of suffering.

Abbreviations

AN	*Aṅguttara Nikāya*
ACT	Anonymous Chinese Translation
CDB	The Connected Discourses of the Buddha (translation of the *Samyutta Nikaya*)
DN	*Dīgha Nikāya*
DPPN	Dictionary of Pāli Proper Names
EA	*Ekottara Āgama*
MN	*Majjhima Nikāya*
MA	*Madhyama Āgama*
MLDB	*The Middle Length Discourses of the Buddha* (translation of the *Majjhima Nikāya*)
PED	Pali-English Dictionary
SN	*Saṃyutta Nikāya*
Sn	*Sutta Nipāta*
Th.I.	*Theragāthā*
Vin	*Vinaya*
Vism	*Visuddhimagga*

Bibliography

Primary Sources

The Pali references have been quoted from the Editions of the London Pali Text Society.

Sīlakkhandhavaggaṭṭhakathā (*Sumangalāvilasini*) Part I (*Devanāgari* Edition), Maharastra: Vipassana Research Institute,1998.
《大正新脩大藏經》第一冊 No. 1《長阿含經》
《大正新脩大藏經》 第一冊 No. 26《中阿含經》
《大正新脩大藏經》第二冊 No. 99《雜阿含經》
《大正新脩大藏經》第二冊 No. 125《增壹阿含經》
《大正新脩大藏經》第二十二冊 No. 1428《四分律》
《南傳大藏經總索引》Part II

Secondary Sources

BURLINGAME, Eugene Watson.
(1922). *Buddhist Parables: Translated from the Original Pāli.* New Haven: Yale University Press.
DASGUPTA, Surendranath.
(1992). *A History of Indian Philosophy* Vol. I. (repri.). Delhi: Motilal Banarsidass
FRAUWALLNER, Erich.
(1993). *History of Indian Philosophy*, Vol. I. (trans.) Bedekar, V.M. (repri.) Delhi: Motilal Banarsidass.
GETHIN, Rupert.
(1988). *The Foundations of Buddhism*. Oxford: Oxford University Press.
(1997). Wrong View (micchā-ditthi) and Right View (sammā-ditthi) in the Theravada Abhidhamma in *Recent Researches in Buddhist Studies.* 211- 229. *Essays in Honour of Professor Y. Karunadasa.* Eds. K. L. Dhammajoti, Asanga Tilakaratne and Kapila Abhayawansa. Colombo: Y. Karunadasa Felicitation Committee in Collaboration with Chi Ying Foundation, Hong Kong.
GOMBRICH, Richard F.
(1996). How *Buddhism Began The Conditioned Genesis of the Early Teachings.* London: The Athlone Press.
(2002). *Theravāda Buddhism: A Social History from Ancient Benares to Modern Colombo.* (repr.). London: Routledge.

HAMILTON, Sue.
(1996). Identity *and Experience: The Constitution of the Human Being According to Early Buddhism*. London: Luzac Oriental.

HARVEY, P.
(2013). *An Introduction to Buddhism: Teaching, History and Practise.*Second Ed. New York: Cambridge University Press.

HORNER, I.B.
(1990). *Women Under Primitive Buddhism*. (repr.). Delhi: Motilal Banarsidass.

KALUPAHANA, David J.
(1977). *Buddhist Philosophy A Historical Analysis*. Honolulu: The University of Hawaii(2nd print.)
(1992). *The Principles of Buddhist Psychology*. 1st Indian edition. Delhi: Sri Satguru Publications.

Nyanatiloka Thera.
(1980). *Buddhist Dictionary: Manual of Buddhist Terms and Doctrines*. Kandy: Buddhist Publication Society.

PADMASIRI DE SILVA, M.W.
(1992). *Buddhist and Freudian Psychology*. (Third Edition). Singapore: University Press, Singapore.

RAHULA, Walpola.
(1974). *What the Buddha Taught*. 2nd ed. New York: Grove Press.

RHYS DAVIDS, Caroline A. F.
(1990). *A Buddhist Manual of Psychological Ethics*. London: Royal Asiatic Society.

WILLIAMS, Paul and TRIBE, Anthony.
(2002). *Buddhist Thought*. (repri.). London and New York: Routledge.

Dictionaries

MALASEKERA, G. P.
(1983). *Dictionary of Pali Proper Names*. 2 Vols. New Delhi: Oriental Books Reprint Corporation (1st Indian edition).

RHYS DAVIDS, T.W., and STEDE, William, (1986). *Pali-English Dictionary*. London: The Pali Text Society.

The *Bhesajjamañjūsā*: A Study on the Pāli Medical Treatise from the Perspective of Applied Buddhism

Dipak Kumar BARUA[*]

The Four Noble Truths of Suffering (*dukkha-ariya-saccāni*), viz. (i) Suffering (*dukkha*), (ii) Origin or Cause of Suffering (*dukkha-samudaya*); (iii) Cessation of Suffering (*dukkha-nirodha*); (iv) and the path leading to the cessation of suffering (*dukkha-nirodhagāminī-paṭipadā*); as enunciated by Gautama (Pāli Gotama) the Buddha (see Vin. I.10; S. I.62, V.420; *Kindred Sayings* I.86) are equally applicable to Medical Science as illness, causes of illnesses, cure from illnesses and steps to be taken for the cure from illnesses. Buddha is, in fact, aware of illness- both physical and mental of His followers. In both the cases, He has prescribed some measures for them. His discourses as collected in the *Vinaya-Piṭaka* bear ample testimony to this effect. After His sacred demise, His unique discourses have been explained by His disciples in the Commentaries and Sub Commentaries. Thus in course of time came into existence a medical treatise like the *Bhesajjamañjūsā* (*Bhes*, Skt. *Bhaisajyamañjūsā*) in Pāli verses composed in sixty *paddhati*-s or chapters (?) by a Buddhist monk-scholar of Sri Lanka during the thirteenth century. Unfortunately, the name of its author is not known. But its colophon notes that this has

* Former Professor and Head, Department of Pali, University of Calcutta, Kolkata, W.B. and former Director, Nava Nalanda Mahavihar, Nalanda, Bihar, India.

been written by a *thera* or senior Buddhist monk-scholar who hails from a Brāhmaṇa family and becomes the 'Head of the Group of Monastic Colleges' in the Śaka Year 1183, i.e. CE 1261 when King Parakkama, i.e. Parākramabāhu II (CE 1236-1270), was reigning in the city of Jambudoni, identified with Dambadeniya in Sri Lanka, as the following colophon reveals:

> *sāke parakkamabujavha-narinda jambuddoṇī puramhi nivasaṁ gajakūṭasaṅkhe brahmanvayo yatirakāsi bhisakk-atantaṁ etañca pañcapariveṇasamūhanātho* (LIYANARATNE 1996: 1).

In the above statement, the author has informed of his profession only without mentioning his personal name. Besides, his modesty has been manifest in the remaining portion of that colophon, wherein he has narrated the purpose of writing the same in the following words:

> *khyātisammānalābhādi nirapekkhena kevalaṁ*
> *idaṁ tantaṁ paratthāya racayantena yaṁ mayā*
> *sambhataṁ kusalaṁ tena āsavānaṁ khayāvadhi*
> *sabbaṁ lokaṁ sukhayituṁ pabhaveyya bhave bhave.*
> (LIYANARATNE 1996: 2)
> "Without expecting material gain, such as, fame and distinctions, but solely for the benefit of others, with the hope that thanks to the merit thus acquired, he may be able to bring happiness to all beings in all his future existences until the Extinction of Inclinations, i.e. attainment of Nibbāna".

But Pandit Aryadasa KUMARASINGHE, a celebrated *Āyurvedic* physician of Sri Lanka and editor of several *Āyurvedic* treatises, based on a colophon opines that the name of the author of the Bhes is Anomadassi Saṅgharāja as the following passage records (LIYANARATNE 1996: 2):

> *siri laṁkāyaṁ chaṭṭha-parakkamabāhu bhūmipālassa samaye* (Parākramabahu II of Dambadiya during 1236-1270 and not Parākramabāhu VI of Kotte of A.C. 1412-

67) *taṁ rājadhānibhūte jambudoṇīnagare vihitavāsena brāhmaṇavaṁsāvataṁsena paṁcapariveṇamelā dhipena dasamahātheravarānaṁ sahassāva- dhāninām aññatame-na sabbatantassa tantena tipiṭakavācissar- ācariyena paṁ-ḍitasiromaṇinā sirimatā anomadassī saṁgharājappavaren-a saṁkalitā bhesajjamañjūsā samattā.*

On the other hand, Ven. Vilegoda Dhammakīrti Śrī Dharmā-nanda or Vilegoda Dhammānanda in the introductory rema-rks of his edition of the *Bhesajjamañjūsā-Sanne* or *Sannaya*, a word-for-word explanation in Sinhala, has noted, without quoting any source or supplying any evidence, that the Bhes has been composed by Pañcamūlapariveṇādhipati Maṁgala Saṁgharāja Māhimi.

About the authorship of the *Bhesajjamañjūsā* has remarked G. P. Malalasekera (1958: 215) as follows: "In a Sinhalese medic-al work, *Yoga-ratnākara*, compiled about the fourteenth cent-ury, a verse in the colophon states that that work was arran-ged on the plan of the *Mañjūsā* (i.e. Bhes), a medical work in Pāli stanzas, composed by Atthadassī Thera about the year A.D. 1267." If this information is correct, the author is undo-ubtedly our Pañca-mūla-pariveṇa-adhipati. However, about the name of the author of the Bhes nothing could be said definitely at the present stage.

A critical edition of the Bhes chapters, 1-18; has been publis-hed under the editorship of Jinadasa Liyanaratne (1996) who has also rendered into English those 18 Chapters with the title *The Casket of Medicine* (2002) (Bhes, Chapters 1-18) publi-shed by the Pali Text Society, Oxford, U.K. The editor-cum-translator of this so far known the only Pāli medical treatise has described the *Bhes* in the under-noted publications:

a) *Catalogue des manuscripts singhalais. Paris, Bibllotheque nationale, 1983, pp.123-126.*
b) *Sinhalese Medical Manuscripts in Paris* in the *Bulletin de l'Ecole Francaise d' Extreme-orient,* 76, 1987, pp.186-189.

c) G. J. MEULENBELD *ed. Medical Literature from India and Tibet.* Leiden, Panels of the VIIth World Sanskrit Conference, Vol VIII, 1991, pp.73-78.

Such information supplied as above has been included with some additional materials by G. J. MEULENBELD (2000: 549-551, Groningen) in his work titled *History of Indian Medical Literature*, Vol IIA.

As mentioned earlier, the name of the author of the Bhes is not known. But its *Sanne* explanation was, in the 18th century, authored by Valivita Saraṇaṁkara (CE 1698-1778) who was the preceptor to two Sri Lankan Kings, viz. Śrī Vijaya Rājasiṁha (CE 1739-1747) and Kīrti Śrī Rājasiṁha (1747-1760). Śrī Vijaya Rājasiṁha conferred on Valviṭa Saraṇaṁkara the title of 'Rājaguru' or 'Royal Preceptor', while the second one appointed him 'Saṁgharāja' or 'Chief Abbot of the Buddhist Order'. During his very young age Ven. Saraṇaṁkara had proved his academic excellence by delivering a discourse in Sinhala and Sanskrit to explain a Pāli verse at the royal court before the King and a foreign Brāhmaṇa ascetic who had been the 'Guest of Honour' on this occasion. As a scholar his fame has reached the shores of Myanmar and Thailand. In fact, the Bhes has been widely known in Burma. This fact is attested by a Burmese Inscription dated B.E. 804, i.e. CE. 1442 (BODE 1909: 108), but which according to Sinhala tradition has to be CE 1348. The Inscription mentions this title in a list of books donated to the Saṅgha along with other materials (BARNETT 1913: 160-61). This fact reveals that religious contacts had been maintained between Sri Lanka, and Burma between the 13th and 18th Centuries. A Burmese edition of the Bhes in 96 pages was published in Rangoon in 1899.

While editing and translating the Bhes on behalf of the PTS, U.K., the following Palm-leaf Manuscripts of the *Bhesajjamañjūsā-Sannaya (Bhes-Sn)* have been considered:

(A) The Manuscript No.1 (M.1) of the Galkandēpuraṇa

Viharaya, Kollegoda, Matara, Southern Province, Sri Lanka, bears no Colophon; but immediately after the text, it concludes, in neat and small letters, with the usual benedictory formula, such as, *siddhir astu, subham astu.*

(B) The M2 of Valiviṭa Pansala, Kandy, Central Province, Sri Lanka, belongs to the Monastery of Valaviṭa Saraṇaṁkara, the author of the *Sanne*, in the Malvatu Vihara Complex, Kandy, records in its colophon:

... *ladā bhesajjamañjūsā naṁ prakaraṇayaṭa kaḷa ṭīkāvan sanyayan apavat va gāthāpota pamaṇak kramayen pāvata avut, pravara dinakarakula gaganatala gata nisākara pratibhāga nikhila narapati-maulimaṇi-bhramara-paricumbita-pādāravinda-dvandopasobhita vū, utum, apagē śrī vīra-parākrama narendrasiṁha nam maharājottamayānam vahanseṭa hasta prāpta viya, ē bhūpālottamayāṇan visin pausathār-amvāsī vū saraṇaṁkarābhidhāna apagē ācāryottamayan visin svakīya siṁhala bhāṇāven mē prakaraṇaya liyavūvot itā yehekayi samārādhita vū upasathārāmavāsī vū saraṇaṁkarābhidhāna apagē ācāryottamayan visin bhaisadyamañjūsa sanyaya ardhayakut nāvata sapayā vaidyaśāstropakārī vū sesut bohō pot balā tamangē śabdaśāstrācārya vū palakumbure arthadassī sāmīn ādhāra koṭa gena mena maharājottamayāṇan vahansegē pratiṣṭhādhāraya mul koṭa śabdaśāstrādiyehi hikmavā gat suvaca kikaru vū taman śiṣya putrayan hā samaga upanyāsavidhi- paddhatiyehi paṭan rogasā-mānyapaddhati (ya) dakvā aṭaḷos paddhatiyak pūrva sanyayan āśraya koṭa gāthā vyākhyāna vaśayen liyā jvarapaddhatiyehi paṭan rasāyana-paddhatiya dakvā desāḷis paddhatiyak suvasē nidāna abhiprāva hā piḷiyan dānagannā piṇisa gāthā sahita heḷu pota vaśayen liyā apagē ñāṇa śakti vū paridden śrī śaka narendra-varṣayen ekvādahas sasiya panas sayata pāmiṇi mē varuṣayehi poson masa ava viseniya nam tithiya lat sandu dina medavasa nikhila nagarāñga śrī samurdhīn sampūrṇa vū kuṇḍasālābhidhāna pura pravarāsanna vū udyānagata vihārayehidī mē bhaisadyamañjūsa sanyaya liyā niṣṭāvaṭa pamuṇu vana ladddeya.*

mē śrī vīraparākarama narendrasiṁha nam maharajānan pramukha koṭa āti śrī laṁkādvīpa vāsīn svargamokṣa sampatehi pihiṭuvana piṇisa miṭa pūrvayen buddho yana akṣara dekakin upalakṣita vū padaya gona arthavarṇanā dvārayen saddharma sārārtha-saṁgraha nam dharma prakaranayak kaḷa seka. eyin svargamokṣa sampatti pratilābhayaṭa piḷivet purannā vū paṇḍita janayangē kāyika roga vyapasamanayaṭa upāyak kaḷa sē nāvata karana lada mē bhaisadyamañjūsa sanyayehi likhita doṣayak hō pūrvāpara virodhayak hō duṭa hot helā no dāka bohō potpat balā nighaṇḍuśāstra vaidyaśāstra śabdaśāstrādiyehi dakṣa vicakṣaṇa paṇḍitavarun hā samaga sākacchā kirimen niṣkāmśābavaṭa pāmiṇa vaidyacārivarayanṭa hastasāra vastuvak cintāmāṇikyayak vāni vū mē bhaisadyamañjūsaya balā ubhayalokārthabhañjaka vū sarva vyādhi upasamanaya piṇisa piḷiyam kirimen sarvārtha saṁsiddhiyata mūla kāraṇa vū nirogibavehi pihiṭā ubhayalokārtha saṁsiddhiya kaṭa yutu. trailokatilaka nikhila guṇaratnākara sugata tathāgata pravara aurasaputrapbhāva prāpta asaraṇajana saraṇa saraṇaṁkarābhidhāna valiviṭa anunāyakasāmīn visin liyavana lada bhaisajjamañjūsayayi.

----------" the *Ṭika* and *Sanyaya* (or *Sanna* or *Sanne*) of the *Bhes* (*ajjamañjūsā*) were lost in the course of time and only the book of *Gāthā*-s reached the hands of King Śrī Vīraparākrama Narendrasiṁha (CE 1707-1739), who requested Venerable Saraṇaṁkara, resident at the Uposathārāma, to render that work into Sinhala. Venerable Saraṇaṁkara then provided half of the *Sanne* afresh, consulted several other medical works, and with the help of his teacher Palkuṁburē Atthadassī Sāmī, and his own pupils, wrote eighteen chapters from the *Upaññāsapaddhati* to the *Rogasāmaññapaddhati* by way of explanation of *Gāthā*-s, making use of previous *Sanna*. He also wrote forty two chapters from the *Jvarapaddhati* to the *Rasāyanapaddhati* in Sinhala along with *Gāthā*-s for the sake of understanding aetiology (*nidāna*) and therapy (*Piḷiyan, P. Paṭikamma*). The whole *Sanne* was completed at the Udayānagata (modern Uyanavatu) Vihāra near the city of Kuṇḍasāle on lunar Monday the 5th in the dark half of the moon in the month of *Poson* (June) of the Śaka year 1656 (1734 CE). The Colophon further adds that previously a treatise on the *Dhamma, Saddharmasārārthasaṁgraha* was written (by Venerable Saraṇaṁkara), based on the term Buddho, in order to ensure to King Śrī Vīraparākrama Narendrasiṁha and the people of Sri Lanka the bliss of heaven and liberation (*svargamokṣa-sampatti*), and that the present *Bhes-sn* was written as a means for learned people striving to achieve that bliss to cure themselves of physical illnesses. The *Bhes-sn* is finally compared to a handy treasure and a crest jewel for physicians" (LIYANARATNE 1996: 5-6). The above Colophon discloses the following facts: (i) The *Sanyaya* or Exegesis of the Bhes has been a team-work supervised by Venerable Valiviṭa Saraṇaṁkara who is assisted by his teacher Palkuṁburē Atthadassī Sāmī and his own disciples, the act of writing is done by one of his disciples, e.g. the king invited 'our esteemed teacher named Saraṇaṁkara, resident at the Uposathārāma' to translate the *Bhes* into Sinhala, and 'our esteemed teacher named Saraṇaṁkara, resident at the Uposathārāma' supplied half of the *Sanne* or *Sannaya* afresh. (ii) It is recorded that Valiviṭa Saraṇaṁkara was a *Sāmaṇera*, 'Novice-Monk', when he composed in CE 1734 the *Sanne* on the *Bhes*, obtained the *Upasampadā*, 'Higher Ordination', and became the *Saṅgharāja*, 'Chief of the Buddhist Order', in B.E. 2296 or CE1752. (iii) The *Bhes* is meant not only for the Buddhist monks, but also for all physicians irrespective of religion.

(C) The M3 of the Etampitiya (spelled also as Ettampitiya), in the District of Badulla, Uva Province, Sri Lanka, supplies the same information as recorded in the M2 and concludes with the words *siddhir astu.*

(D) The M4 of Kantalai, Eastern Province, Sri Lanka, concludes with the following words in the Colophon: *me śrī vīraparākrama narendrasiṁha nam mahārājanam pramukha koṭa āti śrī laṁkadvi...*

(E) The M5 found at Matale, Central Province, Sri Lanka, with the same Colophon as in the M2 ends with the words: *siddhir astu, subham astu, ārogyam astu, sarvarttha sidddhir astu.* MC a preserved in the British Library, London (OR 12137), U.K.

(F) The M6a (OR 12137) preserved in the British Library, London, U.K.

(G) The M6b also preserved in the British Library, London, U.K., in its Colophon after explaining the Colophon verse of the text of the *Bhes,* i.e. *sāke Parakkamabujavha-Narinda Jambuddoni* etc; includes the following additional *Gāthā-s* (LIYARATNE 1996: 16):

> yāva tiṭṭhati selindo yāva cando virocati ।
> tāva tiṭṭhatu lokasmiṁ etaṁ tantaṁ manoramaṁ ।।
> sukhaṁ jīvatu rājā so Siri Vīraparakkama ।
> narindasīho rogehi mutto a candatārakā ।।
> ciraṁ jīvatu rājā so pālento lokasāsanaṁ ।
> kappaṁ tiṭṭhatu rājā so vigatū bhay'upaddavo ।।
> sabbarogavinimmuttā bhavantu sabbapāṇino ।
> vimuttā pana rogehi bhajantu amataṁ padaṁ ।।
> mayā kho lābhasakkāra-nirapekkhena kevalaṁ ।
> kataṁ Sīhalabhāsāya idaṁ tantaṁ pure viya ।।
> paratthaṁ yeva nissāya akāsiṁ suddhacetasā ।
> tena sambhatapuññena pappomi Buddhaṁ uttamaṁ ।।
> lokaṁ pālentu rājāno yathā dhammena sabbadā ।
> sukhattāya janānaṁ va devo sammā pavassatu ।।

This Colophon thereafter continues, with slight variations, as found in the Colophon of the M2 and concludes with the words: *śriyam bhavatu. abhimatā-rthasiddhir astu. iṣṭārthasiddhir astu. vijayo'stu. jayo'stu. ārogyam astu. cirañjīvam astu.*

Incidentally it may be mentioned that a copy of the Bhes written in the Burmese Script on the palm-leaf has been kept in the library of the Cambridge University, U.K., with the shelfmark 'Add MS 1252 (21)' which is not inked and so is very difficult to read. But some of its folios, which are legible, reveal that its text is essentially the same as that of its Sinhala manuscripts.

The manuscript of the *Sanne* or *Sannaya* of the *Bhes* commences with the under-noted *Gāthā*-s:

> mahantaṁ Sugataṁ nāthaṁ lokālokadivākaraṁ ।
> visuddhaṁ karuṇāñāṇaṁ vande lokasivaṁkaraṁ ॥
> ciraṁ jīvatu so raja siri vīraparakkama ।
> narindasīho sakko ' va tejaniddhibalo idha ॥
> mayaṁ sabbe pi niddukkhā rattiṁdivaṁ ananditā ।
> etaṁ Bhesajjamañjūsā likhāma atthato ito ॥

The above Preliminary Verses of the *Sanne* refer to King Śrī Vīraparākrama Narendrasiṁha, who invited the monk Saraṇaṁkara to compose the same.

Before entering into the topics of discussions collected in the Bhes, it is prudent to go through the *Vinaya-Piṭaka* which contains Buddha's admonitions to the monk and nun disciples. This *Piṭaka* has prescribed some medicines for the well-being of the Buddhist monks (*Vinaya-Piṭaka*, 13th Chapter, 6th *Khandaka* of the *Mahāvagga-Bhesajja-Anuññāta-Bhāṇavāra*). This textual portion reveals the applicability of Buddha's discourses or simply the application of 'Applied Buddhism' to humanity. It enjoins the five medicaments, viz. *ghee*, butter, oil, honey, and molasses. The *bhikkhu*-s are permitted to use them at the right time and at other times. They are also allowed to use the fat of bears, fish, alligators, swine, and asses if received at the right time, cooked at the right time, mixed at the right time, to be partaken of with oil. The use of certain roots as medicines are allowed for the *bhikkhu*-s, e.g. turmeric, ginger, orris root, white orris root, *ativisa*, black hellebore, *usīra* root, *bhaddamuttaka*. The use of astringent decoctions as medicine is allowed- *nimba*, *pakkava* (a kind of creeper), *nattamāla*, *kuṭaja* (an antidote to dysentery), etc. The use of leaves and fruits as medicine is allowed, e.g. leaves of *nimba, tulasī, kappāsika, pippala, harītaka, āmalaka,* etc. The use of gums and salts is allowed as medicines, viz. *hingu*, *sipatika*, sea-salt, black salt, rock salt, red-salt, etc. The use of raw flesh and blood is permissible in case of disease. The use of eye ointments is permissible. The *bhikkhu*-s are allowed the use of a little oil on the head, use of a double bag, a decoction of oil. The practice of taking medicine through the nose is permissible. The *bhikkhu*-s are allowed the use of three kinds of pots, e.g. bronze pots, wooden pots, and pots made of the shells of fruits. They are allowed the use of hot baths in water in which the medicinal herbs have been steeped. The use of artificial or natural juice is allowed. The *bhikkhu*-s can cook in-doors. No surgical operation is to be performed within a distance of two inches round the anus and a clyster is not to be used. The *bhikkhu*-s are not to eat elephants' flesh, dogs' flesh, serpants' flesh, lions' flesh, and hyenas' flesh. They are to take rice-milk and honey-lumps. Thus, the *Vinaya-Mahāvagga* long before the composition of the *Bhes* represents a small medical treatise revealing the applied aspect of Buddha's tenets or Applied Buddhism.

The Bhes informs: "Illnesses are twofold: psychical and physical. Out of them, psychical ones are those such as greed and hatred. Remedies for them are given in Religion (i.e. Buddha's Discourses or Buddhism). Physical illnesses are those such as fever and skin diseases. Remedies for them are given in this treatise" (LIYANARATNE 2002:4). The relevant *gāthā* runs as follows:

dvidhābhādhā manokāya-vasen' etesu mānasā।
lobhadosādayao tesaṁ tikicchā āgamoditā।
sarīrā jarakuṭṭhādi tesaṁ ettha bhisajjitaṁ॥ (Bhes I.18)

The above *gāthāa*-s well as its introductory line, i.e. *Namo tassa Bhagavato Arahato Sammāsambuddhassa*- "Homage to the Blessed One, the Worthy and the Omniscient" indicate that the Bhes is out and out a Buddhist text, of which 'Introductory Chapter' also commences: "After duly paying homage to the Teacher, the Healer of mental disease i.e. defilements-*dosa*- such as attachment (*rāga*) this 'Casket of Medicine' (i.e. Bhes) is presented with compassion. Complete with materials drawn from various well-known (about seventy) sources, this work is like a veritable treasure for physicians. Thanks to it, monks who are fellow brethren may gain medical knowledge, and in case of illness, treat each other with the thought, 'May you be healed'. Intelligent people should indeed pray for the state of Permanent Bliss (*Nibbāna*). That state could not, be attained without following the Path presented by the Lord of the *Dhamma*, and that path is extremely difficult to follow for those who are ill. Therefore, to get rid of diseases, one should pay due consideration to this treatise" (LIYARATNE 2002: 1). Its correspondent Pāli *gāthā*-s is as follows (*Bhes* I.1-5):

abhivādiya Satthāraṁ manorogatikicchakaṁ।
sabrahmacārino bhikkhū jātaveyyattiyāmuyā॥
kallā hontū ti rogesu aññamaññatikicchakā।
samuddhaṭapadatthi pasatthānekakosoto॥
sampūritā bhisakkānaṁ hatthasāravasūpamā।
esa Bhesajjamañjūsā kāruññenopanīyati॥
āsiṁsanīyataṁ dhīrehi addhā niccasukhappadaṁ।
adhigantuṁ na taṁ sakkā dhammasāmippaveditaṁ॥
paṭipattiṁ rite sā ca sābādhehi sudukkaraṁ।
tasmābadhanisedhāya kattabbo ādaro idha॥

The Bhes consists of the following sixty chapters (?), each of which is called *Paddhati*, e.g. its first chapter *Upaññāsavidhi-Paddhati*, 'Preface (with) Introductory Chapter'. The titles of these chapters have been mentioned in the following Pāli *gāthā-s* or verses (Bhes I.6-17):

satthassānukkama cādo sukhabodhāya vuccate ।
upaññāsavidhi dabba-rasādīnaṁ vibhāvanā ॥
pasatthācaraṇaṁ 'bhavi ābādhapaṭisedhaṁ ।
annavyañjarūpāni davadabbanirūpaṇaṁ ॥
visāhāro paṭivisaṁ āmabhedanidassanaṁ ।
nānāgaṇagun' uddeso mahākammavicāraṇā ॥
cullakammavidhānañ ca dūtesu gamanesu ca ।
supinesu ca uppāte rogesu ca ariṭṭhatā ॥
vikārasāmaññavidhi nidānasahito jaro ।
yakhumā sarabhedo ca aruci hadyāmayo ॥
pipāsā chaddi kasanaṁ sasanaṁ hidhaṁ āmayo ।
sabibbisikātisāro gahaṇī ca kunāmakaṁ ।
bhagandaro pameho ca sasomo piḷakāyuto ॥
muttāghātosmarīyutto padaṁso mukkhavaddhanaṁ ॥
rattapittaṁ sītapitt' ambilapitteni samyutaṁ ॥
gumbasūlaṁ udāvatto nānāsūlehi saṁyuto ।
udaraṁ sāmbukummañ ca kāmilā paṇḍusaṁyutā ॥
sopho vidradhi visappo kuṭṭhaṁ kimi calāmayo ।
samīrarattañ ca visuṁ cakkhusotāmayā tathā ॥
ghānānanasirovyādhi sopacī sīpadādikaṁ ।
masūrikādibhedō ca vaṇabhaggatikicchakaṁ ॥
sāpasmāraṁ sahummādaṁ yakkhabhūtabhi sajjitaṁ ।
nānāvisappatikāro kappatantaṁ rasāyanaṁ ॥
iti saṭṭhassāvayavā saṭṭhi paddhatisaṁgahā ॥

____ "6-17. At the beginning of the treatise, for the facility of understanding, the sequences (of the Chapters) are given:

(1) 'Introductory Chapter' (or Preface, the disorder-free nature of Air, Fire etc., which is recurrent in Medical

Science and is presented at the beginning or 'Introductory Chapter', *Upaññāsavidhi*, in 143 Verses).

(2) 'Exposition of drugs, taste (*rasa*), etc. (which in *Āyurveda* means not only taste but also the composition, properties, and probable action of the drugs etc. and which refer to potency (*viriya*), digestion (*vipāka*), and specific potency (*pabhāva*) or 'Drugs etc'. (*dabbadi*) in 101versees).

(3) 'Good Living' (*Sadācāra-Paddhati* in 36 verses).

(4) 'Prevention of Disease' or 'Warding off Future Diseases' (*Agāmiroganisedha* in 21 verses).

(5) 'Nature of Food and Food Preparations' (or 'Food and Food preparations', *Annavyāñjana*, grouped under the following 12 *Vaggas*, viz. *Dhaññvagga, Katannavagga, Maṁsavagga, Macchavagga, Sākavagga, Pupphavagga, Phalavagga, Kandavagga, Karīravagga, Khalavagga, Kaṭukavagga* and *Loṇavagga* in 178 verses).

(6) 'Study of Liquid Drugs' (or 'Liquid Drugs', *Davadabba*, grouped under the following 5 *vaggas*, viz. *Toyavagga, Khīravagga, Ucchuvagga, Madhuvagga,* and *Telavagga* in 99 verses).

(7) 'Toxic Food' (*Savisāhāra* in 27 verses).

(8) 'Antidotes' (*Paṭivisa* grouped under the following one *vagga*, viz. *Tikicchamate* in 51 verses).

(9) 'Exposition of Different kinds of Indigestion' (*Āmabheda* in 44 verses).

(10) 'Exposition of Different Groups of Drugs and their Medicinal Properties' (or 'Groups of Drugs', *Gaṇa*, in 140 verses).

(11) 'Study of Major Therapeutics' (or 'Major Therapeutics', *Mahākamma*, grouped under the following 6 *vidhis*, viz. *Snehavidhi, Sedavidhi, Vamanavidhi, Virekavidhi, Nassavidhi,* and *Kharaggividhi* in 171 verses).

(12) 'Application of Minor Therapeutics' (or 'Minor Therapeutics', *Cullakamma*, grouped under the following 7 *vidhis*, viz. *Dhūmavidhi, Gaṇḍūsavidhi, Muddhatelavidhi,*

Ācotanāñjanavidhi, Tappaṇapuṭapākavidhi, Mammavidhi, and *Jalekavidhi* in 146 verses).

(13) 'Fatal Signs in relation to Messengers coming to fetch physicians' (or 'Unfavourable Signs of Messengers', *Dūtāriṭṭha*, in 17 verses).

(14) 'Visiting Patients' (or Unfavourable Signs met on the way', *Gamanāriṭṭha*, in 22 verses).

(15) 'Dreams' (or 'Unfavourable Dreams', *Supināriṭṭha*, in 30 verses).

(16) 'Morbity' (or 'Unfavourable Prodromes', *Uppātāriṭṭha-Uppāta* means 'Abnormal', the Fatal Signs of the opposite of Natural State in 53 verses).

(17) 'Diseases' (or 'Fatal Diseases', *Rogāriṭṭha*, in 61 verses).

(18) 'General Nature of Disorders' (or 'General Treatment of Diseases', *Rogasāmañña*, in 22 verses).

(19) 'Fever with manifest Origin' (*Nidanāsahito Jaro*).

(20) 'Consumption' (with manifest Origin, *Yakhumā*).

(21) 'Vocal Disorder' (*Sarabhedo*).

(22) 'Distaste for Food (*Aruci*).

(23) 'Heart Disease' (*Hadayāmayo*).

(24) 'Abnormal Thirst' (*Pipāsā*).

(25) 'Vomiting' (*Chaddi*).

(26) 'Cough' (*Kasanaṁ*).

(27) 'Difficult Breathing' or 'Dyspnoea' (*Sasanaṁ*).

(28) 'Hiccup' (*Hidaṁ*).

(29) 'Diarrhea with Phlegm' (*Āmayo Sabibbisikatisāra*).

(30) 'Affliction of the Duodenum' (i.e. the Uppermost Extremity or Receiving Ducts of the Intestines *Gahaṇī*).

(31) 'Piles' (*Kunāmakaṁ*).

(32) 'Anal Fistula' (*Bhagandaro*).

(33) 'Diabetes with Pustules and *Somaroga*' (*Pameho ca Sasomo Piḷakāyuto*, a Diabetic Disease, *Bahu-mūtra-roga*, of women, causing wasting of the liquid element of the body, *Āpaḥ*, also known as *Soma*).

(34) 'Obstruction of Urine along with Urinary Calculi' (*Muttāghātosamarīyutto*).

(35) 'Genital Affliction' (*'Padaṁso*).
(36) 'Scrotal Enlargement' (*Mukkhavaddhanaṁ*).
(37) 'Visceral Haemorrhage in conjunction with Cold Bile and Acid Bile' (*Rattapittaṁ sītapitt' Ambilapittehi Saṁyuttaṁ; Rattapitta-* bleeding from the eyes, ears, nose, facial and urinary outlets).
(38) 'Painful Abdominal Tumour' (*Gumbasūlaṁ*).
(39) 'Upward Movement of Air in the Abdomen with various pains' (*Udāvatto nānāsūlehi saṁyutto*).
(40) 'Abdominal Enlargement with *Ambukumma*' (*Udaraṁ Sambukummaṁ, Udara Roga,* i.e. loss of strength, loss of colour of the body, disappearance of the folds of the belly, pain in the bladder, gradual swelling of the legs, gradual enlargement of the abdomen, slimming of the belly above the navel, *Ambukumma*, i.e. probably *Jalakūrma*, 'Water Tortoise' indicating *Jalodara*, 'Ascites').
(41) 'Anaemic Jaundice' (*Kāmilā paṇḍusaṁyutā* or *Kāmalā* and *Pāṇḍu Roga*, 'Morbid pallor').
(42) 'Swelling' (*Sopho*).
(43) 'Abscess' (*Vidradhi*).
(44) 'Erysipelas' (*Visappo*).
(45) 'Skin Disease', particularly 'Leprosy' (*Kuṭṭhaṁ*).
(46) 'Worm' Parasitic Diseases (*kimi*).
(47) 'Air (Nervous) Diseases' (*Calāmayo*); *Samirattaṁ, Vātavyādhi* or Diseases of the Nervous System.
(48) 'Gout' (*Visuṁ*, 'Rheumatism').
(49) 'Eye Diseases'.
(50) 'Ear Diseases' (*Cakkhusotāmayā tathā*).
(51) 'Diseases of the Nose'.
(52) 'Diseases of the Mouth'.
(53) 'Diseases of the Head' (*Ghānānanasirovyādhi*).
(54) 'Elephantiasis with *Upacī*' (*Sopacī Sīpadādikaṁ*, probably *Apacī* or Scrofula).
(55) Smallpox etc '(*Masurikadibhedo ca, Masurika* or Variola).
(56) 'Treatment of Ulcers and Fractures' (*Vaṇabhaggatikicc-*

hakaṁ).

(57) 'Treatment of Diseases caused by beings such as *Yakkhas*, accompanied by Amnesia and Insanity' (*Sāpasmāraṁ Sahummādaṁ Yakkhabhūtabhisajjitaṁ*).

(58) 'Treatment of different types of Poison' or 'Toxicology' (*Nānāvisappatīkāro*).

(59) 'Treatise on Pharmaceutical Preparations' (*Kappatantaṁ*, i.e. Medical Preparations as Tonics made of bananas etc. *Kadali-rasayanādi Kappa-Tantra*).

(60) 'Tonics' (*Rasāyanaṁ*).

Thus, the component parts of Medical Science are gathered in sixty chapters. This is the (end of the) preface (LIYANARATNE 2002: 1-4).

The first eighteen chapters of the Bhes deal with the fundamentals of traditional medicine, while the other forty-two treat of aetiology and therapy.

Since this treatise with sixty chapters appears to be voluminous, for the purpose of illustrating only three chapters, viz. chapter III *Sadācāra-Paddhati* or 'Chapter on Good Living', chapter IV *Agāmiroganisedha-Paddhati* or 'Chapter on Prevention of Disease', and Chapter XVIII *Rogasāmañña-Paddhati* or 'Chapter on the General Treatment of Diseases', have been taken into account.

Further, in order to be brief only some selected verses have been quoted to exemplify the present discussion. The English rendering of these verses have been taken from *The Casket of Medicine*, a Textual rendering already made by Jinadasa LIYANARATNE in order to avoid unnecessary duplication of the work. Still for the convenience of readers corresponding Pāli words have been put under brackets.

As already mentioned, its third chapter titled *Sadācāra-Paddhati* or 'Chapter on Good Living' in the second and third stanzas notes:

> "The healthy person, in order to protect his life, gets up at the holy hour (*brahmamuhuttasmiṁ*, i.e. two hours before sunrise), performs the proper mental, verbal, and physical rites (*manovacanakāyehi*), and masticates without hurting the gums by soft tooth-cleaning sticks (*dantapoṇaṁ muduṁ*) made of Indian beech, *arjuna myrobalaṁ*, *mudur* etc., having astringent, pungent, and bitter taste" (Verses 2, 3).

> "After accomplishing his duties to divinities, teachers, and elders (*devatāguruvaddhesu*) and after paying them homage, he should duly attend to the things which maintain the body" (*dehavattanaṁ* - Verse 7).

> "Having (first) served one's associates, guests, and divinities (*nissitātithidevānaṁ*), one should eat healthy food within limits, at the proper time (eating when all the impurities are completely digested in eating at the proper time), not facing the north" (*anuttaramukho-yevabhuñje kāle hitaṁ mitaṁ*- Verse 23).

Similarly the Fourth Chapter called *Agāmiroganisedha-Paddhati* or 'Prevention of Disease' informs:

> "Due to the suppression of sleep there arise indolence, delusion (*Soppassālasiyaṁ moho*), heaviness of head and eyes. In that case, massage of the limbs and the body and sleep are beneficial" (*aṅgamaddo ca sambāho supinañ ca hitaṁ tahiṁ*- verse 11).

> "Due to the suppression of semen, which is ejaculating on its own (*sayaṁ vimuccamānassa sambhavassa nivāraṇā*), there arise fever, urinary calculi, swelling, loss of manliness, scrotal enlargement and painful urination. For it, eating rice (rice from hill paddy, i.e. paddy grown on dry land) with chicken is recommended" (*tasmiṁ kukkuṭamaṁsena vihitaṁ sālibhojanaṁ*- Verse 17).

This Chapter also records:

> "The person who constantly adheres to healthy food habits and behavior (*niccaṁ hitāhāravihāravihārasevī*) who is circumspect, not attached to worldy desires (desires of five senses- *visayev-asatto*), generous (*dātā*), equally disposed towards all beings, truthful (*saccaparo*), forgiving (*khamāvā*), and who associates with wise men is free from illness" (*garūpasevī ca bhavaty' arogo*- Verse 20).

The Eighteenth Chapter titled *Rogasāmañña-Paddhati*, 'Chapter on General Treatment of Diseases', notes:

> "Disease is the unbalance of the humours, the balance of humours is health" (*rogo tu dosavesammaṁ dosasammaṁ ārogatā*"- Verse 2).
>
> "The health-promoting application of drugs, food, and mode of life (*osadh' anavihārānaṁ, upayogaṁ sukhāvahaṁ*), which are contrary to the cause of diseases and diseases (themselves) and which help such counteraction, should be known as therapeutics (*jāneyyopasayaṁ*). It is also known as disease-compatibility (*rogasātummaṁ uccate*); its opposite disease- incompatibility (*viparītānupasayo rogāsātummasaññitaṁ*)- Homoeopathy and Allopathy are examples of disease-compatibility and disease incompatibility, for the former follows the nature of the disease and latter counters the disease" (Verses 18,19).

The contents and the verses quoted above reveal that the Bhes, composed in Pāli *gāthā*-s presents a glaring example of Applied Buddhism, since it is primarily based on some discourses of Buddha, especially those which have already been collected in the *Vinaya-Piṭaka* and addressed to Buddha's monk as well as nun disciples for maintaining good health free from all kinds of physical and psychological diseases. The Blessed one being very practical could realize that without good and diseaseless health it would be quite impossible for them to pursue higher religious life. That is why on several occasions, He had incidentally asked His lay disciples also to lead the pure life. All such teachings delivered by Buddha subsequently induce His disciples to write a medical treatise like the Bhes.

Abbreviation

Bhes *Bhesajjamañjūā* (see LIYANARATNE 1996).
Vin *Vinaya Piṭaka* (see OLDENBERG 1997)
S *Saṁyutta-Nikāya*(see FEER 1991, 1976)

Bibliography

BARNETT, L. D.
(1913). *A Catalogue of the Burmese Books in the British Museum.* (Ed.). London
BODE, Mabel Haynes.
(1909). *The Pāli Literature of Burma.* London: Royal Asiatic Society.
FEER, M. Léon
(1991). *The Saṃyutta-Nikāya,* Vol.-I. (Re.). Oxford: PTS. (I[st] Pub. 1884)
LIYANARATNE, Jinadasa.
(1996). *Bhesajjamañjūā: Chapters 1-18.* (Ed.). Oxford: PTS.
(2002). *The Casket of Medicine.* (Tr.). Oxford: PTS.
MALALASEKERA, G[unapala] P[iyasena].
(1958). *The Pāli Literature of Ceylon.* (Re.). Kandy, Sri Lanka: Buddhist Publication Society. 1st Pub. 1928.
OLDENBERG, Hermann.
(1997). *The Vinaya Piṭakaṃ. Mahāvagga.* Vol. I (Re.). Oxford: PTS. (Ist ed. 1879)
(1976). *The Saṃyutta-Nikāya Vol-V.* (Re.). Oxford: PTS. (I[st] Pub. 1898)

Kātantra: Pathfinder of Kaccāyana

Suchitra Ray ACHARYYA*

The study of grammatical science is very ancient in India. It can be traced back to the Vedic age. The river of speech was familiar to the Vedic seers is clearly known from the Ṛgvedic verses:

catvāri vākparimitā padāni,
tāṇi vidurbrāhmaṇā ye manīṣiṇaḥ।
guhā trīṇi nihitā neṅgayanti,
turīyaṃ vāco manuṣyā vadanti।। (Ṛg 1/164/45)

"Speech is measured in four quarters, the Brāhmanṇa-s who are wise know them. Three (of three quarters) are hidden and do not listen themselves. Men speak the fourth the quarter of speech."

uta tvaḥ paśyanna dadarśa,
vācamutatvaḥ śṛṇvanna śṛṇotyenām।
uto tvasmai tanvaṃ vi sasre,
jāyeva patya uśatī suvāsāḥ।।(Ṛg 1/71/4)

"And one seer does not see speech, and one hearing does not hear it. And to another she unfolds her body, like a well-dressed and loving wife to her husband."

* Professor (Retired), Department of Sanskrit, University of Calcutta, Kolkata, India. E-mail: suchitraroy7@gmail.com

At the time of Pāṇini Sanskrit was called as *bhāṣā*. The *Aṣṭādhyāyī* of Pāṇini is regarded as one of the marvellous and pioneer productions in the field of Descriptive Linguistics. But the principles of the *Aṣṭādhyāyī* were not followed throughout India. The *Rāmāyaṇa*, the *Mahābhārata* and some *Purāṇa*-s were composed or collected and collated after Pāṇini. It is evident from the fact that the language of these books has deviated from the accepted forms prescribed by Pāṇini. From this we can assume that the composers and collectors of the Epics were either ignorant of Pāṇini or Pāṇini was not popular at that time. This is substantiated by *Kaumāra Vyākaraṇa* or *Kalāpa Vyākaraṇa*. This was popularly studied throughout Kasmir, Bengal, South India, Afganisthan and Tibet. This *Kaumāra Vyākaraṇa* became more popular than the *Aṣṭādhyāyī* for a remarkable period in the different regions of India. *Kaumāra Vyākaraṇa* was more lucid and simple than *Aṣṭādhyāyī*, is one of the best reasons of popularity of this grammar.

Sanskrit grammar is the most wonderful and the best creation of human mind has ever produced. Indian scholars have attained the highest prominence in grammar. They have all through made distinguished contributions towards development of the philosophy of language. Accurate observations about the linguistic usages, about linguistic changes that take place in course of time in different localities are done by them. They had in view not only the language of literature but also the spoken Sanskrit also. The fragments of a work named *Kaumāra* which is now lost have been recovered from Turkistan. In the opinion of Heinrich LÜDERS it was based on the *Kalāpa Vyākaraṇa*. The recovered text differs from the available recension of the latter in minor details. This proves the study of the *Kātantra* system was spread in Turkistan for its popularity.

Pāṇini's *Aṣṭādhyāyī* is a land-mark in the vast field of grammatical science. The popularity of the *Kātantra Vyākaraṇa* was great as a minor system of grammar. It influenced home and abroad- from Central Asia (Turkistan) to Southern India as well as in Tibet. Purāṇa-s are influenced by this grammar. The *Agnipurāṇa*, the *Garuḍapurāṇa*, the *Nāradapurāṇa* and the *Viṣṇudharmottarapurāṇa* contain chapters dealing with the *Kaumāra Vyākaraṇa*. A. B. KEITH (1996: 431) has said:

> "The later schools present no features of essential interest and may be reviewed briefly. The oldest was probably the *Kātantra* "little treatise" called also *Kaumāra* or *Kalāpa* the latter names indicating acceptance of the legend that its author *Śaravarman* wrote under *Śivaś* special favour. The legend which brings him into contact with *Sātavāhana* has been noted and its work questioned. What is conjectured is that in Kasmir and Bengal the work had much influence and that it affected deeply the Pāli grammar of *Kaccāyana* and the Dravidian grammarians. Originally of four books, it appears with supplements both in the Tibetan translation and in Durgasiṃha's Commentary (*Vṛtti*) on which he himself wrote a *Ṭīkā*, a sort of commentary is provided in *Ugrabhūtiś Śiṣyahitānyāsa* (1000 CE). Tibetan tradition ascribes to Śarvavarman the use of the grammar of Indragomin, and this work seems to have been popular among the Buddhists of Nepal, but it is lost, though the reality of its author's existence is certain."

M. WINTERNITZ has made a brilliant review on the system of *Kātantra Vyākaraṇa*. WINTERNITZ (1985: III. 478) says:

> "The *Kātantra* of *Śarvavarman* [a Buḍdhist scholar] is probably the oldest among the grammatical works that without being independent of Pāṇini have attempted to build a new system of grammar. At last this elementary book of grammar, of which the aim was to place in the hands of students a book of rules that

were easier than those of Pāṇini originated in the first century CE. Apparently this work consisted originally of four books or rather four *pāda*-s but was already enlarged by the time of the commentator Durgasiṃha (8th century) through additions that are found in our texts and also in the Tibetan translation. The *Kātantra* springs out from Pāṇini's *sūtra-s* that sometime have been reproduced adversity in it.

The terminology in a great measure is in accord with that of *Pāṇini*. However the Vedic language and accent have not been taken into consideration. This grammar has still recently been studied in Kashmir and in East Bengal, and it must have been popular throughout the centuries in these Indian regions since it was taken also into Tibet and into Central Asia. The fact that *Kātantra* was used by the Pāli grammarian *Kaccāyana* and that it served as model for the indigeneous grammars of the Dravidian languages proves wide circulation of this work.

There are several commentaries on the *Kātantra* and there exist many treatises accessory to it. Without the commentary of Durgasiṃha the text would not have been intelligible. Durgasiṃha wrote further a commentary (*Ṭīkā*) on his commentary (*Vṛtti*). The *Dhātupāṭha* of the *Kātantra* is preserved only in its Tibetan translation. Ugrabhūti's *Śiśyahitanyāsa*, a work that has been mentioned by Ālberunī is a sort of commentary on the *Kātantra*. In it one single chapter has been extended in the form of two. Here *sūtra*-s, one after another are explained in a verbose style, a *sūtra* is omitted here or one or other *sūtra* of Pāṇini is made more complete there. This Ugrabhūti wrote in about 1000 CE, since he was the teacher of Ānandapāla of Kābul who came to the throne in 1001 CE. The *Śabdar-*

> *ahasya*, a treatise on the philosophy of language of Rāmakānta Vidyāvāgiśa too belongs to the *Kātantra.*
>
> The Tibetan scholars say that the *Kātantra* agrees with the *Aindra Vyākaraṇa* of Indragomin. Probably this was the grammar of the Buddhists of Nepal. But it has not come down to us."

Śarvavarman, the author of *Kātantra* or *Kalāpa* School is placed in the first century BCE or first century CE by the scholars. The *Kātantra-Vyākaraṇa* of *Śarvavarman* is one of the oldest and the earliest of the post *Pāṇinian* systems of Sanskrit grammar. Before the composition of *Kātantra* the *Aṣṭādhyāyī* of Pāṇini was regarded as one of the most complete and authoritative Sanskrit grammar.

This *Kātantra* grammar challenged the renowned *Pāṇinian* grammar as it was written in a new system. In this grammar Śarvavarman adopted an independent and new method. In this grammar he rearranged the *sūtra*-s in respect of topic wise. Non use of *pratyāhāra-sūtra*-s and total omission of the rules dealing with the Vedic Sanskrit and accents are speciality of this grammatical system.

In the *vṛtti* of the *sūtra "upajñātam"* (7/562) of the grammar *Harināmāmṛta* of Śrī Jīva Goswami we get '*pāṇininopajñātaṃ prathamakṛtaṃ pāṇinīyam. kālāpaṃ vyākaraṇam.*'

In the *Vālatoṣaṇī* commentary of this grammar we get that the grammar made or composed by Kalāpī *is Kālāpa* grammar. In the *Siddhānta Kaumudī* edited by S. Candrasekhar SĀSTRIGAL published on 1910 from Tricinopali we get *kalāpakamadhīte kālāpakaḥ*. In no other edition of Siddhānta *Kaumudī* we get this. According to this the name of the book should be *Kalāpaka*. We may surmise that the *Kalāpaka* or *Kalāpa* or *Kalāpaka* grammar is the '*āddhya vyākaraṇa*' '*vṛddha kātantra*'. The Sārvavarmik edition *Kātantra* is the modern edition of the same. From this it may be surmised that this stream is very old even older than Pāṇinī. There are many such documents. In the community of '*Daurga*' we get the verse:

> śaṅkarasya mukhād vāṇiṃ śrutvā caiva ṣaḍānanaḥ।
> lilekha śikhinaḥ pucche kalāpa iti kathyate॥

This verse may be taken as the source of the name *Kalāpa.*

The *Kātantra* has another name as *Kaumāra Vyākaraṇa.* This grammar is supposed to have come from *kumāra,* i.e. Lord Kārtikeya. According to some scholars origin of this grammar is supposed to be meant for so called *kumāra*-s or children i.e. beginners. Lucidity and simplicity of this grammar proves that *Kātantra* was the first grammar based on the principle of topic wise division. The importance of topical division lies in the fact that the beginners are more benifited in reading of Sanskrit grammar in this method. Aequiring the fundamentals of Sanskrit grammar through its simple and lucid style students are gaining more than that of the *Aṣṭādhyāyī.* Unless one goes through the entire *Aṣṭādhyāyī* he will not be able to master any topic of Sanskrit grammar. In *Prakriyā*-method if one read some topics of Sanskrit grammar without going through all other topics still he gets an easy access over the particular section he reads. For this reason people started to read *Kātantra* leaving Pāṇini's *Aṣṭādhyāyī.* The followers of Pāṇinian system did utmost efforts to save the system and to prevent the increasing popularity of *Kātantra.* As a result of this struggle among the Pāṇinian and non- Pāṇinian systems a new era was initiated in the history of Sankrit grammar. This was known as *prakriyā* school which gave birth to the five major works one of which is the *Siddhānta Kaumudī* by Bhaṭṭoji Dīkṣita (1600 CE). It is undoubted that the authors of all these works draw their inspirations from *Kātantra.* Even the Pāṇinian-s of the *prakriyā* school are indebted *to Kātantra.*

Kātantra with such a small structure developed into an independent and exhaustive system is a matter of special interest. Though the *Kātantrasūtra*-s are based on the *sūtra*-s of Pāṇini and *Vārtika*-s of Kātyāyana the arrangement of *sutra*-s is quite different from that of Pāṇini. Probably *Kaccāyana* was influenced by *Kātantra* system for its lucidity and *prakriyā* system. Some scholars say that *Kaccāyana* belonged to 5th century CE. Some others say he belonged to later than 7th century CE. Speciality of *Kaccāyana* is that it is influenced by *Kātantra* and *Pāṇini.* Apart from this we know that the grammarian *Śarvavarman* and the commentator Durgosiṃha both were worshipper of lord *Śiva* who is interpreted as Viṣṇu or Buddha. To some extent this may be the reason for which *Kaccāyana*, a Buddhist one became follower of *Śarvavarman*. The complete text is distributed over four major sections, each one again divided into chapters. The first section is known as *Sandhi-Prakaraṇa*, dealing with the euphonic rules of Sanskrit. This section is divided into five chapters. Total number of rules in this section is seventy nine.

In the next six chapters which jointly come under the section of *Nāmacatuṣṭaya Prakaraṇa* the rules on declension are given. In the last three chapters of this section, rules on case compound and *taddhita- suffixes* are discussed. There are 337 rules, in total.

The following section is named as Ā*khyāta Prakarṇa*, divided into eight chapters consisting of 439 rules in total. It deals with the conjugation. Subject distribution is as follows:

i. Definition of some important technical terms
ii. Rules on denominative suffixes etc.
iii. Reduplication
iv. Vocalization
v. Guṇa
vi. Elision of the penultimate nasal.
vii. augmentation
viii. Rules on phonological changes respectively.

In this way, the total number of rules formulated by *Śarvavarman* is 855. The fourth section, viz *kṛt- Prakaraṇa* is a case of later addition by Kātyāyana according to Durgasiṃha. It is divided into six chapters, consisting of 546 rules. Including this section, *Kātantra* contains 1401 rules. Moreover each and every chapter has its own name.

The main purpose of Pāṇini was to write a descriptive grammar of synchronic and diachronic diversities of Sanskrit, to protect it from the ongoing language change as synchronic diversity, different dialectal usages are included. Differences in dialectal usages can be categorized under two broad regions, consisting of Udīcī and Prācām. Pānjāba Gāndhāra and Kāśmīra – all the three are used to belong to Udīcī. Whereas the eastern part of Udīcī is known as Prācām. Diachronically, he had also considered about the Vedic language along with the supra- segmental specifications.

We may compare the name of the chapters of both the grammars *Kātantra* and *Kaccāyana*:

Kātantra	Kaccāyana
Section-1 Sandhi Prakaraṇa Chapter one- Saṃjñā Pāda Five Chapters in the Section one	Section-1 Sandhi Kappe Chapter one- Saññā Five Chapters in the section one
Section- II Nāmacatuṣṭaya Prakaraṇa	Section-II Nāmakappe
Section-III Ākhyāta Prakaraṇa	Section-III Ākhyāta Kappe
Section- IV Kṛt Prakaraṇa	Kṛtvidhāna Kappe

Similarities among the *sūtra*-s of the *Kātantra* and *Kaccāyana*

Kātantra	Kaccāyana
Yato 'paiti bhayamādatte vātadapādānam 2/4/8	Yasmādapeti bhyamādatte vātadapādānaṃ 2/6/1
īpsitaṃ ca rakṣārthānām 2/4/9	rakkhanatthānamicchitaṃ 2/6/3
ya ādhārastadadhikaraṇam 2/4/11	yodhāro tamokāsaṃ 2/6/8
yena kriyate tat karaṇam 2/4/12	yena vā kayirate tat karaṇam 2/6/9
yat kriyate tat karmaḥ 2/4/13	yaṃ karoti taṃ kammaṃ 2/6/10
yaḥ karoti sa kartā 2/4/14	yo karoti sa kattā 2/6/11
kārayati yaḥ sa hetuścaḥ 2/4/15	yo karoti sa hetu 2/6/12

An attempt has been made in this paper to make a comparison between *Kātantra* and *Kaccāyana* from the perspective of vowel.

Pāli cannot be considered a direct descendant of either classical Sanskrit or of the older Vedic dialect. The languages are obviously very closely related. The common charateristics of Pāli and Sanskrit were always easily recognized by those in India who were familiar with both. Indeed, a very large proportion of Pāli and Sanskrit word stems are identical in form, differing only in details of inflection.

i. Skt. 'ai' and 'au' always monophthongize to a Pāli 'e' and 'o' respectively.

Examples : maitrī> metta

auṣadhi > osadha

ii. Skt. 'aya' and 'ava' likewise often reduce to Pāli 'e' and 'o'

Example : dhārayati > dhāreti
avatāra > otāra
bhavati> hoti

iii. Skt. 'avi' becomes Pāli 'e' (i.e. avi > ai >e)

Example: sthavira > thera

iv. Skt. *r* appears in Pāli as 'a', 'i' or u' often agreeing with the vowel in the following syllable 'r' also sometimes becomes 'u' after labial consonants.

Examples: kṛta > kata
tṛsnā > taṇhā
smṛti > sati
ṛsi > isi
dṛṣṭi > diṭṭhi
ṛddhi> iddhi
ṛju> uju
spṛṣṭa > puha
vṛddha > vuddha

v. Skt. long vowels are shortened before a sequence of two following consonants.

Examples: kṣānti > khanti
rājya > rajja
īsvara > issara
tīrna > tiṇṇa
pūrva > pubba

Generally Vowel sounds are classified in two ways. These are "(i) according to quantity and (ii) according to quality. The former depends upon the time taken to utter them in speech. Usually the time is reckoned in terms of one *mora* (*mātrā*) which is the time taken for a short vowel. On this basis we get two kinds of vowels: short vowels needing one *mora* and long vowels needing two *mora*. Sanskrit grammarians have also recognised an extra-long *pluta* vowel of three *mora*, where the length is indicated by the figure 3, as in ī3. This is used for instance, in the long drawing out of the final syllable in calling a person from a distance, e.g. *Devadatta 3 āgaccha*. Modern linguistics recognises an extra-short vowel also, which serves as a help in pronuncing an otherwise difficult combination of consonants. Its duration in time is half a *mora* or *ardhamātrā*. It is generally of the same quality as the following vowel. It is heard for instance, in the pronunciation of the English name *Goldsmith*, as heard in many parts of India. The combination- *ldsm*- presents difficulties and so an extra- short 'i' is inserted, and the word sounds as Gold-smith" (TARAPOREWALA 1978: 123-124).

The more important classification of vowels is according to quality. The nature of the vowel varies with the size and shape of the mouth opening.

The fundamental vowel is 'Ā'. Starting from that position we may make the mouth opening smaller, at the same time raising the front of the tongue higher and higher. This gives us the *front-vowels*. "Similarly by a gradual shutting of the mouth accompanied by the gradual raising of the back of the tongue and a rounding of the lips we get the set of *back-vowels*. In between there is a third set of what may be normal called *mixed-vowels*. There is necessarily an infinite gradation possible in each of these three series but individual languages only recognize a few standard types from each series.

In the front series the highest position is of 'I' and among the *back vowels*, the highest position is that of the 'U'. If we mark out the highest points of the tongue for each of these, Ī and Ū as also that of A the *fundamental vowel*, we get an inverted triangle which is called the *Vowel -Triangle*" (TARAPOREWALA 1978: 124). The sounds marked here are simple sounds (i.e., not diphthongs).

There is another classification based on the height to which the tongue is raised. When the mouth cavity shows the widest opening, the vowels is called open (*vivṛta*). When it shows a narrow opening it is called close (*saṃvṛta*).

Between these extremes there are two well -marked intermediate stages named half open and halfclose.

Of these four the 'Ā' 'E' and 'I' are found in *Sanskrit*. The 'E' is developed in some of the Indian Vernaculars. It is clearly heard in the Bengali word 'Ek'. With 'I' the tongue approaches very near the *hard palate*. It is very close to the contact point of the *palatals*. A very little raising of the tongue would make a contact and give 'Y' (I) We find very close connection between the semivowel 'Ya' and the vowel 'I'.

Again beginning with the fundamental 'Ā' we get in succession 'O' and 'U'. The three grades of openness for the *back-vowels* are rounded.

On the basis of some reason Daniel JONES and other scholars have put down the sounds of these two "long" vowels 'Ī' and 'Ū' as the highest grades in the front and the back-series respectively. In both of these the position of the tongue is perceptibly higher than with the corresponding "short" vowels and the vowelsare "closer" as well. It is very likely that in ancient Sanskrit there was this distinction between these "long" and "short" vowels. But Sanskrit grammarians have definitely laid down that the difference between 'I' and 'Ī' and 'U' and 'Ū' is, merely that of quantity and so we must leave it at that, at least as far as classical Sanskrit is concerned.

In the triangle of vowels the *mixed vowels* are put in the middle but this does not imply that the middle of the tongue has to be raised. There is no rising of the tongue in the centre, but a slight depression. The tip of the tongue and the back are both slightly raised with a slight depression in the blade.

Sanskrit 'A' and 'Ā' are so close that they get confused together. Sanskrit grammarians usually regard 'A' as the "short" and 'Ā' as the corresponding "long" vowel. Still the essential fact remains that they really differ not in quality along but in quantity as well. As these two vowels are pronounced today (even by the *Mārāṭhā*-s) they differ mainly in quality. All simple sounds are capable of a variation of quality or length. But in all languages we get combinations of two or more of these simple vowels. There each is pronounced separately and the combination is felt to be a combination. So all diphthongs are "long" in quantity. In modern English an originally simple vowel is drawn out as it were and is heard as a diphthong. The reverse process is also found. Sometimes an original diphthongal pronunciation is reduced to a simple vowel. In Sanskrit the grammarians tell us that 'E', 'AI' , 'O', 'AU' are diphthongs. But their length is always two *mora*. But as pronounced to-day they may be transcribed respectively: (e), (i), (o) and (u). Thus we see that the diphthongal value of only two of these is clearly perceptible, whereas the other two have been reduced to simple half close vowels. But the *sandhi* rules as well as comparisons with other languages, particularly with the Avestā very clearly establishes the original pronunciation of these four. These were 'AI' 'ĀI' 'AU' and 'ĀU' respectively. So we see that all four have suffered from reduction. The simple sounds 'A' 'E' and 'O' of the Indo European parent language have fallen together in Sanskrit as 'A' so that these four diphthongs of Sanskrit stand for no less than twelve original vowel combinations. What should be noticed particularly is that the simple sounds 'E' and 'O' are later developments in Sanskrit. and do not by any means represent the original *I.E.* sounds. But though these new values have developed, they are all four treated as if they had their original values both in *sandhi* as also in metrical composition.

Lengthening of short Vowel

A. Kaccāyana

Lengthening of Vowel 'A'

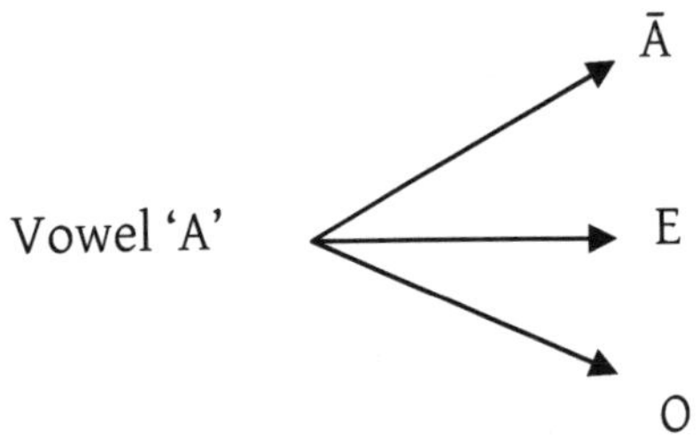

ṇyattatā bhāve tu|| Kc. 2/8/17

By the rule "ṇya-tva-tā bhāvetu" of taddhitakappe of Kaccāyana's Pāli grammar 'A' becomes 'Ā'. So 'anubhāva' becomes 'ānubhāva', 'anindya' becomes 'ānindya'. According to Kaccāyana this lengthening happens *bhāvārthe* that means in the sense of mode. Here quantitative change occurs.

Example:	Sanskrit	Pāli
	anubhāva	ānubhāva
	anindya	ānindya
		A> E
	yadatra	yadetha
	atra	etha
	antapura	antepura
	vāla	vāle
	diśati	desesi
	phalgu	pheggu

Here we find some examples of Pāli words where we find the vowel 'A' of the Sanskrit words becomes 'E'. In the second syllable we find the vowel 'A' becomes 'E' due to accentuation.

A>E

Suhisakāro e|| Kc. 2/1/50

Sanskrit	Pāli
sarva+ sup	savvesu
yad+ sup	yesu
tada+sup	tesu
kim+sup	kesu

Here *sarva* is an a-ending pronominal word which becomes *savva* in Pāli. Locative case-suffix "*sup*" is added with this making the form as *savvesu*. This occurs by the rule "*suhisvakāro e*". Here final vowel of the word 'savva' is 'a' which is lengthened and becomes 'e'. That means vowel 'a' becomes a long vowel.

Similarly *yesu, tesu, kesu* develop by the rule "*suhisvakāro e*". Final consonants of these words are elided as all the words in Pāli become vowel-ending. It is a qualitative change.

A> O

Yo karoti sa kattā|| Kc. 2/6/11

Sanskrit	Pāli
pācakaḥ	pācako
kutaḥ	kuto
antara	anto
tiraska	tirokkha
naraḥ	naro

Kaccāyana makes the rule "*yo karoti sa kattā*". According to the Pāli grammarian he who does is *kartā*. That means he is subject.

We find Skt. *naraḥ* becomes *naro* in Pāli. Skt. *duṣtaḥ* becomes *duṭṭho*. That means vowel 'A' becomes 'O'. It is a qualitative change.

Lengthening of Vowel (I)

Vowel 'I' → E
Vowel 'I' → O

I > E

Sanskrit	Pāli
dvi	dve
mahiṣī	mahesi
vimadhya	vemajha
iṣṭi	eṭṭi

Here we find Skt. word *dvi* is changed into *dve* in Pāli. Probably short 'I' of the word is changed into short 'E'. In the same way Skt. *mahiṣī* becomes *mahesi* in Pāli. Here 'I' of the second syllable of the word *mahiṣi* becomes 'E' in Pāli making the form as *mehesi*. Thus vowel 'I' of the 1st syllable of the Skt. word *vimadhya* becomes *vemajha* in Pāli. The vowel 'I' of the 1st syllable of the Skt. word *iṣṭi* becomes *eṭṭi* in Pāli. In all these above mentioned word short 'I' of the Skt. word is changed into short 'E' in Pāli.

(I > O)

ādito oca|| Kc. 2/1/18

By the rule "*ādito oca*" (2/1/18) Skt. word *ādi* becomes *ādi* and *ādayo* in Pāli. Here 'I' of the final syllable of the word becomes 'O' in Pāli. Here lengthening takes place making the form "*ādayo*" in Pāli.

Lengthening of Vowel 'U'

Vowel 'U' ⟶ **'O'**

(U> O)

Sanskrit	Pāli
Purāṇa	porāṇa
Uṣṭra	Oṭṭha
Ulkā	Okkā
puttlikā	potthalikā

The Skt. words *purāṇa, uṣṭra, ulkā*, and *puttlikā* become *porāṇa, oṭṭha, okkā* and *potthalikā* in Pāli. In all these four words change occurs in the 1st syllable. Here accent is shifted on the first syllable.

B. Śarvavarman

Lengthening of Vowel 'A'

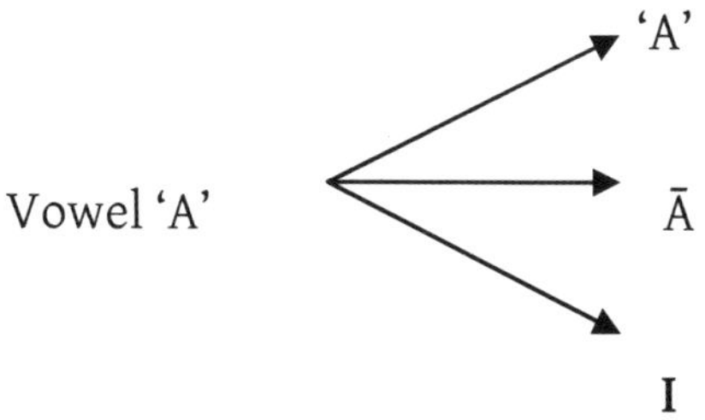

(A> Ā)

Striyāmādā।। **Śv 2/4/49**

aja+ā > ajā
eḍaka+ā > eḍakā
eṭaka+ā > eṭakā

Here feminine suffix 'ā' is the cause of lengthening. It is a quantitative change.

(A> Ā)

Ṅasirāt।। **Śv 2/1/21**

The rule of Kātantra grammar is *Ṅasirāt* (2/1/21) by which develops the form *vṛkṣāt*. Development is this following way.

vṛkṣa+ṅasi > vṛkṣa+āt > vṛkṣāt. By this way short vowel 'A' develops into 'Ā'. It is a Quantitative change.

(A> Ā)

Nirddhāraṇe ca ǁ **Śv 2/4/36**

In the sense of specification, i.e. one from the rest, sixth and seventh case-endings are employed.

Examples: vṛkṣa+ām > vṛkṣāṇām
puruṣa+ām > puruṣāṇām
gacchat+ām > gacchatām
go+ām > gavām

Here we find that vowel 'A' becomes 'Ā'. That means Quantitative change takes place here.

(A> Ā)

Yasmai ditsā rocate dhārayate vā tat sampradānam ǁ **Sv. 2/4/10**

The person who is benefited by the action signified by √*dā*, √*ruc* or to whom someone owes, is dative (*sampradāna*). Gives a cow to the Brahmin, Devadatta likes sweet, he owes a cow to Viṣṇumitra, the virgin reveals (her desires) to the pupil.

Examples:
brāhmaṇāya gāṃ dadāti
(brāhmaṇ > brāhmaṇāya)
Devadattāya rocate modakaḥ
(devadatta> devadattāya)
Viṣṇumitrāya gāṃ dhārayate
(viṣṇumitra > viṣṇumitrāya)

In this sūtra vṛtti we get the words Viṣṇumitrāya, chātrāya, brāhmaṇāya, devadattāya, yajñādattāya, as the examples of sampradānam or 4th case ending devadattā+ ṅe> devadattā+e > devadatta+ay > devadattāya. The final vowel "A" of the word *devadatta* develops as (Ā) as a result of vowel sandhi. It is lengthening indicating quantitative change.

(A> Ā)

ṇya gargādeḥ ।। Śv. **2/6/2**

Examples: daśaratha+ iṇ> dāśarathi
garga+ iṇ > gārgiḥ
jamadagni+iṇ > jāmadagnya

The words; *garga, vatsa, jamadagni* etc. become *gārgya, vātsya* and *jāmadagnya* accordingly. In all these words 'A' becames 'Ā' by the rule "*vṛddhirādau saṇe*" (2/6/49) making a quantitative change in the aforesaid word. *Ggargādi* belongs to *ākṛtigaṇaḥ*.

(A> Ā)

Surāmi sarvataḥ।। Sv. **2/1/29**

Examples: sarva+ām (stri) = sarvāsām
ya+ām (stri) = yāsām
tad+ām (stri)= tāsām

The word *sarva* becomes *sarvāsām* genitive plural in feminine. Genitive Plural case suffix '*ām*' takes place after the pronoun '*sarva*'. The vowel 'A' of the word '*sarva*' is lengthened and changed into 'Ā'.

(A>Ī)

Nadādyañcivāhavyanasyantṛsakhinântebhyaī।। Śv. **2/4/50**

Examples: Nada+ ī > nadī

Here feminine suffix 'Ī' is added to the word *nada* making the form '*nadī*'. Here feminine suffix 'Ī' is the cause of the lengthening here. It is a qualitative change.

(A>E)

Ina ṭā।। Śv. 2/1/23

Ṭā changes *ina* into after 'A' ending bases

Examples: vṛkṣa+ ṭā > vṛkṣeṇa
vṛkṣa+ bhyas > vṛkṣebhyaḥ
vṛkṣa+ ṅi > vṛkṣe

The stem here 'vṛkṣa' by the rule "**Ina ṭā**" (2/1/23) after a-ending word *ṭā* becomes *iṇa.* So *vṛkṣa+iṇa* becomes *vṛkṣeṇa* making final 'A' lengthened into 'E'. The stem is here *vṛkṣa* . The case-suffix 'bhyas' denotes 4th case-ending plural number. This '*bhyas*' becomes '*bhya*': in 4th case-ending plural of 5th case-ending plural. By this rule final (A) of the a-ending word *vṛkṣa* becomes (E) as because this is in plural form and before a "*dhuṭ*" sound. So the vowel (A) becomes lengthened being changed into (E).

The stem *vṛkṣa* is an A-ending word. *ṅi* of the 7th case-ending singular remains as 'I'. So final 'A' of *vṛkṣa* + i of 7th case ending singular becomes lengthened vowel (E) by sandhi making the form *vṛkṣe.*

yavebhyaḥ gāṃ rakṣati that means *yavebhyo gāṃ niṣedhati.* In the Kalāpa grammar of Śaravarmā we get the rule "*īpsitañca rakṣārthānām*" (2/4/9).

When one will apply *rakṣārthaka* root then desirable and undesirable things are matter *apādānakāraka* that means fifth case-ending is added with the stem.

That means it remains as *yava+bhyas.* Final 'a' of the a- ending *yava* becomes (e) as it comes before a "*dhuṭ*" sound '*bha*' of the *bhyas*, fifth case- suffix in plural. "*Dhutṭ*" means all the mutes and sibilants.

(A>E)

Ya ādhārastadadhikaraṇama॥ Śv. 2/4/11

The place of rest or locus or support is termed as Locative (*adhikaraṇa*). Sits on the mat; oil is in sesame; gangāyām ghoṣaḥ ; milkman lives on the bank of Ganga.

Examples: kaṭe āsta (kaṭa> kaṭe)
teleṣu tailam (tila> tileṣu)

Here we find that vowel (A) becomes (E). That means Qualitative change takes place here owing to the above *sūtra* which belongs to *Kalāpa Vyākaraṇa.* Here we get the examples *kaṭe* and *tileṣ, kaṭa+ṅi* (locative singular) leads to *kaṭa+i* which ultimately becomes *kaṭe* as a result of sandhi between vowel '*A*' of *kaṭa* and vowel '*I*' of the case-suffix. *Tila+sup* (locative plural) becomes *tileṣuc* hanging the final (A) of *tila* to (E).

(A>E)

Yena kriyate tat karaṇam॥ Śv. 2/4/12

To accomplish an action, what is needed (as the best ingredient), is termed as instrument (*karaṇa*).

Manasā merum gacchati that means 'mentally goes to the mountain.' *Paśunā rudraṃ* yajate 'worships *Rudra*, with animals,' *gotreṇa gārgyaḥ' gārgya* by clan, '*dvi-droṇena dhānyam krīṇāti* 'buys crops by exchanging an amount equivalent to two *droṇas*'.

Examples : dātra+ṭā = dātreṇa
prāya+ṭā= prāyeṇa
gotra+ṭā= gotreṇa

The vowel (A) of the word "*dātra*" becomes (E) in instrumental singular case. By the rule "*Yena kriyate tat karaṇam*" here instrumental case takes place in *karaṇa* or instrument "dātra", "ṭā" is replaced by "*ina*". Then *sandhi* takes place and makes the word "dātreṇa" Thus "a" is lengthened and becomes "e".

(A>E)

Yaḥ karoti saḥ kartā।। Śv. 2/4/14

The concept, which accomplishes the action, is termed as agent (*kartā*). *Chātreṇa hanyate* 'killed by the student'. Here the student accomplishes the action of killing. Therefore it is considered as the agent of the action. Since it is a passive construction, the agent is marked with the third case ending Similarly, *Caitreṇa kṛtam* 'done by caitra'.

Examples: chātreṇa hanyate (chātra > chātreṇa)
Caitreṇa kṛtam (Caitra > Caitreṇa)

Here *chātreṇa* occurs by anuktakartari tṛtīyā. Here the sūtra is "Yaḥ karoti saḥ kartā"

But the sentence *Chātreṇa hanyate* is in passive voice. In passive voice *kartrā* is known as *anuktakartā*. Instrumental case occurs in *anuktakartā*.

The word "*chātra*" becomes *chātreṇa*. The vowel "a" of the word *chātra* being lengthened becomes "e".

(A>E)

Tṛtīyādau parādiḥ।। Śv.2/1/7

In case- *ṭā* or any of the remaining endings is added, an augment, having- 'a' as the indicatory marker, is however, introduced as the initial segment of the ending.

Examples: sarva+āma = sarveṣām

The word "sarva" becomes *sarveṣām* genitive plural. Genitive plural case-suffix "ām" takes place after the pronoun "sarva". The vowel "a" of the word *sarva* is lengthened and changed into "e".

(A>E)

Jas srva iḥ॥ **Śv. 2/1/30**

Jas changes into *–i.*

Examples: sarva+jas > sarve

viśve+jas > viśbe

Here the sūtra is "**Jas srva iḥ**". *Jas* is nominative plural case suffix. By this rule *jas* is changed into "i", Then "e" comes as a result of sandhi.

So we get the vowel "e" which is seemed a lengthened form of the vowel "a" of the word. It is a Qualitative change.

Lengthening of Vowel (i)

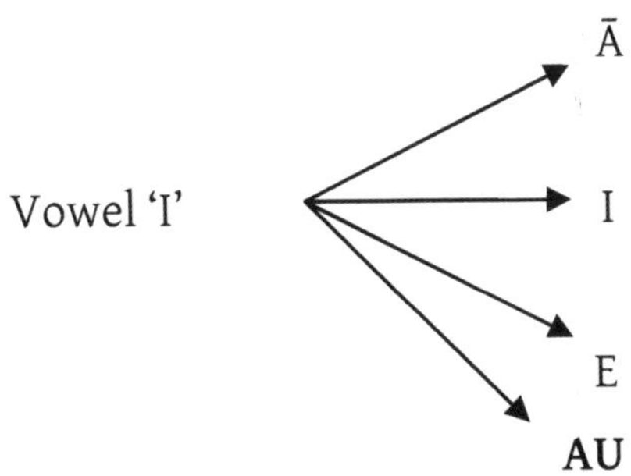

(I>Ā)

Ghuṭi tvai॥ **Śv. 2/2/24**

Before *ghuṭa*, however, (i of *sakhi*) is substituted by 'e'

Examples: sakhi+au > sakhāyau
Sariva+ jas > sakhāyaḥ

The stem here is a masculine word *sakhi.* By the rule. " ghuṭi tvai" (2/2/24) *au* and *jas* become 'ā' after 'i' ending word. So sakhi+āu becomes *sakhāyau* and sakhi+jas becomes *sakhāyaḥ.*

Here case- suffix 'ā' is the cause of the lengthening. It is a Qualitative change.

(I>Ā)

Panthimanthyabhukṣīṇām sau || **Śv. 2/2/35**

Examples: Pathin+su > panthā
Mathin+su > manthā

Here we find that vowel (i) becomes (ā). That means qualitative change. Here the sutra is "Panthimanthyabhukṣīṇām sau" (2/2/35). *su* is nominative singular case suffix. Development is this following way.

Pathina+su >panthā, mathin+su > manthā. By this way short vowel (i) develops into (ā). It is a qualitative change.

(I>Ī)

śasoऽkāraḥ saśca toऽstriyām || **Śv. 2/1/52**

Examples: agni+śas > agnīn
paṭu+śasa > paṭūn

Here the sūtra is **śasoऽkāraḥ saśca toऽstriyām** (2/1/52) and *śas* is accusative plural case-suffix. Here the vowel 'i' of the word 'agni' becomes the vowel 'ī' of the word 'agnīn' by the case suffix. So (ī) is the cause of the lengthening here. It is a quantitative change.

(I>E)

ṅasiṅasoralopaśca || **Śv. 2/1/58**

Before ṅasi and ṅas too final i and u are substituted by e and o respectively and 'a' of 'ṅasi' and 'ṅas' is elided.

Examples: agni+ṅasi > agneḥ
agni+ṅas > agneḥ

Here we get the masculine word agni which becomes *agne* by this rule **ṅasiṅasoralopaśca** (2/1/58) in the ablative and genitive case suffix. So the initial vowel (i) of the word *agni* becomes (e) making the word agneḥ. It is a qualitative change.

(I>E)

Patirasamāsa।। **Śv. 2/2/2**

Example: Pati+ṅe > patye

The stem here is masculine word *pati.* i- ending word *ṅe* becomes e, by the rule *patirasamāsa* (2/2/2). So pati+ṅe in the dative case becomes *patye.* Here case suffix (e) is the cause of the lengthening here. It is a qualitative change.

(I>AU)

ṅirau।। **Śv. 2/1/60**

Example: Agni+ṅi >agnau

Here the masculine word *agni* becomes *agnau* by the case-suffix *ṅi.* By this rule *ṅirau sapūrvaḥ* (2/1/60), (i) becomes (au) to the locative singular case. It is a Qualitative change.

(I>Au)

Sakhipatyoraṅi।। **Śv. 2/1/61**

Sakhi+ṅi > sakhyau
Pati+ ṅi > patyau

The stem here a masculine word *sakhi* and *pati* by the rule "**Sakhipatyoraṅi**" (2/1/61) after 'i' ending word 'ṅi' becomes 'au'. So sariva+ṅi > sakhyau and pati+ṅi becomes *patyau.* Here case-suffix 'au' is the cause of the lengthening. It is a qualitative change.

Lengthening of Vowel (u)

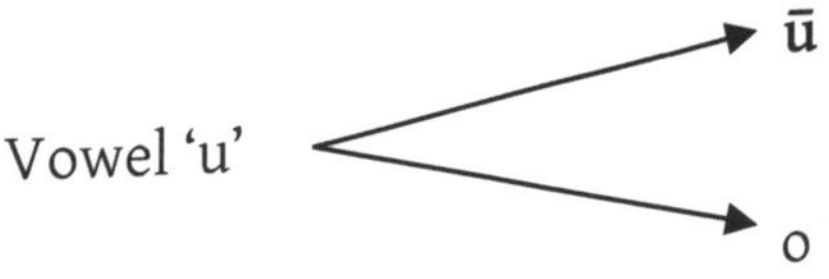

(U> Ū)

Aukāraḥ pūrvam।। Śv2/1/51

Examples: paṭu+ au > paṭu
Sādhu+au > sādū

Here the masculine words are *paṭu* and *sādhu*. The vowel 'u' of the word *paṭu* becomes (ū) and similarly the vowel (u) of the word *sādhu* becomes (ū) in nominal dual case-suffix. By the rule "**Aukāraḥ pūrvam**" (2/1/51) (u) becomes (ū**).** It is a quantitative change.

(Ū> U)

Dīrghamāmi sanau।। Ś**v.**2/2/15

Dhenu+ām > dhenūnām

By this rule "**Dīrghamāmi sanau**" (2/2/15) the vowel (u) becomes (ū) in the feminine word. The vowel 'u' of the word *dhenu* becomes the vowel 'ū' of the word 'dhenūnām' in genitive plural case-suffix. Here case - suffix (ū) is the cause of lengthening. It is a quantitative change.

(U>O)

ṅasiṅasoralopaśca।। Śv. 2/1/58

Example: dhenu+ṅasi > dhenoḥ
Dhenu+ṅas >dhenoḥ

Here we get the feminine word "dhenu" which becomes "dhenoḥ" by this rule "**ṅasiṅasoralopaśca**" (2/1/58) in the ablative and genitive singular case suffix. So the initial vowel (u) of the word 'dhenuḥ' becomes (o) making the word *dhen-*

uḥ. So (u) is lengthened and becomes (o). It is a Qualitative change.

Shortening of Long Vowel

A. Kaccāyana

Shortening of Vowel (ā)

Vowel (ā) ⟶ (a)

(Ā> A)

Sahādi yoge ca|| Kc. 2/6.17

Examples :	Sanskrit	Pāli
	gārgena	gaggena
	sārdham	saddhiṃ

By this rule third case-ending occurs by the words 'saha' and 'artha' Kaccāyana gives examples *sahāpi garggena saṅgho uposatha kareyya, vināpi gaggena*. Here we find Sanskrit *gārgena* becomes *gaggena*. Here long vowel '*ā*' becomes '*a*', but the grammarian does not explain the cause. Linguistically we can say that the long sound comes before a conjunct group. So shortening takes place. 'sārghama' becomes 'saddhima' Vowel 'ā' becomes 'a', that means shortening takes place.

Shortening of Vowel (ī)

Vowel (ī) ⟶ (i)

(Ī> I)

Aghorassamekavacana yosva pica|| Kc 2/1/33

Examples:	Sanskrit	Pāli
	striyaḥ	itthiyo

Here case suffix *yo* comes which denotes nominative plural case. So stri+yo> *itthiyo* in Pāli. So, stri> ithi (ī > i). It is shortening here and quantitative change.

Shortening of Vowel (ū)

Vowe (ū) ⟶ **(u)**

(Ū> U)

Aghorassamekavacana yosva pica|| Kc 2/1/33

Examples:	Sanskrit	Pāli
	vadhūm	vadhuṃ

Here case suffix *aṃ* comes which denotes accusative singular case. So vadhū+aṃ > vadhuṃ in Pāli. So it is shortening here and quantitative change also.

B. Śarvavarman

Shortening of Vowel (ā)

Vowel (ā) ⟶ **(a)**

(Ā> A)

Tausore|| **Śv 2/1/38**

Examples: śradhā+ṭā > śraddhayā

śradhā+os> śraddhayoḥ

The feminine word is śradhā. Here case suffix *ṭā* comes which denotes instrumental singular case. So śradhā+ṭā becomes '**śraddhayā**' making final (ā) shortened into (a)

Similarly, by the rule "tausore" the feminine word *śradhā*, which becomes *śraddhayoḥ* by the case suffix *osa*. So it is shortening here and quantitative change also.

Shortening of Vowel (ī)

Vowel (ī) ⟶ **(i)**

(Ī> I)

Sambuddhau hrasvaḥ|| **Śv. 2/1/46**

The final vowel of **ī** and **ū**-ending bases which are designated as nadī becomes short before vocative singular ending.

Example: nadī sambodhane > nadi

Final vowel ī of an ī-ending word becomes i, if the vocative case suffix comes after it. e.g. nadī+su (vocative)= nadi.

In case of nadi shortening takes place due to accentuation.

Shortening of Vowel (ū)

Vowel (ū) ——————→ (u)

(Ū> U)

Sambuddhau hrasvaḥ॥ Śv. 2/1/46

Example: vadhū sambodhana >vadhu

Final vowel ū of an ū-ending word becomes u, if the vocative case suffix comes after it. e.g. vadhū+ su (Vocative)= vadhu. In case of *vadhu* shortening takes place due to accentuation.

Treatment of Sonant

A. Kaccāyana

The Vowels ṛ, ḷ are absent from Pāli. They are represented by other vowel sounds.

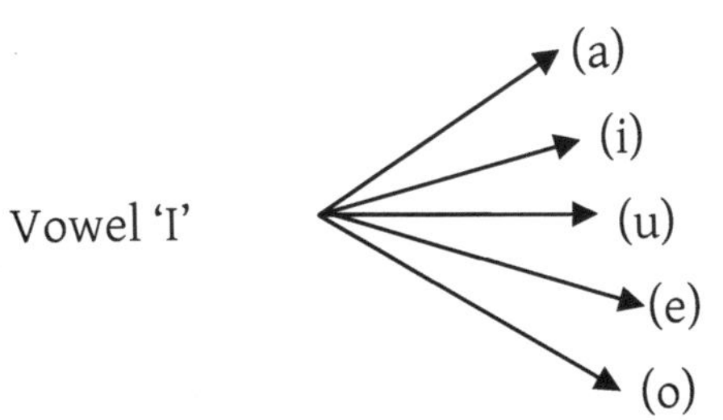

(Ṛ> A)

Sanskrit	**Pāli**
amrta	amata

hrdaya	hadaya
trṣita	tasita
grha	gaha
mrtyu	maccu

(Ṛ > I)

Sanskrit	Pāli
mrga	miga
rṇa	ina
krśa	kisa
drṣṭaṃ	diṭṭaṃ
trpti	titti
brṅgāra	bhiṅkāro

(Ṛ> U)

Sanskrit	Pāli
prcchati	pucchati
mrdu	mudu
rtu	utu
vrṣṭi	vuṭṭhi
vrttānta	vuttnto

(Ṛ > E)

Sanskrit	Pāli
grha	geha
grhapati	gehapati
rājagrha	rājageha

(Ṛ > O)

Sanskrit	Pāli
sammrṣa	sammosa

Here, the Pāli words *amata, taṇhā, isi, igaveda, usabha, mudu, geha, gehapati, sammosa* get their forms followings Pkt. words probably.

B- Śarvavarman

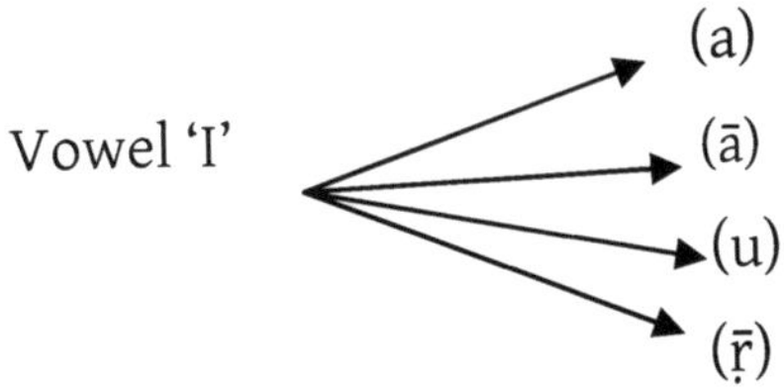

(Ṛ > A)

Ghuṭi ca।। Śv 2/1/67

ṛ is changed into *ar* before *ghuṭ*

Example: pitṛ+au > pitarau
pitṛ+jas > pitaraḥ

Here we find that the ṛ-ending word becomes 'a' in nominative dual and plural case suffix. By this rule "Ghuṭi ca" (2/1/67) ṛ of the masculine word becomes 'a'. It is a Qualitative change.

ṛ of the ṛ-ending masculine and feminine words becomes 'a' in locative singular case, i.e. mātṛ+ṅi> mātari.

(Ṛ> A)

Āca na sambuddhau।। Śv. 2/1/70

In *sambudhi*, of course ā of ār in place of ṛ is negated so that the substitute for ṛ is not ār but ar.

Example: katṛ> kartaḥ in sambodhane

ṛ of the ṛ-ending masculine word becomes 'a' in vocative singular case- suffix (su).

(Ṛ> Ā)

Svasrādīnām ca|| Śv. 2/1/69

Example: svasṛ+ au > svasārau

By this rule "**Svasrādīnām ca**" (2/1/69), ṛ-ending word becomes 'ā' in nominative dual case-suffix. It is a Qualitative change.

(Ṛ> U)

ṛdantāt sapūrvaḥ|| Śv. 2/1/63

With the final ṛ of ṛ-ending bases, **a** of **ṅasi** and **ṅas** are jointly substituted by **u.**

Examples: pitṛ+ṅasi > pituḥ
pitṛ+ṅas > pituḥ

The stem here is a masculine word 'pitṛ'. By the rule "**ṛdantāt sapūrvaḥ**" (2/1/63) ṅasi and ṅas become (u) after ṛ-ending word. So, pitṛ+ ṅasi becomes pituḥ and pitṛ+ṅas becomes pituḥ. It is a Qualitative change.

(Ṛ > Ṝ)

Agnivacchasiḥ|| Śarvavarman 2/1/65

ṛ- ending bases are declined as agni, before śas i.e to say a of śas is substituted by ṛ while -s- is substituted by n.

Examples: pitṛ+ śas> pitṝn

mātṛ+śas > mātṝ

By this rule "**Agnivacchasiḥ**" (2/1/65), ṛ–ending masculine and feminine words become long ṛ in accusative plural case suffix. Here the vowel long ṛ is the cause of the lengthening. It is a Quantitative change.

Treatment of Diphthong

A. Kaccāyana

The vowels 'ai' and 'au' are absent from Pāli. They are represented by other vowel sounds. In this case the Pāli words which are originated from Skt. words follow the rules of Pkt.

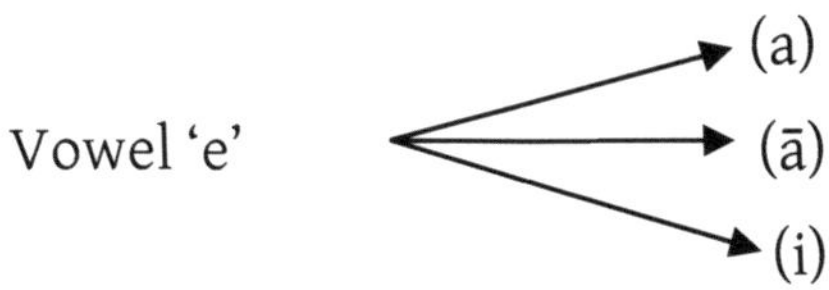

(E > A)

Sanskrit	Pāli
mleccha	milakkha

(E > Ā)

Sanskrit	Pāli
keyūra	kāyūra

(E > I)

Sanskrit	Pāli
udvela	uvvila

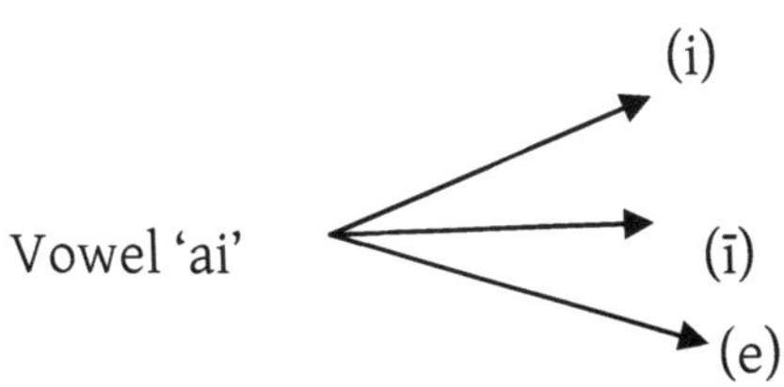

(AI > I)

Sanskrit	Pāli
saindhavo	sindhavo
caitraḥ	citto
aiśvaryaṃ	issariyaṃ

(AI > Ī)

Sanskrit	**Pāli**
graiveyaṃ	gībeyyaṃ

(AI > E)

Sanskrit	**Pāli**
airāvaṇa	erāvaṇa
maitre	mettā
vaiyākaraṇaḥ	veyyākaraṇo
tailaṃ	telaṃ
kaivarttaḥ	kevaṭṭo
naiyāyikaḥ	neyyāyiko
aitihyaṃ	etiyhaṃ

Vowel (au) → (u)
Vowel (au) → (o)

(AU > U)

Sanskrit	**Pāli**
kṣaudraṃ	khuddaṃ
autsukyaṃ	ussukkaṃ
auddeśikaḥ	uddesiko
sautrikaṃ	suttikaṃ

(AU > O)

Sanskrit	**Pāli**
audarikaḥ	osriko
gautama	gotama
audumbaraṃ	odumbaraṃ
dauvārikaḥ	dovāriko
pauraḥ	poro
saugandhikaṃ	sogandhikaṃ

B. Śarvavarman

Vowel (O) → (**ā**)
→ (au)

(O > Ā)

go+ au > gāvau go+jas > gāvaḥ

Here we find the vowel 'o' becomes the vowel 'ā' in nominative dual and plural case-suffixes.

By the rule "**gorau ghuṭi**" (Śv. 2/2/33) the vowel "o" of the word "go" becomes "au" when it is followed by "ghuṭ" i.e case suffix "au" etc. Then sandhi takes place by the rule "au āva" (1/2/15) making the form as "gāvau". Here sandhi causes the change of "o" into "ā".

(O > AU)

gorau ghuṭi।। Śv. 2/2/33

Before **ghuṭ** in 'go' **au** substitutes the final **o.**

Example: go+au > gāvau
go+ jas > gāvaḥ

By this rule 'o' of the word 'go' becomes "au". Then by the rule "au āva" (1/2/15) "gau" becomes "gāv", followed by the "ghuṭ" "au". Finally the form becomes "gāvau". It is a quantitative change.

Initial vowel Lopa

'a' Lopa

Due to want of stress initial vowels or syllables are sometimes dropped in Old-Indo-Aryan. This phenomenon persisted in the Middle Indo-Aryan Stages.

Skt. agni > Pāli gini

Skt. alāpu > Pāli lāpu
Skt. alābu > pāli lābu

'i' Lopa

Skt. iti > Pāli ti
Skt. idāni> Pāli dāni

'u' Lopa

Skt. udaka > Pāli daka
Skt. upavasatha > Pāli posatha.

Appendix

Sajñā which are used by Kaccāyana & Śarvavarman

Śarvarman	Kaccāyana
1. Nāma/ ghut Sūtra- pañcadau ghuṭ (2/1/3) The first five case-endings are together known as ghut. In neuter gender jas and śas are also known as ghut.	1. nāma/ śabda- Sūtra- tadanuparodher (2/1/5) yathā yathā tesa[m] jinavacanānaṃ anuparodh[e] tathā idha liṅañca nipacc[a]te, atra 'liṅga' śabdasyārth[a] nāma/śabda
2. sambuddhi- Sūtra- āmantrite sisambuddhiḥ (2/1/5) First case ending singular –su, when added, in vocative is called saṃbuddhiḥ.	2. ga-saṃjñā- Sūtra- ālapane si gasaññ[ā] (2/1/6) ālapanatthe si gas[a]ñño hoti. Bhoti aye, bho[ti] kaññe, bhoti kharādiye. Here, ālapana= sambodhan[a] Si= prathamā ekavacana
3. nadī- Sūtra- īdūt strākhyau nadi	3. jha-saṃjñā, la-saṃjñā- Sūtra- ivaṇṇuvaṇṇājjh[a]

(2/1/9) ī and ū ending bases, to mean something feminine are treated as *nadī*, and declined accordingly.	(2/1/7) Ivaṇṇuvaṇṇā iccete jha; asaññā honti yathāsaṃkhyaṃ. isinā, daṇḍino, aggino, gahapatino, setuno, bhikkhuno, sayammbhno. Here i, ī-kārānta puṃliṅga śabdānām nāma 'jha', u', ū-kārānta puṃliṅga śabdānām nāma 'la'.
4. śradhā- Sūtra- ā śradhā (2/1/10) The ā ending bases, (to mean something feminine), are treated as śraddhā, (and declined accordingly)	4. pa-saṃjñā- Sūtra- te itthikhyā po (2/1/8) Te ivaṇṇuvaṇṇā yadā itthikhyā, tadā pasaññā honti. rattiyā, itthiyā, dhenuyā, vadhuyā. Here, I, ī-kārānta strīliṅga śbdānām u, ū-kārānta strīliṅga śbdānāmaśca pa-saṃjñā bhavati
5. upadhā- Sūtra- antyātpūrva upadhā (2/1/11) The penultimate sound (= immediate antecedent of the final sound) of a liṅga (base) is known as upadhā.	5. gha saṃjñā Sūtra- āgho (2/1/9 Ākāro yadā itthikhyo, tadā ghasañño hoti. saddhāya, kaññāya, vīṇāya, gaṅgāya, disāya sālāya, mālāya, tulāya, dolāya, pabhāya, sobh-

6. anuṣaṅga- Sūtra- vyañjanānno'nuṣaṅgaḥ (2/1/12) The-n-sound, which is the immediate antecedent of the final consonant, is known as anuṣaṅgaḥ.	āya, paññāya, karuṇāy nāvāya, kapālikāya.
7. dhuḍ Sūtra- dhuḍvyāñjanamanantaḥ sthānunāsikam (2/1/13) Except semivowels (antasthāḥ, i.e. y, r, l, v) and nasals (anunāsika, i.e. n, ñ, ṇ, n, all other consonants are known as dhuḍ.	

Bibliography

BANERJEE, Satya Ranjan.

1992. *Kaccāyana Kata Pāli Vyākaraṇam*. Ed. Calcutta: Sanskrit Sahitya Parishat.

BARUA, Dijendralal.

1956. *New Elements of Pāli Grammar*. Kolkata: University of Kolkata.

GHOSH, Subhra Basu.

2003. *Sanskrit Phonetics in the light of Modern Phonology*. Calcutta: Sanskrit Book Depot.

BASU, S.C.

1963. *Aṣṭdhyāyī of Pāṇini*. (Vol. I-II). Delhi: Motilal Banarsidass.

BELVALKAR, S.K.

2015. *Systems of Sanskrit Grammar*. Ed. Delhi: New Bharatiya Book Corporation. 1st ed. 1976.

BHANDARE, Vasant. V.

1986. *Sanskrit Speech Habits and Pāṇini: With Special Reference to Sandhi, Samāsa and Roots-chapters of Pāṇini's Aṣṭādhyāyī.* Delhi: Takshila Hardbounds.

BURNELL, A. C.

1975. *On the Aindra School of Sanskrit Grammarians*. Mangalore.

CARDONA, George.

1999. *Recent Research in Pāninian Studies*. Delhi: Motilal Benarsidass Private limited.

CHATTERJEE, Suniti Kumar.

1983. *On the Development of Middle Indo Aryan*. Kolkata: Government Sanskrit College, Kolkata.

DEVASHARMA, Kalijivan.

1995. *Śabdaśāstrer Itihāsa.* Kolkata: Ramkrishna Mission Institute of Culture.

DVIVEDI, Janakiprasad.

1997. *Śarvavarman. Kātantra Vyākaranam.* Ed. Varanasi: Sampurnanda Sanskrit University.

GUPTA, K. M.

2006. *Linguistic Approach to Meaning in Pali.* New Delhi: Sundeep Prakashan.

HAZRA, K. L.

1994. *Pali Language and Literature: A Survey and Historical Study with Canonical and Non Canonical Pali Texts (Emerging Perceptions in Buddhist Studies).* New Delhi: D.K. Print World Ltd.

RAY, Biswapati.

2000. *Kaumāra Vyākaraṇa: A Critical Study*. Kolkata.

SATPATHY, R. K.

1999. *Pāṇinian and Kātantra systems of Grammar: A comparative study.* Delhi: Bharatiya Vidya Prakashan.

SHASTRI, Bidhusekhar.

1318 (Baṅgābda). *Pāliprakāsh.* Bolpur.

TARAPOREWALA, Irach Jehangir Sorabji.

1978. *Elements of the Science of language*. Kolkata: University of Kolkata.

TIWARI, Lakshmi Narayan and SHARMA Birbal.

1989. *Kaccāyanavyākaraṇa*. Ed. Varanasi: Tara Book Agency. 1989. (First ed. 1962).

On the Authorship of *Kaccāyana*, the Oldest Pāli Grammar

A. Ruiz-Falqués*

1. Single or multiple authorship of *Kaccāyana*

The *Kaccāyana* (Kacc) Pāli grammar was composed around the sixth century CE, most probably in India, for it was unknown in Sri Lanka until a later date. This work, partly original and partly based on Pāṇini and Kātantra (Kā) is the oldest extant Pāli grammar. It is also the most influential *vyākaraṇa* text in the history of Theravāda Buddhism. The authorship of this text, however, remains disputed. An old Sinhalese tradition identifies Kaccāyana with Mahā Kaccāyana, the disciple of the Buddha and alleged author of the *Nettippakaraṇa* and the *Mahānirutti* (Ap-a 491, $_{17\text{-}21}$ (ad Ap 531); A I 23, $_{16\text{-}28}$). This view is today dismissed by most scholars. Even orthodox Theravādin-s find it difficult to accept that an imperfect treatise such as Kacc could have been written by an impeccable *arahant* such as Mahā Kaccāyana. The name Kaccāyana, therefore, must represent a different author. Pind suggests that Kacc could be the work of one or more compilers rather than authors: "Kacc is a compilation of various hands" (Pind 2012: 75). This is the reason that scholars have described it as chaotic and devoid of any systematic arrangement. Now, when we say "various hands" it is not clear whether we mean a definite or indefinite number of authors. A more or less established consensus among scholars, after D'Alwis (1863:

* Ph.D. University of Cambridge. E-mail: ar607@cam.ac.uk

104–105), divides the work in three layers of text. In the Pāli grammatical tradition, each layer is ascribed to a particular author. Thus, the *sutta* text, that is to say, the grammatical aphorisms, are ascribed to a certain Kaccāyana, the *vutti* ("gloss", Kacc-v) is ascribed to a certain Saṅghanandin, and the *payoga* ("examples") section is ascribed to a certain Brahmadatta. These three texts make the Kacc proper. The *Nyāsa* of Vimalabuddhi, otherwise known as *Mukhamattadīpanī* (Mmd) is considered the fourth layer of the corpus, but I will not concern myself with this work, as it has a textual tradition of its own.

In order to illustrate the threefold nature of Kacc, let us examine Kacc 336 *sare an* "[when deriving a compound], before a vowel *an* [replaces *na*]". The following is the text that we would find in a manuscript:

> *sare an. nassa padassa tappurise uttarapade sabbasseva anādeso hoti sare pare. anasso. anissaro. anariyo. aniṭṭho.*[1]

Here we can distinguish three sections. The main rule, *sare an*, is the first. What follows is a gloss giving the context that applies to the rule, that is to say, conditions from previous *sutta*-s that implicitly "recur" (*anuvattanti*) or "are still valid" (*vattanti*), that is why this second section is called *vutti*. Finally, we have a series of words that exemplify the "application" (*payoga*) of the rule.

Some *sutta*-s in Kacc include even another type of section at the end. This section consists of questions and answers about the purpose and scope of the words used in the previous sections. For instance, Kacc 9 *parasamaññā payoge*:

> *parasamaññā payoge. yā ca pana sakkataganthesu samaññā ghosā ti vā aghosā ti vā tā payoge sati ettha pi payuñjante. ga gha ṅa ja jha ña ḍa ḍha ṇa da dha na ba bha ma ya ra la va ha ḷa iti ghosā. ka kha ca cha ṭa ṭha ta tha pa pha sa iti*

1 I follow the PTS critical edition (= PIND 2013).

aghosā. ghosāghosa icc anena kv attho. vagge ghosāghosānaṃ tatiyapaṭhamā (Kacc $3,_{1\text{-}8}$).

The initial statement *parasamaññā payoge* is the *sutta*, which means "Concepts of others [should be used] when they apply". The *vutti* explains that concepts, such as *ghosa* "aspirate" and *aghosa* "unaspirate", defined in Sanskrit treatises, are to be used when there is occasion to apply them (*payoge sati*). We subsequently find a list of *ghosa* and *aghosa* consonants. This part already belongs to the *payoga*. The last section consists of a question about the purpose of saying "*ghosāghosā*" and the answer giving the place in Kacc where these two concepts are used [i.e. Kacc 29]. That type of section could also be considered *payoga*, for it specifies the scope for the application of the *sutta*. In this case and in other cases, it is very important to observe how the *payoga* does not comment upon the *sutta* (allegedly composed by Kaccāyana) but upon the *vutti* (allegedly composed by Saṅghanandin). In his critical edition of the text, PIND establishes a simpler division that overlooks this fact. He separates the *sutta* text, that is Kacc, from the rest, which he calls *Kaccāyanavutti* (Kacc-v). According to PIND, it is practically impossible to determine the authorship, single or multiple, of Kacc. That is why, I think, he has adopted a straightforward and practical policy when editing the text.

In this paper I do not intend to solve the question of the Kacc authorship. I will simply problematise it taking into consideration some facts that have so-far been overlooked.

2. Origin of the fourfold division of the *Kaccāyana* system

James D'ALWIS was the first modern scholar to raise the question of the triple authorship of Kacc. In his essay on this grammar, he quotes a passage from the "*Kaccāyanabheda-ṭīkā*", actually meaning, as PIND already pointed out, the *Kaccāyanabheda-navaṭīkā* (Kacc-bh-nṭ, not to be confused with the old *Kaccāyanabheda-porāṇaṭīkā*). D'Alwis quotes the entire passage, which deals with the number of *sutta*-s in every chapter of Kacc and it basically contains a quotation of an older work, now lost, called *Kaccāyana-dīpanī*. Ariyālaṅkāra, the author of Kacc-bh-nṭ points out that the number of *sutta*-s according to *Kaccāyana-dīpanī* does not match the number of Kacc *sutta*-s embedded in the *Nyāsa*. And he adds the famous passage, including another quotation that may come from *Kaccāyana-dīpanī* as well:

> *imāni suttāni mahā kaccāyanena katāni vutti ca sanghanandi sankhātena mahā kaccāyaneneva katā payogo brahmadattena kato ti. vuttañ cetaṃ:*
>
> *kaccāyanakato yogo vutti ca sanghanandināpayogo brahmadattena nyāso vimalabuddhinā ti* (Kacc-bh-nṭ 129, 15-30).

D'ALWIS translates:

> These aphorisms were composed by Mahā Kaccāyana. The *Vutti* were [*sic*] composed by *Mahā Kaccāyana* himself, (who was also) called Saṅghanandi; - and the illustrations by Brahmadatta.

So it is expressly stated - that 'The aphorisms were made by Kaccāyana, the *vutti* by Sanghanandi, the illustrations by Brahmadatta and the *nyāsa* by Vimalabuddhi' (D'ALWIS, 1863: 105).

D'ALWIS adds, in a footnote, that the interpretation of the author of Kacc-bh-nṭ, identifying Mahā Kaccāyana and Sanghanandi, is probably a misunderstanding of the source, where clearly four layers of text are implied. D'ALWIS therefore believes that Kacc-bh-nṭ is wrong. Other scholars, such as MALALASEKERA, VIDYABHUSANA, DEOKAR and PIND,[2] have also

[2] MALALASEKERA (1958: 180) says: "In the *Kaccāyanabheda*, written by Mahāyasa Thera of Thatōn about the thirteenth century, there occurs a memorial verse: 'The aphorisms were made by Kaccāyana, the *Vutti* by Saṅghānandi. The illustrations by Brahmadatta. And the *Nyāsa* by Vimalabuddhi.'" To the best of my knowledge, that verse is

dismissed the interpretation of Kacc-bh-nṭ and prefer what they consider to be the original meaning of the quotation given in Kacc-bh-nṭ, that is, they do not identify Kaccāyana with Saṅghanandin, and they do not believe that the *sutta* and the *vutti* are the work of the same author.

A tradition similar to the one quoted by Ariyālaṅkāra is found in the *Saddhammasaṅgaha* (Saddhamma-s IX, 18-20, 35). This work is a "bibliography" written in the fourteenth century by the Thai monk Dhammakitti (or maybe by Ñāṇakitti, fifteenth century[3]). The passage reads as follows:

> *kaccāyano kato yogo saṃghanandi pavuttikā,*
> *ṭīkā vimalabodhī ca brahmaputto ca kārakā.*
> (SADDHĀNANDA, 1890: 63)
>
> Kaccāyana composed the *yoga* ["rule"], Saṅghanandin the *pavuttikā* ["notes"], and Vimalabodhī the *ṭīkā* ["commentary"], and Brahmaputto the *kāraka* ["section on factor of action"].

The author of Saddhamma-s had allegedly studied at the Mahāvihāra of Laṅkā (*laṅkāramamahāvase*[4]) and it is likely that the stanza ultimately comes from Laṅkā, not Burma, but this is difficult to ascertain.

Nandapañña's *Gandhavaṃsa* (Gv), a Burmese catalogue

---

not found in Kacc-bh. VIDYABHUSANA (1901: xxvi) says: "'The Yoga (*Sūtra*) was written by Kaccāyana, the commentary by Saṅghanandī, the examples were added by Brahmadatta and the gloss by Vimalabuddhi.' From the manner in which the *sutta*, *vutti*, *payoga* and *nyāsa* are intimately connected with one another, I am inclined to believe that the entire work was written by Kātyāyana himself. At any rate the *sutta*, etc. were written simultaneously." Even though VIDYABHUSANA is clearly not aware that the *Nyāsa* is a different text, it is important to keep in mind that this great scholar had the intuition of a single authorship. DEOKAR (2008: 7) and PIND (2012: 71) also distinguish four authors in that quotation.

3 NYANATUSSITA, 4.3.1.

4 SADDHĀNANDA, 1890: 90.

written probably around the seventeenth century[5] but source of many other bibliographies and one of the most consulted in modern Pāli, mentions Kaccāyana as the author of the "Kaccāyanagandho". Gv does not mention Saṅghanandin, nor Brahmadatta (or Brahmaputta). It however mentions Vimalabuddhi as the author of Mmd.[6]

Ariyālaṅkāra probably had some reasons to believe that Kacc and Kacc-v are the work of the same author, and to consider the *payoga* as a different work, a latter addition. It seems as if he already expected three authors, and that is why he forces the meaning of the stanza in such a counterintuitive way. Indeed he is quoting the stanza in order to back up his judgement. He might be wrong in his interpretation, but he might still be right in seeing three, and not four, authors in the core text of the Kacc System.

In Western scholarship FRYER argued, as early as in 1882, in favour of Ariyālaṅkāra's position (although he ascribes the stanza to Ariyālaṅkāra himself). VIDYABHUSANA also maintained that the text known as *Kaccāyana* was the work of a single person (see previous note). In the following section I will examine some features of Kacc and Kacc-v that can explain why some scholars tend to believe in a single author or editor.

3. Points of structure

It is necessary in the first place to examine the structure of the text as a whole. The structure of Kacc *sutta* is the same as Kātantra and many other grammars of the so-called Aindra class. Originally the work consists of four books: *Sandhi, Nāma, Ākhyāta* and *Kibbidhāna*[7]. Introductory verses are found in the beginning of the 1st, the 3rd and the 4th books. Those in the 3rd

5 NYANATUSSITA, 4.3.3.

6 Gv, 60: *vimalabuddhi nāmācariyo mukhamattadīpanī nāma nyāsapakaraṇaṃ akāsi.*

7 For the so-called Aindra System see BURNELL, 1885 *passim.*

book, according to PIND (2013: 146), are later additions. Kacc structure is based on the complete version of *Kātantra*, including the last book on *kṛt* suffixes, allegedly authored by a certain Kātyāyana, not by Śarvavarman (SAINI 1999: 18). The title *Sandhikappa*, which should be the title of the first book only, is found in Kacc manuscript colophons at the end of every chapter (... *sandhikappo niṭṭhito*), the fact is that tradition consistently refers to this grammar as *Kaccāyana* (DEOKAR 2008: 10). Taking the title from the introductory stanzas, with slight variations, is a normal practice.

As early as in Vimalabuddhi's *Mukhamattadīpanī* (probably around the 10th century CE) we find that Kacc is treated a compilation of four treatises. The original fourfold sectioning developed into an artificial eightfold division already recognised by Vimalabuddhi. Furthermore, Vimalabuddhi's recension of Kacc (and Kacc-v) is not exactly the same as the recension of the text called simply *Kaccāyana* in Sri Lanka and Burma. But the textual transmission of Kacc and Kacc-v is the same. They are consistently called Kaccāyana in mss.

The commentarial pattern or method of Kacc-v is the same throughout the four books. We find the same set of (optional) fields:

(1) A paraphrase (*vutti*)

(2) Examples introduced by *tamyathā* or equivalent

(3) Counter examples introduced by *kasmā* or equivalent

(4) Purpose or scope of the *sutta* introduced by *kv attho* or equivalent

(5) Comments on *anuvṛtti*, meaning of *ca* or *vā*, etc. for instance: Kacc-v ad Kacc 35: *casaddaggahaṇena iheva makārassa pakāro hoti.*

Regarding the text of PIND's Kacc-v specifically, it is

considered that:

1) It is made of different layers in Kacc/-v, each layer is the work of one single author.

2) It is made of different sections in Kacc/-v, each section is the work of one author.

According to PIND, it is questionable that Kacc-v is the work of a single author and he gives the following explanation:

> [T]he *sandhi* chapter differs from the other chapters in the way it paraphrases each *sutta*. In contrast to the other chapters which use the verb *āpajjate* to indicate that a grammatical operation obtains, the *sandhi* chapter invariably uses *pappoti*, e.g. *lopaṃ pappoti* or *papponti* at Kacc-v 12 through 17, contrasting with *lopaṃ āpajjate* or *āpajjante*, e.g. at Kacc 220. They also differ with respect to the formulation of the contrastive sections of the exegesis of Kacc: in the *sandhi* chapter this section is invariably introduced by *kasmā*, elsewhere by *kimatthaṃ*. This difference in style seems to indicate that the commentary on the *sandhi* chapter has a different author from the rest of the work (PIND 2012: 90).

The difference in terminology seems obvious. But the difference of style in Kacc-v I and II-IV is merely lexical. The meaning of the technical terms is the same. The method of grammatical analysis is also the same. In fact, the only differences PIND accounts for are:

Kacc-v, book I	**Kacc-v books II-IV**
pappoti	*āpajjate*
kasmā	*kimatthaṃ*

In this context, *pappoti* and *āpajjate* are synonyms. Furthermore, there are other formulae to express the same idea in

Kacc-v. For instance, even within the *Sandhikappa*, the obtaining of a substitute can be expressed in different ways:

> Kacc-v ad. Kacc 32: *ekāre hakāre ca pare niggahītaṃ kho ñakāraṃ pappoti vā*
>
> Kacc-v ad. Kacc 34: *niggahītassa kho sare pare makāradakārādesā honti.*

Sandhikappa probably translates Kā's *āpadyate* either with acc. + *pappoti* or with *(x)-ādesa hoti* or simply *(x) hoti*. Compare:

> Kā, I.4.60 *mo 'nusvāraṃ vyañjane*
>
> Kā-v *makāro punar anto vyañjane pare anusvāram āpadyate.*
>
> Kacc, 30 *aṃ byañjane niggahītaṃ*
>
> Kacc-v *niggahītaṃ kho byañjane pare aṃ iti hoti.*

This does not necessarily imply that the commentary is written by two different authors. Variation might be a feature of the author's style, a mixed style that reminds us of the Sanskrit commentator Kātyāyana or the Kātantra commentators. The same applies to *kasmā* and *kimattham* which seem to be synonyms.

Finally, Kacc-v uses the expression *kv attho* "where is it used?" in order to exemplify the scope of a rule. This expression (*kv attho*) is not different in books I, II and III, but interestingly, it changes to *kimpayojanaṃ* in book IV.

Compare the examples:

	I Sandhi	II Nāma	III Ākhyāta	IV Kibbidhān a
A) Introduce	kv attho	kv attho	kv attho	kimpayo-janaṃ

s examples of scope of a sutta				
B) Introduces examples from the canon	kasmā	kimatthaṃ	kimatthaṃ	kimatthaṃ

From this we could conclude that Kacc-v is an aggregate of layers, every layer being the work of different authors according to the section. But despite some variations in terminology, I think Kacc-v proves fairly consistent as a commentary. In fact, VIDYABHUSANA, who was well versed in logic and grammar, had the impression that "the entire work was written by Kaccāyana himself". We should also take into account that variations and variant readings occur also in Kā and Kā-v, and in other commentaries of long tradition. That may be the result of a textual tradition that transmitted the text in separate books, not as a whole, as it is the case with Kacc/-v. Orality, in the handing down of these treatises, can also be an important factor of lexical variation.

4. Author of what?

The question, however, still remains: author of what? PIND assumes a clear cut difference between *sutta* and the rest – which is conventionally called Kacc-v. But, as I have shown, this is not what an internal analysis of Kacc-v reveals and this is not the opinion of other grammarians. Ariyālaṅkāra, for instance, sees a unity in the *sutta* and the *vutti* "gloss", whereas he considers the rest as a *payoga* – and obviously he knows that Mmd is a different work. I think that some features point to a singularity of author of the *sutta* and the *vutti*, if not the *sutta* together with *vutti* and *payoga*. I will subsequently offer some examples of the way *sutta* and *vutti* are intimately connected and could be considered the work of the same author, an author that was creating a Pāli version of *Kātantra* and *Kātantravṛtti* (or perhaps a version of some Buddhist *Kātantra* such as the *Kaumāravyākaraṇa*) (see LÜDERS, 1930). I will also show some problems with this view.

Alleged misunderstandings of Kacc-v:

[A] Misunderstanding of *vā*

Example 1 – *vā* in Kacc 273

The beginning of the *kāraka* section in Kacc starts with the definition of *apādāna*:

> Kacc 273 *yasmād apeti bhayaṃ ādatte vā tad apādānaṃ*

Kacc-v comments upon the *sutta*:

> *yasmā vā apeti yasmā vā bhayaṃ jāyate yasmā vā ādatte taṃ kārakaṃ apādānasaññaṃ hoti.*

Etc. SENART, ignoring the *vutti*, translates:

> On apelle *apādāna* (*ablatio*) [la relation syntactique où se trouve] l'objet dont on s'éloigne ou dont on s'effraye (SENART 1871: 125).

SENART skips the translation of *ādatte*, and remarks:

> Malgré le scholiaste, suivi par M. Kuhn, je ne crois pas possible de dédoubler l'expression *bhayaṃ ādatte*; il faudrait dans ce cas un premier *vā* après *bhayaṃ* (SENART 1871: 125).

SENART also points out that this extra *vā* in Kacc-v is not to be found in Pāṇini's or *Kātantra*'s *sūtrapāṭha*. He is right: in Kā II.214 there is only one *vā*. But this missing *vā* is implicit in Durgasiṃha's Kā-v. It is evident that Kacc and Kacc-v follow the same text:

> Kā II.214 *yato 'paiti bhayam ādatte vā tad apādānaṃ*
>
> Kā-v ad Kā II.214 *yasmād apaiti, yasmād bhayaṃ bhavati yasmād ādatte vā tat kārakam apādāna-saṃjñaṃ bhavati.*

Kacc-v follows the interpretation of Kā-v. This example shows the three different contexts where *apādāna* is applied, and they are the ones we find in Kacc-v. This instance seems to indicate that Kacc *sutta* and *vutti* are composed together following the model Kā and Kā-v.

Example 2 – *vā* in Kacc 281

A similar example is found again in the *kāraka* section (although there are instances of this alleged "over interpretation" all over the work).

> Kacc 281 *yena vā kayirate taṃ karaṇaṃ*
>
> That with which something is, for instance (*vā*), done, is the instrument (*karaṇaṃ*).

My translation follows the interpretation of Kacc-v, where this *vā* has usually the meaning of "for instance":

> Kacc-v ad Kacc 281 *yena vā kayirate yena vā passati yena vā suṇāti taṃ kārakaṃ karaṇasaññaṃ hoti.*

SENART (1871: 142) says: "Il est difficile de croire que le *vā* du *sūtra* ait réellement le sens que semble lui attribuer le scholiaste" ("It is difficult to believe that the *vā* of the *sūtra* actually has the meaning that the commentator seems to ascribe to it") and later on, in the same comment: "Le grammarien pāli aurait cherché à rendre par la particule *vā* l'intention contenue dans le superlatif du grammarien sanskrit" ("The Pāli grammarian would have tried to express, by means of the particle *vā*, the intention that is implied in the superlative of the Sanskrit grammarian"). This *vā* is not found in the Kā or Kā-v. But we know that Kacc and Kacc-v, in the *kāraka* section, are a faithful copy of Kā and Kā-v. Why should Kacc add a particle devoid of information? A closer look reveals that the particle *vā* in Kacc 281 actually reflects Kā-v ad Kā II.218: *dātreṇa dhānyaṃ lunāti. manasā meruṃ gacchati. tatha paśunā rudraṃ yajate*, etc. The author of Kacc knows that the verb *kayirate* (S. *krīyate*) means actually any action, as the examples in Kā-v indicate. That is why he adds *vā*. Kacc *sutta* seems to be based not on Kā but on Kā through its *vṛtti*.

[B] Misunderstanding of *ca*

Example 3 – *ca* in Kacc 20

Kacc 20 *do dhassa ca*

Kacc-v *dha iccetassa sare pare kvaci dakārādeso hoti. ekaṃ idāhaṃ bhikkhave samayaṃ.*

"And *dh* becomes *d*"

"*dh*, when followed by vowel, becomes *d* sometimes [*ca* triggers *vā*= *kvaci* from Kacc 13]"

The commentary goes on with a list of other instances of consonantic change (*vikāra*). This is, according to Senart, an "overuse" of the particle *ca*: "cet abus, que nous rencontrerons fréquemment par la suite, d'un mot ou d'une particule qu'il étend et dénature au point de faire dire à l'auteur une foule de choses, souvent fautives, qui n'étaient nullement dans sa pensée" (SENART 1871: 18). But if we think of the *vutti* as the gloss only, we realize there is no "abus". The gloss sticks to the meaning of the *sutta*. The flaw is in the *payoga* layer, where the list of extensions ("foule de choses ... fautives" i.e. "many wrong things") is found. If this is a mistake, then, it should not be ascribed to the *vuttikāra*.

Example 4 – *ca* in Kacc 366

Kacc 366 *tad assatthī ti vī ca*

Kacc-v *tad ass atthī ti icc etasmiṃ atthe vīpaccayo*

hoti.

medhā assa atthi tasmiṃ vā vijjatī ti medhavī. evaṃ māyāvī.

casaddaggahaṇena sopaccayo hoti. sumedhā assa atthi tasmiṃ vā vijjatī ti sumedhaso.

Again, we can observe that the "abus" of the particle *ca* is not found in the *vutti* "gloss" proper, but in a sort of *vārttika* comment at the end, which should be considered part of the *payoga*. This example shows clearly two different layers in what is conventionally called Kacc-v. In one of them we find a rigorous gloss of the *sutta*, with proper examples. In the second layer we find a correction or extension of the *sutta*. This correction (called "abus" by SENART) is based on the extension of the rule triggered by the particle *ca*. Vimalabuddhi (Mmd 317, 8) explains the examples derived from *ca* separately: *caggahaṇaphalaṃ sayam eva vakkhati* "the results of the use of *ca* will be explained independently". I think it is clear that the first layer of the *vutti* does not trespass the rule.

[C] Problematic passages

Example 5 – *tudampatī* in Kacc 341

Kacc 341 *jāyāya tu daṃ jāni patimhi*

Kacc-v *jāyāya icc etāyaṃ tu daṃ jāni ete ādesā honti patimhi pare. tudampati. jānipati.*

This passage has been presented as the proof that Kacc-v misunderstands the text of Kacc and therefore they cannot be the work of the same author or editor. Indeed, the *vutti* reads *tu* with *daṃ*, and the result is the artificial word *tudampatī*. This word is accepted in CHILDERS Dictionary and PED sv. *tudampatī* as a dual, *tu* > *du* (!), and also in other grammars such as DUROISELLE and MULLER. Moggallāna (Mogg-p 187: 26-28) says: *yam pana kaccāyanavuttiādisu tudampatī ti udāharan ti nāyam payogo āgame niruttiyañ ca tādisassa payogassāsambhavato*, "the example *tudampatī* that we find in the *vutti* and other commentaries is not found in the scriptures, because there is no such a usage in the language (*nirutti*)". We do find, however, variant readings without *tu*:

C^{e}(1) *jāyāya pati dampati*

C^{e}(2) *jāyā ca pati ca dampati*[8]

These Sinhalese variants may be corrections based on Mogg criticisms.

Alternatively, the word *tu* could be an interpolation fruit of the contamination of the lexicon *Abhidhānappadīpikā* 242 *padas ab*:

> *jāyāpatī janipatī jayampatī* <u>tu dampatī (or tudampatī ?)</u>

The *Abhidhānappadīpikā-ṭīkā* refers to Kacc 341 as an authority:

> *catukkaṃ patipatinīnaṃ yuge "dārā pume bahutte ca, daṃ kalatre napuṃsake"ti* [Cintāmaṇiṭīkā 16.38] *amaramālā, jaṃsaddo tvabyayo dāravacano. tasmā "jampati, dampatī"ti pi bhavitabbaṃ, idha pana* <u>*kaccāyanamatenodāhaṭā.*</u> *jāyā ca pati ca jāyāpati. itarītarayogadvando. jāyā ca pati ca jānipati, tathā jāyampatiādayo, jāyāsaddassa patimhi pare jāni,* <u>*tudañ ca, jāyañ ca yadādinā.*</u>

The particle *tu* could be an old interpolation into both *sutta* and *vutti*. If we remove it, the text makes perfect sense:

> *Kacc 341 *jāyāya daṃ jāni patimhi*

> *Kacc-v *jāyāya icc etāyaṃ daṃ jāni ete ādesā honti patimhi pare. dampati. jānipati.*

---

8 PIND, 2013: 119 fn 19.

It is nevertheless striking that the tradition has accepted the "wrong" reading without doubts. Even Vimalabuddhi reads the example *tudampatī*. This may point to some meaningful solution that I cannot see. In any case, this faulty example could have survived until today precisely because Vimalabuddhi did not purge it in his edition. *Rūpasiddhi* and its *ṭīkā* also accept it. The case is, no doubt, problematic, but in my opinion this example is not enough to prove that Kacc and Kacc-v are the work of a different authors.

Example 6 – *mantā* in Kacc 7

The following is an instance of Kacc using material not from Kā but from Kā-v.

Kacc 7 *vaggā pañcapañcaso mantā*,

The word *mantā* is not found in the Kā equivalent Kā I.1.10 *te vargāḥ pañca pañca pañca*, but it is actually found in Kā-v *ad loc. te kādayo māvasānā varṇāḥ pañca pañca pañca bhūtvā pañcaiva te vargasaṃjñā bhavanti*, followed by Kacc-v ad Kacc 7: *tesaṃ kho byañjanānaṃ kakārādayo makārantā pañcapañcaso akkharavanto vaggā nāma honti*. Notice how Kacc-v translates Kā-v using synonyms: *māvasanā* = *makārantā*; *vargasaṃjñā* = *vaggā nāma*; *varṇāḥ* = *akkhara-*. The word *mantā* in the *sutta* and *vutti* of Kacc seems to derive from Durgasiṃha's *vṛtti*. Again, it seems that the author of Kacc and Kacc-v was working directly not only from Kā but Kā-v.

5. Conclusions

Even though it is at present impossible to determine whether the author of Kacc *sutta* and the *vutti* is the same, I have shown in this article that there are some reasons to follow the Burmese savant Ariyālaṅkāra and postulate a single authorship for these two works. For two things are clear: first, the text called Kacc-v in PIND's edition is made, at least, of two layers (identified by the tradition), and second, not only the *vutti*, but also the *sutta* text follows the text of

Kātantra-vṛtti. It makes sense, therefore, to think that if the author of Kacc *sutta* had the *Kātantra-vṛtti* in front, he could have adapted this text as well. This would explain the great consistence of *sutta* and *vutti*, a consistence that is lost when we move to the *payoga*, probably written, as the tradition maintains, by some other grammarian, conventionally known as Brahmadatta.

REFERENCES

Primary Sources

Kacc	*Kaccāyana* = PIND, 2013.
Kacc-v	*Kaccāyanavutti* = PIND, 2013.
Kā	*Kātantra* = DWIVEDI, 1997–2005.
Kā-v	*Kātantra-vṛtti* = DWIVEDI, 1997–2005.
Gv	*Gandhavaṃsa* = KUMAR, 1992.
Mmd	*Mukhamattadīpanī*= *Nyāsapāṭh*, Yangon, Sudhammavatī cā pum nhip tuik Press, 1933.
Saddhamma-s	*Saddhammasaṅgaha* = SADDHĀNANDA, 1890.

Secondary Sources

D'ALWIS, J.
(1863). *An introduction to Kachchāyana's grammar of the Pāli language, with an introduction, appendix, notes, etc.* London

BURNELL, A. C.
(1875). *On the Aindra School of Sanskrit grammarians*. Mangalore.

DEOKAR, M. A.
(2008). *Technical terms and technique of the Pali and the Sanskrit grammars*. Varanasi: Central Institute of Higher Tibetan Studies.

DWIVEDI, J.
(1997—2005). *Kātantravyākaraṇa of Ācārya Śarvavarmā, with four commentaries: Vṛtti and Ṭīkā by Śri Durgha Singh; Kātantravṛttipañjikā by Śri Trilocanadāsa; Kalāpacandra*

by Kavirāja Suṣeṇaśarmā; Samīkṣā by the editor. Sarnath, Varanasi.

KUMAR, B.

(1992). *The Gandhavaṃsa: A History of Pali Literature*. Delhi: Eastern Book Linkers.

MALALASEKERA, G. P.

(1960). *Dictionary of Pāli Proper Names*. London: Luzac and Co.

NYANATUSITA.

(2008). *Reference Table of Pali Literature*, electronic edition by the author: http://gretil.sub.unigoettingen.de/gretil_elib/

PIND, O. H.

(2013). *Kaccāyana and Kaccāyanavutti*. Bristol: PTS.

(2012). Pāli Grammar and Grammarians from Buddhaghosa to Vajirabuddhi: A Survey. XXXI, 57-124. *Journal of Pali Text Society*.

SADDHĀNANDA, N.

(1890). Saddhamma Samgaho. 21–90. *Journal of Pali Text Society*, IV.

SAINI, R. S.

(1999). *Post-Pāṇinian systems of Sanskrit grammar*. Delhi: Parimal Publications.

SENART, E.

(1871). *Kaccàyana et la littérature grammaticale du Pâli*. Paris: Journal Asiatique.

VIDYABHUSANA, S. C.

(1901). *Kaccayana's Pali Grammar: Edited in Devanagari Character and Translated into English*. Calcutta: Mahabodhi Society.

A Comparative Study of the Pāṇinian Grammar and the Three Grammars of Pāli

Mahesh A. DEOKAR*

At the outset, it should be mentioned that the scope of this topic is very wide. This would make it impossible to cover all the points in detail in such a small span. Hence, the present paper will be restricted to some significant issues concerning the Pāṇinian and the Pāli grammars. It is largely based on my book entitled *Technical Terms and Technique of the Pali and the Sanskrit Grammars*.

The Pāṇinian Grammar

Pāṇini's *Aṣṭādhyāyī* is a well known grammar of the Sanskrit language written in Sanskrit. Due to its systematic and exhaustive treatment of the language, it is still considered as the best grammar of Sanskrit. Economy with precision is the hallmark of its composition. It has provided a well-tested and ready model for composing a grammar of any language. This is evident from a number of grammars of vernacular languages modeled after it.

Pāṇini's grammar developed into a full-fledged system of the *Vyākaraṇa śāstra* (Science of Grammar) through the contributions made by the subsequent scholars. These include supplementary aphorisms (*vārttika*-s) by Kātyāyana, commentaries such as the *Vyākaraṇa-Mahābhāṣya* by Patañjali and the

* Professor and Head, Department of Pali, Savitribai Phule Pune University, Pune, Maharashtra, India.
E-mail: latamahesh@gmail.com

Kāśikā-vṛtti by Vāmana and Jayāditya, and *Prakriyā* works which rearrange the Pāṇinian rules in the *Aṣṭādhyāyī* considering the derivational process, such as the *Rūpāvatāra* of Dharmakīrti, the *Prakriyākaumudī* of Rāmacandraśeṣa and the *Siddhāntakaumudī* of Bhaṭṭojī Dīkṣita. Besides these, there are works such as the *Vākyapadīya* of Bhartṛhari, the *Vaiyākaraṇasiddhāntamañjūṣā* of Nāgeśabhaṭṭa and the *Vaiyākaraṇabhūṣaṇasāra* of Kauṇḍabhaṭṭa etc., which deal with the philosophical aspect of the language.

The Pāli Grammatical Tradition

The origin of the Pāli philology can be traced back to the time of the Aṭṭhakathā-s, the Pāli commentaries on the Tipiṭaka. The Pāli Aṭṭhakathā-s of Buddhaghosa, Dhammapāla and Buddhadatta contain occasional discussions on a syntactical problem (cf. Sv, part 1, p. 33. Cp. P II.3.5, II.3.18, II.3.37), a particular construction (Cf. Sp 209, 13-210, 1 (= Ps III 297, 14ff), Mp III 298, 18-299,3; Sp 288, 12-15; and Sv 425, 26ff, Ps III 327, 16, Sv 569, 15ff, Spk I 209, 4–5), or the derivation of a particular word (cf. for instance, Buddhaghosa's explanation of the words *indriya* and *bhagavā* at Vism p. 491-492 and Pj I, p. 107ff respectively, also cp. P V.2.93 and VI.3.109) or the like. It is possible to show that in substance these discussions presuppose the Pāṇinian grammar. The main feature of this type of discussions is that they identify syntactical or other features of Pāli with similar features of Sanskrit (Pāli: *Sakkaṭabhāsā*) described by Pāṇini in his *Aṣṭādhyāyī*. This in turn rules out the possibility of the existence of any pre-Buddhaghosa Pāli grammars, as is believed by scholars like R. O. FRANKE (1902) and others. It is, however, surprising that many of these important observations made in the Aṭṭhakathā-s did not find due recognition in the early grammatical literature. Later when the grammatical tradition developed, some of these analyses were absorbed in the treatises of

Moggallāna and Aggavaṃsa.[1] But there are still many interesting observations, which did not receive a place in these Pāli grammars. These occasional grammatical discussions found in the Aṭṭhakathā-s mark the initial phase of the Pāli philology.

The second phase is marked by the emergence of the indigenous Pāli grammatical literature. It begins with the compilation of Kaccāyana's grammar (6th–7th century CE). The subsequent grammarians tried to improve upon the *Kaccāyanavyākaraṇa* by formulating new rules, or reformulating the rules embodied in the *Kaccāyanavyākaraṇa* or the supplementary aphorisms in the *Kaccāyana-Vutti*, so as to improve upon their grammatical description of many phonological, morphological, and syntactical features. This was done on the basis of a comprehensive collection of examples from the canonical and the post-canonical literature. There are a number of post-Kaccāyana treatises such as the *Mahānirutti*, the *Cūlanirutti* and its commentary *Mañjūsā*, the *Niruttipiṭaka*, the *Saṅgaha*, the *Mahāsandhippakaraṇa* and the *Cūlasandhi*, which are no longer extant but are occasionally referred to in works such as Vajirabuddhi's *Mukhamattadīpanī*. It appears that these treatises, though lost, had a great impact on the subsequent Pāli grammarians. For instance, Patañjali's *Mañjūsā*, which was written in the form of *kārikā*-s and modeled after Bhartṛhari's *Vākyapadīya*, has influenced the description of the *kāraka* system in the *Rūpasiddhi* and the *Saddanīti*.

---

1 Buddhaghosa's analysis of the syntactical constraints on the tense of the verb when constructed with the sentence complements *atthināma* (Sp 209, 13-210, 1(=Ps III 297, 14ff), Mp III 298, 18-299, 3), *kathaṃ hi nāma* (Sp 288, 12-15.) and *yatra hi nāma* (Sv 425, 26ff, Ps III 327, 16, Sv 569, 15ff, Spk I 209, 4–5) is incorporated by Moggallāna and Aggavaṃsa at MV 6.3 and Sadd 893 respectively. Similarly, Buddhaghosa's analysis at Vism 216, 4ff of the series of words ending in *-ika* occurring in a sentence *svākkhāto Bhagavatā dhammo sandiṭṭhiko akāliko ehipassiko opanayiko paccattaṃ veditabbo viññūhīti* was also incorporated by Moggallāna and Aggavaṃsa at MVu 4.29 and Sadd 764 respectively.

This process of evolution reached its peak in the second half of the 12th century with the compositions of the *Moggallāna-vyākaraṇa* (1165 CE) of Moggallāna and the *Saddanīti* of Aggavaṃsa (second half of the 12th century CE). What followed thereafter was a creation of a number of commentaries and sub-commentaries modeled on these three texts. Thus, it is a constantly developing tradition spread over a period of more than thousand years. Some of the salient features of this tradition are:

1. It presents itself as a complete and an independent grammatical system having its own set of ancillary texts such as the *dhātupāṭha,* the *gaṇapāṭha* and the *ṇvādivutti.*

2. Unlike the grammars of the Prakrit languages, these grammars deny the historical relation between Pāli and Sanskrit and try to depict Pāli as a language independent of Sanskrit. One obvious drawback of this denial is that the Pāli grammarians failed to explain some grammatical phenomena, which were a result of that relation. For instance, they could not explain why the initial syllable of some verbal roots is duplicated when they are preceded by a vowel, e.g. *niggaho, paggaho* etc. The well-known reason for this phenomenon is that the underlying Sanskrit forms are *nigraha* and *pragraha* respectively. Note that the Prakrit grammars such as Vararuci's *Prākṛtaprakāśa* describe the Prakrit languages in the context of Sanskrit with an underlying assumption that they evolved out of Sanskrit.

3. The Pāli grammatical tradition follows the basic structure of the Sanskrit grammar and draws heavily upon them in the matter of technique, technical terminology, grammatical concepts, and the manner of description.

4. Though the initial phase of the indigenous Pāli philology developed independent of the Pāli Aṭṭhakathā-s, there is a growing tendency of incorporating the grammatical obse-

rvations of the Aṭṭhakathā-s and thereby linking these grammars with the existing exegetical literature.

Aim and Nature

It is quite well known that the grammar held a prestigious position among all the ancient Indian sciences. It is considered to be one of the *Vedāṅga*-s (auxiliary sciences of the Veda-s). Grammar also has a similar status in the Buddhist tradition. It is said in the *Dhammapada* (24.19):

> *vītataṇho anādāno niruttipadakovido* ।
> *akkharānaṃ sannipātaṃ jaññā pubbaparāni ca* ॥
> *sa ve antimasarīro mahāpañño mahāpuriso'ti vuccati* ॥
>
> He who is without thirst and without affection, who understands the words and their interpretation, who knows the order of letters (those which are before and which are after), he has received his last body; he is called the great sage, the great man.

According to the Pāli grammarians, the main aim of the Pāli grammar is to understand the exact meaning of the Buddha's teachings, which is the true path of salvation.

> *seṭṭhaṃ tilokamahitaṃ abhivandiyaggaṃ* ।
> *buddhañca dhammam amalaṃ gaṇamuttamañca* ॥
> *satthussa tassa vacanatthavaraṃ suboddhuṃ* ।
> *vakkhāmi suttahitam ettha susandhikappam* ॥
> (Introductory verse of the *Kaccāyanavyākaraṇa*. Also cf. introductory verses 7-13 in the *Padamālā* section of the *Saddanīti*.)

Later in the tradition, Dhammasenāpati in his *kārikā*-s explains the purpose of learning grammar as:

> *saddānusāsanassa kiṃpayojanaṃ ticevade* ।
> *rakkhohāgamalahūpāyāsandehatthamevaca* ॥

> (*Kārikāpāli*, kārikā 28 as quoted by TIWARI & SHARMA 1989: 44).
>
> If one asks what is the purpose of the science of grammar, then (it should be answered), that it is for the sake of protection (of the canon), comprehension, canonical injunctions, easy means, and clear understanding.

This clearly follows the pattern of the Mahābhāṣya:

> *rakṣohāgamalaghvasaṃdehāḥprayojanam* । (I.1)
>
> The aim [of grammar] is: a) *rakṣā*: the protection [of the Vedic texts]; b) *ūha*: the [suitable] adaptation [of a *mantra* according to the requirements of a particular ritual]; c) *āgama*: [complying with the] Vedic tradition; d) *laghu*: simplicity/economy [in acquiring/ transmitting knowledge of the correct speech forms]; e) *asaṃdeha*: removal of doubt.

However, the pedagogic model accepted by Kaccāyana suggests that the emergence of the indigenous Pāli grammar was probably prompted by the need to prepare a textbook for monastic community teaching broad features of Pāli in the simplest possible way. The fact that the *Kaccāyanavyākaraṇa* and the *Kaccāyana-Vutti* are not composed in the tradition of the *Aṭṭhakathā*-s supports this assumption (Cf. PIND 2011: 86). As per this aim, the Pāli grammars were composed in such a way as would meet the requirements of its students. Śarvavarman's *Kātantravyākaraṇa* was the best model of such a type of grammar before the compilers of the *Kaccāyanavyākaraṇa*. The *Kaccāyanavyākaraṇa* was composed in such a way that the rules are arranged according to their topics. A section dealing with *sandhi* is given at the beginning. The technical terms used in a particular chapter are generally given at its beginning. Each section is composed in such a way as would form an independent unit. Thus, if students are interested in learning only a particular section such as nominal inflection or compounds or verbal inflection, they do not have to go through the complete text as in the case of the students of the *Aṣṭādhyāyī* or the *Cāndravyākaraṇa*. Later grammarians such as Aggavaṃsa and Moggallāna have followed the same pattern as that of the *Kaccāyanavyākaraṇa* in their treatises. Thus, the nature of the Pāli grammars is that of a guiding manual.

The basic aim of the *Aṣṭādhyāyī* is to recapitulate essentials of Sanskrit grammar and to present them in the most succinct form in order to facilitate memorization rather than to teach grammar of Sanskrit in a simple, easy manner. The rules of the *Aṣṭādhyāyī* are interdependent in such a way that any rule of the *Aṣṭādhyāyī* presupposes knowledge of the rest of the text. This interdependence of the *sūtra*-s in the *Aṣṭādhyāyī* makes impossible its gradual understanding. Thus, the form of the *Aṣṭādhyāyī* is not that of a students' textbook on the Sanskrit grammar but that of a highly sophisticated digest meant for those alone who are proficient not only in Sanskrit language but also in its grammar.

Arrangement

The Pāli grammarians have followed the traditional topic-wise arrangement of the rules as used in the *Kātantravyākaraṇa*. All the three grammars begin with a list of alphabets followed by a section on the technical terms and the operational rules. The rest of their grammars can be divided into two parts. The first part deals with the nominal derivatives whereas the second part deals with the verbal derivatives. The sequence of topics followed in the *Kaccāyanavyākaraṇa* and the *Saddanīti* is exactly identical with that of the *Kātantravyākaraṇa* (for details, cf. DEOKAR 2008: 14–16, 24–27, 46–49).

Although Moggallāna has accepted the basic structure of the *Kaccāyanavyākaraṇa*, he has introduced some changes in the sequence of some sub-topics (for details, cf. GORNALL 2012:

69ff). In his grammar, sections dealing with *kāraka*-s and *vibhatti*-s are shifted before the section on the nominal inflection. This appears to be a more logical arrangement. The section on primary derivatives is shifted before the verbal inflection. It seems that the change in the sequence of the section dealing with the primary derivatives and the one dealing with the verbal derivatives is prompted by the arrangement of the *Aṣṭādhyāyī* and the *Cāndravyākaraṇa*. Thus, the Pāli grammarians have arranged their texts according to various grammatical categories such as compounds, primary derivatives, secondary derivatives etc.

Grammars of Pāṇini and Candragomin are governed by the two main principles of *anuvṛtti* 'ellipsis' and *vipratiṣedha* 'opposition'. These grammarians have also followed the topic-wise arrangement wherever it does not violate these two principles (for details, cf. DEOKAR 2008: 39–42, 53–55). Modern scholars have classified Pāṇini's grammar into two main sections, namely, analytical and synthetic. The analytical part, which forms the core of his grammar, analyses the language into some basic elements such as morphemes. In the synthetic part, there are rules, which are helpful in deriving words from morphemes and sentences from words. Thus, Pāṇini's emphasis is on the derivational procedure.

Grammatical Description

1. Alphabet

The Pāli grammarians follow the traditional method of listing alphabets, which is already met with in the *Kātantravyākaraṇa*. The alphabets are given at the beginning of every grammar (cf. Kacc 2, Sadd 1, and MV I.1). The number of alphabets found in the *Kaccāyanavyākaraṇa* and the *Saddanīti* is 41 whereas *Moggallāna* has listed 43 alphabets including short *e* and short *o* (for the detailed discussion on the number of alphabets in Pāli, cf. GORNALL 2012: 137ff). By listing all the alphabets, the Pāli grammarians have provided a complete picture of the Pāli phonetics.

Pāṇini and Candragomin, on the other hand, have introduced some changes in the already existing list of alphabets to suit their purpose of forming abbreviations. Their grammars begin with rules in which the alphabets are listed with the indicatory letters *ṇa, ka* etc. These rules are traditionally known as the *pratyāhārasūtra*-s. What these rules list are not phones but phonemes. These *pratyāhārasūtra*-s do not present a complete picture of the Sanskrit phonology, as they do not list all the existing sounds of the Sanskrit language, e.g. sounds such as *visarga, anusvāra, upadhmānīya, jihvāmūlīya*, which are traditionally known as *ayogavāha*-s, have not found any place in these rules.

2. Treatment of *Sandhi*

The Pāli grammarians have generally dealt with three types of *sandhi*: a vowel *sandhi*, a consonantal *sandhi*, and miscellanea, which includes non-transformational, i.e. *pakatirūpa sandhi*, *sandhi* of pure nasal (*niggahīta sandhi*), *sandhi* resulting into a hiatus-bridger (*āgama sandhi*), *sandhi* concerning two words (*pada sandhi*) and the *sandhi metricausa.* The Pāli grammarians' treatment of *sandhi* greatly differs from the treatment given by Pāṇini on the following points:

i. Method of carrying out *sandhi*:

In their grammars, both Kaccāyana and Aggavaṃsa have laid down procedural rules for carrying out the *sandhi* operation (cf. Kacc 10-11, Sadd 28-29). According to this method, the *sandhi* operation is carried out in two steps. In the first step, the preceding syllable is separated from its vowel and placed below it. In the second step, the same syllable is combined with the following syllable after effecting the necessary changes. This procedure clearly suggests the existence of a graphic practice of presenting a particular *sandhi* form. The *Kātantravyākaraṇa* (I.1.21–22) and Vararuci's *Prākṛtaprakāśa* (3.1–2) also presuppose a similar practice. Such a procedure is, however, absent in the *Moggallānavyākaraṇa* and other Sanskrit grammars.

ii. Absence of the governing rule *saṃhitāyām* ('in a continuous utterance'):

Following the *Kātantravyākaraṇa* and other non-Pāṇinian schools, the Pāli grammarians have discarded the governing rule *saṃhitāyām* ('in a continuous utterance') which provides the ground for making *sandhi* in Pāṇini's Aṣṭādhyāyī.

iii. Absence of the technique of the *ekādeśa* ('single substitute'):

Like the *Kātantravyākaraṇa*, the Pāli grammarians have also not followed the *ekādeśa* technique of Pāṇini. For example, in Pāṇini's grammar, the *sandhi* between *na + upaiti* is formed by replacing both, the final *a* of *na* and the initial *u* of *upaiti*, with a single substitute *o* as per the rule *ādguṇaḥ* (P VI.1.87). The same form can be derived in the system of the *Kātantravyākaraṇa* by applying Kt I.2.3: *uvarṇe o*. Here the initial *u* of *upaiti* is elided and at the same time the preceding phoneme *a* is substituted by *o*. The procedure followed by the Pāli grammarians to derive the *sandhi* form *nopeti* from *na + upeti* is different than the *Kātantravyākaraṇa*. According to them, first the final *a* of *na* is dropped and then the initial *u* of *upeti* is substituted by *o*. In the same vein, Pāṇinian *pararūpa* and *pūrvarūpaekādeś* as are reduced merely to the elision of the preceding or the following vowel respectively (cf. Kacc 12, Sad 30, 32-33, MV I.26).

iv. Absence of a complicated procedure:

The Pāli grammarians' treatment of *sandhi* is guided by a desire to simplify complicated grammatical procedure adopted by the Sanskrit grammarians in arriving at the final form. Hence, as far as possible, they connect the root form directly with the surface form. This tendency of simplifying the grammatical procedure by weeding out the intermediate procedures is evident in other sections as well.[2]

Aggavaṃsa stands alone among the Pāli grammarians in giving a separate treatment to the phonetic changes caused by the metrical composition (Sadd 158-159). Similarly, Aggavaṃsa alone has dealt with the *sandhi* peculiar to a particular form of literature (cf. Sadd 70, 134, 156 and 160).

3. Nominal Inflection

As in the *Kātantravyākaraṇa*, in all the Pāli grammars, the nominative singular suffix is *si* instead of *su* accepted by Pāṇini and Candragomin. The ablative singular *smā* (Skt. *smāt*) and locative singular *smim* (Skt. *smin*), which are peculiar to pronouns in Sanskrit, are included in the basic list of nominal case terminations since in Pāli they are commonly shared by nouns and pronouns. Some linguistic categories such as *sarvanāmasthāna* and *bha*, which are conceived by Pāṇini in order to explain the strong, the medium, and the weak categories of the nominal inflections, are missing in Pāli grammars.

4. Syntax

The Pāli grammarians' treatment of *kāraka*-s is in no way exhaustive. The *kāraka* section of these grammars deals only with the general facts about the syntax of the Pāli language and does not enter in the subtleties as recorded in Pāṇini's *Aṣṭādhyāyī*. As shown by KAHRS (1992), Pāli grammars do not always provide a correct picture of the Pāli syntax. On a

---

[2] E.g., the nominative singular form *buddho* can be derived in two steps by applying a single rule in both Kaccāyana and Moggallāna's grammars, namely *so* (Kacc 104) and *sisso* (MV 2.111): *buddha* + *si*, *buddha* + o, *buddho*. In Pāṇini's grammar, one has to follow at least four steps to arrive at the nominative singular form *rāmaḥ*: *rāma* + *su*, *rāma* + *s* (*u* is dropped by P I.3.2: *upadeśe 'j anunāsika it*, P I.3.9: *tasyalopaḥ*), *rāma* + *ru* (*s* changes to *ru* by P VIII.2.66: *sasajuṣoruḥ*), *rāmaḥ* (*ru* changes to *visarga* by P VIII.3.15: *kharavasānayorvisarjanīyaḥ*).

number of occasions, the syntactic peculiarities of Sanskrit are superimposed on Pāli.

Pāṇini clearly maintains a dichotomy between *kāraka* and *vibhakti*. His *kāraka*-s stand for the deep or underlying relation of a noun to the verb and the *vibhakti*-s stand for the representation of *kāraka*-s in the surface structure. This dichotomy is somewhat blur in Pāli grammars. Although Kaccāyana and Aggavaṃsa have dealt with the *kāraka*-s and the *vibhatti*-s separately, on a number of occasions, they have mixed these two categories. For example, the ablative in connection with the prefixes *apa* and *ā* is treated as a *kāraka-vibhatti* by Kaccāyana and Aggavaṃsa whereas in Pāṇini's *Aṣṭādhyāyī*, it is treated as an *upapadavibhakti* (cf. *dhātunāmān-am upasaggayogādisva pi ca*: Kacc 274); *vajjanatthā papariyoge*: Sadd 560); *pañcamya pāṅparibhiḥ*: P II.3.10). Like Candragomi-n, Moggallāna has merged the *kāraka* and the *vibhakti* sectio-ns together. He has not laid down rules defining various *kāraka* categories. His main focus is on the allocation of cases.

5. Compounds

Kaccāyana and Aggavaṃsa's treatment of compounds is general in nature like that of Śarvavarman. Although Mogga-llāna has dealt with certain specific cases, his treatment of compounds is not as exhaustive as that of Pāṇini who provides rules for particular cases.

Technical terminology used by Kaccāyana and Aggavaṃsa to denote six types of compounds is similar to that of Pāṇini and Śarvavarman. Like Candragomin, Moggallāna has avoi-ded the use of the traditional terminology denoting the types of compounds. He appears to recognize only four main cate-gories of compounds such as *Avyayībhāva, Tappurisa, Bahub-bīhi* and *Dvanda*, which are designated in his grammar as *asaṃkhya, amādi, aññattha* (Skt. *anyārtha*) and *cattha* (Skt. *cārtha*). Following the *Cāndravyākaraṇa*, compound is called *ekattha* (Skt. *ekārtha*) in Moggallāna's grammar (cf. CV II.1.

For a detailed comparison of the compound sections of the *Moggallānavyākaraṇa* and the *Cāndravyākaraṇa*, cf. DEOKAR 2009: 7–16).

On occasions, Aggavaṃsa and Moggallāna's description of the Pāli compounds is misleading, since some compounds that are described by them are not instantiated in the Pāli literature. For example, compounds like *tiṭṭhagu* etc. (Sadd 697 and MV 3.7). Besides, some compounds, which are classified by the Pāli grammarians as *Avyayībhāva-s*, do not actually possess that status in Pāli, e.g. *adhicittaṃ*. The Kacc-Vu has misinterpreted the rule *jāyāyatudaṃjānipatimhi* (Kacc 341) and has derived the ghost form *tudaṃpati.* Aggavaṃsa has repeated the same mistake in the rule *jāyāyakvacitu-daṃjānipatimhi* (Sadd 731).

6. Secondary Derivatives

The Pāli grammarians' treatment of *taddhita* is extremely cursory compared to that of Pāṇini. Pāṇini's treatment of *taddhita* is spread over 1110 rules in the *Aṣṭādhyāyī* whereas the same topic has been dealt with in 62 rules in the *Kaccā-yanavyākaraṇa*, 114 rules in the *Saddanīti* and 142 rules in the *Moggallānavyākaraṇa*. Even in this section, the Pāli grammarians have only considered some of the important *taddhita* meanings and suffixes. Thus, their treatment of *taddhita* is like a brief summary of Pāṇini's *taddhita* section.

Composition of Pāṇini's *taddhita* section is very complex due to the interweaving of *arthādhikāra*-s ('governing meaning') and *pratyayādhikāra*-s ('governing suffix'). Such a complex structure was, however, not adopted by the Pāli grammarians for the sake of simplicity.

7. Treatment of Verbal Inflection

Kaccāyana and Aggavaṃsa have followed the *Kātantravyākaraṇa* and other non-Pāṇinian Sanskrit grammars in accepting the familiar significant terms like *adyatanī, śvastanī, bhaviṣyantī* etc. for the ten Pāṇinian *lakāra*-s.

To bring simplicity, the Pāli grammarians have totally discarded the Pāṇinian notion of substitution in case of the *lakāra*-s. They have simply given eight sets of twelve suffixes each and then in the following rules have taught the necessary alterations in these suffixes.

While the theory of substitution is discarded in respect of the *lakāra*-s, it is more closely adhered to by them in respect of the verbal morpho-phonemics. However, the level of substitution found in the *Aṣṭādhyāyī* is higher than the Pāli grammars. Among the Pāli grammars too, the level of substitution is higher in the *Moggallānavyākaraṇa* compared to that of the *Kaccāyanavyākaraṇa* and the *Saddanīti.* To illustrate, Pāṇini has taught only one causative suffix *ṇī* (P III.1.26: *hetumatica*) against two (*ṇi* and *ṇā pi*) taught in MV (5.16: *payojakavyāpāreṇāpica*) and four (*ṇe, ṇayaṇāpe, ṇāpaya*) in the *Kaccāyanavyākaraṇa* and the *Saddanīti.* Thus, Pāṇini teaches only one basic suffix and then derives different surface forms by way of introducing morphophonemic changes.[3] Kaccāyana and Aggavaṃsa, on the other hand, have directly linked the four different surface forms to four suffixes. On a number of occasions, they prescribe a substitute for the whole root instead of splitting the root into smaller phonemic units as done by Moggallāna (cf. for instance, *jaramarānaṃ jīrajiyyamiyyāvā:*

3 Cf. for instance the derivation of the verb nāmayati in Pāṇini's grammar: nam + ṇic = nam + i (hetumatica P III.1.26), nām + i (aco'ñṇiti P VII.2.115), nām + i + ti (lasya P III.4.77, tiptasjhi° P III.4.78), nām + i + śap + ti (kartariśap P III.1.68), nām + e + a + ti (sārvadhātukārdhadhātukayoḥ P VII.3.84), nām + ay + a + ti (eco 'yavāyāvaḥ P VI.1.78), nāmayati. Also cf. the derivation of the word adhyāpayati: adhi + i + ṇic, adhi + i + i, adhi + ā + i (krīṇjīnāṃṇau P VI.1.48), adhi + āp + i (artihrīvlīrīknūyīksmāyī° P VII.3.36), adhi + āp + i + ti (tiptasjhi° P III.4.78), adhi + āp + i + a + ti (kartariśapP III.1.68), adhi + āp + e + a + ti (sārvadhātukārdhadhātukayoḥ P VII.3.84), adhi + āp + ay + a + ti (ikoyaṇaci P VI.1.77, eco 'yavāyāvaḥP VI.1.78), adhyāpayati.

Kacc 507, *sadassasīdattam*: Kacc 611; *sadassasīdo*: Sadd 1213; and *jarasadānamīmavā*: MV 5.123, *jaramarānamīyaṅ*: MV 5.174).

8. Treatment of Primary Derivatives

The Pāli grammarians' treatment of the primary derivatives is also of a general nature. The *kṛdanta* section of Pāṇini's *Aṣṭādhyāyī* is spread over 590 rules excluding the rules of morphophonemic changes (P III.1.1-3.4.76). Compared to this, the treatment of primary derivatives including rules related to the morphophonemics is spread over 100 rules of the *Kaccāyanavyākaraṇa* (526-625), 125 of the *Saddanīti* (1106-1230), and 179 of the *Moggallānavyākaraṇa* (5.1-79).

In the *Kaccāyanavyākaraṇa* and the *Saddanīti*, the technical name *kit* is given to a number of primary suffixes excluding the gerundive affixes and the finite verbal endings. Note that in Pāṇini's *Aṣṭādhyāyī*, the gerundive suffixes are also included among the *kṛt* suffixes.

The Manner of Description: General and Particular Rules

It is quite well-known that Pāṇini has adopted the technique of generalization and particularization to compose his grammar. He developed it to such perfection that he could describe a large number of linguistic facts in the shortest possible manner (cf. *kiṃcit sāmānya viśeṣavalla kṣaṇam pravartyaṃ yenālpena yatnena mahato mahataḥ śabdaughān pratipadyeran* । Mbh I.6). This most scientific method of the language description was later adopted by all the systems of grammar and the Pāli grammarians were no exception. However, it should be mentioned that while describing compounds and syntactic relations, the rules formulated by the Pāli grammarians are rather general in nature and not specific. On the other hand, while describing the morphophonemic changes, Kaccāyana and Aggavaṃsa have formulated separate rules for individual cases even when generalizations were possible. For example, the morphophonemic changes taught in rules Kacc 579-581 were explained by Moggallāna using one general rule, MV 5.95. Thus, although the Pāli grammarians have followed the same manner of description by way of general and particular rules, their level of generalizations is not as high as that of Pāṇini.

The *Sūtra* Style

The *sūtra* style of composition represents a genre belonging to ancient Indian literature. A Pāṇinian *sūtra* is regarded as a perfect model of the *sūtra* type of composition. Brevity leading to the most condensed formation is the soul of Pāṇini's *sūtra* style.

The Pāli grammarians have also adopted the *sūtra* style of composition. L. N. TIWARI (1989: 393-401) has shown that around 215 rules of the *Kātantravyākaraṇa* and around 300 of the *Aṣṭādhyāyī* (including the overlap with the *Kātantravyākaraṇa*) are reproduced in the *Kaccāyanavyākaraṇa* with necessary alterations. Still there are more than half of Kaccāyana's rules that are without parallel in Sanskrit and therefore, can be treated as original ones. Here it should be noted that although a number of rules from the *Kaccāyanavyākaraṇa* correspond to the rules of the *Aṣṭādhyāyī*. Kaccāyana generally follows the descriptive style of the *Kātantravyākaraṇa*.

Like the *Kātantravyākaraṇa*, many rules of the *Kaccāyanavyākaraṇa* are not composed in a compressed *sūtra* style of Pāṇini. But at the same time, Kaccāyana has not followed the *kārikā* style of composition found in the *samāsa* and the *taddhita* sections of the *Kātantravyākaraṇa* (cf. *syātāṃ yadi pade dvetu yadi vāsyurbahūnyapi*। *tānyanyasyapadasyārthe bahuvrīhiḥ*।। Kt II.5.9; *añña padatthesu bahubbīhi* Kacc 330; *vibhakti saṃjñā vijñeyā vakṣyante'taḥparaṃtuyā* Kt II.6.24; *tvādayo vibhattisaññāyo* Kacc 249).

Aggavaṃsa's *Saddanīti*, which is basically modeled on the *Kaccāyanavyākaraṇa* and the *Kaccāyana-Vutti*, is more elaborate and exhaustive. In the *Saddanīti*, we come across two types of rules, namely, the rules that are composed in a *sūtra* style and the rules that are composed in the commentarial style using the sentence format (cf. *yaṃ ivaṇṇ onavā* : Sadd 51 and *kvaci sare vyañjane vāodantānaṃ nāmānam akārantattaṃ pakati* : Sadd 163).

In the matter of rule formation, Moggallāna follows the pattern of Pāṇini and Candragomin. Many of Candragomin's rules and even their *Vṛtti* by Dharmadāsa are reproduced *verbatim* by Moggallāna (for a close correspondence between the rules and the commentaries of the *Cāndravyākaraṇa* and the *Moggallānavyākaraṇa*, see FRANKE 1902-03: 71–95). However, the influence of the *Kaccāyanavyākaraṇa* and the *Kātantravyākaraṇa* on the sections dealing with the technical terms, *sandhi*, and nominal inflections is beyond doubt. Although Moggallāna has not made use of the *pratyāhāra*-s, he has used other technical devices of Pāṇini and Candragomin such as use of indicatory letters etc. He has also adopted the Pāṇinian technique of compressing more than one statement into a single rule with greater efficiency than Kaccāyana and Aggavaṃsa. Cf. for instance, Moggallāna's rule I.48 *tavaggavaraṇānaṃ ye cavaggabayañā*. It comprises a number of phonetic changes, which are taught individually by Kaccāyana and Aggavaṃsa.

To sum up, it can be said that on account of following the more traditional and unsophisticated way of the *sūtra* formation, the *sūtra*-s of the Pāli grammarians have not become as compressed as Pāṇini's. Consequently, they are simpler and less cryptic than those of Pāṇini.

Nominal Style

In the rule formation, the Pāli grammarians have adopted the nominal style like that of Pāṇini. In this type of composition, the helping verb is either missing or is to be supplied from outside, e.g. *sarā sare lopam* (Kacc 12). Here one has to supply a helping verb *papponti* to get a complete sentence: *sarā kho sabbe pi sare pare lopaṃ papponti* (Kacc-Vu 12).

Among the Pāli grammarians, Moggallāna is a meticulous follower of this style. Kaccāyana and Aggavaṃsa have, however, made occasional use of a finite verbal form e.g., *viyojaye* (Kacc 10), *naye* (Kacc 11), *sijjhanti* (Kacc 393), *ṭhapeyya, naye, papponti* (Sadd 28-30), *nipaccate* (Sadd 849) etc. Such grammatical aphorisms are more like a statement than a traditional *sūtra.*

Meta Language

The meta-linguistic use of the ablative, the genitive, and the locative, which originated in Pāṇini's grammar, is retained in the Pāli grammars. Here too, the genitive indicates the actual place for the grammatical operation (cf. *harassagiṃ se*: Kacc 476; *jiharānaṃgim*: MV 5.102). The locative denotes operations applying to what precedes (cf. *sarā sare lopam*: Kacc 12; *sarā lopaṃ papponti sare*: Sadd 30; *saro lopo sare*: MV 1.26), and the ablative denotes operations that apply to what follows (cf. *karatoririyo*: Kacc 556; *karāririyo*: MV 5.51). Moggallāna is very consistent in the use of these cases. Kaccāyana and Aggavaṃsa on the other hand are not so meticulous in this regard.

Other Technical Devices

In the matter of other technical devices used by Pāṇini such as ellipsis (*anuvṛtti*), section headings (*adhikāra*), and indicatory letters (*anubandha*-s), though the Pāli grammarians have generally followed the footsteps of Sanskrit grammarians, Moggallāna's usage matches more with that of Pāṇini. Like Śarvavarman, the Pāli grammarians have avoided the use of abbreviations (*pratyāhāra*) and common denominators, like *la* etc., which are very efficiently used by Pāṇini to achieve brevity. On a number of occasions, Kaccāyana and Aggavaṃsa's usage of the particle *ca* is unscientific. Moggallāna, on the other hand, has used it with greater skills. The Pāli grammarians have used more option markers compared to that of Pāṇini. However, they failed to preserve the subtleties regarding the levels of optionality found in Pāṇini's grammar. With regard to the principles governing the selection of rules, the Pāli grammarians have accepted the Pāṇinian principle of exception. Although the principle of posteriority is also accepted by them, the area of its application is limited. Out of the other Pāṇinian principles, only the principle of *antaraṅgatva* (interiority) is referred to by Moggallāna. The *siddha-asiddha* dichotomy is all together missing in the Pāli grammars.

Conclusion

The Pāli grammarians' choice of instructional grammar over the theoretical one is prompted by their motive behind writing these grammars. This in turn has affected their choice of model grammar. Thus, Kaccāyana and Aggavaṃsa preferred the *Kātantravyākaraṇa* above the *Aṣṭādhyāyī*. Moggallāna tried to strike a balance between simplicity and technical precision by synthesizing both the models.

Abbreviations

CV	Cāndravyākaraṇa
Kacc	Kaccāyanavyākaraṇa
Kt	Kātantravyākaraṇa
Mp	Manorathapūraṇī
MV	Moggallānavyākaraṇa
MVu	Moggallānavutti
P	Pāṇini's Aṣṭādhyāyī
Pj	Paramatthajotikā
Ps	Papañcasūdanī
Sadd	Saddanīti
Sp	Samantapāsādikā
Spk	Sāratthapakāsinī
Sv	Sumaṅgalavilāsinī
Vism	Visuddhimagga

Bibliography

Primary Sources

Aṣṭādhyāyī of Pāṇini in Roman Transliteration. Sumitra M. KATRE. Austin: University of Texas Press. 1987.

Cāndra Vyākaraṇa of Candragomin. Ed. by Kshitish Chandra CHATTERJI. Pune: Deccan College Postgraduate & Research Institute. 1961.

Kaccāyanavyākaraṇa. see TIWARI and SHARMA 1989.

Kaccāyana-nyāso by Ācariyo Vimalabuddhi Thero (Paṭhamo Bhāgo). Ed. by Bhikshu SATYAPĀLA. Delhi: Buddha Triratna Mission. 1991.

Kalāpa-vyākaraṇam. Ed. by Janaki Prasad DWIVEDI.Varanasi: Central Institute of Higher Tibetan Studies, Sarnath. 1988.

Kātantravyākaraṇa of Ācārya Śarvavarmā. Vol. I-III.1, Ed. by Jānkī Prasāda DWIVEDĪ. Varanasi: Sampurnanand Sanskrit University. 1997-2000.

Moggallāna Vyākaraṇa. Bhadanta Ananda KAUSALYAYANA. Hoshiarpur: Vishveshvaranand Vedic Research Institute. 1965.

Saddanīti: La Grammaire Pālie D'Aggavaṃsa. Ed. by Smith HELMER. Oxford: The Pāli Text Society, 2001. (First Edition Vols. I-III - 1928-1930, Vols. IV-V (1949, 1954, 1966).

The Vyākaraṇa Mahābhāshya of Patanjali. Vols. I-III. F. KIELHORN. Bombay: Government Central Book Depot. 1883-1892.

Secondary Sources

DEOKAR, Mahesh A.

(2008). *Technical Terms and Technique of The Pāli and The Sanskrit Grammars*. Sarnath, Varanasi: Central Institute of Higher Tibetan Studies.

(2009). The Treatment of Compounds in the MoggallānaVyākarana *vis-à-vis* CāndraVyākaraṇa. In: *The Ocean of Buddhist Wisdom* (Vol. IV). Ed. B. N. LABH. 7-16. Delhi: New Bharatiya Book Corporation.

FRANKE, R. Otto.

(1902). Geschichte und Kritik der einheimischen Pāli-Grammatik und –Liexicographie. Strassburg: Trübner.

(1903). *Moggallāna's Saddalakkhaṇa und das Cāndra-vyākaraṇa.* In: Journal ofthe Pāli Text Society. 1902–1903. London, 70–95.

GORNALL, Alastair M.

(2012). *Buddhism and Grammar: The Scholarly Cultivation of Pāli in Medieval Laṅkā.* An Unpublished Ph.D. Dissertation Submitted to the University of Cambridge.

KAHRS, Eivind.

(1992). Exploring the Saddanīti. *Journal of the Pāli Text Society.* Oxford. Vol. XVII, 1–212.

PIND, O. H.

(2011). Pāli Grammars and Grammarians From Buddhaghosa to Vajirabuddhi: A Survey. *The Journal of the Pāli Text Society*, Vol. XXXI. 57–124.

TIWARI, Lakshmi Narayan and SHARMA Birbal.

(1989). *Kaccāyanavyākaraṇa.* Ed. Varanasi: Tara Book Agency. (I[st] ed. 1962).

Translating *Sutta*-s from Pāli to English: Some Methodological Reflections

K.T.S. SARAO*

Why do we ever translate from one language to another? The simple answer is: Because we do it for people who do not understand a word of the original language. Further, as pointed out by RAFFEL, we translate "to interest and to educate, to please and to inform, the modern reader who knows not a word of the original tongue" and "to recreate, for someone without the linguistic ability to do the job for himself" i.e., for the "philologists, historians, archaeologists, and other essentially non-literary persons" (RAFFEL 1971: 11, 62, 150). The translator's job is not philology but literature and his interpretation should be identical with the original text's intention, i.e., the effect that the translation has on its readers should be the same as the one that the original text had on its readers. As pointed out by Hans VERMEER, "each text is produced for a given purpose and should serve this purpose" (quoted at AVELING 2002: 5).

A language can be understood properly only through the study of sentences. Isolated words, like stems and roots, are just mere abstractions devised by the grammarians to analyze a language. Only a sentence has an exact meaning because it is the natural unit of speech and the smallest unit which

* Professor and Head, Department of Buddhist Studies, University of Delhi, Delhi, India. E-mail: ktssarao@hotmail.com

has a precise and specifically expressed meaning. Thus, for translating from one language to another, the basic ground rule is to translate sentence by sentence i.e., by finding close equivalents of sentences. As far as words are concerned, it is not always possible to provide close equivalents for words and the generalized meanings of words are enormously vague and therefore, the study of words in itself can only be of limited use in the understanding of a language. In other words, anything less than a sentence can have many meanings and hence would amount to being unclear. Thus, one is not surprised when Alice in *Alice in Wonderland* wonders "whether you can make words mean so many different things." Besides, as once Bertrand RUSSELL pointed out "no one can understand the word 'cheese' unless he has a non-linguistic acquaintance with cheese" (RUSSELL 1950: 18). But, of course, the choice of words within a sentence is very important because the choice of a single word can determine the essence of an entire *sutta*. Moreover, no dictionary or thesaurus can ever be a fully adequate guide in translating. In fact, "dictionaries cannot provide translators with ready-made solutions to all their problems" (see KASPAREK 1983: 86).

The task of translation is viewed by some as a profession unworthy of an honourable scholar for such a person betrays the beauty of the original text. Burton RAFFEL, a well-known translator notes with regret: "How angry I seem to make some people" (RAFFEL 1971: 147). According to I.B. SINGER, "There is no such thing as a good translator. The best translators make the worst mistakes. No matter how much I love them all, translators must be closely watched" (see GOLDBLATT 2002: 10). And Milan KUNDERA goes even further and compares translators with rapists and traitors (see GOLDBLATT 2002: 10). In fact, the exact vulgar wording of KUNDERA is "Ye translators, do not sodomize us!... '*Traduttore-traditore*' (Translator = traitor)" (see GOLDBLATT 2002: 10). Whatever may be the meaning of all this, translators, including monks who were responsible for carrying Buddhist texts to different parts of Asia, during the course of their *dhamma*-work metamorphosed the very languages into which they translated the Buddhist *sutta*-s by importing from the source languages into the target languages, loanwords and calques of grammatical structures, idioms, and vocabulary.

So far as the question of translating Pāli *sutta*-s into English is concerned, the person who takes up the difficult and risky task of translation must be, above all else, not only an expert in the subject of Buddhism but also an expert in the original (i.e., Pāli) as well as the target (i.e., English) languages. As pointed out by Roger BACON back in the thirteenth century, for a translation to be true, the translator must know both languages (quoted at KASPAREK 1983: 85-86). It is expected that the translator must have a profound understanding of the etymological and idiomatic correlates between the two languages; and a finely tuned sense of when to meta-phrase ("translate literally") and when to paraphrase, so as to assure true rather than spurious equivalents between the source- and target-language texts (KASPAREK 1986: 135). As a matter of fact, to be a competent translator one must not only be bilingual but also bicultural because a language is not just a collection of words and of rules of grammar and syntax for generating sentences, but also an immense cultural mosaic whose mastery "comes close to being a lifetime job" (PEI 1949: 424).

It is generally acknowledged that if the target language is the native language of the translator, then the chances of the translation being of better quality are much higher. For instance, Martin LUTHER, credited with being the first European to translate the Bible into German, suggests that one translates satisfactorily only towards one's own language (KELLY 1979: 86). The chances of the quality of translation further improve if, instead of one competent individual, the task of translation is performed by a team of competent scholars. The reason for this is that some of the biases of the individual which are bound to sneak into his/her translation can be to some extent filtered out by the other team members.

The translator's primary *dhamma* is to serve two constituencies faithfully: original language and its corresponding culture as well as the target language and its corresponding culture– a task not so easy to perform. The translator works as a bridge over which a culture is carried over. In fact, a translator is an artist and the job of translation an art. However, it cannot be overlooked that there are limits to an art too. Buddhist monks who translated the Indian Buddhist texts into Chinese often calibrated their translations to better suit aspirations of Chinese society in which notions such as filial piety were central. Moreover, there was the more difficult problem of finding equivalents for philosophical words and terms. For instance, the concept of *anattā*. Though the notion of *anattā* was not subjected to the rigorous examination that it received in India, its meaning was greatly enlarged by thinkers in Chinese, Tibetan, Korean, and Japanese Buddhism and consequently made profound impact on Buddhist thinking in these countries. Early Chinese thinkers found it difficult to come to terms with the Buddhist notion of *anattā* leading some of the thinkers to defend the existence of an enduring self. Whereas Indian Buddhists had built their notions of self by means of empiricism, anti-*Brāhmaṇism* and analytic reasoning, Chinese Buddhists did so by means of non-analytic insights, utilising pre-established epistemology and cosmogony. One major transformation was the Chinese reinterpretation of the concept of *shen*– initially an agent of thought which perished with the body– into an eternal essence of human spirit, a soul. Though the notion of an eternal soul was later challenged by the Chinese Buddhist scholars, the notion of a permanent agent of perception throve in China. Though the West has its own scholarly tradition with regard to 'person' but concepts such as *āsava*, *dhamma*, *jhāna* are not easy to translate into English or any of the other West European languages. The difficulty in finding equivalents for such words can be gauged from the fact that efforts have been made to translate the words *āsava* with English words such as "flows", "discharge", "leaks", "cankers", and "intoxicants" etc. all of which are unsatisfactory equivalents.

As languages change over time, when a *sutta* in a classical language such as Pāli is to be translated into a foreign and modern language such as English, the task of the translator is further compounded. However, poetry presents special challenges to translators, given the importance of a text's formal aspects, in addition to its content. RAFFEL points out that a scholar who translates poetry, "preserves that which is easiest to preserve and loses that which is hardest to preserve (i.e., keeps the scholarship clean, but muddies and destroys the poetry)" (RAFFEL 1971: 51). Douglas HOFSTADTER argues that a good translation of a poem must convey as much as possible of not only its literal meaning but also its form and structure (for instance, meter, rhyme, or alliteration scheme) (see DOKOUPIL 2009: 10). However, as mistakes are an unavoidable consequence of poetry in translation, some experts in the field even go so far as to proclaim that "poetry by definition is untranslatable" (JAKOBSON 1959: 118).

Commonly, the mode of translation that is employed is appropriation, domestication, imitation, omission, elimination, rewriting and/or implicitation of part of the text; expansion or explicitation of source information, either in the main body or in the foreword, footnotes or a glossary; exoticism i.e., the substitution of stretches of slang, dialect, nonsense words etc., updating and/or replacing outdated or obscure information due to its situational or cultural adequacy through the recreation of a context that is more familiar or culturally appropriate in the target language. Such methods are collectively called adaptation (see BAKER and SALDAHNA 1998: 3-4). Adaptation, though represents the source text, it is a sort of free translation which is justified in terms of the need for adaptation to cater the tastes and habits of the target culture. However, many historians and scholars take a negative view of this 'les belles infidèles' and dismiss it as a distortion and falsification. Obviously such an exercise lacks transparency. But, as can be seen, adaptational re-creation becomes unavoidable in circumstances where cross-code breaks down i.e., where there are simply no lexical equivalents in the target language; situational or cultural inadequacy where the context or views referred to in the original text do not exist or do not apply in the target culture; genre switching i.e., a change from one discourse type to another (e.g. from scholarly audience to illiterate masses); disruption of the communication process i.e., the emergence of a new epoch or approach or the need to address a different type of readership (see BAKER and SALDAHNA 1998: 3-5). Having said that, the fact remains that it is after all a falsification!

Broadly speaking, translation is of two kinds, faithful and transparent. Faithfulness is the degree to which a translation delivers correctly the meaning of the source language without distorting it i.e., it is a "word-for-word" rendering and if need be, by overlooking the natural features of the target language. Transparent translation appears to a native speaker of the target language as if it were written in his own language as it conforms to the grammar, syntax, and idiom of the target language. Such a paraphrased and "idiomatic" translation, though conveys the essential ideas communicated in the original language, it nevertheless violates its grammar, syntax, and idiom. Interestingly, a French critic in the seventeenth-century coined the phrase "les belles infidèles" to suggest that translations, like women, can be either faithful or beautiful, but not both. However, now the times have changed as the two qualities are not necessarily seen as mutually exclusive. A competent translator can blend the two quite judiciously. Thus, a typical modern day translator of a religious text while adhering as closely as possible to the source text and adopting expressions from it to provide "local color," stretches the limits of the target language at the same time to produce an unidiomatic text. In such a situation, translation of the *buddhavacana* into English is actually a trial of the teaching of the Buddha as it is opened up to an audience which is utterly different from the audience to which it was originally uttered. Thus, the *sutta* is in a way uprooted from its *lieu de naissance* (*janma-bhūmi*) the Majjhimadesa, and sent into a sort of exile. In other words, it is a trial to reveal the kernel of *buddhavacana* in a foreign language such as English. When it comes to translating poetical part of the *buddhavacana* into English, the situation becomes quite hopeless. It has been suggested that as in such an exercise, the meter and the rhyme is completely lost, it results in a "mosaic of barbarism" (quoted at BERMAN 2000: 290 from Émile ALAIN, *Propos de littérature,* Paris: Paul HARTMANN 1934: 56). Points out Antoine BERMAN, "the deformations of translation are more accepted in prose... For they operate on points that do not immediately reveal themselves. It is easy to detect how a poem... has been massacred. It isn't so easy to see what was done to [prose]... especially if the translation seems "good." The deforming system functions here in complete tranquillity" (BERMAN 2000: 287).

One of the most prominent modern day advocates of a "non-transparent" i.e., faithful translation is the French scholar Antoine BERMAN, who in one of his brilliant essays, has identified at least twelve deforming tendencies which remain unconsciously inherent in most prose translations (BERMAN 2002: 288-297). According to him, "ethnocentric" translating is questionable as it "deforms" the original text by assimilating it to the target language and culture. Bad translation is not merely domesticating, but mystifying; "generally under the cloak of transmissibility, [it] performs a systematic negation of the foreignness of the foreign work... Good translation shows respect for the linguistic and cultural differences of the foreign text by developing a "correspondence" that enlarges, amplifies and enriches the translating languages" (see VENUTI 2000: 219). The twelve deforming tendencies suggested by BERMAN are rephrased here as follows (see BERMAN 2002: 288-297):

1. **Rationalization**: This mainly deals with the syntactical structure of the original, beginning with *punctuation* which is the most meaningful and changeable element in a prose text. Through rationalization sentences and their sequences are recomposed and rearranged according to a certain idea of discursive *order.* Wherever the sentence structure is relatively free (i.e., wherever it does not respond to a particular idea of order), there is the risk of it being subjected to a rationalization contraction. As it is not possible to recreate the "bushy undergrowth" of the sentences, despite the richness of their content, rationalization destroys them as if they were weeds. "Rationalization makes the original pass from concrete to abstract... by reordering the sentence structure... It is content to *reverse* the relations which prevail in the original between formal and informal, ordered and disorderly, abstract and concrete. This conversion is typical of ethnocentric translation: it causes the work to undergo a change of *sign*, of *status*- and seemingly without changing form and meaning" (289).
2. **Clarification**: Whereas the original text does not have a problem marching into the *indefinite*, there is always an inclination in the target language to enforce the definite. As translation is expected to be a "little clearer than the original," most of the translators follow the obvious principle of clarifica-

tion. Of course, clarification is intrinsic to translation to the extent that it contains some degree of explication. However, as pointed out by HEIDEGGER (M. HEIDEGGER, *Questions I*, Paris: Gallimard, 1968: 10), "In translation, the work of thinking is transposed into the spirit of another language and so undergoes an inevitable transformation. But this transformation can be fecund, because it shines a new light on the fundamental position of the question" (quoted at BERMAN 2000: 289). The aim of explicitation is to render "clear" something that does not wish to be clarified in the original text.

3. **Expansion**: Translation is invariably 'inflationist' as it has a tendency to be longer than its original. Rationalizing and clarifying necessitate expansion, an *unfolding* of what is "folded" in the original text. In fact, "*the addition adds nothing* ... it augments only the gross mass of the text, without augmenting its way of speaking or signifying. The addition is no more than babble designed to muffle the work's own voice. Explicitations may render the text more "clear," but they eventually obscure *its own mode of clarity*. The expansion is, moreover, a stretching, a slackening, which impairs the rhythmic flow of the work" (BERMAN 2000: 290). Consequently, the text becomes "bloated and uselessly titanic... [and above all] expansion aggravates the initial shapelessness of the work" (BERMAN 2000: 290).
4. **Ennoblement**: Rhetorization and "poetization" consists in producing "elegant" sentences by utilizing the source text as *raw material*. Thus the ennoblement is only a rewriting, a "stylistic exercise" base on and at the expense of the original text. Consequently, we have an end product that is "readable," "brilliant," rid of its "original clumsiness" and "complexity" so as to enrich and heighten the "meaning" (BERMAN 2000:

290-291).

5. **Qualitative Impoverishment**: Prose and poetry create, in their own strange and unusual ways, what can be called *surfaces of iconicity.* But the terms, expressions, and figures of the original text get replaced with terms, expressions, and figures in the target text that lack their sonorous richness (BERMAN 2000: 291). When translating the Pāli *gaṇikā* with *courtesan*, the meaning can certainly be rendered, but none of the phonetic-signifying truth of the word. And when this practice of replacement, which is most often unconscious, is applied to an entire *sutta*, to the whole of its iconic surface, it decisively erodes a good portion of its signifying process and mode of expression, on the basis of which a *sutta* speak to its audiences.
6. **Quantitative Impoverishment**: Every *sutta* presents a certain *proliferation* of signifiers as well as signifying chains. As the translation contains *fewer* signifiers than the original text, there is a lexical loss. The translation that pays attention to the lexical texture of the work, enlarges it by adding articles and relatives, explicative and decorative signifiers that have nothing to do with the lexical texture of the original. "Translating results in a text that is at once *poorer* and *longer*. Moreover, the expansion often works to mask the quantitative loss" (BERMAN 2000: 292).
7. **The Destruction of Rhythms**: Every poem and every *sutta* has its own rhythm. Translation destroys the distinctive rhythm through actions such as arbitrary revision of the punctuation (BERMAN 2000: 292).
8. **The Destruction of Underlying Networks of Signification**: A typical *sutta* contains an element of concealment, an "underlying" text, where certain signifiers correspond and link up leading to the formation of all sorts of network below the "surface" of the text of the *sutta* itself. "It is this *subtext* that

carries the network of word-obsessions. These underlying chains constitute one aspect of the rhythm and signifying process of the text. After long intervals certain words may recur, certain kinds of substantives that constitute a particular network, whether through their resemblance or their aim, their "aspect."... If such networks are not transmitted, a signifying process in the text is destroyed.... To sketch out a visual domain, for example, an author might employ certain verbs, adjectives and substantives, and *not others*." (BERMAN 2000: 292-293).

9. **The Destruction of Linguistic Patternings**: The introduction of various elements through rationalization, clarification, and expansion etc. results in the destruction of the systematic nature of the text that goes beyond the level of signifiers, metaphors, etc. and extends to the type of sentences, the sentence constructions employed. However, "asystematic nature is not apparent and in fact is concealed by what still remains of the linguistic patternings in the original" (BERMAN 2000: 292-293).
10. **The Destruction of Vernacular Networks or Their Exoticization**: All great prose is rooted in the vernacular language. The effacement of the vernaculars that takes place in the process of translating a text causes a serious damage to its textuality. The traditional method of preserving vernaculars is to *exoticize* them, say for example, by italicizing to isolate what does not exist in the original. "Unfortunately, a vernacular clings tightly to its soil and completely resists any direct translating into another vernacular.... An exoticization that turns the foreign from abroad into the foreign at home winds up merely ridiculing the original" (BERMAN 2000: 294).
11. **The Destruction of Expressions and Idioms**: Prose abounds in images, expressions, figures, proverbs,

etc. which derive in part from the vernacular and get destroyed even when their "equivalents" are used. "To play with "equivalence" is to attack the discourse of the foreign work. Of course, a proverb may have its equivalents in other languages, but... these equivalents do not *translate* it" (BERMAN 2000: 295).

12. **The Effacement of the Superimposition of Languages:** The superimposition of languages in a text involves the relation between dialect and common languages. However, "the superimposition of languages is threatened by translation. The relation of tension and integration that exists in the original... between the underlying language and the surface language... tends to be effaced (BERMAN 2000: 296).

In the light of the above stated, for the purposes of translating from Pāli to English, it may be said that one useful way of translating could be to provide morphological translation and leave the rest to the reader's judgement. In Pāli, the general classification of speech is done in four parts:

1. *Nāma*: Nouns, pronouns, and adjectives are included in the category of *nāma* and are declined as *nāma* (noun). In dictionaries and vocabularies nouns are usually listed in their stem forms, less often in the form of the nominative singular.
2. Verb (*ākhyāta*): Verbs are usually given under the form of the third person singular of the present tense (indicative active).
3. Prefix (*upasagga*): The prefixes, of which there are about twenty, are regarded as a separate part of speech in Pāli. The various verbs, consisting of prefix+root, have all to be learned separately as regards meanings. Although the separate prefixes and roots can be assigned meanings, usually rather broad and vague ones, the meaning of a prefix+root cannot usually be accounted for adequately as simply the

product of the two separate meanings. A good many roots are also used without prefixes, but prefixed forms are much more frequent in Pāli. A number of verbs have two or three prefixes to their roots.

4. Indeclinable (*nipāta*): Conjunctions, prepositions, adverbs, and all other indeclinables are included in the category of indeclinables. Indeclinable words are those that do not take any inflections (for instance, *evaṃ*).

In Pāli all the words are derived from a limited number of roots i.e., all words are analyzable into roots plus suffixes. A root is an element, not further analyzable at the grammatical level, having a very vague and general meaning. A root does not exist in its pure state except in dictionaries and grammar books. An infinite number of stems (*dhāturūpa*) may be derived from any root by the addition of suffixes and by certain changes to the root itself, for instance by lengthening the vowel, substituting a compound vowel, inserting a nasal, reduplicating the root or contracting a semi-vowel+*a* into the vowel corresponding in place of the semivowel. Each verb has a variety of stems for its different parts (tense, participles etc.), all bearing the same meaning except for the grammatical distinctions of tense. After this derivation of the word stems by the addition of suffixes (*paccaya*) to roots, inflectional endings (*vibhatti*) are added to form actual words (*pada*) as they occur in sentences.

There are three genders of nouns and adjectives: masculine, feminine, and neuter. Pronouns are not regarded as a separate class of words but as a kind of noun, although their inflections do not entirely coincide with those of nouns. As a rule 'substantive' nouns have only one gender each, whereas 'adjectives' and pronouns have all three genders according to the nouns with which they 'agree' as attribute-words: the inflections of adjectives are the same as those of nouns of the corresponding gender, hence they are not regarded as a separate class of words. In the vocabulary given along with each verse, the abbreviations nom., acc., ins., dat., abl., gen., loc., and voc. are used to designate the cases described above; and sg. and pl. are used for singular and plural. In the case of verbs, the root (*dhātu*) is given with the preceding sign √, and 1.sg., 2.sg, 3.sg., 1.pl., 2.pl., and 3.pl. mean first person singular, second person singular, third person singular, first person plural, second person plural, and third person plural respectively. Various forms of the verb such as gerund, gerundive, infinitive, aorist, optative/potential, imperative, passive, active, intensive, desiderative, causative, indicative, imperfect, perfect, future are indicated.

Here is an example of morphological translation rendered keeping in mind the above stated observations:

> *na antalikkhe na samuddamajjhe*
> *na pabbatānaṃ vivaraṃ pavissa*||
> *na vijjatī so jagatippadeso*
> *yatthaṭṭhito muñceyya pāpakammā*||Dhammapada 127||
>
> **Translation**
>
> Not in the sky, not in the middle of the ocean, not having entered a hole in the mountains, is there that spot in the world where being one would be freed from the evil deed.

Morphological Explanation

na [indec. part.]= no, not.

antalikkhe: *antalikkha* [ntr.]= sky. *antalikkhe* [loc. sg.]= in the sky.

na [indec. part.]= no, not.

samuddamajjhe: *samudda* [masc.]= ocean. *majjha* [adj.]= middle. *samudda+majjha= samuddamajjha* [adj.]= middle of the ocean. *samuddamajjhe* [masc. loc. sg.]= in the middle of the ocean.

na [indec. part.]= no, not.

pabbatānaṃ: *pabbata* [masc.]= mountain. *pabbatānaṃ* [gen. pl.]= of mountains.

vivaraṃ: *vivara* [ntr.]= hole. *vivaraṃ* [acc. sg.]= hole.

pavissa [ger. derived from *pa* [indec. strengthening pfx.]+√*vis* (to enter)]= having entered.

na [indec. part.]= no, not.

vijjatī: *vijjati* [3. sg. pr. indic. act. of √*vid* (to find, to know)]= is found, exists. *vijjatī* is m.c. for *vijjati.*

so [masc. nom. sg. of demonstr. pron. *ta* (it, that)]= he.

jagatippadeso: *jagata* [ntr.]= world. In cpd. *jagatī* [fem. Its cpd. form is *jagati*] is used. *padesa* [masc.]= place, spot, district. *jagati+padesa= jagatippadesa* [euphonic sandhi, masc.]= a spot in the world. *jagatippadeso* [nom. sg.]= a spot in the world.

yatthaṭṭhito: *yattha* [rel. adv. of place]= where. *ṭhita* [adj, pp. of √*ṭhā* (to stand)]= stood. *yattha+ṭhita= yatthaṭṭhita* [adj, euphonic sandhi]= where being. *yatthaṭṭhito* [masc. nom. sg.]= where being.

muñceyya [3. sg. pot. pas. derived from √*muc* (to free)]= might be freed.

pāpakammā: *pāpa* [ntr.]= evil, wickedness. *kamma* [ntr.]= deed. *pāpa+kamma= pāpakamma* [ntr.]= evil deed. *pāpakammā* [abl. sg.]= from the evil deed.

In a translation such as this, quite a few pitfalls are avoided, though of course, the verse has lost its meter and rhyme but the translation retains most of its originality otherwise. Such a translation is also able to serve a far wider audience than otherwise.

Talking further about translation from Pāli to English and taking some examples from the translations done by the Pali text Society, it may be said that attempts to provide the English equivalent of every word, including proper names, is quite unnecessary and also misleading. For instance, words such as *Gijjhakūṭa* should not be literally translated as proper names, apart from being meaningful words, have their sound importance. Hence *Gijjhakūṭa* is much more than *Vulture's Peak*. Same is true of technical words which do not have their equivalents in English. The fact that English languages has largely is a product of Western socio-religious, cultural, and philosophical milieu, it is not easy to find equivalent words in it for many technical Pāli words. In such cases, the original word must be retained and the meaning in the context ought to be given in the morphological explanation as shown above in the case of a verse from the *Dhammapada*. Thus, words such as *āsava*, *dhamma* need to be retained in their original form. Furthermore, it has been sometimes suggested that there are quite a few words in Pāli which are impossible to explain or understand. They can only be experienced. Hence, a word such as *vipassanā* can be understood only through it practice. Thus, perhaps a practising Buddhist scholar can make a better translator.

References

AVELING, Harry.
(2002). "'Mistakes' in Translation: A Functionalist Approach," A Paper Prepared for the Third Workshop on "The Art of Translation." London, 19-20 September 2002.

BAKER, M and SALDAHNA, G.
(1998). *Routledge Encyclopedia of Translation Studies*. (eds.). Abingdon, UK: Routledge.

BERMAN, Antoine.
(2000). Translation and the Trials of the Foreign. In: Lawrence VENUTI (ed.), *The Translation Studies Reader*. 284-297. London: Routledge.

DOKOUPIL, Tony.
(2009). Translation: Pardon My French: You Suck at This.

Newsweek, May 18, 2009: 10.

GOLDBLATT, Howard.

(2002). The Writing Life. *The Washington Post,* Book World, Sunday, April 28, 2002: 10.

HERMANS, Theo.

(1997). Translation as Institution. In: A. PYM, M. SCHLESINGER and Z. JETTMAROVA (Eds.), *Sociocultural Aspects of Translating and Interpreting.* 3-20. Amsterdam, Philadelphia: Benjamins.

JAKOBSON, Roman.

(2000). On Linguistic Aspects of Translation. In: Lawrence VENUTI, (ed.), *The Translation Studies Reader.* 113-118. London: Routledge.

KASPAREK, Christopher.

(1983). The Translator's Endless Toil. *The Polish Review*, Vol. XXVIII, no. 2, 84-87.

(1986). Prus' Pharaoh and Curtin's Translation. *The Polish Review*, Vol. XXXI, nos. 2–3, 127-135.

KELLY, L.G. (1979). *The True Interpreter: A History of Translation Theory and Practice in the West.* New York: St Martin's Press.

NORD, Christiane.

(1997). *Translating as a Purposeful Activity: Functionalist Approaches Explained.* Manchester: St Jerome.

PEI, Mario.

(1949). *The Story of Language.* New York: Lippincott Co.

RAFFEL, Burton.

(1971). *The Forked Tongue: A Study of Translation Process.* The Hague: Mouton.

RUSSELL, Bertrand.

(1950). Logical Positivism. *Revue Internationale de Philosophie*, Vol. 4, 3-19.

SPIVAK, Gayatri Chakravorty.

(2000). The Politics of Translation. In: Lawrence VENUTI (ed.), *The Translation Studies Reader.* 397-416. London: Routledge.

VENUTI, Lawrence.

(1995). Call to Action. In Lawrence VENUTI, *The Translator's Invisibility: A History of Translation.* 307-313. London: Routledge.

(2000). *The Translation Studies Reader.* (ed.). London: Routledge.

VINAY, Jean-Paul and JEAN Darbelnet.

(2000). A Methodology for Translation. In: Lawrence VENUTI (ed.), *The Translation Studies Reader.* 84-93. London: Routledge.

The Origin of Buddhism in Sāṃkhya-Yoga Sister Systems

M(ohan) G(ovind) DHADPHALE*

A Prefatory Note:

I acknowledge the fact that the readers of the present article at many a time find the views of the celebrated scholars like H. OLDENBERG, H. JACOBI, S. K. BELVALKAR, A. B. KEITH, G. C. PANDE repeated at many places. This was a bit inevitable because the different contexts require such repetition, contextual variations being responsible to these apparent repetitions. The second important point is the distinction between "Sāṃkhya, original and classical" (see SCHRADER 1955). The theistic Sāṃkhya was known and implied in the Bhgavad-Gītā XIV: 3-4. The classical Sāṃkhya came into existence under the influence of Buddhism, Jainism and Mīmāṃsā. This Atheistic Sāṃkhya is implied in this article.

Preface:

I turned to the subject of this article primarily because I was inspired by *Buddhism* (Ch. II) by Ananand K. COOMARASWAMY (1943) book entitled *Hinduism and Buddhism*, where the veteran touched upon many a similarity between Sāṃkhya system and Buddhism and naturally, the question as to who borrowed from whom becomes extremely important. Atheistic

* Professor (Retired), Fergusson College, Pune, Maharashtra, India, former Honorary Secretary, The Bhandarkar Oriental Research Institute, Pune, India.

attitude being common to these two is the starting point. Next comes the apparent similarity between the twelve *nidānā*-s of the *Pratītyasamutapāda*, the pivot of Buddhism and the evolved products of *Prakṛti* (primordial matter) in Sāṃkhya. COOMARASWAMY rightly observes that the question whether Buddhism borrowed from the classical Sāṃkhya represented in Īśvarakṛṣna's *Sāṃkhyakārikā*-s which is next to impossible as there is more than a thousand years of difference between the Buddha and Īśvarakṛṣna. Thus we will have to speak of the epic Sāṃkhya (especially of the *Bhagavad-Gītā*) and whatever Sāṃkhya tenets the Buddha received from his first teacher Āḷāra/Arāḍa Kālama and Sāṃkhya based Yoga-doctrine from Uddaka Rāmputta the second teacher of Gautam the Śākya. COOMARASWAMY also referred to Hermann JACOBI's (1898) article in ZDMG (LII.1-15) where the German scholar found clear traces of borrowing of the twelve *nidāna*-s from the evolution-series of the Sāṃkhya principal of primordial matter (*prakṛti-vikṛtayaḥ*). COOMARASWAMY being justifiably impartial did not forget to refer to the non-agreement points in another German scholar H. OLDENBERG (1892) as also his critique of JACOBI (1898). COOMARASWAMY also notes that Āḷāra's version of Sāṃkhya not even once refers to the word *guṇa* (strand). Perhaps this is to be explained in the light of Paul OLTRAMARE (1906: 243-5) where the French scholar holds that the doctrine of *guṇa*-s is a later accretion to the Sāṃkhya but unfortunately he fails to give any evidence for his conjecture (see also STRAUSS 1913: 257 ff, who points out the affinity of Arāḍa's views to those of the epic). OLTRAMARE was not a scholar who will give up his views because of the attack of criticism. He explained his position by saying that the matter was confined only to the explanation of misery (*duḥkha*) and yes Īśvarakṛṣna's *kārikā*'s start with exactly the same problem "*duḥkhatrayābhighātāt jijñāsā tadapaghātake hetau*". These are first Two-Nobel Truths i) *Dukkha* and 2. *Dukkha-Samudaya*. This gist is given to facilitate the readers understand the longish and complex nature of the main article.

The Indian philosophical schools are mainly divided in two groups: the *āstika* (orthodox) and *nāstika* (heterodox). Now the subject of this article shows that the orthodox sister-systems (*smānatantre*, as they are referred to in Sanskrit terminology) are the origins of a heterodox system namely Buddhism. How can this be possible? The answer is not far to seek. In the gedanken kresis or thought fermentation, there are many amalgamations in the orthodox and the heterodox system. The free and frank thinkers of Indian are not bound stick fast to either orthodox or heterodox philosophical traditions.

We know that being disgusted with cramped house hold life and to experience the fresh air of renunciation, "*sambādhoyaṃ gharāvāso, rajassāyatanaṃ iti; abbhokāso va pabbajjā, iti disvāna pabbaji*" was the answer given by Gautma the Śākya, to king Bimbisāra (vide Sn 408). Gautam went from home to homeless state (*agārā anagāriyaṃ*, Sn 276) at the age of twenty-nine (*ekūnatiṃso vayasā*, D II.151), wearing yellow robes when his wife and son were sleeping. He renounced the family life when he was in tender young age and his hairs were black. He renounced the family life much against the wishes of his weeping parents and thus chose the way of a recluse, searching for what is good, seeking the peerless way of desirable peace...(BREWSTER 1926: 23-24).

The Tipiṭaka before us today does not represent what the Buddha himself might have said. His monks out of their respect and devotion for their teacher (*satthā*) have likely put in his mouth certain sayings which a modest and humble person like Gautama the Buddha would never say about himself so very boastfully. The verses are from Vinaya *Mahāvagga* when after obtaining enlightenment under the Bo-tree Gautama is said to have about himself:

na me ācariyo atthi, sadiso me na vijjati ।
sadevakasmiṃ lokasmiṃ, natthi me paṭipuggalo ।।
ahañhi arahā loke, ahaṃ satthā anuttaro ।
ekomhi sammāsambuddho, sītibhūtosmi nibbuto ।। (Vin I.8)

> I do not have any teacher; no one exists who is like me. In this world along with the world of gods there is no rival for me. Awakened, I am in the world, the teacher supreme am I, I alone am all-awakened, become cool am I, nirvana-attained.

We know that after renunciation Gautama in search of spiritual knowledge tried to find for himself a suitable *guru* (spiritual teacher) which fact is quite in keeping with the time-old Indian tradition. Thus the account of past renunciation life of Gautama tells us that he first went to learn from Āḷāra Kālāma, who was a Sāṃkhya teacher and having found him not quite satisfactory he further proceed to Uddaka Rāmaputta, who was a teacher of Yoga philosophy. Sāṃkhya and Yoga are complementary to each other, Sāṃkhya stating the basic theory of how an endeavourer who is sentient, pursed and try to seek release from *prakṛti*, which is insentient primordial matter constituted by the three strands (*guṇa*-s)- *sattva*, *rajas*, and *tamasa* while the Yoga tells us about the spiritual way of gaining this separation (being liberated from the clutches of *prakṛti*) from the insentient primordial matter by following meditation, *samādhi* etc. The Yoga terminology is much the same as the later Buddhist-Yoga terminology.

As for the Sāṃkhya teacher Āḷāra Kālāma, his highest achievement was *akiñcāyāyatana*, i.e. a state when nothing whatsoever is the higher for attainment. Gautama achieved this very quickly but found it as only one of the early stages (*āyatana*-s) on the way of ultimate highest goal, i.e. *Nirvāṇa*. However Gautama gave it a place in the formless abodes beginning with *ākāsāyañcāyatana* and ending with *saññāvedayita-nirodha* which R. C. CHILDERS (1875: 288) in his *A Dictionary of the Pali Language* renders with a perfect wording namely "Yogic Coma", a term which in Greek means 'a deep sleep' which we will be justified in translating into Sanskrit as '*susupti*' about which when the person awakened he says '*nāhaṃ kiñcidavediṣam*'.

Aśvaghoṣa in his *Buddhacarita* describes the philosophy of Āḷāra Kālāma as a variety of Sāṃkhya, a Sāṃkhya where there is no reference to *guṇa*-s or strands? What sort of a variety of Sāṃkhya can it be? For it is altogether and absolutely not possible of even to think a Sāṃkhya version devoid of *guṇa*-s, so much essential constituents, the *guṇa*-s being of *prakṛti*, without which (i.e. *prakṛti*) one can never think of Sāṃkhya-philosophy.

To this difficult and impossible appearing obviously as insurmountable the Russian Buddhist scholar Th. STCHERBATSKY (1934) in his highly revealing article in IHQ (10: 737-760) entitled "The Dharmas of the Buddhists and the Guṇas of the Sāṃkhyas". The substance of the article being that Āḷāra Kālāma used the term *dharma* in place of the usual term *guṇa*. We have in Sanskrit also such synonym-compounds as *guṇa-dharma* and *nyāya-nīti*, while in marketing we have *bazar-hāṭa* (both meaning a market), *udyoga-dhandā* (both meaning business) and in English bag and baggage. The word *dharma* (for *guṇa*) occurred first in the *Kaṭhaopaniṣad*.

The essence of Buddhist philosophy can be summaries in a single gāthā:

> *ye dhammā hetuppabhavā, hetuṃ tesaṃ tathāgato āha* ।
> *tesaṃ ca yo nirodho, evaṃvādi mahāsamaṇo'ti* ।। (Vin I.40; Ap I.25; Peṭ 10)
>
> Those things which proceed from a cause, of these the Truth-finder has told the cause, and that which is

their stopping- the great recluse has such a doctirine. (tr. HORNER 1971: 54)

JACOBI (1898: 1) long ago maintained that Buddhism was "aus den Sāṃkhya-yoga hervorgegangen" (emerged from the Sāṃkhya-yoga) being "eine individuelle umgestaltung des sāṃkhya" (a remodling custom of Sāṃkhya). It is argued not only by JACOBI but also by a few other scholars of comparative philosophy that the Buddha could have been as little far from the influence of Sāṃkhya-doctrine as any medieval author from Aristotelian thought. When he incorporated in his philosophy so much matter from Sāṃkhya he could not have kept himself uninfluenced by Yoga's theoretical basis namely Sāṃkhya. Thus both of his teachers Āḷāra Kālāma (the Sāṃkhyan) and Uddaka Rāmaputta (Yogist) have been successful in leaving on Gautama's thinking a permanent influence on Gautama's ḅasic philosophy. Even Nīlakaṇtha the commentator on *Mahābhārata* appears to be quite justified in seeing a referee to Buddhism in the *Mahābhārata* (Śp. 219, 32 ff).

Both the Sāṃkhyana-s and Buddhists begin with the enquiry of *dukkha* and its *nirodha* (cessation). The Four Nobel Truths are (1) *Dukkha*, (2) *Dukkha-samudaya*, (3) *Dukkha-nirodha* and the (4) *Dukkhanirodhagāminī paṭipadā*. The very first *kārikā* of Iśvarakṛṣṇa is "*duḥkhatrayābhighātāt jijñāsā tadapaghātake hetau*". Attempts have been made to derive the Twelve *Nidāna*-s of *Pratityasamutpāda* from the evolvements of *Prakṛti* right from the time of JACOBI, OLDENBERG, KEITH and S. K. BELVALKAR. The attempts consist of efforts to find out the forerunners of twelve constituents of *Pratityasamuttapāda* (Causal Nexus or Dependent Origination) in the evolvements of Sāṃkhyan Prakṛti or Primordial matter.

Since the doctrine of Twelve Links is generally held to be the heart of Buddhist Philosophy, it is natural that scholars will be interested to know that its authorship obviously goes to the Buddha about whom it is said that the knowledge of the Dependent Origination with its twelve links was dawned upon him when he was in deep concentration under the Bo-tree in the Bodha-Gayā. In fact the enlightenment which made Gautama the Śakya a Buddha or 'Awakened One' consisted of his knowledge of the *Pratityasamutapāda*. In other words it was the *Pratityasamutapāda* which alone was the *saddhamma* (good religious doctrine). The Buddha is said to have pointed out this fact to the monks Vakkali (either Valkalin or a Balkhrin) in the *Apadāna* (ii. 467). The Gātha is as follows:

> *yo hi passati saddhammaṃ, so maṃ passati paṇḍito* ।
> *apassamāno saddhammaṃ, maṃ passampi na passati* ॥

So the excellent and unique gift that the Buddha gave to the world is *dhamma-ratana*, which is nothing else but the principle of *Paṭiccasamuppāda*. But this can be the view of only a pious devoted Buddhist. The scholars of religions give more importance to reason rather than faith. They are bound to try to see the origin of *Paṭiccasamuppāda* in the Indian philosophical schools, much earlier than the rise of Buddhism.

In fact the doctrine of Twelve Nidāna-s (links) called *Paṭiccasamuppāda* is necessitated to explain fully the nature of the Four Nobel Truths (*cattāri ariyasaccāni*). Now according to STCHERBATSKY (1927: 55) the doctrine of Dependent Origination offered to explain the Four Nobel Truths which two complimentary concepts we generally think are essentially Buddhist are not so. The formula of the Four Nobel Truths is found also recurring in Non-Buddhist Indian philosophical currents like, Medicine, Yoga etc. In support of this claim STCHERBATSKY (1927: 55) quotes from the *Nyāyavārt* "*etāni catvāry arthapadāni sarvāsv adhyātmavidyāsu sarvācāryair varṇayanta iti*". Leaving merely *adhyātmavidyā*, I shall like to support STCHERBATSKY from the Indian medical school. We know that in the Pāli canon the Buddha is many a time called a surgeon (*salla-kattā*, Skt. *śalyakartā*) who removes the *dukkha-salla* from the patient's heart. The Tathāgata is also called *vaidyarāja* (*Lalitavistara* Pp. 4, 107, 275, 351, 448, 458), *bhisakko* (Skt. *bhiṣak*) a medicine man is one of the eight *adhivacana*-s of the Buddha. The *sutta* (Catukkanipāta: Brāhmaṇadhammayāgasutta) from the *Itivuttaka* (101) has "*ahamasmi, bhikkhave,....anuttaro bhisakko sallakatto...*" the best physician.

In fact it is interesting to note that their existing *Vyādhisūtra* which explicitly compares the Four Nobel Truths with the medical tetrad; viz. Disease (*roga*), Diognosis (*nidāna*), Cure (Health State) and Medical Treatment (*Upāya*). This treatise is quoted by Yaśomitra and taken note by DE LA VALLÉE POUSSIN (1903: 578-580) (see also *Abhidharmakośa* Vol. IV. P. 121, fn. 4). We should note that the Buddhist medical term *dhātu* (element) is also borrowed from the pre-Buddhist medical science. In all this discussion we should not lose sight of the fact that the Sāṃkhya which we are claiming as the source of Buddhism has given us for the first time the concept of the three *guṇa*-s namely *sattva*, *yajas* and *tamas* (referred to by the *Bhagavadgitā* by the term "*guṇa-saṃkhyāne*"). The three *guṇa*-s are compared by many scholars with the three humors in the Greek Philosophy. The cardinal humours being breath, phlegm (*kapha*), yellow bile (*pitta*) and temperament (read: *vaidyā vadanti kapha-pitta-marudvikārān*, etc.). Thus the Āyurvedic *tṛdoṣa* concept is based on the Sāṃkhya *triguṇa*-concept.

Various scholars differ in their identifications, while a few are not quite ready to find any semblance between the links of *Pratītyasamutapāda* and the evolvemnats of Sāṃkhya-*Prakṛti*. A.B. KEITH (1924) is most prominent among these, while S. K. BELVALKAR (1938) does present a chart of the similarity has chosen to keep a man whether he accepts it or not. Rightly it is said "*maunaṃ sarvārtha sādhanaṃ*", "not to articulate any definite opinion achieves many a thing".

The Buddhist masters knowing well that their 'ism' in at least certain facts has been inspired by the Sāṃkhya-doctrine are always seen alert to find that their source is free from inner inconsistencies. Thus a Buddhist medieval master Manoratha in one of his *kārikā*-s raises a possible inconsistency in the Sāṃkhya. His inner motive must have been that the Sāṃkhyan-s by giving a reasonable and irrefutable answer silences such stray objections. Says Manoratha (Yuktidipika, a commentary on Īśvarakṛṣṇa's Sāṃkhyakārikā):

> *vinā sargeṇa bandho hi puruṣasya na yujyate* ।
> *sargastasyaiva mokṣārthamaho sāṃkhyasya sūktatā* ॥
>
> "without emanation or starting creation (*sarga*) the *puruṣa*, the sentient being is not bound, or poisoned, while it is in the same breathe also maintained that the creation flow or primordial matter *Prakṛti* is meant for the release of the same *purṣa*. What a logical statement of the Sāṃkhya?"

What Manoratha was saying was not untrue. The situation is that Prakṛti or Primordial Matter is constituted by the three *guṇa*-s, *sattva, rajas* and *tamas.* So far these three are in equipoise the emanation (creation) does not start. But something happens (this is the weak link in Sāṃkhya doctrine) so that the balance between the three *guṇā*-s comes to an end thus *prakṛti* begins to evolve. The first evolvement is *buddhi* (or *mahān*). Now the *puruṣa* finds its images reflected in the mirror of *buddhi* and imagine that he is no more free but bound. *Prakṛti* then shows all her dance to the *puruṣa*. But just as a female dancer after completing her dance retires to the wing or as the cow gives milk for her young one the calve, *prakṛti* herself struggles for the *mokṣa* of the *puruṣa*. Thus *prakṛti* does two quite opposite things in the case of *puruṣa*, the bond and the release; will it be a cogent statement (*suutatā*) for the Sāṃkhya-s? Naturally asks our Manoratha.

Now comes, the brilliant and unimpeachable answer to this seeming contradiction from the side of the Sāṃkhya masters. It is my strong conviction that they based their wise explanation of this inconsistency pointed out by Manoratha on *śruti* from the *Śvetaśvtara Upaniṣad* says which points out the two sorts of free *puruṣa*; one when he was naturally free from the clutches of the creation of *prakṛti* (*vinā sargeṇa bandho hi puraṣasya na yujyate*), a natural freedom of *puruṣa* and the second freedom brought out by the efforts of *prakṛti* herself, which Iśvarakṛṣna in his *Sāṃkhyakārikā* refers to in the words *puruṣavimokṣa-nimitaṃ tathā pravṛttḥ pradhānasya* (*pradhāna-prakṛti*). This is the second type of the freedom of *puruṣa* brought out by the kind efforts of *pradhāna*.

These two types of freedom must have been suggested to the Sāṃkhya-master Iśvarakṛṣṇa- the *śṛtimantra*, pertinent in this context in the *Śvetāśvatara Upaniṣad* which S.K. BELVALKAR and R.D. RANADE (1997) in their *History of Indian Philosophy: The Creative Period* where they designate this Upaniṣad as *locus classicus* of Sāṃkhya (a classical source of Sāṃkhya). The said Mantra is:

> *ajāmekāṃ lohitaśuklakṛṣṇāṃ*
> *bahvīḥ prajāḥ sṛjamānāṃ sarūpāḥ* ।
> *ajo hyeko juṣamāṇo 'nuśete*
> *jahātyenāṃ bhuktabhogāmajo'nyaḥ' (Śvetāśvatara Upaniṣad 4.5) iti* ॥

The verse is very important for many salient points viz. (1) the Sāṃkhya philosophy is a dualistic one maintaining the permanency of two of its characters the *prakṛti* and many *purṣas*. (2) The both are called *ajā* and *aja*-s respectively meaning the female goat and male goat as well as unborn (and therefore) permanent. (3) One Puruṣa (out of many) enjoys (experiences) the *trigunātmika prakṛti* while the other after having enjoyed her abandons her permanently. 4) Thus there emerge two types of free *puruṣa*-s, one who when not had fallen prey to the alluring binding of the *prakṛti* and the other one who having enjoyed (experienced) her, abandons her permanently not being any more susceptible to the alluring bondage of *prakṛti.* This freedom (*vimokṣa*) is permanent. To give a modern example (not quite a fitting one but helpful in understanding the Sāṃkhya stand), a man (*puruṣa*) marries a dancing charming maiden; but once he enjoys her dance on the stage of the world gives her divorce and never marries again). Thus, this divorcee is permanently free from the bondage of marriage. He has realized entirely the futility of marriage forever. Thus, he was for two times quite free, before his marriage and after giving a divorce to his beautiful dancer wife. She also realizing the fact in a way tries to help her once married husband by allowing him a divorcee permanently, knowing that a marriage means a permanent bondage.

Now what remains to explain is the answer given by the Sāṃkhyan-s to Manorath the Buddhist. The verse is as follo-ws:

> dṛśyadarśanabhāvena prakṛteḥ puruṣasya ca।
> apekṣā śāstratattvajñairbandha ityabhidhīyate॥
> evaṃ vināpi sargeṇa yasmādbaddhaḥ pumānguṇaiḥ।
> tasmādviphalatāṃ yātu manorathamanorathaḥ॥
> *Yuktidīpikā*

The answer given by the Sāṃkhyan is very subtle and deep. What they say is it is not necessary to start creation or emanation of *prakṛti* so that *puruṣa* sees his image reflected in the very first evolvement *mahāna* or *buddhi*-s and illicitly thinks (imagines) that he is now no more *svastha* or *svatantra* (free) but *prakṛtistha* and therefore , *a-savstha* or bound. This expectancy (a likely position) yet lurks there and therefore, actual creation (*sarga*) matters little. Any time the *puruṣa* is likely to see its image in *buddhi*, when the equipoise of *guṇa*-s is somehow lost and the *prakṛti* begins to evolve.

Well, after all this is who are neither Sāṃkhyans nor Buddhists are certainly amused by such small skirmishes or sham fights between the Sāṃkhya and Buddhist adherents who know well that they are far from real adversaries and bound internally by a common bond. The *kārikā*-s quoted above are from *Yuktidīpikā*, a valuable commentary on Iśvarakṛṣṇā's *Sāṃkhya-kārikā*-s.

I appreciate the neologism used by C. A. F. RHYS DAVIDS 'anchistolohy' (*antarābhavāvsthā*) and not the usual eschatology or the study of the lost things, obviously the last birth matters. (*purva-janma/gata-janma*). Among the six supernatural powers *cha abhiññā*-s one is *pubbenivāsa-sati-jñāṇaṃ* (knowing the memories of the earlier stations). In the *Bhagavadgītā* Śrikṛṣṇa also firmly tells Arjuna:

> *bhūmi, me vyatītāni janmāni tava ca'rjuna. tānyahṃ veami sarvāni, na tvam vettha parantara.*
>
> We two have passed through many earlier births. I know (remembered) them all, not you, oh "one who is troublesome to his enemies.

In Upaniṣada we find a pregnant woman called "*andhruvagṛhitā*". Here the word called *andhara* means embryo. It was a belief that this *gandharva* or embryo can answer the questions put to him, he can foretell many things. The word *gandha* must have the sense of 'smell' for which another word is used *vāsanā*. When we carry fragrant flowers in our handkerchief, the handkerchief continues giving the fragrance. So is the case of soul or subtle body it carries with it the smell (memory) of the earlier with it the smell (memory) of the earlier birth. This Iśvarakṛṣṇa, the classical Sāṃkhyan called *bhāvairair adhivā stim lingam. Gandharva* or *liṇga, sūkṣma śarīra* is in Arabic *rūh* (which means fragrance and self). Kālidāsa, who accordingly my preceptor the late T. G. MAINKAR (1962) was none else but Iśvarakṛṣṇa, also in his *Abhijñānaśākuntalam* says "*taccetasā smarati nūnaṃ abodhapurvam bhāvasthitāni janaāntara sambhṛtāni*".

Many more similarities between Buddhist and Sāṃkhya-Yoga systems can be illustrated. But the instances quoted above are, I believe, will not fail to prove that the origin of Buddhism is ultimately related to the Sāṃkhya-Yoga doctrine. With all this one has to admit that Buddhism developed far beyond the frame of Sāṃkhya and Yoga. And yet Kapil the promulgator must have a strong hold in Buddha's time. Gautama was born in Lumbini near Nepal territory but the capital city of Śākyan municipality was called Kapil-vatthu (the stay of Kapil). This has a lot of significance.

Before taking into consideration the correspondence between the evolvements of *prakṛti* and the twelve links of the *Pratītyasamutapāda* A. B. KEITH discuss the essential fact of the atheism between the Sāṃkhya doctrine in its classical form and the atheism implied the question whether this doctrine of atheism is borrowed by Sāṃkhyans from Buddhism or whether the Buddhism is the borrower. The origin of non-belief in God being natural to Sāṃkhyans like the word like *deva* in Pāli expressions *sadevakasmiṃ*, *lokasmiṃ*, definitely do not mean the God as the creator of the Universe, *katta* (doer), *nimmātā* (maker), and the giver of *sukha* (happiness) and pain (*dukkha*) etc. KEITH (1924: 24) speaks of the "Sāṃkhya system in its classical form". But we know that the classical Sāṃkhya as presented by Iśvarakṛṣṇa in his *Sāṃkhya-kārikā* is quite silent about the 'atheism'. It was the late B.G. TILAK in his extremely original article, which presents a lost *Sāmkhyakārikā*, which the great scholar has reconstructed from the *Bhāṣya* on the *Kārikā*-s that speaks of the atheism of the Sāṃkhya. We also know that the Yoga philosophy, a practical commentary school to the theoretical Sāṃkhya system speaks of *Īśvara*, which is likely to mislead to many readers who are not sufficiently careful about its real meaning. The word *Īśvara* in the Yoga doctrine does not mean God but only a certain *puruṣa* who is not spoiled by *kleśa*, *karma*, *vipāka* and *āśaya* (all these terms being shared by the primitive Buddhism). KEITH further points out that though the Sāṃkhya system abandons the existence of the absolute, it still carefully retains the principal of spirit (*puruṣa*) and nature (*prakṛti*). The doctrine of Buddhism on the other hand, has in effect abandoned these two conceptions and has left itself with only the fleeting series as a quasi-reality, from which the development of the doctrine of void (*śūnya*) is a natural enough state. In so many Mahāyānic texts it is often said "*yaḥ pratītysamutpādaḥ sūnyatāṃ tāṃ pracksṃahe*" (see *Madhyamakasastra* XXIV: 18).

If anyone tries to derive the tenets of Buddhism from the classical Sāṃkhya represented by text of *Sāṃkhyakārikā*, the text is definitely later than the origin of Buddhism. Such an attempt, therefore, will be a glaring instance of anachronism. But, there is in the epic *Mahābhārata* evidence of the existence of Sāṃkhya at an early period than the *Sāṃkhyakārikā*. The classical Sāṃkhya speaks of a single *prakṛti* and many *puruṣā*-s. The antagonists of the Sāṃkhya who maintain the plurality of *puruṣa*-s (puruṣa-bāhulyaṃ) and singleness of *prakṛti* ridicule such a position by saying that in such a case we will have to admit that if one woman becomes pregnant all women will simultaneously become pregnant, an unpalatable fun indeed. So the original Sāṃkhyan-s in order to avoid this absurdity assume a separate *prakṛti* for each *puruṣa*. This assumption no doubt will serve the purpose of removing the entailing absurdity but then we will have to assume that according to the *Maulikāḥ Sāṃkyāḥ* every *puruṣa* (a conscious individual) live in his own world and if we find instances of corresponds between these different worlds the instances are mere coincident. But then how many coincident will be there and their assumption leave any meanings to the world 'coincidence'?

However, we should try to understand the position that the

Maulikāḥ Sāṃkhyāḥ took in long past, in any case before the Christian era and its importance for only recently a group of American linguists tried to pose the theory (say hypothesis at this stages) that the users of different languages live in different worlds and yet can carry out activities with each other. The idea of a different language meaning a different world was anticipated by our *Maulikāḥ Sāṃkhyaḥ* in their assumption of the principle of *pratipuruṣaṃ bhinnā prakṛtiḥ* (a creditable contribution).

What result from all this discussion entailing many a controversy is the fact that both Sāṃkhya and Buddhism have a chequered historical development. Thus KEITH (1924: 25) considers that there is absolutely no difficulty in deriving Buddhism from the earlier doctrine of the *Upaniṣad* (by which he must have meant the Upaniṣadic Sāṃkhya thought). Herman OLDENBERG in his book translated into English under the vague title "Buddha" (3rd ed., Pp. 433 ff) though to a certain extant criticizes JACOBI (1898: XLII I.15) who asserts that the only means therefore, of proving that Buddhism is really dependent on the Sāṃkhya is to find the existence in some important Buddhist doctrines of characteristics which are very definitely connected with the Sāṃkhya and which if not necessarily in themselves peculiarities of the Sāṃkhya school; are nevertheless treated by it in a special manner. The attempt to bring this really conclusive form of argument to bear JACOBI further gives importance to the influence that Āḷāra Kālāma, Gautama first teacher made on him. Āḷāra was a Sāṃkhynist and we know that the first impression is a lasting impression. Though Gautama was discriminate and did not accept all that Āḷāra tried to teach him but at least the basic dualism between sentient ones (*cetana puruṣa*-s) and insentient primordial matter (*a-cetanā prkaṛti*) must have been deeply rooted in Buddha's thought. We know from Aśvaghoṣa's *Buddhacarita* that the conception of three *guṇa*-s without which we cannot think of anytime of Sāṃkhya is not even once referred to by Aśvaghoṣa in the system of Āḷāra. Relying on this essential difference between what is generally supposed to be the basic Sāṃkhya and Āḷāra Kālāma's version of Sāṃkhya, A. B. KEITH (1924: 27) is extremely disturbed, who somehow tries to solve the anomaly by suggesting that Āḷāra's Sāṃkhya version is to be traced to a certain unknown Sāṃkhya under-current which did not think the existence of the *guṇa*-s to constitute the *prakṛti.*

But KEITH who is a scholar who will never accept any view unless there is sufficient historical data to prove it remark that, "It is clear, however, that this argument cannot safely be pressed: the historical accuracy of the views of Aśvaghoṣa is not confirmed by the information we have. Arāḍa is known to the sacred books of Buddhism, but his doctrine are never set out in any way corresponding to the picture of him in the Aśvaghoṣa, and we cannot therefore say that the account of Aśvaghoṣa has any value at all, not merely for the actual teaching of Arāḍa, but for the existence of any time of a scholar Sāṃkhya, which denies the existence of the *Guṇas*. It may be doubted if any such school of Sāṃkhya ever was known (KEITH 1924: 23)". True! But as I have said earlier the revealing article of the Russian scholar STCHERBATSKY, "The "Dharmas" of the Buddhists and the "Guṇas" of the Sāṃkhyas" perhaps had escaped the notice of KEITH. There the Russian scholar STCHERBATSKY amply proves that the Buddhists preferred to use the word *dharma* as a synonym of *guṇa*. I am sure A. B. KEITH might have greatly relieved of his doubt as to how can Arāḍa's version of Sāṃkhya as presented in the *Buddhacarita* of Aśvaghoṣa could speak of Sāṃkhya without even once using the word *guṇa*. The tension is relieved by the fact that instead of the term *guṇa* the word *dharma* is used by the Buddhists ultimately relying on Sāṃkhya (and Yoga too).

The *Pratītyasamutpāda* series begins with *avidyā* (either ignorance, nescience or what does not exist *na vidyate iti a-*

vidyā). This *avidyā* further results serially *saṃskāra*-s, *vijñāṇa*, *nāma-rupa*, *saḍāyatana*, *sparśa*, *vedanā*, *jarā-maraṇa*, *duḥkkha-davrmanaśya* etc. In the view of JACOBI all the twelve *nidāna*-s belong to one birth and one life (this view is not admitted by many scholars), who as we will see further divide the twelve links into three groups- past, present and future (see *Pratitya-saumtapāda hṛdya-kārikā* jointly authored by GOKHALE and DHADPHALE 1978).

Avidyā in both Sāṃkhya and Yoga alike the cause of the binding of spirit. It consists in the failure to realize the external distinction of spirit and nature. In Buddhism it means in failure to realize the Four Nobel Truths beginning with *dukkha*.

The *saṃkhāra* (Skt *saṃsakāra*) is a term borrowed by Buddhism from Sāṃkhya and Yoga where it means impressions made upon the intellect by such activities as thinking, feeling, willing and action from which in due course other phenomena of the life of the soul spring forth. The Buddhist conception of the *saṃsakāra*-s is a varying one, but it is sometimes clearly analogues to its correspondent Sāṃkhya one. The Pāli commentators explain it as "*saṃkharantī'ti' saṃkhāra*: (Because it makes something) it is called a maker of fashioner, molder, shaper).

Name and form (*nāmarūpa*) are to be considered as being equivalent to the principle of individuation and they naturally grow out of *vijñāṇa*, which is nothing else but the intellect of Sāṃkhya, which has *vijñāṇa* as one of its functions. Moreover, the derivative character of the Buddhist system as KEITH (1924: 20) calls it shows itself very clearly in the fact that both for ignorance and for *saṃskāra*-s an intellect must be assumed, which it merely admits after *saṃskāra*-s in the form of *vijñāṇa*. From individuation (*ahaṃkāra*), the Sāṃkhya allures on the one hand, the organ of sense and the fine elements (*tanmātrāṇi*), from which arise the gross elements (*pañca mahābhūtāni*). All this is in briefly is noted in the *Sāṃkhya-kārikā* (*prakṛter mahān, mahato' haṃkārah, tataḥ gaṇaśca ṣoḍaśaḥ, tasmādapi ṣoḍaśakāt pañcabhyo pañcabhūtāni*).

This is rendered plausible by the cosmic principle of individuation, as name and form; the sense and their corresponding objects are derived simply and without any justification as regards the individual.

The next element in the Buddhist series is contact or touch (*sparśa* or *phasso*). It means the contact of the senses with their corresponding objection (*cakṣur vijñāna, śrotra-vijñāna* etc.) which is in the same way recognized in Sāṃkhya-Yoga sister systems; from it results the feeling of pleasure, pain and neither the one nor the other; which is the same as the feeling (*vedanā*) of the Buddhist series. From feeling arises desire in both the systems, Sāṃkhya and Buddhist. From desire (rather craving) arises the motive to rebirth (*bhava*) or 'becoming', for which the twin systems Sāṃkhya-Yoga use the term *a-dīṣṭa* (unseen) or *dharmādharma* and in the Buddhist series *upādāna* or clinging.

I am aware that the series of twelve *nidāna*-s is interpreted on the basis of the old Buddhist texts in a different way by OLDENBERG (vide Buddha, 5th ed. Pp. 257-295.). However, even 'the oldest Buddhist texts' on which OLDENBERG relies are not unanimous about the order of twelve links, even the relation between the twelve *nidāna*-s is not uniform (see KEITH 1924: 96; RHYS DAVIDS 1907: 160; DUTTA 1941: I. 66-167; PANDE 2015: 436-441). OLDENBERG as he asserts interprets the twelve *nidāna*-s on the basis of the "old Buddhist Texts" lays stress on the fact that *vijñāna* is conceived as coming into existence at the time of conception as the result of the *saṃskāra* or impressions, which have been formed in the mind through ignorance in the former birth leaving out discussion the intermediate states. We at once jump to the fact that the 'consciousness' of any individual is imbued with the idea of individuality, which again comes from former experiences, which in their turn are derived from the lack of the correct knowledge. This is a tempting suggestion, but it is open to the serious objection that it goes a good deal beyond what is recorded and introduces in all probability too refined a psychology (Allgemeine Geschichte der Philosophie. I. II. 164-168). His view is that *vijñāna* is cosmic and produces all reality (cf. M. Walleser, Die Philosophische Grundloge des ālteren Buddhismns, pp. 4aff; but see Oldenberg Buddha, p. 263, foot note 1.).

Paul DEUSSEN goes so far as to hold that the systems of twelve links is the conglomeration of two quite different elements; the last group of members from craving (*tṛṣnā-taṇhā*) onwards is a formulation of the ground of the origin of misery (i.e. *duḥkha-samudaya*; not *samudāya*); the group from the second to the seventh explains psychologically the growth of the eight, craving, while the conception of ignorance is borrowed from the *vedanā* and placed at the head of the series.

Having known OLDENBERG, JACOBI, OLTRAMARE (1909) and Paul DEUSSEN (1894), A. B. KEITH (1924: 25-26) remarks that:

> "The only conclusion that can be drawn from the evidence is that some of the conceptions of Buddhism are very closely allied to those of the Sāṃkhya. The most important correspondence is that in the conception of the relation of ignorance (*avidyā*) and *saṃskāras*, the impressions thus left on the mind, which cause it in the view of the Sāṃkhya to attain ever new births, until at last the true knowledge is reached, and there ceases to be the possibility of rebirth, as the source being cut away no more impressions can be formed. This conception corresponds very closely with the Buddhist, and the use of the term *Saṃskāra*, which is not a very natural one, possibly points to direct borrowing. A second similarity of great import-

> ance is the precise correspondence of the two ideas, of the Sāṃkhya that the essential knowledge is to realize that anything empiric is not I, and of the Buddhist that it is essential to free oneself from the delusion that there is anything which is or belongs to the self (*ātmā-attā*)."

Thus beginning from OLDENBERG and reaching A. B. KEITH many a Buddhist scholar by and large accepted the Sāṃkhya-creation orders having influenced a lot the Buddhist core doctrine of *Pratītyasamutapāda*. A. B. KEITH (1924: 27) of all these scholars has his own reservations for he concludes by saying that "it seems best, therefore, to draw the conclusion that Buddhism did not draw the inspiration from the Sāṃkhya in the form in which it appears even in the epic, for there the doctrine of isolation of spirit and nature and of the three *Guṇas* is fully and completely evolved." We can safely admit the reservation expressed by A. B. KEITH.

It is obvious that the Buddhist Yoga doctrines are far earlier than the classical *Yoga-sūtra* of Pātañjali. The Idea of the four *Brahamihāra* are already mentioned in the Pāli-*nikāya*-s and what Pātañjali did is only to accept them and put them in the *sūtra* form. There is of course abundant later evidence of the knowledge of the Buddhist teachers of Sāṃkhya and Yoga too, as in the case of Nāgārjuna (see WOODS: 1914: xviii). That the Sāṃkhya system was known to *Dīghanikāya* was disproved by RHYS DAVIDS (1907: 27). Louis DE LA VALLÉE POUSSIN (1929, 1936-37), the well known French Buddhist scholar has repeatedly demonstrated the dependence of the *Yoga-sūtra*-s of Pātañjali on scholastic Buddhism.

Our discussion in this article mainly tries to indicate two points.

1. The influence of Sāṃkhya on Buddhism, and
2. The influence of Yoga on Buddhism.

If certain Indian thinkers themselves deny that the Sāṃkhya played any important role in shaping Buddhist philosophy, the majority of scholars nevertheless do consider the influence of Yoga techniques on Buddhist as incontestable.

Two great orientalists F. Max MULLER and OLDENBERG were the first to reject the tradition which was until then accepted by many scholars both oriental and occidental that Buddhism derives a lot of thought- material from Sāṃkhya system (a fact which may be due to the teaching of Āḷāra Kālāma, the first preceptor of Gautama). Richard GARBE (1897: 3-5) in his *Die Sāṃkhya Philosophie* attempts to justify the tradition by indicating the eight points common to Sāṃkhya and Buddhism among which he stresses the following: Both Buddhism and Sāṃkhya are enumerative philosophies by which GARBE means that these two make exaggerated use of classification, enumerations and schemata: both are pessimistic and begin with the existence of *dukkha* (sorrow), anti-sacrificial and anti-ascetic; both hold that spirit must not be confused with psycho mental experience; both regard liberation (*kaivalya/ nirvāṇa*) of the supreme goal to be achieved in life. GARBE thinks that Sāṃkhya cannot have borrowed all its ideas and all its schemata from Buddhism since Buddhism is decidedly later than Sāṃkhya, the roots of which we can easily trace to the Upaniṣadas. The further point which GARBE indicates that Sāṃkhya cannot have borrowed from Buddhism anything since Buddhism refused to give clear answers on at least ten important philosophical questions (the *dasa avyakatāni*) by the Buddha. The Buddha's thinking behind this being that these points have little to do with main goal of liberation. JACOBI (1896) in his important book *Der Ursprung des Buddismus aus dem Sānkhyaa-Yoga* not only accepts GARBE conclusions but also gives them added support by bringing out the intimate relation between the twelve *nidāna*-s of Buddhism and the categories of the Sāṃkhya. OLDENBERG who in his "*Buddha*" had denied Sāṃkhya influence on Buddhism criticizes JACOBI's statements (Buddstischen Studien, p. 693) and questions whether the Buddha, though steeped in yoga ascetic practices, had also adopted the Sāṃkhya tenets. He refutes JACOBI's opinion of Sāṃkhya influence on Buddhism at greater length in his "Zur Geschichte der Samkhya-Philosophie", NKWKG 1917-1919, Pp. 178-223. But as Louis DE LA VALLÉE POUSSIN pointed out OLDENBERG gradually convinced himself of the influence of Sāṃkhya on Buddhist thought.

These I call real scholars who are always ready to give up their wrong views and correct themselves by accepting the right ones; they always believe "Socrates is dear but truth is dearer". Max MULLER also gave up his view that Āryan was a separate race and accepted the truth that "Āryan" was only a separate "language-family". I confess, I do not know whether he too changed in course of time his view about Sāṃkhya influence on Buddhism. The changed view of OLDENBERG was also shared by Richard PISCHEL (1910: 10, 65 ff); (cf also F. Lipsius, "Die Sāṃkhya-Philosophie als Vorläuferin des Buddhismus", JSG 15, 1928, 106-114; Tuci II Buddhism, pp 58ff; see also Eugen HULTZSCH (1927: 78-83); Walter LIEBENTHAL (1934), Jakob Wilhelm HAUER (1927), Satischandra Vidyabhusana (1907: 571-578).

The *Bhagavadagitā* of which the second (and altogether important) *adhyāya* is known as Sāṃkhya-Yoga and as S. K. BELVERKAR repeatedly explained "the Sāṃkhya is an old nomenclature of knowledge", the knowledge in that Yoga is primarily the Upaniṣadic doctrine of *vedanā*, which teaches that the bodies though being mortal, the Soul (*Ātman* or *Brāhman*) is eternal. Further the *Bhagavadgitā* uses more than once the word *Brahma-Nirvāṇa* which T. G. MAINKAR (1955) in his *Gītā Bhāṣya-Prakāśa* superbly characterizes "Brāhmo-Buddhist" compound.

JACOBI is of the opinion that Aśvaghoṣa's testimony represents a genuine historical tradition. He (1898) returns to the subject in his study "Über das Verhältnis der buddhistischen Philosophie zu Smankhya-Yoga und die Bedeutung der Nidānas" in which he makes his opinion more explicit; "Buddhism appears not as a copy but a personal re-interpretation of Sāṃkhya, the latter was not the model after which Buddhism was constructed, but rather the soil on which it grew" (JACOBI 1898: 1).

For the time being let us conclude this article which has become "longish" by putting Sāṃkhya categories (evolvements of *prakṛti*) and their most probable parallels in the Buddhist *Pratītyasamutapāda*. Here too, there is no unanimity between the scholars in citing the parallels.

I have chosen the mostly agreed once which are mainly divided time wise, i.e. the (A) the Past, (B) the Present and the (C) Future.

Past:

1. *Avidyā* (Ignorance)
2. *Sṃsakāra*-s (Latent dipostions)

Present:

3. *Vijñāna* (Rebirth Consciousness)
4. *Nāma-rūpa* dependent on each other (Name and Form)
5. *Ṣaḍāyatana* (Six Organs of Knowledge)
6. *Saprśa* (Contact)
7. *Vedanā* (Feeling)
8. *Tṛṣṇā* (Craving)
9. *Upādāna* (Rooted ideas)
10. *Bhava* (Action or Character)

Future:

11. *Jāti* (Birth)
12. *Jarā-maraṇa-śoka-paridevanā-duḥkha-daurmanskatā* (Old age-death-sorrow-lamenting-pain, dejection of mind).

The whole round of the twelve-*nidāna*-s is technically known as *bhava-cakra*. The wheel moving constatntly round and round. The school babies enjoy the pleasure of sitting a play-instrument known as "Marry-go-round". Our pessimistic makes it for adults "a sorry-go-round".

The "Wheel of Law" is an ancient and orthodox idea which has even been preserved in a pictorial form in Ajantā caves and elsewhere too (for more details see RHYS DAVIDS 1907: 153). Vācasapatimiśrā in his commentary *Bhāmati* on *Brahma-sūtra*-s (II. 2.19) gives a somewhat different explanation of the *Pratītyasamutpāda*, "1) *tatra eteṣu sṭsu yā ekasmjña, piṇḍa-samjñā...pudgalasaṃjñā...sā iyaṃ avidyā.* 2) *tasyāṃ avidyāyāṃ sattyāyāṃ ragadveṣamohāḥ viṣayeṣu pravartante ...vastuviṣaya vijñaptiḥ vijñānam.* 3) *vijñāt catvāro rūpiṇaḥ upādāna skandhāh.* 4) *nāmarūpaṃ nirupyate śarīrasyaiva kalalabuddudā avasthā.* 5) *nāmaraūpa saṃmiśritāni saḍayatanaṃ.* 6) *nāmarūpendriyāṇāṃ trayāṇāṃ sannipātaḥ sparśaḥ.* 7) *sparṣāt vedanā sukhādikā.* 8) *vedanāyāṃ sattyāṃ kartavyametat sukhṃ mayā iti adyavasānaṃ tṛṣṇā,* 9) *tata upādānaṃ vākkāyaceṣṭa bhavati,* 10) *tato bhavo bhavtyasmājjanmeti bhao dharmādharmau,* 11) *tadhetukaḥ skan-dhaprādubhāvo jātiḥ,* 12) *janmohetuka uttare jarā-maraṇādyaḥ* etc. Two others commentaries namely *Brāhmāmṛta varṣiṇi* and *Brahmavidyā bharṇa* have given their own slightly diverg-ent explanation of the twelve links of the Buddhist "Depend-ent Origination". Thus we have seen many common ideas between Sāṃkhya-Yoga and Buddhism.

Later Buddhism developed four distinct schools of Philoso-phy. Viz. (1) Sarvāstivāda- all things in the world are real and can be perceived through sense organs which is a purely realistic school like the Sāṃkhya. (2) Vaibhāṣika- this school also admits the external world as really existing; the only thing that differs from the earlier one is that they deny the direct perception and the existing external world and make it a subject of *anumāna* (inference). But the third school

Vijñānavāda makes the world formed of ideas and not realities while the fourth one considers the universe as purely *śunya*, empty.

The Sāṃkhya-s were realists and consider the world as real. This is an important point of difference between Vijñānavādins and Śūnyatāvadins, which we, while admitting the Sāṃkhya as an original model of Buddhism should never forget otherwise we could have said the same thing about Saṃkara's *māyā-advaita-vāda* and Buddhism as *yuyaṃ ca bauddhāśca samānasaṃsadaḥ you (śāmkarism),* and the Buddhists sit in the same party meeting and further *vedāntā yadi śāstraṇi bauddhaiḥ kimaparādhitaṃ*. So let us say about Sāṃkhya and Buddhism as *sāṃkhyāśca bauddhāśacho samānasaṃsadaḥ.*

As per my personal opinion about whether the Sāṃkhya-cateogories (of creation) helped the enlightened one to formulate his doctrine of *Pratītyasamutpāda*, it is definitely positive. The first teacher, the Sāṃkhyan Āḷāra Kālāma , though Gautama left him, left permanent Impression on Gautama's mind of the Sāṃkhya process of creation.

Why I am so very emphatic about this fact is not only the modern critical foreign scholars like JACOBI (ZDMG lii, I-15), which was criticized first by H. OLDENBERG (Buddha) (3rd ed.) Pp. 443ff; Z.D.M.G. lii 681-694) but later as a sincere scholar corrected his view, PISCHEL, A. B. KEITH (he would like to derive Dependent Origination from Epic Sāṃkhya). Now according to JACOBI when he accepts that in the ultimate analysis the *Pratītyasamutpāda* doctrine, the very core-doctrine of the Buddhist Philosophy, the Sāṃkhya theory of *guṇa*-s had yet to develop or assimilate. As I have mentioned earlier the revealing article by SCHERBATSKY (1934) the word *guṇa* was not used. In its place the typically Buddhist word *dhamma* (*dharma*) was used of. But the prominent points of dissimilarity between the Buddhist doctrine of causal nexus and Sāṃkhya- categories of creation though scholars try to establish a correspondence between Buddhist *avidyā* and Sāṃkhya *prakṛti* (primordial matter), the prakṛti is really the original cause; it is not caused by any other factor. The *Sāṃkhyakārikā* says, "*mulaprakṛtiravikṛtiḥ, mahadādyāḥ, prakṛtivikṛtaya. Sapta ṣaḍaśakastu vikārāḥ, na prakṛtirna vikṛtiḥ pumān*।" The concept of puruṣa idea comes closer to the Vedāntic doctrine of *jīvātmā*.

Now a new point that I shall like to place before the scholars is that trying to find a correspondence between the *nidāna*-s and the *prakṛti* and its products is not a modern (mostly western) piece of research but was also found in India at least before the time of the celebrated commentator on *Piṭakan*-texts, the great Buddhaghosa. This is plain from Buddhaghosas Encyclopedia of Buddhism known as *Visuddhimagga*. He zealously refuted any influence of Sāṃkhya on *Paṭiccasamutappāda* (vide. KERN 1896: 46f.; Pousin 1913: VII fn 2).To refute this view of the Sāṃkhya creation theory on the formulation of Dependent Origination, Buddhaghosa pointed out (Vism 525) ignorance (*avijjā*), the traditional first link of the twelve *nidāna*-s, can no way be regarded as similar of *prakṛti* (*pakati*) of the *pakativādin*-s (i.e. the Sāṃkhya Philosophers) as *avijjā* was never considered by the Buddhists as the primary cause of the world (*mūlakāraṇaṃ*), nor was it uncaused (*akāraṇaṃ*). In the Nikāya-s the chain does not start always with *avijjā* as its first member. *Avijjā* ows its origin from impurities or *āsava*-s (defilements). The reason advanced by Buddhghosa for making the chain start by *avijjā* as its first member was that the Buddha used ignorance of truth (*avijjā*) or desire for rebirth (*bhavataṇhā*) for commencing (*sīsabhāvaṃ*) his discourses in *Paṭiccasamuppāda* as the chain was without any beginning or end (*vaṭṭakathā*) or *anamatagga* (*anv-a-mata-agga*) (i.e. its specific beginning being not known) (Vism 525). Thus though theoretically *avijjā* was not the starting point of *bhava /saṃsāra-cakka* it is one of the terms found suitable by the author of the formula to begin the chain. It could as well be commenced with *bhavataṇhā* (ibid 525, *purimā, bhikkhave koṭi na paññāyati avijjāya (or bhavataṇhāya) ito pubbe avijjā (or bhavataṇhā) nāhosi. atha pacchā saṃbhavatī'ti. evaṃ c'etam, bhikkhave, vuccati, atha ca pana paññāyati idapaccayatā avijjā (or bhavataṇhā)* (S II.178, 149). In the Saṃyuttanikāya (II. 101-3; Mahāniddesa (I.25-26) the starting point of *Paṭiccasamuppāda* is *āhāra* (food).

Abbreviation

A	*Aṅguttaranikāya*
Ap	*Apadāna*
D	*Dīgha-nikāya*
M	Majjhima-nikāya
Peṭ	*Peṭakopadesa*
S	*Saṃyuttanikāya*
Sn	*Suttanipāta*
Mbh	*The Mahābhārata;* Ed. V.S. SUKTHANKAR et al., 19 vols., Poona 1933-1966.

References

BELVALKAR, S. K.
(1938). *Brahmasūtra Bhāshya: Selections translated into English.* Poona Oriental Series No. 13. Pune.
(1934). Development of Buddhist thought, AP 5, 1934, 306 ff.
BELVALKAR S. K. and RANADE R. D.
(1997). *History of Indian Philosophy: The Creative Period.* New Delhi: Munshiram Manoharlal Publishers Pvt. Ltd.
Brewster, E. H.
(1926). *The Life of Gotama the Buddha: Compiled exclusively from the Pali Canon.* London: Kegan Paul, Trench, Trubner & Co. Ltd. New York: E. P. Dutton & Co.
CHILDERS, R. C.
(1875). *A Dictionary of the Pali Language.* London: Trubner & Co. Reprint. Delhi: Asian Educational Services 2003.
COOMERSWAMY, Ananand K.

(1943). *Hinduism and Buddhism.* New York: Philosophical Library.

DE LA VALLÉE POUSSIN, Louis.

(1903). Vyādhisūtra on the Four Āryasatyas. *The Journal of the Royal Asiatic Society of Great Britain and Ireland*, pp. 578-580.

(1913). *Théorie Des Douze Causes.* Londres: Luzac & Co.

(1936-37). Le Bouddhisme et le Yoga de Patañjali. *Mélanges Chinois et Bouddhiques 5.* Pp. 223-242. Bruxelles.

(1929). Notes bouddhiques: XV: Les deux nirvanas d'après la Vibhasa. BCLS 5th series, 367-374. English version in IHQ 6, 1930, 39-45.

DEUSSEN, Paul.

(1894). *Allgemeine Geschichte Der Philosophie.* Leipzig: F. A. Brockhaus.

DUTTA, Nalinaksha.

(1941). *Early Monastic Buddhism.* Vol. 1. Calcutta: Calcutta Oriental Book Agency.

GARBE, Richard.

(1897). *Die Sāṃkhya Philosophie*. Leipzig.

GOKHALE, V.V. and DHADPHALE, M. G.

(1978). Pratityasaumtapāda hṛdya-kārikā. *Principal V. S. Apte Commemoration Volume.* Ed. by M. G. DHADPHALE. Pune: Deccan Education Society.

HAUER, Jakob Wilhelm.

(1927). *Das Laṅkāvatāra-sūtra und das Sāṃkhya.* Stuttgart: W. Kohlhammer.

HORNER, I. B.

(1971). *The Book of the Discipline.* Vol. IV Mahāvagga. London: Luzac and Company Ltd.

HULTZSCH, Eugen.

(1927). Sāṃkhya and Yoga im Śiśupālavadha. *Aus Indiens Kultur: Festgabe für Richard von Garb.* Ed. J. von Negelein. 78-83. Erlangen: Palm and Enke.

Jacobi, Hermann.

(1896). Der Ursprung des Buddismus aus dem Sānkhyaa-Yoga. *Nachrichten von der königlichen Gesellschaft der Wissenschaften zu Göttingen,* philologisch-historische Klasse, 43-58.

(1898). Über das Verhältnis der buddhistischen Philosophie zu Smankhya-Yoga und die Bedeutung der Nidānas. *Zeitschrift der Deutschen Morgenländischen Gesellschaft* (ZDMG). Vol. XLII, 1-15.

Keith, A. B[erriedale].

(1923). *Buddhist Philosophy In India and Ceylon.* Oxford: At the Clarendon Press. Reprint 1995, New Delhi: Asian Education Service.

(1924). *The Sāṃkhya System: A History of the Sāṃkhya Philosophy.* Calcutta: Association Press. London: Oxford University Press.

KERN, Hendrik.

(1896). *Manual of Indian Buddhism.* Strassburg: K. J. Trübner.

LIEBENTHAL, Walter.

(1934). *Satkārya in der Darstellung seiner buddhistischen Gegner: Die prakṛti-parīkṣā im Tattvasaṃgraha des Śāntarakṣita zusammen mit der Pañjikā des Kamalaśīla übersetzt und ausführlich interpretiert.* Beiträge zur indischen Sprachwissenschaft und Religionsgeschichte 9. Stuttgart-Berlin: W. Kohlhammer.

Lipsius, F.

(1928). Die Sāṃkhyaphilosophie als Vorläuferin des Buddhismus. JSG 15, 106-114.

MAINKAR, T. G.

(1962). *Kālidāsa, His Art and Thought.* Poona: Deshmukh Prakashan.

OLDENBERG, Herman

(1892). *Buddha: His Life, His Doctrine, His Order.* Translated from the German by William Hoey. London: Williams and Norgate.

OLTRAMARE, Paul.

(1906). *L'histoire Des Idées Théosophiques Dans L'inde.* Paris: Ernest Leroux.

(1909). *La Formule bouddhique des douze causes.* Genève: Librairie Georg & C.

Pande, Govind Chandra.

(2015). *Studies in the Origins of Buddhism. 3rd Reprint.* Delhi: Motilal Banarsidass.

Pichel, Richard.

(1910). *Leben und Lehre des Buddha.* Leipzig: Drud und Derlag von B. G. Teubner.

RHYS DAVIDS, T. W.

(1907). *Buddhism its History and Literature.* American Lectures on the History of Religion First Series 1894-1895. 2nd ed. New York, London: G. P. Putnam's Sons.

SCHRADER, F. Otto.

(1955). Sāṃkhya, Original and Classical. *Brahmavidya.* Vol. XIX. Parts 1-2, Pp- 1-3. The Adyar Library Bulletin.

STCHERBATSKY, TH.

(1922). *The Central Conception of Buddhism and the Meaning of the Word "Dharma".* 1st Ed. London. Reprint. Delhi: MLBD. 1988.

(1927). *The Conception of Buddhist Nirvāṇa.* Leningrad: Publishing Office of the Academy of Sciences of the USSR.

(1934). The "Dharmas" of the Buddhists and the "Guṇas" of the Sāṃkhyas. *Indian Historical Quarterly.* Vol. X, 737-760.

STRAUSS, Otto.

(1913). Zur Geschichte des Samkhya. *Vienna Oriental Journal.* XXVII, no. 3-4, 257-275.

WOODS, James Haughton.

(1914). *The Yoga System of Patañjali: Or the Ancient Hindu Doctrine of Concentration of Mind.* Cambridge, Massachusetts: The Harvard University Press.

Vidyabhusana, Satischandra,

(1907). Sāṃkhya Philosophy in the Land of the Lamas. *Journal of the Royal Asiatic Society of Bengal*. Vol. III, 571-578.

Online Sources

Śvetāśvatara Upaniṣad *http://gretil.sub.unigoettingen.de/gretil/1_sanskr/6_sastra/3_phil/vedanta/brssgo1u.htm*

Yuktidipika *Nyāyavārtikagretil.sub.unigoettingen.de/gretil/1_sanskr/6_sastra/3_phil/samkhya/yuktdipu.htm*

Two Traditions of Female Renunciation in South Asia: Challenges and Prospects

Gihani De Silva*

Introduction

Female renunciation is a radical refutation that challenges the traditional assumed roles of mother and wife. South Asian patriarchal social orders do not encourage women to renunciate their lay life. However, there are number of women could be seen who challenge to the above assumed conservative roles by dedicating their lay lives for monasticism. This essay mainly discusses about female renunciants in Buddhist and Hindu traditions in Sri Lanka and India. Renunciants in both traditions have been less studied and encounter similar difficulties in these mainstream religions. Therefore, it is noteworthy to review, whether how these renunciants challenge to the challenges they encountered from a feminist perspective. First, the essay focuses on the brief history and recent scholarship on female renunciation in both traditions. Then, attention move towards the social image of female renunciation. Specifically, how these renunciants challenge to this negative image. In other words, it will be discussed about female renunciants who have brought their religious vocation to the mainstream. For instances,

* Lecturer in Sociology, Department of Sociology, Faculty of Social Sciences & Languages, Sabaragamuwa University of Sri Lanka, Sri Lanka. Email: gihani.desilva@yahoo.com

Hindu female *guru*-s and revival of *bhikkhunī* order in Theravāda Sri Lanka will be briefly illustrate in this regard. Therefore, this study employed both secondary data and primary data (empirical data). Empirical data were collected by conducting interviews and observing Hindu female ascetics in Trivandrum and Amritapuri in Kerala and Sri Lankan Buddhist nuns (*dasasilmātā*-s and *bhikkhunī*-s).

Social History on Buddhist Nuns

Buddhism is a path of transcendental emancipation, as well as a social philosophy with a reformist role on existing social practices. Buddhism originated in the Gangetic valley in Eastern India, which almost a change of nomadic era in stabilizing agrarian development. By 8th century BCE the old agrarian social order was undergoing a dramatic transformation (Sponberg 1992: 4). In this era, it produced an agrarian surplus based on trade and urban mercantile class. Therefore, this period was undergoing urbanization and the beginnings of states. Parallel to these social reforms, there were ideological transformations. No longer could prevail Brahmana rituals integrate with these ideological concerns of the social reforms which derivatives through rapid urbanization (Kosambi 1965). New large numbers of religious and philosophical principles were derived to fill the ideological vacuum. According to Sponsberg (1992: 4), "the emergence of a new sense of self-consciousness or individuality, especially among those who were on the margins, socially or spiritually, of the prevailing Brahmanic culture was another key development within the era." It was a time that demanded not just new answers, but a new ethos.

In this regard, it seemed to be an interrogation of social system, identification of suppressed figures and represent them, and going beyond the Brahmanic standpoints were common features of above newly emerged religions. They believed in human's spiritual power than monotheism, creativities and polytheism. Women's status under Brahamanic epoch is well known and elaborated by many scholars. For instance, classic Hindu *Dharmashāstra*-s of the Manu-Smṛti, popularly known as the 'Laws of Manu,' is the best known as anti-feminist literature. It describes the dependable life of a woman, "by a girl, by a young woman, or even by an aged one, nothing must be done independently, even in her own house" (BÜHLER 1886: V.147). "In childhood a female must be subject to her father, in youth to her husband, when her lord is dead to her sons; a woman must never be independent" (BÜHLER 1886: V.148). However, historians questioned how for these laws were in force at the time of Buddha. Because *Dharmashāstra*-s were said to be compiled later when Hinduism dominated (DE SILVA). There was an ancient tradition in India, which is known as 'going forth.' This way of life was always held in very high esteem, however, it was reserved only for the higher castes; kings, Brahmin-s, merchants etc. They had to live their life according to four *āśrama*-s:

1. *Brahmacāri*: as youths, their duty is to practice celibacy and study the Vedas.
2. *Gṛhastha*: when they decide to marry they become family men who have a duty to look after their wife and children.
3. *Vānaprastha*: At middle age when the duty to look after the family is complete they may go to live in solitude or in the forest in order to develop a spiritual practice. At this point, business and responsibility is handed over to successors.
4. *Saṃnyāsi*: Finally, those who detach from everything and go forth, living a monastic or ascetic life (see DHAMMACARO).

However, these practices were reserved mostly for men. Women were banned from learning and especially studying the Vēda-s. It was regarded as a secret scripture whose wisdom was only for men. Women were likened to Sūdra-s and slaves. A woman could not attain heaven through any merit of her own. Thus, she could not worship or perform a sacrifice by herself. She could reach heaven only through implicit obedience to her husband, be he debauched or devoid of all virtues (see DEWARAJA 1994).

Many women, who of course did not have a right to practice spirituality in such a way, were drawn to the opened and equality of that which the Buddha taught. Women were quick to take advantage of the opportunity encouraged by the Buddha, than any of the other mendicant teachers of that day according to the canonical texts. In this regard, Buddhism has challenged and critical of the 'semi slavery' status of women in India at that time. The hostile attitude towards the women, both in religion and in society was repeatedly criticized and condemned by the Buddha on numerous occasions. However, while granting a very high position for women in many Buddhist scriptures, at the same time there are many occasions, which are still controversial in nature. According to Uma CHAKRAVARTI (1996: 32), "general tore of Buddhist literature is antagonistic to women."

However, Buddhist teaching emphasis not only women can reach the same levels of enlightenment as men, but also they are able to follow the same path. Thus, *bhikkhunī*-hood is one of the important achievements of Buddhist women at that time. But, the women who seek the *bhikkhunī*-hood had to face many challenges, as Buddha was reluctant to establish the order. But, Ānanda-thera could manage to change the Buddha's mind and by most unflagging efforts of Mahāprajāpati and Ānanda thera *bhikkhunī* order was established. However, the Buddha insists that *bhikkhunī*-s take upon themselves "*Aṭṭha Garu Dhamma*" (eight rules) which places the *bhikkhunī-s* in a position decidedly under the authority of the *bhikkhu*-s. CHAKRAVARTI (1996: 32) firmly states that, in fact, "in the entire early Buddhist literature only Ānanda seems to have genuinely believed in the principles of equity between men and women. Therefore, real feminist was Ānanda, but not Buddha."

Nevertheless, Buddha himself opened the doors for women's entrance to monastic life. Women flocked by the thousand to join the order of *bhikkhunī*. *Bhikkhunī*-hood is very much similar to a bridge over a great river by means of which one is able to cross the river of *saṃsāra* to meet the bank of *Nirvāna*. Thus, women joined for all sorts of reasons for the order. Many women joined in desire for liberation. This was a great opportunity opened them to renunciate lay life rather become mothers or mistress.

The global level expansion of Buddhism was initiated because of the third *Dhamma* council in the regime of Emperor Asoka in the 3rd century BCE. Sri Lanka benefitted from the above successful missionary work by Mahinda-thera, the son of Emperor Asoka and it mostly effect on the shaping of entire social-cultural patterns of the country. He was successful in converting the King and civilians to the new religion. As incidental sequel, Sri Lankan women become the most active members of this new religion. The establishment of the *bhikkhunī* order proves this. Thus, it becomes a great achievement of Sri Lankan women. Even the Sri Lankan *bhikkhunī*-s were involved in international missionary work in China. Thus, the present Dramaguptaka *bhikkhunī* tradition in China is believed to be granted from Sri Lanka. However, after flourishing its golden age, *bhikkhunī*-s were disappeared. As stated by R. A. L. H. GUNAWARDANA (1979: 39), "nuns left the stage of history as quietly as they had occupied it, and there are no clues to help the curious historian to determine the causes or the circumstances of their disappearance." Whatever the causes were, chronicles are completely silent as to what led to the disappearance of the *bhikkhunī* order after thirteen centuries of its succession.

A new phase of Buddhist female clergy was initiated in the Buddhist revival period in the early 20th century called as *dasasila-mātā* movement. However, it is an alternative form of female renunciation in between status of fully ordained *bhikkhunī*-s and lay women. They are not recognized into the *saṅgha*. Thus, Thessa Bertholemeuz (1994: 3) who did a lengthy study on Buddhist nuns in Sri Lanka calls them as 'lay nuns.' This movement started with the assistance of Sinhala Buddhist elites and then spread into other social strata. However, *dasasila-mātā* movement splits into another new group when *bhikkhunī* order was claimed to be reestablished by an international and local feminist inspired groups. However, this newly established *bhikkhunī* order is not legally sanctioned by the conservative *Mahānāyaka saṅgha* in Theravāda Sri Lanka.

Recent Scholarship on Buddhist Female Renunciation

Although, Buddhist nuns do have a long institutionalized history compared with Hindu female ascetics, until 1980s, it was not gained much attention within the social and the academic spheres. Female renunciation has given neither noteworthy space in the textual tradition of Buddhism nor in Anthropological field research. The early Western academia was interested in the textual tradition, as Kawanami (2013: 1) states, "they focused on restoring the textual traditions more acceptable and enhance philological understanding of its doctrines." Therefore, female renunciants were invisible as they were not the official custodians of doctrines. They were neglected and evade from the ethnography of mainstream Buddhism until recently. For instance, Buddhist female renunciants did not fit comfortably into the structuralist paradigm of binary oppositions that dominated academic discussions in early Sri Lankan Anthropological work. They were revolved largely around the popular binary categories such as 'the great tradition' and 'the little tradition,' 'worldly' and 'otherworldly,' 'sacred' and 'secular,' 'orthodox' and 'syncretistic,' 'Buddhist' and 'animistic' (ABEYSEKARA 2002: 30). Elizabeth NISSAN (1984: 32-49) states that, "studies dealing with monasticism and asceticism in Sinhalese Sri Lanka are the studies of the Buddhist monkhood. Scholarship has followed Sinhalese cultural representation in this respect associating the ascetic with male, and the ecstatic with female." In this respect, while male attract to the robe, female shoved and confined into the practices such as possession largely. Accordingly, *bhikkhu* came to represent the great tradition within the religious sphere, while women represented the little tradition.

"Feminist-inspired Anthropology" was developed in the late 1970s as a response to this male led Anthropology of Buddhism. It enhanced sensitivity developed towards studying women of other cultures and religious traditions. Although it was intended to challenge the male led conceptual paradigm, it has created some troubles with the advent of the liberal feminist approach. Feminism probably originated in the late 19th century with the debate on "whether women should be confined to the private realm of home and family or be welcomed into the public realm of business and politics" (YOUNG 1999: 2). It has emerged in various forms of feminism by the second wave of feminism in the 1970s. "In religious circles, feminists call for women's inclusion in liturgical or theological language, education, leadership, ritual and symbolism" (YOUNG 1999: 2) in the religious dimension of feminism. Therefore, religious feminism or feminist study of religion was crucial to achieve the equal position in the religious sphere by focusing not only on theoretical transformation but also with the practices of living traditions. 'Religious feminism' has marked as a turning point, which has claimed for reinterpretations to the mainstream religious traditions with core values of patriarchy. Under the sphere of religious feminism, Buddhism and its practices were largely concerned. This was termed as 'Buddhist feminism.' Rita Gross (1992: 127) describes Buddhist feminism as "the radical practice of the co-humanity of women and men."

As mentioned by J. J. Clark (1997), "the interest in the study of Buddhism in the West has grown considerably during the nineteenth century" (quoted in Cheng 2007: 9). According to Walters (1994), "the early voices of feminist studies of Buddhism were waylaid by male agenda (quoted in Cheng 2007: 9). As Cheng (2007: 9) observes, "Western discovery of Buddhist women, focuses largely on the texts, on the history of women and the study of feminine images and symbols within Buddhist texts." Thus, feminist curiosity in Buddhism much considered in Western women's experience with Buddhism. For instance, Sandy Boucher's (1988), *Turning the Wheel: American women creating the New Buddhism* can be shown in this regard.

Rita M. Gross's (1993) in *Buddhism after Patriarchy: A Feminist History, Analysis, and Reconstruction of Buddhism* as one of the groundbreaking ethnographical study considered many critics to this day. As she remarks, her primary task in this book was "feminist revalorization of Buddhism, feminist theology in general the task of revalorization involves working with the categories and concepts of a traditional religion in the light of feminist value" (Gross 1993: 3). Salgado (2013: 9) argues that, "Gross's works, through instructive in their approach to the subject, relate better to Buddhist practitioners of a certain profile living in the 'developed' world rather than to those living elsewhere." Thus, Gross has tried to reconstruct Buddhism that appropriate to the modern Western world by explicating the Buddhist doctrines through feminist lenses. However, she gives less attention to identify the agency of female renunciants as changing agents in Asian countries. As Kawanami (2013: 6) states, "some feminist theologians had made their experience of socio-religious exclusion central to their academic work, and by doing so, transported their own political and ideological baggage to the study of women in other cross-cultural and religious settings." Therefore, these studies has employed 'East/West' or 'Us/Other' structuralist binary rhetoric.

"Feminist discourse on religion may unintentionally set up imperial boundaries that homogenize differences among women and/or subjugate women of different backgrounds, by assuming that all women's interest are identical" (CHENG 2007: 6). One can query this as a new type of colonizing; DONALDSON and KWOK (2002: 3) observe the feminist study of religion is sometimes "replicating the colonial gaze in the name of serving a feminist agenda." Accordingly, theoretical and empirical analysis of liberal Western feminist largely based on Western values and tried to impose them into non-Western social setting by ignoring the values embedded within these different cultural settings. Thus, the voices of the subjects in these 'other' or non-Western cultural settings has been subsided and subjugated by distorting their real interests. Because according to DELPHY (2008) and SCOTT (2007), "in Western discourses, religious women are considered too oppressed to speak for themselves or too dominated to express a real 'free choice'" (quoted in ACCIARI 2014). Therefore, these oppressed subjects were often to be represented by dominant discourses. This approach is highly criticized by postcolonial feminism and third world feminism.

Intervention of Western liberal feminists in an issue of Asian Buddhist female renunciants has been challenged by postcolonial feminism. Postcolonial feminism can be referred as one of the intellectual trend in feminism, which has emerged in 1980s. "Postcolonial feminists, along with minority feminists in both the East and the West, demand for gender recognition as insiders" (YOUNG 1999: 17). Hence, the outsiders (e.g. White feminists) hardly understand the voices of such minority-oppressed women. As MOHANTY pointed that, first world feminist constitutes women as a homogeneous group instead of considering the cross-cultural disparities. "The homogeneity of women as a group is produced not on the basis of biological essentials, but rather on the basis of secondary sociological and anthropological universals" (Mohanty 1991: 56). They argue that, "Western feminism often carries a flavor of white/Western superiority and does not necessarily bring liberation to minority/colored/ third World women, for they are in turn oppressed by prejudice in Western feminism" (Cheng 2014). The first world women's intervention in speaking for women cross culturally on their struggles and troubles that they encounter in day today life is questioned by this new intellectual trend of feminism. This has led to develop an alternative way of studying about Buddhist female renunciation and related issues by the contemporary academia.

Hindu Female Asceticism

"Within Hinduism, asceticism as an institutionalized way of life is closely associated with the pursuit of salvation (*mokṣa* - liberation) or release from transmigration (*saṃsāra*) through world renunciation (*saṃnyāsa*; see–*āśrama* and *saṃnyāsa*) or the abandonment of all activities constitutive of life in the world, ritual, and otherwise" (Clémente-Ojha 2011: 60). Thus, asceticism is only allowed to men in twice born three *varaṇa*-s and other caste categories such as *Sūdra* and women of all *varṇa*-s are excluded from the above definition. Does this mean there is no space for women to gain spiritual development? The answer is 'no,' as it allowed in marriage life. According to the Hindu culture, the ideal female is a married woman. Because only male can perform rituals while female assist him. Women have to conduct themselves according to *strīdharma* (*dharma* of the women). Indeed, they are not just performing ritual in outside the home, but within everyday household activities. Thus, "women can lead a form of ascetic life while pursuing their domestic calling" (Clémente-Ojha

2011: 60). Therefore, the asceticism is considered as an important female expression in female religiosity. It gives her a sense of self-worth. "It places some value on "good" women's roles. Such symbolism can enhance the individual's sense of self-worth by showing her existence as part of imitative of some larger reality" (McGuire 2002: 139).

In an ideal sense, Hindu women dedicate their lives to marriage life. As Leslie (1989) stated, "married life can thus be seen ideally as a form of renouncement for women" (quoted in Clémente-Ojha 2011: 61). According to Mallison (1979) "it can also be seen as a path to holiness within the world" (quoted in Clémente-Ojha 2011: 61). The woman who follows the *stridharma* becomes a *saint*. Moreover, she is ideally brings well-being to her husband, family and community, ideal female figures such as Sītā and Sāvitrī depicted in old scriptures. "Women, by nature, are endowed with animating power-*śakti*, which, when disciplined by ritual practices and service directed towards their husbands, protects them from harm" (Courtright 2011: 167). Further, they take vows (*varta*-s) for the welfare of their husbands. According to McGee (1987) as quoted by Pintchman (2010: 427) a *varta* is, essentially, "a religiously sanctioned votive observance, that is, a rite performed at a particular time with a particular desire in mind." Even in the contemporary India, "women tend to see *varta* observance as continuous with their *stridharma*, their *dharma* as women..." (Pintchman 2010: 427).

If the husband dies, "in a culture and religion that places such importance on marriage as the foundation of society, it is not surprising that the widow occupies an anomalous position: she is the carrier of inauspiciousness" (Courtright 2011: 167). Thus, "widowhood in Hindu India is associated with vivid images: the widow who burns on her husband's funeral pyre, the child widow and the ascetic widow" (Chen 2011: 174). Specifically, "the logic of *satī* is related to notion of – *dharma* that are appropriate to married women, or *pativra*-

tādharma" (Courtright 2011: 166). This practice is prohibited. However, "...it has romanticized both in India and the West, while *satī* remains a potent symbol of female abjection" (Courtright 2011: 172). "The orthodox Hindu model for widows who did not commit *satī* and did not remarry was to lead a chaste, austere, ascetic lifestyle" (Chen 2011: 174). Some of them stay in their own household by spending an ascetic way of life and others may move into a community of widows where they could perform rituals for the benefit of her husband in their next life. However, most widows do not become ascetics. Because, widowhood cannot be conserved as a sufficient qualification to lead the life of an ascetic. In fact, a good proportion of female ascetics are celibate. According to Olivelle (1977) as quoted by Clémente-Ojha (2011: 65), "renunciation is defined more by what it is not, rather than by what it is." However, it implies unhide the value of female asceticism at all. However, stated in some other places, "renouncing the world means renouncing married life and key aspects of socially defined women-hood... In the traditional Hindu society, for a woman who refuses to marry or who walks out of her marriage, religious career is the best alternative" (Clémente-Ojha 2011: 61).

In Hinduism until the 20th Century, there were no well organized institution for female ascetics. "Through the history of Hinduism, women wanting to become ascetics struggled against considerable odds" (Clémente-Ojha 2011: 63). Thus, institutionalized Hindu female asceticism is not much visible phenomena until recently. "In most cases they either lived on the broader of monastic institutions or within the framework of rules that are designed by males for other males and are essentially male oriented" Clémente-Ojha 2011: 63). Although it can be inferred there were some Hindu female ascetics, we have little knowledge about the number or their renunciant lives. Here, *bhakthi* traditions were important, as they were mainly unconcerned about gender. "Legendary women poet-saints of the *bhakti* period such as Mirā-bāi, Mahadeviyakka, and Andal cultivated an emotional relationship with a god envisioned as husband and thus rejected ordinary marriage; they faced social disapproval during their lifetimes even if they are now revered as saints" (quoted in KANDELWAL 2009: 1008).

1980s can be regarded as an epoch, which took much scholarly attention towards Hindu female asceticism. If move towards the recent works on Hindu female asceticism, Urusula KING (1984) has documented about social change and the admission of women to asceticism recently. Lawrence BABB (1984) focused on Brahma Kumari-s and "describe Brahma Kumari feminism in its cultural context." Further, Denton Lynn TESKEY (1991) has brought the scholarly attention about the Hindu female ascetics in contemporary India. Ethnographies on female ascetics can be taken as the most recent development. Thus, Sinclair-Brull's (1997) *female ascetics* is a length study, which focuses on female ascetics in Śaradā Mandiram in Kerala. Denton Lynn TESKEY's (2004) *Female Ascetics in Hinduism*, brings documentation on female renunciation in Benares. She "approaches the study of female asceticism by focusing on features of two *dharmas,* two religiously defined ways of life: that of woman-as-householder and that of the ascetic, who, for various reasons, falls outside the realm of householdership" (TESKEY's 2004). Sondra HAUSNER's (2007) *Wandering with Sadhus* illustrates about a larger renunciants community concerning about the issues of gender and sexuality. Moreover, Antoinette DENAPOLI (2009) has published a recent essay on women Hindu renouncers in Rajasthan, with a focus on the construction of personal narratives. All above scholarly work on Hindu female asceticism has brought the phenomenon on female asceticism into the mainstream Hinduism.

Female Renunciation in contemporary South Asia: Challenges and Prospects

Although the above studies have shown the blooming status of female renunciation, the social image related to the female renunciation not yet changed a lot. Women are not being encouraged to renunciate their lay life in South Asia. Thus, still marriage is an institution women should spend their whole life. There is no fully accepted space to think beyond mistress or mother. Thus, most women are aspiring to obtain a good husband, in laws and children. But, if someone who reject this social norm to achieve their spiritual liberation is not welcome by her family and the society. The Buddhist nuns and Hindu female ascetics, whom I have interviewed in Sri Lanka and India, stated the difficulties they met when they decide to renunciate. For instance, Kusala *dasasilmātā's* story (who is highly dedicated to mediation) depicts such constraints she encountered,

> After my graduation ceremony, I worked as a teacher at an International School for a period of one year. It was a hubris environment. Soon I got frustrated with everything. Meanwhile, I met a *bhikku* who meditates. I used to go to that temple for getting instructions for meditation. Soon I felt that I should give up the lay life. But my parents and brother against my idea. But I never changed my mind. I resigned from the job and stayed at home and refused to take any food. I was sick and parents thought that I would commit suicide. Then they allowed me to do what I want.[1]

Meanwhile, it is interesting to see how *Matha* Amritha became a famous female *guru* while facing many difficulties. *Matha* Amritha was born into a poor fishing family in Kerala in 1953. She came to know that, she is spiritually connected with Krishna Bhava.[2]

---

1 Interview with Kusala *dasasilmātā* (age 35) on 2015.04.22.

2 Informal discussion with lay devotees and several female ascetics-white clad women, who stayed in the Amritapuri on 2015.03.10.

> ...Thereafter Sudhamani regularly appeared in Krishna Bhava, during which people flocked to meet her on the beach near her home. But a group of youths from the surrounding villages, calling themselves the "rationalists" were against her and tried to harm her. Seeing the harassment that his daughter was being subjected to, amma's father took pity on her and converted the family cowshed to make a proper place for her to meet people.[3]
>
> ....Sudhamani's elder brother, unable to comprehend her exalted state, chastised her terribly. One day in a fit of anger because of the gatherings around his sister, he threw her out of the house. From then on Sudhamani lived outdoors by herself.[4]

However, her endless dedication to spiritual vision has made her into a "Universal motherhood" with millions of disciples all over the world. Female *guru* is a relatively recent development in Hinduism as it is a male defined space. "Most female *gurus* tend to be seen as the embodiment of motherhood because of their maternal feelings" (Clémente-Ojha 2011: 66). Thus, they attract many devotees and create their own monastic space due to their charismatic personalities. Similarly, when the head female ascetic (*Mathaji*) in Trivandrum decided to renunciate lay life, her family members were reluctant to let her to do it.[5] Thus, she had to ask for the permission repeatedly. In another story, Dhammadinna *dasasilmātā's* father at first rejects her to be ordained saying that, "renunciation is for the destitute women."[6]

---

3 "Life of Amma- Krishna Bhava." Accessed on May 05, 2015. http://www.amritapuri.org/amma/life/krishna.

4 "Life of Amma- Union with the Divine Mother." Accessed on May 05, 2015. http://www.amritapuri.org/amma/life/union.

5 Interview with female ascetic (*Matha*) on 2015.03.08.

6 Interview with Dhammadinna *dasasilmātā* (age 48) on 2015.04.29.

Above stories emphasis that renunciation is not an easy path to be taken by women in both traditions. However, this endless dedication is not well reputed by the society instead, they are seen as 'destitute women.' For instance, as I have observed, number of Sri Lankan teledramas and novels depicts that, when women or girls face troubles in their family relationships or love affairs, ultimate solution is to be a 'Buddhist nun.' Although this can be a solution for those who face such troubles, it undermines the status of female renunciation. However, according to empirical data, many stories of renunciants emphasis that, not all the women are renounce due to helplessness, but there are a number of dedicated women who seek spiritual liberation from the very young age.

Moreover, another assumption that makes very negative image is about the role of female renunciants. According to the commonly believe assumption, these renunciants just stays in *ārāma* (nunneries), *maṭha* or *āśrama* without involving any duties or responsibilities. Nevertheless, below explanation prove the multiple roles performed by renunciants in both traditions not only to enhance their own spiritual liberation but also their surrounding communities' welfare. Here, it will be mainly documented on Buddhist nuns' role. The social engagement of Buddhist nuns is not a new phenomenon at all. Social engagement or activism can be defined in various ways. Although the meaning of the term "activism" may appear obvious, interpretations of the term vary in different cultural and historical contexts. As Karma Lekshe Tsomo (2009) states, "In the Buddhist context, activism may include overt social and political activism—advocacy, marches, and civil disobedience—and also include quiet activism, such as counseling, caring for the needy (orphans, and the sick, frail, elderly, and destitute), community action projects, and a range of temple activities."

"Without fanfare, Buddhist temples were both the primary providers of social services and cultural centers for their surrounding communities. This tradition has continued up to the present day, expanding and becoming more visible in recent years" (Tsomo 2009). The recent surge in Buddhist social activism, especially in Sri Lanka, can be attributed to many salient factors. Religious rituals are the main role that performs by Buddhist nuns. As ritual specialists, they engage in *Buddha pūja* (offerings to Buddha), *Bōdhi pūja* (offerings to Bō tree), *Sēla viyāpāra* (merit making offerings), *Pirith* chanting (recitation or chanting of the word of the Buddha), preaching sermons, and attending for *Dāna* (alms giving). Most of the time the laity gives adequate sponsorship for these religious rituals and therefore, *ārāma* are so busy with full of devotees in full moon *Poya* days and weekends. In addition, Buddhist nuns as educators are confined mostly to teaching in the schools and *Pirivena* (Buddhist *dhamma* education centers). The most preferable activity among the responsibilities is the teachings as not only a service but as a means of surviving. It is obvious that, they prefer teaching as a form of social work, especially teaching young children. Some of the Buddhist nuns conduct meditation programs in *ārāma* for laity. For most of these works, they do not get financial assistance from the government or other organizations.

At the community level, *ārāma* nowadays become centers for social services. It is the most and dedicatedly engaged activity by present Buddhist nuns. They are going voluntarily to hospitals for aid sick and children. According to Subba *dasasilmāta*, hospital service (*Rohal Sevaya*) is one of her daily routine activities.[7] In addition, some of these Buddhist nuns cure the people who suffering from various fears by using *Pirith* who come to *the ārāma*. Sumedha *bhikkhunī* helps laity as a healer.[8] They go to *Dāika* (female lay devotees' houses), when they are sick. Female lay devotees come to *ārāma* often

7 Interview with Suba *dasasilmātā* (age 53) on 2015.04.23.

8 Interview with Sumedha *bhikkhuni* (age 58) on 2015.04.24.

and take care of these Buddhist nuns. Sussane Mrozik in her study "We Love Our Nuns: Affective Dimensions of the Sri Lankan *Bhikkhunī* Revival" (2013) also focuses on the affective ties between laity and *bhikkhunī*-s which proves the multiplicity of *bhikkhunī*-s tasks and laity as its beneficiaries. What she stresses as the underlying reason for such development is that "the *bhikkhunī*-s have developed a reputation in Sri Lanka for being exceptionally virtuous (*silvat*)..." (Mrozik 2013: 87).

The most noteworthy activity that these renunciants are taking is informal counseling. Thus, laywomen freely have relationships with Buddhist nuns, as there were no social barriers. The lay community happily accepts that the Buddhist nuns start to do counseling. According to *bhikkhuni* Metta there are a number of women coming to *ārāma* asking help for various problems.[9] Most of them are in young ages. Even married women are coming by abandoning their children and husband. In such cases, nuns do not allow these women to stay for a long time in *ārāma*. They advise them and help to rejoin with their own families again.

However, said role is problematic, as these renunciants do not have sufficient knowledge of counseling. Even some of them do not know about it well. As nuns have less educational opportunities, they do not get the chance to learn about psychology, counseling or social work. However, as I have observed, this informal counseling service can be improve into formal level to minimize societal problems in rural level. Rural communities are undergoing various changers due to social problems such as family disorganizations, increasing of divorces and separations, suicides, early marriages, abortions, etc. in contemporary Sri Lanka. Thus, Buddhist nuns could contribute in minimizing these social problems efficiently. Moreover, women's associations in rural level can

---

9 Interview with Metta *bhikkhuni* (age 45) on 2015.04.25.

be empowered through the guidance of Buddhist nuns. Finally, it should be remember to remark that, counseling or doing social work is not prescribed role for Buddhist nuns, but present complex social atmosphere cause and even ask them to involve in above roles.

According to empirical findings in India, prove that female ascetics in Trivandrum, Kerala are highly educated and specialized in various roles. As the head ascetics (*Matha*) told me every and each *Ashram* is for specific purposes.[10] For instance, Trivandrum Math is providing educational center and boding place for girls who do their higher studies, as Trivandrum itself an education center in the state of Kerala. All the activities in the Math are highly scheduled and girls are well disciplined. Thrissur Math is educating students at a school. Some other *Ashrams* are do have orphanages for children, old ages homes etc. Moreover, Matha Amritha *Ashram* provides cultural and spiritual activities, health care, education, social welfare and nature care.[11] As a female *guru* Matha Amrita has gained attention towards her projects all over the world due to her charismatic personality.[12]

Finally, if these female renunciants in both religious traditions take the leadership role in community work, they will be better accepted. These pious renunciants have sacrificed their lay life on behalf of religious commitment. However, their activities have transformed neither into commercialized forms nor even these nuns solely going away from achieving ultimate spiritual attainments though they engage in such multiple roles. According to the research findings, these renunciants are willing to dedicate their lives for social activities. Thus, they have brought their religious vocation into

---

10 Interview with head ascetic (*Matha*) (age 80) on 2015.03.08.

11 See more in "Humanitarian Activities." Accessed on May 05, 2015. http://www.amritapuri.org/activity.

12 Fieldwork on 2015.03.11-12.

mainstream with identifying their own monastic spheres and expanding it dramatically.

Bhikkhunī Issue

Reintroduction of '*bhikkhunī* ideal' in Theravāda tradition is motivated by the transnational Buddhist women's movement. According to Tomalin (2013: 108), "transnational Buddhist feminist networks, which cut across different Buddhist traditions and locations, also play a significant role in strengthening and promoting Buddhist feminism across the globe." Those emerging transnational Buddhist feminist networks created a good wet-ground for reviving the *bhikkhunī upasampadā* in Theravāda tradition, as it was declined. For instance, the first International conference for Buddhist women held in Bodhagaya, India in 1987 given much attention to feminist issues in Buddhism. Thus, the higher ordination ceremonies took place in Saranath in 1996 and in Bodhgaya in 1998 can be considered as succeed of expectations of the above International forums.

"The issue of the ordination of women is one of the most controversial issues because of its great symbolic importance and because the role of the clergy is powerful than lay roles. The significance of the ordination of women is that it presents an alternative image of women and an alternative definition of gender roles" (McGuire 2002: 135-136). Therefore, present *bhikkhunī* higher ordination debate occurs within this context for reclaiming its rights where it has declined (such as Sri Lanka, India, and Burma) or never established (such as Cambodia, Laos, and Thailand and Tibet).

The *bhikkhunī* order which declined from around the 11th century in Sri Lanka, has emphasized the necessity of four fold Buddhist community, including *bhikkhu*, *bhikkhunī*, *upāsaka* and *upāsikā* in Theravāda tradition. The disappearance of *bhikkhunī-hood* caused difficulties for Buddhist women to renunciate their lay life within the institutionalized religious sphere as it is solely controlled by the patriarchal hierarchies. According to feminist scholars, institutional patriarchal religious hierarchies needed to keep religious women under a subjugated and submissive framework, where women were restricted for achieving their spiritual liberation in institutionalized manner. Therewith, the conservatives or opponents considered the very attempt of reestablishment of *bhikkhunī* higher ordination (*upasampadā*) as a violation of law of Buddha or defilement of pure Theravāda Buddhism. Therefore, the conservative sangha authorities in Sri Lanka do not legally sanction this new *bhikkhunī* movement. Nevertheless, the new *bhikkhunī* movement, empowered by its transnational Buddhist feminist networks could not be easily brought to an end by those supreme authorities... "as an inevitable or unstoppable movement..." (DE SILVA 2009: 25). Therefore, Sri Lankan Buddhist renunciants are continuously ordaining into this new order without considering the above obstacles.

Conclusion

Female renunciation took less attention in both academic and social milieus until 1980-s. This could be seen in Buddhism and Hinduism. However, women have to struggle over their monastic rights throughout the history. Even the achievements they gained is constrained and controlled by the male institutionalized authorities of these mainstream religious traditions. But, women do challenge to these constraints. Because they do know about the way, they should expand their monastic spheres. That is why they could be concern as challenging and changing agents of these religious traditions in South Asia. For instance, they do not concern about the negative social image that impedes becoming renunciants. After joining these orders, they do involve in multiple duties. Moreover, Hindu female *gurus* and newly ordained *bhikkhunī*-s challenge to these mainstream religions, as they were the formerly male defined monastic spaces. Therefore, female renunciation is a continuously changing social phenomenon in contemporary South Asia.

References

Abeysekara, Ananda.
(2002).*Colors of the Robe: Religion, Identity, and Difference.* Columbia: University of South Carolina.

Babb, Lawrence.
(1984). Indigenous Feminism in a Modern Hindu Sect. *Signs*, 9, 3: 399–416.

Bartholomeusz, Tessa.
(1994). *Women under the Bo Tree.* New York: Cambridge University Press.

Boucher, Sandy.
(1988). *Turning the Wheel: American women creating the new Buddhism.* Boston: Beacon Press, 1988.

Bühler, G[eorge].
(1886). *The Laws of Manu.* Oxford: At the Cladrendon Press. Under the *Sacred Book of the East.* Ed. by F. Max Müller, Vol. XXV

Chakravarti, Uma.
(1996). *Social dimensions of early Buddhism.* New Delhi: Manushiram Manoharlal Publishers Limited.

Chen, Martha Alter.
(2011). Widowhood. In *Brill's Encyclopedia of Hinduism.* Ed. by Knut A. Jacobsen. Vol. III Society, Religious Specialists, Religious Traditions, Philosophy. Leiden: Brill.

Cheng, Wei-Yi.
(2007). *Buddhist Nuns in Taiwan and Sri Lanka: A Critique of the Feminist perspective.* London and New York: Routledge.

Clémente-Ojha, Catherine.
(2011). Female Ascetics. In *Brill's Encyclopedia of Hinduism*, Ed. by Knut A. Jacobsen. Vol. III Society, Religious Specialists, Religious Traditions, Philosophy. Leiden: Brill.

COURTRIGHT, Paul.
(2011). Sati. In *Brill's Encyclopedia of Hinduism*, Ed. by Knut A. JACOBSEN. Vol. III Society, Religious Specialists, Religious Traditions, Philosophy. Leiden: Brill.
DE SILVA, Premakumara.
(2009). Discourses and Counter Discourse(s) on the New *Bhikkhunī* Order in Sri Lanka: An Ethnographical Inquiry. *Nivedani*. 25-41.
DENAPOLI, Antoinette.
(2009). By the Sweetness of the Tongue: Duty, Destiny, and Devotion in the Oral Life Narratives of Female Sadhus in Rajasthan. *Asian Ethnology*, 68(1), 81–109.
DENTON, Lynn T.
(1991). Varieties of Hindu Female Asceticism. In *Roles and Rituals for Hindu Women*. Ed. by J. Leslie. Rutherford. NJ: Fairleigh Dickinson University Press.
(2004). *Female Ascetics in Hinduism*. New York: State University of New York Press.
DONALDSON, Laura E. and KWOK Pui-lan.
(2002). *Postcolonialism, Feminism and Religious Discourse*. New York and London: Routledge.
GROSS, Rita.
(1992). *Buddhism After Patriarchy: A Feminist History, Analyze and Reconstruction of Buddhism*. Albany, NY: State University of New York.
GUNAWARDANA, R.A.L.H.
(1979). *Robe and Plough: Monasticism and Economic Interest in Early Medieval Sri Lanka*. Tucson: Arizona University Press.
HAUSNER, Sondra L.
(1979). *Wandering With Sadhus: Ascetics in the Hindu Himalayas*. Bloomington and Indianapolis: Indiana University Press.
KANDELWAL, Meena.
(2009). Research on Hindu Women's Renunciation Today: State of the Field. *Religion Compass*, 3/6, 1003-1014.

Kawanami, Hiroko.
(2013). *Renunciation and Empowerment of Buddhist Nuns in Myanmar-Burma: Building a Community of Female Faithful.* Leiden: Koninklijke Brill NV.

King, Ursula.
(1984). The Effect of Social Change on Religious Self-Understanding: Women Ascetics in Modern Hinduism. In *Changing South Asia.* Ed. by K. Ballhatchet and D. Taylor. 69–83. London: School of Oriental and African Studies.

Kosambi. D. D.
(1965). *The Cultural and Civilization of Ancient India in Historical outline.* London: Routledge and Kegan Paul.

McGuire, Meredith B.
(2002). *Religion: The Social Context.* Belmont: Wadsworth Thomson Learning.

Mohanty, Chandndra T.
(1991). Under Western Eyes: Feminist Scholarship and Colonial Discourses. In *Third world and the politics of Feminism.* Ed. by Chandra T. Mohanty, Ann Russo and Lourdes Torres. 51-80. Bloomington and Indianapolis: Indiana University Press.

Mrozik, Sussane.
(2013). We Love Our Nuns: Affective Dimensions of the Sri Lankan Bhikkhunī Revival. *Journal of Buddhist Ethics.* 57-95.

Nissan, Elizabeth.
(1984). Recovering Practice: Buddhist Nuns in Sri Lanka. *South Asia Research* 4, no. 1, 32-49.

Pintchman, Tracy.
(2010). Vratas. In *Brill's Encyclopedia of Hinduism*, Ed. by Knut A. Jacobsen. Vol. II. Sacred Texts and Languages, Ritual Traditions, Arts, Concepts. 427-434. Leiden: Brill.

Salgado, Nirmala S.
(2013). *Buddhist Nuns and Gendered Practices: In Search of Female Renunciants.* New York: Oxford University Press.

SINCLAIR-BRULL, Wendy.
(1997). *Female Ascetics: Hierarchy and Purity in an Indian Religious Movement*. Surrey: Curzon Press.
SPONBERG, Allan.
(1992). Attitude toward women and feminine in early Buddhism. In *Buddhism, Sexuality and Gender*. Ed. by Jose Ignacio CABEZON. 1-36. New York: State University Press.
TOMALIN, Emma.
(2013). Gender Buddhism and Bhikkhuni Ordination: Transnational Strategies for the Feminist Transformation of Religion in the 21st Century. In *Religion, Gender, and the Public Sphere*. Ed. by Niamh REILLY and Stacey SCRIVER. New York: Routledge,
YOUNG, Katherine K.
(1999). Introduction. In *Feminism and world Religion*. Ed. by Aravind SHARMA and Katherine K. YOUNG. Albany, N.Y.: State University of New York Press.

Sources Accessed from Internet

ACCIARI, Louisa.
(2014) "Recognizing Religious Women as Feminist Subjects: The Case of Catholic Feminists in Brazil." Accessed May 05, 2014. http://blogs.lse.ac.uk/gender/2013-/09/23/recogniziizing-religious-women-as-feminist-subjects-the-case-of-catholic-feminists-inbrazil/.
CHENG, Wei-yi.
(2014). "Western Buddhist Feminist Oppressors." Accessed May 16, 2014. http://dharmafolk.org/ 2008/11/24/westernbuddhit-feminist-oppressors/.
DE SILVA, Swarna.
(2015). "The Place of Women in Buddhism." Accessed May03,2015,http://www.enabling.org/ia/vipassana/Archive /D/DeSilva/WomenInBuddhism/womenInBuddhismSwarna DeSilva.html.

DEWARAJA, L. S.

(1994). *The Position of women in Buddhism.* Kandy: Buddhist Publication Society. Accessed May 08, 2015.http://www.accesstoinsight.org/lib/authors/dewaraja/wheel280.html.

DHAMMACARO.

(2015). "Female Monks in Buddhism." Accessed April 27,2015.http://www.buddhapadipa.org/buddhism/female-monks-inbuddhism/. "Female Ascetics in Hinduism," Accessed May 05, 2015, "http://www.sunypress.edu/p-3981-femaleascetics -in-hinduism.aspx.

TESKEY, Denton Lynn

(2004). *Female Ascetics in Hinduism.* Accessed 05 May, 2015, http://www.sunypress.edu/p-3981-female-ascetics-in hinduism.aspx.

TSOMO, Karma Lekshe.

(2009). Socially Engaged Buddhist Nuns: Activism in Taiwan and North America. Journal of Global Buddhism 10, 459-485, Accessed on 22nd of May 2015,http://www.globalbuddhism.org/10/tsomo09.html.

"Humanitarian Activities." Accessed on May 05, 2015. http://www.amritapuri.org/activity.

"Life of Amma- Krishna Bhava." Accessed on May 05,2015.http://www.amritapuri.org/amma/life/krishna. "Life of Amma- Union with the Divine Mother." Accessed on May 05, 2015. http://www.amritapuri.org/amma/life/union.

Pāli Language Teaching Methods in Myanmar

Ram NIWAS alias HlaTun*

Introduction

Myanmar people had been familiar with Pāli language since the arrival of Buddhism. Since that time to until now Myanmar people have been striving hard to learn and understand Pāli texts. Here in the country two types of teaching methods are still using for proper teaching of Pāli language, the traditional monastic Pāli teaching and modern Pāli language being used at universities. The first is a traditional method that has been adapted by Buddhist monks throughout successive periods and the second one invented by the well-versed scholars of Pāli language from western countries and it was introduced to Myanmar during the British colonists. The modern Pāli language teaching method is used to teach the University students. The traditional Pāli language teaching methods, which are accepted and adapted by the majority of the monk students such as *Mandalay Teaching Method* (MTM), *Pakokku Teaching Method* (PTM), modified traditional method developed by Venerable *Ashin Janakābhivaṃsa* and modern teaching method used in the Department of Oriental Studies.

Traditional Pāli Language Teaching Method

Nowadays, Myanmar stands first among Theravāda Buddhist

* Professor and Associate Head, Department of Pali Language & Literature, State Pariyatti Sasana University (Yangon), Myanmar.
E-mail: ramniwas.dr@gmail.com

nations world-wide in many aspects. In fact, Theravāda Buddhism has flourished in Myanmar due to the energetic attempts of successive learned monks whose effective teaching methods have ensured the nearby perfect authenticity and originality of *Gotama* Buddha's teaching. Since Pāli language teaching had passed a significantly long period starting from Bagan era (round about 11th century CE) to present day, varied according to different institutions, different localities and different times despite the same aim of each method. The only one aim of teaching Pāli language is to understand the Buddha's teaching. MTM and PTM teaching methods are found to be the most famous.

Mandalay Method of Teaching

Among the traditional teaching methods, the *Mandalay* is the most basic and the most influential. "If one is not skilled in grammar, one cannot be skilled in literature". Traditionally, a Pāli language learner has to learn the core texts that form the architecture of Myanmar monastic high school level curriculum. They were *Kaccāyana*'s *Pāli* grammar, the *Abhidhammatthasaṅgaha* and the *Pātimokkha*. *Kaccāyana*'s grammar was to provide a good knowledge of Pāli grammar, while the *Abhidhammatthasaṅgaha* was to give him a summary of the *Abhidhamma Piṭaka*. The *Pātimokkha*, on the other hand, was taught as a preparation for the *Vinaya Piṭaka*. These three texts, known simply in Myanmar as *thatda* (grammar), *thingyo* (compendium) and *vinee* (discipline) respectively, were thus considered a preparation course for higher study. Teaching of *Kaccāyana*'s grammar, the monk students had to memorize all *sutta*-s by heart. The parsing is the separating how to become of a Pāli word gradually therefore, it is an important fact to learn Pāli grammar. Based on *Kaccāyana* grammar, *Piṭaka* learning is made step by step. Day courses are on the *Sutta* and *Vinaya* studies and evening courses on *Abhidhamma*. While learning by heart *sutta*-s in *Kaccāyana*, the students have to read in opposition to the *Abhidhamma*-

thasaṅgaha. Then, translating into Myanmar to understand the meanings of *Sutta* (A brief description, rules), *Vutti* (elaborated version of *sutta*) and *Udāharaṇa*, parsing and analyzing *Citta* and *Cetasika* etc. When a student has learnt almost *Kaccāyana Saddā* at a time, he has to study mainly the declension together with *Rūpasiddhi*. Apart from its emphasis on grammatical study, the *Mandalay* method studies the *Abhidhamma* by drawing tables on board. In this way, at the traditional Pāli teaching, Pāli grammar and *Abhidhammatthasaṅgaha* is taught as the basic foundation.

Then only the student who had studied the foundation course, he has to study *Aṭṭhakathā* (commentary) texts. According to the verified version of the Sixth Buddhist Council, it is learnt that the total number of original Pāli scriptures delivered by the Buddha himself is 40, while there are 51 *Aṭṭhakathā*-s and 26 *Ṭīkā* (sub-commentary). Thus, a Pāli learner finds it very difficult to learn such a large number of scriptures effectively and successfully. Even though he spends 15 or 20 years on learning these scriptures, it is still difficult for him to learn all of them. Accordingly, the Pāli lectures of ancient times i.e. the lecturer *Sayadaws* (teacher monk) usually selected some of the *Aṭṭhakathā*-s to be taught in detail. As for the remaining treatises they used to instruct them as references. Those texts are *Pārājika Aṭṭhakathā*, *Aṭṭhasālinī Aṭṭhakathā* and *Sīlakkhandha Aṭṭhakathā*. In the *Mandalay* teaching method, if *Aṭṭhakathā*-s were studied, Pāli would have been studied that means. When *Pāli* and *Aṭṭhakathā* are studied together, the teacher has to explain the definitions in *Aṭṭhhakathā*, therefore, *Aṭṭhakathā*-s are studied mainly. In teaching detail it was profoundly and widely taught through detailed analysis of words by grammatical method, explanation of sentences through *Codana* and *Sodhana* methods after classification of them, analysis through prosody and metaphorical method and criticism through *Abhidhamma* methods such as *Paṭṭhāna* method and *Nāsa* method etc. Thus *Mandalay* teaching method is reflected much of the ability and expertise of the teacher.

In teaching a Pāli canon, the lecturer *Sayadaw* uses such methods as *Yawzanar nee* (method of word to word translation of Pāli into Myanmar side by side), *Kyanyoengachet*, *Chakkathapanā*, *Pucchahtwat-tetnee*, *Code*, *Anusandhi*, *Saṁvaṇṇanā*, and *Nirutti* etc. to make a clear interpretation of a Pāli phrase. So, this method ornamented with such numerous ways is called *Mandalay* teaching method. The lecturer *sayadaw* usually selects some sentences with complex structure and unfamiliar words from a certain scripture and gives a detailed discussion based on various concepts of Pāli texts, commentaries and sub-commentaries etc. in addition to various meanings and interpretations of various Pāli texts.

These procedures of traditional Pāli teaching method were adopted in Myanmar monasteries since the reign of ancient Myanmar kings. Learning and teaching of the Buddha's doctrines had reached a peak during *Ratanabon* Period of the late *Konbaung* era when King *Mindon* appreciated Buddha's literature and made energetic efforts to flourish Buddhism.

In the history of Buddhism in Myanmar, there are a lot of monks and laymen who are skilled in Pāli with *Mandalay* method. Therefore, this method gives benefit to be the steadfast Pāli learning in Myanmar.

Pakokku Method of Teaching

Pakokku method of teaching was first introduced to the learners by the first *Yesagyo Sayadaw* Venerable *Ganthasāra*, who had used it since his arrival to *Pakokku*. This method had been used by his successive disciples until now. So, this method is known as *Pakokku* style of teaching method.

Being a higher study centre, the *Pakhokku* tradition did not teach a foundation course. But some basic texts such as *Kaccāyana*'s *Pāli*, the *Abhidhammatthasaṅgaha* and the *Pātimok-*

kha, were learnt by heart in *Pakokku* method. When the course of study of three *Piṭaka*-s is studied, *Pāli* text is taught mainly together with *Aṭṭhakathā* and *ṭīkā* texts to be able to translate into Myanmar. Therefore, the main purposes of *Pakokku* teaching method are "to end the course of study of three *Piṭaka*-s" and "to know the meaning whenever Pāli is seen".

Pakokku style method seems to be a proof to be the truth of a saying that indicates "A single *Pāli* word can convey many interpretation and definitions as many as ten and so". Accordingly various interpretations of a Pāli word given by as many sources as possible are analyzed. A variety of interpretations and meanings of a certain Pāli words are taken from various sources available and they are analyzed in an interesting way using a step by step procedure starting with elicitation of ideas (brain storming), motivation of readiness to learn, presentation of problems and giving solutions to them, having learnt Pāli texts for about two years through this method. Moreover, they are very likely to grasp their meaning clearly. In fact, *Pakokku* method can help the learners clearly interpret any Pāli word. Thus, they can learn all Pāli scriptures with thorough understanding under the supervision of the teacher. Consequently, this method can provide the learners with a strong basis of Pāli grammar and *Ahhidhammatthasaṅgaha* so that they can study the three *Piṭaka*-s thoroughly and effectively. In other words, the learners are exposed to Pāli language through scriptures of Pāli, *Aṭṭhakathā*-s, and *Tīkā*-s etc. If this method is effectively used, the learners will be able to study relatively many Pāli texts from the three *Piṭaka*-s even within an academic year. Thus, the core syllabus of Pāli literature made up of the five *Nikāya*-s preached by the Buddha himself is taught to the learners in a comprehensive manner by integrating with other interpretation and elaborations made by the compilers of *Aṭṭhakathā*-s and *ṭīkā-s* in a relatively short time. Such kind of teaching method is also known as "mastering the *Tipiṭaka*".

Another significant characteristic of *Pakokku* style teaching method which is distinct from other methods is that it does not encourage the stressful condition of examination system. Instead of focusing its emphasis on getting the certificate of passing an examination, it intends to teach the learners a complete core of Pāli texts, through a comprehensive approach so that they can master in Pāli language. So, *Pakokku* method of teaching puts its emphasis on process rather than a product.

Some well versed scholars of Pāli literature such as Venerable *Ashin Janakābhivaṁsa* of *Mahāgandhayone* monastery, Venerable *Ashin Neminda*, the holder of *Tripitakadhara* title (bearer of the scriptures) in Myanmar, Venerable *Rājindha*, the head monk of *Phayarphyu* Teaching Institution, Venerable *Sobhita*, the head monk of Koesaung teaching Institution, and Venerable *Kosala*, the compiler of many *Buddhavaṁsa* etc. had set good examples to highlight the effectiveness of *Pakokku* style method, which enabled them to master and excel at Pāli literature.

Ashin Janakābhivaṁsa's Pāli Teaching Method

Ashin Jankābhivaṁsa was a well-versed compiler of *Bhāsāṭīkā* and the abbot of the famous *Mahāgandhārāma* Monastery of *Amarapūra*, *Mandalay* Region, Myanmar. He had modified the traditional Pāli teaching method based on his own experiences as a young learner. The teaching method adopted by *Sayadaw* was the one suggested by Venerable *Mahāsīlavaṁsa*, the well-versed scholar of Ava era. The beginners were taught Pāli language using the method as easy as possible. Such method gave them only very basic meaning and concise interpretation in teaching fundamentals of Pāli language. Only after these, learners became more and more proficient in Pāli language, introduced to more comprehensive and subtle meanings of Pāli words.

Having established Mahāgandhayuṁ monastery in Amarapū-ra in CE 1941, he taught the new method combined with both *Pakokku* and *Mandalay* methods to students in order to be systemically skillful without having any difficulties. The syll-abus integrated by *Ashin Janakābhivaṁsa* for his monastic institution comprises the five levels: 1-Pre-school, 2-(a) Prim-ary (Part-1), (b) Primary (Part-2), 3-Basic level, 4-Intermidi-ate Level and, 5-Higher Level.

In Pre-School level, the attributes of Triple Gems, rules and regulations of monasticism, *Pālisikkhā* (A Basic *Pāli* Composi-tion) and a concise Pāli Grammar are taught. In *Pālisikkhā*, some important parts of the speech are extracted to be studied. In terms of a concise Pāli grammar, extracted declin-ing of nouns, and conjugating of the verbs from *Kaccāyanavy-akaraṇa* and *Rūpasiddhi* are taught in brief too.

In Primary level, *Dhammapada* Commentary, a basic Pāli Grammar, *Kathasallapasikkhā* (a basic spoken Pāli) are taught. Here in this level, only three chapters; *Sandhi* (combination of Pāli words), *Nāma* (various kinds of Nouns, Pronouns, Adjectives, Conjunction, Preposition and Adverbs), *Akhyāta* (Verbsa), *Kita* (Primary derivatives or Participles) and *Kāraka* (Eight cases in Declension of Nouns) are taught in detail. *Kathāsallāpasikkhā* is designed to make fluent inspoken Pāli and it is more helpful to be skilful in reading and writing as well. By learning this way, Pāli language skill is improving since one year.

At the basic level, *Mahāvagga Pāli, Aṅguttara Nikāya, Dhamma-pada* Commentary, Basic *Pāli* Grammar (*Samāsa* and *Taddhita*) and basic *Abhidhamma* are taught. Now Pāli study becomes higher and it is carefully built to go further forward towards the advanced Pāli text.

Another study of previous *Dhammapada* chapters is prepared to review the stories from the Pāli grammatical and *Abhidha-*

mma point of views in more detailed and methodical way. Remaining chapters of Basic *Pāli* Grammar, *Samāsa* and *Taddhita* are taught. Now the whole book of *Pāli* grammar is studied here. The candidate, who has successfully completed this level, is allowed to sit for *Sakyasīha*, i.e. First Level Examination.

After that *Cūḷavagga-Pāli* and *Parivāra-Pāli*, *Aṅguttara Nikāya*, *Dhammapada* Commentary and Basic *Abhidhamma* are taught in intermediate level. All chapters of basic *Abhidhamma* are thoroughly taught. The candidate, who has successfully completed this level, is allowed to sit for *Sakyasīha,* Second Level Examination and the Basic Governmental Pāli Examination.

During the Higher level of their study, the learners can continue to learn considerable high standard treaties such as *Pārajika-Pāli* and *Pācittiya-Pāli*, *Aṅguttara Nikāya* and *Dhammapada* commentary. In this level the whole text of *Aṅguttara Nikāya* and *Dhammapada* commentary have been completely studied. The candidate, who has successfully completed this level, is allowed to sit for *Sakyasīha* Third Level Examination and the Intermediate Governmental Pāli Examination. It is a surprise that, within three years, the following original Pāli text; five books of *Vinaya Piṭaka*, three books of *Aṅguttara Nikāya* and two books of *Dhammapada* commentaries, have been proficiently done.

Moreover the syllabus saves the time and makes the student more skillful and well-versed in Pāli and *Abhidhamma*. Now he can easily go for a further study to sit for higher governmental examinations where he would seek much more time to explore the knowledge of language, contemporary communication methods and skills. Actually, this integrated syllabus is thoughtfully and well-built for the purpose of understanding of the essence of *Dhamma* through Pāli language in a short time and it is also meant to practice the *Dhamma* in the meantime.

Even though the syllabus integrated by *Ashin Janakābhivaṁsa* is mainly effective for the Pāli study. It is partly accepted in the several monastic institutions in Myanmar and it still needs to polish up. Meanwhile Pāli is a popular language among the Buddhists in the world today and widely studied in easy way constructing the new syllabus and building the infrastructures for the study.

Examination Method

The traditional teaching methods include *Mandalay* and *Pakokku* style while other more updated methods are used to enable the learners to pass some examinations, which are supposed to assess the Pāli language competence of the learners. Such examinations are *Pathamabyan* examination, *Dhammācariya* examination, *Nikāya* examination and *Tipiṭakadhara* selection examination bearer of scriptures: the one who memorizes and masters in the three Piṭakas etc. This method is supposed to be intended the exam result than literacy. In this method *Mandalay* and *Pakokku* may be use. Nowadays, the government leads in holding annual *Pariyatti* examinations. The *Saṁgha* and the people also make enormous efforts to hold private examinations. Therefore, this method is being mostly used in the present age.

Modern Pāli Language Teaching Method in Universities

Modern Pāli language teaching was first introduced to Myanmar learners in State High schools, college and university by international teachers and lecturers who taught Pāli language during the reign of British colonists. The British government established the Yangon College in the year 1885. Yangon College offered six courses on six major subjects namely English, Pāli, Philosophy, Mathematics, Physics and Chemistry. All subjects had to be taught in English which was the medium of instruction at colleges and universities. Pāli as the major subject was no exception. In addition to the use of English, modern contemporary teaching methods being used in international colleges and universities were first introduced to Pāli language teaching. Accordingly, this method was known as modern teaching method and it has long been being used by the Department of Oriental Studies since that time to up to now. The Westerners had started taking interest in Pāli language since the early 19th century. As they were interested in Buddhism, they started to learn *Pāli* literature during the 19th century.

The Teaching Method used by the Department of Oriental Studies

Since methodology plays an important role in studying an academic subject, the Department of Oriental Studies is teaching *Pāli* language by using the suitable teaching methods in line with the modern age. So that university students can master over the Pāli language in writing and speaking as a result of full understanding so that they can follow the advice and admonition given by Buddha in their daily activities.

The Pāli grammar teaching method used by universities at present is the one, which mainly rely on such references as modern concepts suggested by Charles Duroisells's "*A Practical grammar of the Pāli language*", V. Perniola's "A Grammar of the *Pāli* Language", Wilhelm Geiger's "*A Pāli Grammar*", Lily de Silva's "*Pāli Primer*" and A. P. Buddhadattha's "*The New Pāli Course*" etc. It is a direct and simple method that uses linguistics so that the learners can master over Pāli language in the prescribed academic years. Thus, they will be able to realize and value the profound significance of Pāli literature and the Buddha's teachings. In studying Pāli literature teaching method which is used by the Department of Oriental Studies, it is found that the courses are designed to teach the learners the basic Pāli grammar and syntax in an easy way together with a variety of Pāli scriptures, which involve History of Pāli literature, History of Buddhism, Buddhist philosophy, Buddhist Ethics, Inscriptions, Epigraphy, and a comparative study between Pāli, Sanskrit and Prakrit languages etc.

Apart from studying Pāli grammar and literature, the learners are required to study basic *Pāli* grammar and *syntax* in an easy way, which influenced Myanmar language and literature, the two main components of Myanmar culture. To be proficient in Pāli language proficiency over Sanskrit and Prakrit languages is required. In this way Linguistics is also taught to students of Oriental Studies, so that they can study the links among Indo European languages. In fact, linguistics was first introduced to the department of Oriental Studies at the universities. Philological method can help the learners to decide right or wrong making a comparison with Sanskrit and Prakrit languages. Such a miscellany of course-contents despite just a little bit of each constituent theme can enable the learners to study Pāli language and literature in an easy way. So, this modern method of Pāli language teaching seems to be on a par with international teaching methods, to a certain extent, but not large. This method is supposed to be a short cut method, which mainly focuses on providing the learners with instant reading materials rather than lengthy and move difficult courses conveying subtle and serious themes. In other words, the modern teaching method puts its emphasis on breadth that is how many materials the learners can study regardless of their low level of difficulty rather than on depth that is how well the learners can master Pāli language in whatever level of difficulty.

Discussion

It has been presented in this paper that Pāli language teaching methods in Myanmar can be divided into two types; the traditional monastic Pāli language teaching method and the modern teaching methods used in Universities. Traditional Pāli language teaching method, however, puts its emphasis on the mastery of Pāli grammar based on three factors namely *Sutta*, *Vutti* and *Udaharaṇa* with the use of such reliable grammar references as *Kaccāyana Saddāgyi*, *Rūpa Siddhi* and *Moggallāna* etc. Besides, other necessary courses such as dictionary, prosody and rhetorical composition etc. for studying *Kavilakkhaṇa* are taught to the learners, too. In fact, Myanmar traditional Pāli language teaching method is a comprehensive one, which can enable the learners to swim across the sea of Pāli language successfully. Learners of the Pāli language, especially the monks can write in Pāli languag-e very well; they can compose verses in Pāli and they can compile expositions and commentaries in Pāli. Consequently, the expositions and grammar texts prepared by well-versed Pāli scholars of Myanmar concerning with Buddhist philosophy have played a leading role in the history of Pāli literature in Myanmar.

On the other hand, the modern Pāli language teaching method is being used at the Department of Oriental Studies with the following objectives:

1. to teach Pāli language to the students until they acquire basic mastery over *Pāli* grammar,
2. to widen the scope of their knowledge by providing them with informations such as administration system, economics, social structure, politics, education, trade and commenced agriculture of ancient India before and during the life time of *Gotama* Buddha described in Pāli literature,
3. to be able to construct exact and correct Pāli phrases and sentences using philosophy and to be able to understand the similarities and the differences between Pāli and Sanskrit (or) between Pāli and Prakrit language,
4. to study the historical background of long-lasting literature, which has come into existence since BCE 600 and to study how Pāli language spread to Asian countries including Myanmar,

5. to know, understand and follow Buddhist philosophy in daily activities.

Unlike the traditional monastic Pāli language teaching method, the modern (or) contemporary Pāli language teaching method used at the Universities does not use Pāli grammar references as their manuals. But it adopts the international Pāli language teaching method which also includes teaching of two other related subjects to Pāli language namely Sanskrit and Prakrit. This is the major difference between the traditional and modern approach to Pāli language. As there was no detailed analysis like giving a scrutinized explanation about the structure of a word with reference to *sutta*-s in the modern Pāli language teaching method, it can be said to be a less-rigid form than the traditional method.

In Pāli language teaching at present, the modern and traditional teaching methods are integrated at State Pariyatti Sāsana Universities and other Buddhist Universities. In addition, Pāli Language teaching modern method is supposed to be better than the traditional. It can provide the students with a comprehensive knowledge of multi disciplinary nature such as Pāli grammar selected extracts of Pāli, Sanskrit and Prakrit, History of Pāli language and Buddhist Philosophy, Buddhist Ethics etc.

At present, international students at international universities are studying Pāli language with modern method. The teaching, learning methods used at the Department of Oriental Studies are being upgraded in accordance with the international teaching methods sought through research work.

Conclusion

Among many purposes and objectives of learning Pāli language the most important one should be to fully comprehend the profound significance of Buddha's Dhamma to be followed and practiced Pāli literature consists of numerous moral lessons of the mundane world and a variety of guidelines and instructions of the supra mundane world (spiritual life) where the way of life is pure and noble with no defilement *puthujjana*-s tend to have. Moreover, Buddha had given admonition to ordinary people (or) laity concerning with what they must know, had to know and nice to know such as social relationships, economics, education, ethics, obligations, good morality and do's and don'ts for one's prosperity etc. Likewise, Buddha also pointed out the ways to escape from *saṁsāra* (or) an endless round of rebirths so that all living beings can enjoy emancipation.

It is assumed that students can be proficient in Pāli language in a relatively short time if the selected method to be used is suitable for their ability and readiness. If so, they can have a chance to realize the high value of advice and admonition given by Buddha described in Pāli texts and they will be able to follow and practice them in their daily activities. Thus they will become benevolent and their lives will be blameless, comfortable and worthwhile. They will also become responsible citizens and leaders of the future. In conclusion, a nation made up of such reliable youth folk with good morality and a wide scope of knowledge obtained from learning Pāli literature can be proud of its high status among the other nations of the World.

Reference

DHAMMASAMI Khammai.
(2004). A *Study of Monastic Education in Burma and Thailand from the Seventeenth Century to the Present.* PhD Thesis. University of Oxford.

JANAKABHIVAMSA, Ashin
(2007). *Tatbhavathathana (One Life in Sasanara) [Autobiography].* Re. Amarapura: Mahagandhayon Press.

KARRUNIKA, Ashin
(2008). *Dhammacartiyamyatshu.* Yangon: Department of Religious Affairs.

KELATHA, Ashin

(1970). *Mahāvisutārāma Nikāya Sāsanāwin*, Yangon: Department of Religious Affairs.
(1982). *Mandalay Sāsanāwin* Vol.II. Yangon: Department of Religious Affairs.

KHAINE Khaine, Than.
(2010). Yesagyo Sayadawgyi Ashin Ganthasara, the Architect of Pakokku Sasana Inventor of Pakokku Teaching Method. *Universities Research Journal.* Vol.3, No. 6. Yangon.

KHIN, Thein Ma
(1972). *Pāli Education in Myanmar under the British Colonists (1885-1941).* M.A. Thesis. University Yangon.

The Scholars' Papers. (2000). Yangon: Department of Religious Affairs.

The Syllabus and Curriculum of the Department of Oriental Studies (2013-2014).

Buddhism and Pāli Studies in Bangladesh: A Brief Historical Survey

Sukomal BARUA*

Bangladesh is a multi-cultural and multi-religious country shared by Muslims, Hindus, Buddhists and Christians and some animist groups. It is noteworthy that the Buddhist community of Bangladesh comprises various ethnic entities, such as BARUA, SHINHA BARUA, MARMA, RAKHAIN, CHAKMA, TANCHANGYA, KHEYANG, LUSAI etc., who reside in different regions, speak different languages, practice different colorful popular rituals and follow Theravāda Buddhist tradition since its inception. In this paper, I have focussed on the brief history of Buddhism and Pāli studies as well as the patronization of Buddhist practices in Bangladesh by various rulers.

It is difficult to ascertain, when Buddhism was first introduced into Bangladesh. Though popular beliefs, traditions and legends report that Buddhism was introduced into this country during the lifetime of the Buddha, there is almost no historical validity of it. Paucity of archaeological evidence from Bangladesh proper makes it difficult to say anything on the condition of Buddhism in Bangladesh during the early centuries of the Common Era. However, we can guess the probable date and routes of the introduction of Buddhism into

* Former Chairman, Department of Pali and Buddhist Studies, University of Dhaka, Dhaka, Bangala Desh.
Email:skbaruadu@gmail.com

Bangladesh by examining various Buddhist literary works, traditions, folk beliefs, historical treatises and archaeological findings.

The *Mahāvagga* relates that Tapussa (SinghaleTapassu) and Bhallika, two merchants from Okkala or Orissa offered cake and honey to the Buddha at Uruvelā and became his first lay devotees (*tena kho pana samayena tapussabhallikā vāṇijā ukkalā...bhagavantaṃ etadavocuṃ - "paṭiggaṇhātu no, bhante, bhagavā manthañca madhupiṇḍikañca...*Vin I.3). Orissa was a part of ancient Bengal. So, many believe that Buddhism was introduced into Bangladesh through them. But this evidence is not enough to support the view that Buddhism was introduced into Bangladesh during the Buddha's period. According to the chronological history of Burma and Arakan, the Buddha visited that land two times. Basing on this point, the Buddhists of Bangladesh firmly believe that the Buddha stayed at Cakrasala, a place in Chittagong, when he went to Arakan and Burma. The Chinese pilgrim Hiuen Tsang (see BEAL 1906: II.194), who visited Indian sub-continent during the seventh century reports that he heard during his visit from the people that the Buddha stayed seven days at Karṇasuvarna, Punḍravardhana for three days and seven days for Samata, the three famous regions of ancient Bengal. It is mentioned in *Avadānasataka* and *Divyāvadāna* that Anāthapinḍika, a famous patron of the Buddha gave his daughter Sumagada in marriage to a son of Niganṭha of Punḍravardhana and the Buddha came to Punḍravardhana on the invitation of Sumagada with a view to convert the family members of her father-in-law's house. These two books also inform that at that time the Buddha ordained the inhabitants of Punḍravardhana to his religion. This incident is also found in the *AvadānaKalpalatā*, a book written in the eleventh century (see VAIDYA 1956: 231). But these legends cannot be taken as true facts and have almost no historical validity.

The *Aṅguttaranikāya* (I. 24) mentions the name of two monks: Vaṅganta-putta and Vaṅgisa. Scholars think that they were so named as they hailed from the Bengal region. In *Saṃyutta-nikāya* (V. 89, 168-70) it is mentioned that the Buddha came over Setaka-*nagara* or town of Sumbha and delivered various sermons. *Telapatta Jātaka* (see FAUSBØLL 1962: I.393-401) also reports that the Buddha visited Desaka-nagara and preached *Janapadakalyāṇi-sutta* there. Both, Setaka *Nagara* and Desaka were the part and parcel of ancient Bengal.

During the life time of the Buddha, Majjhimadesa was a great Buddhist cultural center. Pāli Tipiṭaka reports that the Buddha toured over many parts of Majjhimadesa and delivered sermons. It is mentioned in Tipiṭaka that the Eastern boundary of Majjhimadesa extended up to Kajaṅgala, a place near Rājmahal-hill, which was the eastern boundary line of ancient Bengal. *Aṅguttara Nikāya* (Vol. I. 54) mentions that the Buddha visited Kajaṅgal two times and stayed in Mukeluvana where he preached *Indriyabhāvanā-sutta*. *Divyāvadāna* (see COWEL and NEIL 1970: 21), a book compiled in 2nd or 1st BCE, mentions that the eastern boundary of Majjhimadesa extended up to Punḍavardhana. According to *Vinaya Piṭaka*, Kajaṅgal was the eastern frontier of Aryāvarta. Aryāvarta was famous for Buddhistic activities and ordination. Prabodh Chandra BAGCHI (ND: 411) and Egaku MAYEDA (1964: 92) also hold that the eastern boundary of Mjjhimadesa extended up to Punḍravardhana. Historian like A.K.M. SHAMSUL ISLAM, V.A. SMITH, R.S. TRIPATHI, R.K. MOOKERJI stand witness that the northern part of Bengal known as Punḍravardhana was included into the territory of the empire of King Asoka.

We also found in *Asokāvadāna* that an anti-Buddhist *Nigaṇṭha* had dawn a picture depicting the Buddha's humiliation under his feet. Hearing the news King Asoka inflicted punishment upon the culprit. This book also mentions that King Asoka sent his brother Vitāsoka as a monk to a monastery of Punḍravardhana and Mahinda and Saṅghamitā, the son and daughter of King Asoka went to Sri Lanka from Tāmralipti, a sea port of Bengal. Chinese pilgrims report that they saw many of them in Samatata and Puṇḍravardhana, two ancient regions of Bengal. In 1931, a piece of stone inscription was uncovered at Mahasthangarh where the word "*samvaggiya*" is mentioned. Niharranjan ROY and B.M. BARUA considered the inscription as Asokan inscription and they interpreted the word "*samvaggiya*" as Chavaggiya, a group of monks, contemporary with the Buddha, frequently mentioned as being guilty of various Vinaya offences (for detail see MALALASEKERA 1974: I.926). Considering the fact, ROY and BARUA opined that Buddhism was introduced into Bengal region in early Asokan period. However, VOGEL, BHANDARKAR (1931: 87) and K. R. NORMAN, who are the authority on Asokan inscription, denied the Mahasthangarh inscription as Asokan inscription. Moreover, phonetically the word "*samvaggiya*" cannot change into "*saravaggiya*" or into "*chavaggiya*". Anyway, all these facts suggest that Buddhism had probably obtained a footing in northern part of Bengal during the time of Asoka. But due to the lacking of archaeological findings many scholars feel doubt as to introduction of Buddhism in Bengal before Common Era. The fact strengthened their doubt: when we notice the references of *Buddavaṃsa* and *Mahāparinibbāna Sutta* of the *Dīgha-Nikāya* where it is mentioned that some Kings and clans divided the Buddha's holy relics after the great demise of him at Kusinārā and built holy *stūpa*. But mention of Bengal king is not found in those books.

The first archaeological evidence as to the existence of Buddhism in Bengal was found at Sanchi (see BÜHLER 1894: 108). Two votive inscriptions dated 2nd century BCE, uncovered at Sanchi. It is known from those inscriptions that two inhabitants of Puṇḍravardhana defrayed the expense of the boundary wall and main gate of Sanchi *stūpa*. Scholars regard these votive inscriptions as the direct evidence of the spread of Buddhism in Bengal region. The second archaeological evidence was the Cetiyagarh-inscription, dated 2nd or 3rd century CE. It is found at Nagarjunakonda. In this inscription Vaṅga, the ancient name of Bengal, was mentioned as an important center of Buddhism. The inscription records the foundation of some religious constructions for the benefit of monks from Sri Lanka who had converted many countries including Bengal. Historians are unanimous and have identified this inscription as the basic document of propagation of Buddhism in Bengal region. It is, therefore, reasonable to believe that at the time of the compilation of this inscription Buddhism had already been firmly rooted in Bengal. Furthermore, the flourishing condition of Buddhism at the beginning of Gupta period can be assumed from the travel account of Chinese pilgrims Fa-hien (see WALTERS 1904: 184-5), who came to visit Indo Bangladesh subcontinent at the beginning of the 5th century. He stayed two years at Tāmralipti and saw twenty-two *saṅghārāmā*-s, all of which were inhabited by *bhikkhu*-s. Fa-hien informed that during his visit the law of Buddhism was flourishing. He copied here many sacred books and drawn Buddhist images. Tao Ching, another Chinese traveler is also given the same description. The accounts of these two pilgrims are amply corroborated by the archaeological evidence of the Gupta period, discovered at Gunaighar in Comilla. In this inscription following information is found:

> *"For enhancing the religious merits of myself and my parents, on the request of Maharaja Rudradatta, a slave to our feet, in the village of Kantedadaka situated in the "Northern Mandala," eleven Patakas of uncultivated lands in five plots are granted by Me, by means of a copper plate as an Agrahara in absolute possession; for providing perpetually for perfumes, flowers, lights, incense, etc. thrice a day unto the Lord Buddha in the abode of the Vaivarttika congregation of monks (belonging) to the Mahayana, established by the Buddhist monk of the Mahayana,*

> *Acaryya Santideva, in the Asrama-'Vihara (dedicated) to Arya-Ava- lokitesvara, which (Vihara) was being constructed in the part of.... by that (king) for the sake of that Acaryya; and for the enjoyment of garments, food, beds, seats, medicines for the sick etc. by that congregation; and also for repairing breaks and cracks in the Vihara"* (BHATTACHARYYA 1930: 57).

This inscription also refers two other monasteries in neighboring area. Many Mahāyāna statues of Gupta period have been uncovered that suggests that Buddhism was in flourishing condition during Gupta period.

After Fa-hien many Chinese pilgrims came to visit in Bengal region between 4th century and 7th century CE, to acquire knowledge on Buddhism and its culture. Their accounts constitute the earliest first-hand account of the state of Buddhism in Bangladesh. They visited almost all the important centers of Buddhism in ancient Bengal (Bangladesh) and spent a pretty long time over here. Among them Hiuen-tsang is mention worth (see BEAL 1906: II. 193f). His account contained vivid description of monastic establishment and the state of Buddhism practiced at that time in Bengal. Historians think his travel account to be the most authentic of all such accounts recorded by the Chinese pilgrims. His sources also considered as basic evidences of the state of Buddhism in Bengal.

The first Buddhist royal dynasty of Bengal was Khadga dynasty. We came to know about the Khadga dynasty from two copper plates discovered along with bronze votive *stūpa* at Asrafpur, a place situated 30 miles North-East of Dhaka, issued by Deva Khadga, the 3rd ruler of Khadga Dynasty who ruled over Samatata in the period between 630-700. This was confirmed by an inscribed Sarvani image discovered from Deulbari, a village 22 miles south of Comilla town. In the inscription of the image names of three rulers of Khadga dynasty is mentioned. Respectively they are: Khadgodyama, his son Jata Khadga and his son Deva Khadga. Both copper plates mention the name of queen of Devakhadga as Prabhavati and his son Rajaraj-bhatta. In the copper plates the Buddha has invoked. The Khadga kings were both followers and patron of Buddhism. They reigned in Samatata mightily for 70 years. During the period Buddhism enjoyed great royal favor. This supported by the report of the Seng-chi, a veteran Chinese traveler from China. About the condition of Buddhism in Samata during his visit he mention in his itinerary: *"the king used to make everyday hundred thousand images of Buddha with earth and read hundred śloka-s of mahāprajñāpāramitā-sūtra. He also used to take out procession in honor of Buddha with an image of Avaloketeśvara at the front and make pious gift. In the city, in his name, there were more than thousands monks and nuns"* (BEAL 1911: XI). Discoveries of images of Avaloketeśvara from Belasa, Vajrapāṇi Bodhisattva from Subhapur, Jambhala from Viharamandala, Dhyāni-Buddha from Bagherpur and goddess Marīci from Barakamta corroborate that Buddhism was strongly practiced in Samatata during the time of Khadgas.

After the Khadga, the next Buddhist dynasty ruled in Samata of Bengal was the Deva Dynasty. Their capital was Devaparvata. The obverse of the plate mentions the name of three successive rulers of the dynasty: Sri Sāntideva, his son Sri Viradeva and his son Ānandadeva. All the kings mentioned in the plates as '*Paramasaugata*'. The discovery of the Salban-Vihār in the Lalmai-Mainamati range near Comilla testifies that Buddhism was flourishing at the time of Deva rulers. The monastery which was about 550ft. square, with 115 cells, was built by Deva king Bhāvadeva, son of Sri Ānandadeva. A large number of Buddhistic images uncovered from the ruins of the monastery expose the flourishing condition of Buddhism in Samatata.

Around the 9th century, during the Pāla reign, Samatata was ruled by Chandra Dynasty, restore its independent. Thirteen copper plates issued by the rulers of Chandra dynasty exposed the genealogy of the dynasty. We came to know the name of seven rulers of the dynasty. They are: Purnachandra, Suvarnachandra, Trailokyachandra, Sri Chandra, Kalyanachandra, Ladachandra and Govinachandra. During their rule, Tantric Buddhism developed widely that gave birth to Buddhist mystic songs. These songs latter influenced and helped to develop Bengali language and literature (ROY : 412).

The great Pāla rulers, who ruled from 8th to 12th century in Bengal and Bihar were the great patrons of Buddhism. It was the time when Buddhism reached the highest peak in Bengal, and new centers of Buddhist learning were established in Bengal. Gopāl, the first king of this dynasty, was a devout Buddhist. In the Khalimpur copper-plates, he was mentioned as '*paramsaugata*'. According to *Manjusṛimūlakalpa*, he offered valuable gifts to the Buddhist *saṅgha*. During his reign Odantapuri monastery was established and in his reign many Buddhist teachers flourished in Bengal. He erected numerous monasteries in his territory and maintained them by royal expenditure. Somapura-Mahavihāra (Paharpur) was established at the time of the reign of Dharmapāla (770-810 CE). Somapura Mahavihāra was one of the biggest monasteries in Indian subcontinent at that time. Dharmapāla's Khalimpur copper-plate contains the *dharmacakra* along with wheel flanked by antelopes on both sides, with the symbol of the first preaching of the Buddha. He also founded the famous Vikramaśilā Mahavihāra. Tāranāth, a famous Tibetan historian, makes him the founder of fifty religious institutions. Archaeological findings support the statements of the Tibetans. The successors of Dharmapāla were also the great patrons of Buddhism. The other monasteries built by other Pāla rulers are : (i) Jagaddala Mahāvihāra in Varendri (northern Bengal), (ii) Vikrampuri Mahavihāra (Bikrampur, Dhaka), (iii) Pattikeravihae (Mainamati-Lalmai range), (iv) Paṇḍita Vihāra in Chittagong, (v) Devikotavihāra (Bangarh, West Dinajpur), (vi) Traikuṭavihāra in Radha (Western Bengal) etc.

From the coins, copper-plates and other evidences, it is proved that Buddhism was in a flourishing condition during the reign of Pāla-s. The other Pāla kings are: Devapāla, Śūrapāla, Vigrahapāla-I, Nārāyaṇapāla, Rājyapāla, Gopāla-II. Mahīpāla-I, Nayapāla-I, Vigrahapāla-III, Rāmapāla and Madanapāla were also great devotees of Buddhism. But the fact remains that though the Pāla rulers were Buddhists, their state policy was secular and Buddhism and Brahmanism existed side by side in this period. The discoveries of many mages of both Buddhist and Brahmanical deities in stone and metal testify the rich cultural heritage of Bengal. Under the Pālas and Chandras Mahāyāna Buddhism in Bengal developed into a highly esoteric Tantrism (MAJUMDAR 1971: 423).

So the archaeological, historical evidence suggest that owing to the all out royal patronization Buddhism flourished all over the Bangladesh during the rule of Buddhist dynasties, i.e; between 6th and 12th Centuries and especially in the Pāla period enjoyed the status of a state religion. During their rule many Buddhist centers were founded, which played a very important role in Bengali lives, which attained great reputation in Buddhist world of the day as centers of learning and culture. These institutions can be termed as "monastic-cum-universities." These universities proved to be fertile ground for the introduction and development of Tantric Buddhism. Among the monastic universities Sompuri Mahāvihāra, Salban Vihāra, Odantapuri Vihāra, Vikramśilā Mahāvihār, Nālandā Mahāvihāra, Vasu Vihāra, Paṇḍita Vihāra, Jagaddala Mahāvihāra etc. earned high reputation. Scholars from home and abroad came to these institutions to earn knowledge on Buddhism and its culture. Many of the ruins of these can still be found in Bangladesh. Besides, these institutions gave birth too many world reputed Buddhist scholars, who played a vital role to spread Buddhism in Bengal, Nepal and Tibet. Among them following are distinguished: Atisa Dīpaṅkara Srigyāṇa, Śilabhadra, Sāntarakshita etc. Atisa Dīpaṅkara occupied a place of distinction in the religious history of South-East Asia, especially in Tibet and Indo-Bangladesh subcontinent. Not only for his contribution to the propagation of Buddhism, but also for his scholarship, purity of his character and simplicity of his writings. He brought closer Tibet and Indo-Bangladesh subcontinent through cultural exchange and mutual understanding between two counters. During the Pāla period, painting, architecture and sculpture greatly flourished in Bangladesh. It can be said that the Pāla period is a golden period endowed with great glory and prosperity of Buddhism and its culture in Bangladesh.

During the period, Mahāyāna Buddhism went through a comprehensive process of transformation caused by the Tantric conceptions and Tantra based religious norms and practices. During thc period the Tantric Buddhist scholars like Chandragomin, Sāntideva, Jetari, Saraha, Tilo-pa, Naro-pa, Lui-pa, Kannu-pa, Sabara, Bhususka, Kukkuri, Atisa Dīpaṅkara and the like had unique contribution to the development of Buddhist Tantric movement in Bengal region. The most of the leaders mentioned here hailed from Bengal and have been celebrated in Buddhist Tradition as *Siddha*. In their hands, Tantric Buddhism of Bengal attained a stage where its assimilation to Brahmanism was an easy matter. During the period Buddhism metamorphosed into religion which was mainly based on worship of various gods and goddesses and took the form of popular cult. At that time Tantric Buddhism divided into four sects, they are: Mantrayāna, Vajrayāna, Kālacakrayāna and Sahajyāna. As result, the gap between the two religions, Buddhism and Brahmanism, were gradually narrowing.

On the doctrinal level too, Tantric ideas and ideals bringing Buddhism and Hinduism together. As a result, the worshippers were unable to distinguish between Buddha and Viṣnu, Avaloketeśvara and Śiva, and Tārā and Pārvati. Using this opportunity, the Hindu priest designed all out policies to merge Buddhism into Hinduism by accepting Tantric ideals and views, and adopting its rites and rituals. In fact, the chief objective of them behind doing so was to eradicate Buddhism by monopolizing Buddhism and its norms and customs. It would not be exaggerated to say that they were almost completely successful in achieving this. In this regard T. W. Rhys Davids (1907: 245) holds, "[H]owever, the Tantric Buddhism developed during the Chandras and Palas of the south-east Bengal and the contemporary Palas of north Bengal was gradually assimilated with Brahmanical Tantrism due to vigorous efforts of the Vramans." It is noteworthy that the Chandra kings were succeeded by the Varmans in East Bengal, who were the followers of Brahmanical religion. On the other hand, the Pāla-s were also ousted by the Sena-s, who were also the followers of Brahmanism. In the Sena and post Sena period, the Buddhist Tantra lost its own characteristics, as the Buddhist Tantric scholars had to make adjustment with Brahmanical Tantra in order to maintain their very existence in their homeland. As a fact, we find various Śaiva-Buddhist mixed cults in eastern India like the Kaula, Nātha, Avadhūta, Sahajiya and Baul. In fact, tantric sects ramified in so various sub-sects that it came to be regarded as distinct school of thinking.

After the fall of the Buddhist dynasties, especially Pāla dynasty, Buddhism of Bangladesh was no more patronized by ruling class but actively suppressed. After the Pāla-s, the Sen and Varmans, who were the orthodox followers of Brahmanical cult, ascended throne of Bengal. Their regimes can be termed as the "Dark Age" for Buddhism. At that time Buddhist institutions went under Brahmanic influence and gradually plunged into the bottomless pit of destruction and Buddhism was pushed into a critical phase of its existence, which worsened by Muslims. When the war-loving activities of the Turkish hero Bhaktyar Khilji brought down the Buddhist institutions, Buddhism and its culture fell obscure. In fact, during the Muslim rule starting from 13th century, the history of Bangladesh mainly concerned with rapid progress of Islam. Islam was spread here by mass conversion. But when political pressure came from mighty Hindu kings of South India, the Muslims invaders stopped converting Hindus, but joined their hands with the Hindu Brahmins to uproot Buddhist remnant from Bangladesh (for more details see BARUA 1999: XIII.13-31).

After the 13th century Buddhism reduced to a minority religion in Bengal. There were many factors expediting the decline of Buddhism, which once overwhelmed the mainstream life of Bengal people. Among them the mention worthy were: Anti Buddhist policy of Brahmanical kings and Brahmins, corrupted Tantric practices, destruction of Buddhist institution by Muslim invader, loss of royal and popular support. In spite of the oppression Buddhism was not altogether abolished from Bangladesh even in the Muslim rule. Many Buddhist of the time managed to sustain their existence in the face of Brahmanic and Muslim oppression. Especially, there lived large number of Buddhists in the littoral and in the hilly regions such as Chittagong and Chittagong Hill Tracts. The most important cause of this was the regions being adjacent the Buddhist kingdom of Arakan. Though they could sustain their existence, they could not retain the glory of the past and Buddhism maintained its flickering existence mixed with Tantric cult, Hindu and Islamic rituals.

In the British period this syncretism was ended among the Saṅgha, and the Theravāda tradition was revived. This revival was the outcome of various simultaneous occurrences, particularly the British domination of the entire Bengal-Arakan-Burma area, which created a favorable climate for exchange and communication between Buddhist communities. The Buddhists of Arakan who are strict followers of Theravāda traditions, passed on their influence to the Bengali community. The process of reawakening was supported greatly by the guideline of *saṅgharāja* Saramedha of Arakan and his disciples (*bhikkhu*-s) of Bangladesh. The Lay devotees were also wholeheartedly devoted to the reconstruction of Theravāda Buddhism from this period on.

At present Bangladesh is one of the most significant grounds for Theravāda Buddhism. This is an outcome of the efforts of monks and devotees. Among the monks, who played vital role to the revival of Theravāda Buddhism, the noteworthy were : Chandramohan Mahāthera, Gyanalaṅkāra Mahāsthavira, Kripāsarana Mahāsthavira, Gunālaṅkāra Mahāsthavira, Kalikumar Mahāsthavira, Punnananda Mahāsthavira, Aggamahāpaṇḍita Dharmavansa Mahāsthavira, Prajñaloka Mahāsthavira, Jynaniswara Mahāsthavira, Agrasar Mahāthera, and Vansadipa Mahāsthavira; and the most worthy lay devotees were: Nazir Krisna Candra Chaudhury, Zamindar Haragovinda and Birendra Mutsuddi etc.

In the academic arena B(eni) M(adhab) BARUA (1888-1948), an outstanding personality of Bangladesh played a vital role. BARUA was born in a noble Buddhist family of Mohamani Pahartali of Chittagong District. He earned high reputation all over the world for his excellent academic works. He was the proud Bangladeshi who obtained first D.Litt. degree among the Asians in 1917 from the London University. *History of Pre-Buddhistic Indians philosophy - from the Vedas to the Buddha* is considered by scholars as a remarkable work of him on Indian philosophy. He also earned reputation as a profound scholar on Asokan inscription. He edited many complicated and obscure edicts and inscriptions. He served as a veteran Professor of Pāli and Ancient India History in the Calcutta University from 1917 to 1948.

Nowadays, there are 1250 monasteries in Bangladesh. Besides, many organizations have been established to promote Buddhist culture. Among the organizations: Bangladesh Bauddha Samiti, Bangladesh Bauddha Kristy Pracer Sangha,

Bangladesh Buddhist Federation, Bangladesh National Buddhist Youth Federation, Uttar Vanga Bauddha Parisad, Bangladesh Bauddha Juva Parisad, Parvatya Bauddha Sangha, Rakhain Maram Sangha Council and Anoma are mention worthy for their dynamic activities towards the community. Moreover, these organizations publishing books, periodicals, journals, magazines, memorials and pamphlets and holding seminars, symposium and meeting on Buddhism and its culture to enrich the religious feelings. Among the journals, the Kristy, the Dipankar, the Saugata, the Anoma, the Jyoti etc. are worth mentioning. Uttar Vanga Bauddha Parisad is playing an important role to the propagation of Buddhism in Northern Bangladesh. This organization has established Benuban Vihar in 1996 in the district of Rangpur. The Buddhists of this region are neophytes, who have been started to take refuge in Buddhism from 1994 and on onwards.

As the follower of Theravāda Buddhism, the Buddhist community of Bangladesh observes many religious ceremonies and festivals, which are intimately associated with the life and teachings of Buddha, throughout the year. They observe Purnima ceremonies, Uposatha, Vassavasa (rain retreat), Kaṭhina Civara Dāna Ceremony (yellow rob offering ceremony), Saṅghadāna, Aṭṭhaparikkhāra-dāna and hold Paritta recitation with due respect and religious fervor. They also observe national ceremonies, festivals and days sharing with other communities. They also follow all national and international rights and law. It is citable that from the emergence to 1987, Bangladesh enjoyed the status of a secular state, but in 1988, the majority religion Islam proclaimed as state religion. However, the Constitutions of Bangladesh has reserved all rights for the minorities to preach and practice their respective faith, rites and rituals freely. Bangladesh government provides them with all national facilities. Recitation from the holy Tipiṭaka is done in the National Assembly along with the Al-Quran and the holy book of other communities. Bangladesh Television and Bangladesh Betar (Radio) telecast holy words from the holy Tipiṭaka twice in a week. Bangladesh government declared Buddha's Birthday as a National Holiday and other big religious days as an optional holiday for the Buddhists. Moreover, National dailies publish supplementary volume in Buddha's birth festival.

Buddhism and Pāli literature are studied in the schools, colleges and universities. In the Dhaka and Chittagong University Master, M.Phil. and Ph.D. degree are conferred on Pāli and Buddhist studies. Besides, 'Bangladesh Sanskrit and Pali Education Board' is founded for the study of Buddhism and Pāli. Now there are 115 Pāli Tols and Colleges in Bangladesh where *Bhikkhu*-s, *Sāmaṇera*-s and lay Buddhist acquiring knowledge on Sutta, Vinaya and Abhidhmma Piṭaka as well as Pāli language and literature.

The Buddhists of Bangladesh learn Pāli as a sacred language. However, it is not known when and where the first book in Pāli was written. At present Pāli language and literature are taught at Buddhist institutions as well as at colleges and universities. In Bangladesh the study of Pāli language and literature started primarily to meet religious needs.

Acharya Chandramohan substantially contributed to Pāli education in Bengal by establishing the first Pāli *tol* at Mahamuni-Pahartali of Chittagong in 1885 with the financial support of Zamindar Haragovinda Mutsuddi. The second Pāli *tol* was established at same place in 1902 by the efforts of Sarananda *Bhikkhu*, a Buddhist monk from Sri Lanka. Later on, many *tols* were established in villages such as Rajanagar, Satbaria, Mirzapur, and Unainpur. In 1908 arrangements were made to teach Pāli at Chittagong Collegiate School, and Dharmavangsha Mahasthavir was appointed to teach Pāli and Buddhist Studies. Gradually opportunities were created to study Pāli at the many schools of Chittagong. As a result, more Pāli *tols* were established in Chittagong during the first two decades of the 20th century.

In 1899, a Pali Department was opened at the University of Calcutta. The study of Pāli was also introduced in the University of Dhaka (1921), University of Rajshahi (1955) and University of Chittagong (1968) etc.

During British rule, a number of Buddhists of Bengali origin established Buddhist Mission Press (1930) in Rangoon where the study of the *Tripiṭaka* in Benagli was initiated. Prajnalok Mahasthavir and Sudhanshu Bimal BARUA played a vital role in this regard.

Pāli was also introduced at the College level, and three colleges were given permission to teach Pāli : Presidency College and Vidyasagar College in Kolkata and Chittagong College. The scholars who taught at these Colleges included Mahamahopadhyay Satish Chandra Vidyabhushan, Amulyacharan Ghosh, Nirod Ranjan Mutsuddi, Prankrishna Bhikkhu and Dharmavangsha Mahasthavir.

In the later years, Pāli educations were introduced at Feni College (1926-27), the first Pāli Professor was Lalit Kumar BARUA; Calcutta City College (1932)-Devabrata CHAKRAVARTI and Nirmal Chandra BARUA were the Professor of Pāli in this College; Calcutta Ripon College (at present Surendranath College-1935)-Jyotish Chandra GHATAK was appointed in the position of first Professor of Pāli. Later on, in Bangladesh Pali education were also introduced to Kanungupara Sir Ashutosh College (1943)-the first Professor was Surendra Lal BARUA and thereafter Mr. Munindra Lal BARUA was appointed and Sanskrit Government College (1958) at Calcutta. The provision of Pāli studies and teaching provided at Maharaja Munindra Chandra College in Calcutta in 1943, and Provash Chandra MAJUMDAR joined as a Professor of Pāli in this College. Later on, he was appointed as a reader in the Department of Pali in the University of Calcutta.

In 1958 Pali Department was opened in Sanskrit College by the earnest effort of Dr. Gaurinath SHASTRI. The four Professors are: Dr. Herambanath CHATTOPADYAY, Dr. Binoyendranath CHOWDHURI, Dr. Sukomal CHAUDHURY and Dr. Sadhan Chandra SARKAR. Dr. Herambanath CHATTOPADYAY complied with even the responsibility as the Head of the Department. At that time the opportunity of learning Pāli was created in Ramthakur College of Tripura (see Barua 2001: XIII.140f).

In 1962, a special educational institution was established in the name of Tripura Pali Institute at Venuvana Vihāra of Agartala. The founder of the institute was Principal Srimat Aryamitra *Bhikkhu* of Venuvana Vihāra. The noble deed of Ven. Aryamitra and this institute is unforgettable in preaching Buddhism and Pāli language study. The syllabus of "*Vangiya Sanskrit Siksha Parisad*" at Calcutta was followed in Tripura Pali Institute. The educational institutions which are now imparting Pāli education in Bangladesh are as follows: Rangunia College (Rangunia, Chittagon), Rangunia Hasina Zamal Women College (Rangunia, Chittagong), Noapara College (Rauzan, Chittagong), Agrasara Women College (Rauzan, Chittagong), Karnaphuli College (Chandraghona, Chittagong Hill Tracts), Shah Alam College (Rangunia, Chittagong), Padua College (Rangunia, Chittagong), Imam Gazzali Degree College (Rauzan, Chittagong), Hazi Nurul Islam Women College (Boalkhali, Chittagong), Hulain Saleh-Noor College (Patia, Chittagong), Ali Ahmed Bir-Bikram College (Chandanaish, Chittagong), Ashalata College (Rauzan, Chittagong), Dighinala College (Khagrachari, Chittagong Hill Tracts), Mahalchari College (Khagrachari, Chittagong Hill Tracts) and Rangamati Government College (Rangamati, Chittagong Hill Tracts) etc.

Conclusion

If we accept the view that the eastern boundary of Majjhimadesa extended up to Puṇḍravardhana, there is every possibility that Buddhism was introduced in Bangladesh during

Buddha's period, especially in the northern part of the country called Puṇḍravardhana. For example, Majjhimadesa was a life center of Buddhism during the lifetime of Buddha, and Buddha visited and delivered his sermons in many parts of this territory. Besides, the geographical situation of Bangladesh is very close to the places of Buddha's preaching. Moreover, the traditions about Asoka recorded in *Divyāvadāna*, *Aśokāvadāna* and also by Chinese Pilgrim Huien-Tsang, make it highly probable that Buddhism was not unknown in Bangladesh during the reign of great emperor Asoka. But it is the irony of fate that we do not have any archaeological evidences to support the matter. The earliest authentic historical evidence of Buddhism in the geographical area of modern Bangladesh is the Cetiyaghar inscription found at Nagarjunkonda, which suggests that Buddhism was a living force in Bangladesh during the 2nd or 3rd century. Besides, historical and archaeological materials, travelogues of Chinese travelers who visited Indo-Bangladesh subcontinent between 5th and 7th centuries CE, report that both Hinayāna and Mahāyāna modes of Buddhism were firmly established and Bangladesh was highly endowed with many renowned monastic establishments.

The available archaeological and textual evidences suggest that between 7th and 12th centuries, known as Pāla period, Buddhism enjoyed unprecedented patronage from ruling dynasties and flourished all over the Bangladesh in every aspect of the mainstream life. However, during the same period significant changes occurred in the Buddhism of the region caused by Tantric influence. This brought about massive popularization of Buddhism, which at the same time undermined its distinctiveness. After 12th century, especially after the fall of Pāla dynasty, Buddhism in Bengal region was overshadowed by many adverse conditions such as the anti-Buddhist policies of Sen and Varman dynasties and Muslim oppression. As a result, Buddhism reduced into a minority religion. In spite of the oppression, Buddhism was not completely abolished from Bangladesh but took the form of syncretic religion. In the British period Buddhists got opportunity to revive their religion due to the secular outlook of the British. In this period, Theravāda Buddhism reformed after the fashion of the Buddhism of Arakan-Burma. In this regard, *Bhikkhu*-s and lay devotees of Bangladesh also played a vital role. Moreover, Buddhist Studies again introduced in the schools, colleges and universities of Bangladesh. Thus, it can be concluded that Buddhism of Bangladesh takes present form passing through many phases of deviation and development.

Abbreviation and Bibliography

A	*Aṅguttara Nikaya*
S	*Saṃyutta Nikaya*
Jā	*Jātaka*
Div	*Divyāvadāna*
Vin	Vinayapiṭaka

BARUA, Dilip Kumar.

(1999). The Causes of Decline of Buddhism in Indo-Bangladesh Sub-continent. *Journal of the Pali and Buddhist Studies*. Vol. XIII, 13-31. Japan.

BARUA, Sukomal

(2001). Pali Studies in Bangladesh and its impact on our education system. *Journal of the Pali Bukkyu Bunkagaku*. Vol. XIII. Aichi Gakuin University, Japan.

BEAL, Samuel.

(1884). *SI-YU-Ki: Buddhist Record of the Western World. Translated From the Chinese of Hiuen Tsiang (A.D. 629)*. Vols. I-II. London: Trübner & Co.

(1911). *The Life of Hiuen-tsang by the Shaman Hwui Li*. London: Kegan Paul, Trench, Trübner & Co. Ltd.

BHATTACHARYYA, Dinesh Chandra.

(1930). A Newly Discovered Copperplate from Tippera [The

Gunaighar Grant of Vainyagupta: The Year 188 Current (Gupta Year)]. *The Indian Historical Quarterly*. Vol. 6:1, 45-60.

BHANDARKAR R. D.
(1931-32). Mauryan Brahmi Inscription of Mahasthan. *Epigraphica of Indica*. Vol. XXI. 83-91. Ed. by Hiranananda SASTRI, K. N. DIKSHIT and N. P. CHAKRAVARTI. Delhi.

BÜHLER, G.
(1894). Votive Inscriptions from the Sānchi Stūpas. *Epigraphia Indica: A Collection of Inscriptions Supplemented to the Corpus Inscription Indicarum of the Archeological Survey*. ed. by Jas. BURGESS. Vol. II. 87-116. Calcutta.

COWEL, R. C. & NEIL, R. A.
(1970). *Divyavadana*. (Ed.). Amasterdam.

FAUSBØLL, V.
(1962). *The Jataka: Together with its Commentary*. Vol. I .London: P. T. S. 1st Pub. 1877.

MAJUMDAR, R. C.
(1971). *History of Ancient Bengal*. Calcutta: G. Bharadwaj & Co.

MALALASEKERA, G.P.
(1974). *Dictionary of Pāli Proper Names*. Vol. I-II. London: PTS. 1st Pub. 1938.

MAYEDA, Egaku.
(1964). *History of the Formation of Original Buddhist Texts*. Tokyo.

RHYS DAVIDS,T. W.
(1907). *Buddhism*: London.

ROY, Niharranjan.
(1400 Bengali Year). *Bangalir Itihas*. Calcuta:

VAIDYA, P. L.
(1959). *Avadāna Kalpalatā by Khemendra*. Vols. I-II. Darbhanga: Mithila Research Institute.

WALTERS, Thomas
(1904). *On Yuan Chwang's Travels in India 629-645 A.D.* Edited by T. W. RHYS DAVIDS and S.W. BUSHELL. London: Royal Asiatic Society.